The Way It Was With Me

The Way It Was With Me

by

SENATOR GLEN H. TAYLOR

LYLE STUART INC.

Secaucus, N.J.

Queries regarding rights and permissions
should be addressed to Lyle Stuart Inc.
120 Enterprise Ave., Secaucus, N.J. 07094.

Published by Lyle Stuart Inc. Published simultaneously
in Canada by George J. McLeod Limited
Don Mills, Ontario.

Manufactured in the United States of America

Library of Congress Cataloging in Publication Data
Taylor, Glen Hearst, 1904–
The way it was with me.
Includes index.
1. Taylor, Glen Hearst, 1904–   2. United States
—Politics and government—1933–1945. 3. Idaho—
Politics and government. 4. Legislators—United States
—Biography. 5. United States. Congress. Senate—
Biography. I. Title.
E748.T275A38   328.73′092′4 [B]   79-13549
ISBN 0-8184-0288-1

To Dora

Contents

I
EARLY DAYS
9

II
SHOW BUSINESS
105

III
INTRODUCTION TO POLITICS
145

IV
UNITED STATES SENATOR
271

V
RUNNING WITH WALLACE
339

VI
POST-WALLACE DAYS
361

Index
415

I

Early
Days

FIRE!   Mama always called Papa "Mr. Taylor." Not only in mentioning him, but in addressing him personally. The only happening to alter this quaint formality that I recall occurred in 1910.

This was the year of the most disastrous forest fires in history. Things became so tinder-dry that forests practically exploded. Many people blamed the unprecedented disaster on Halley's comet, which put in its appearance that year. I had heard so much talk and conjecture about the celestial phenomenon that even I, although I was only six, stood out in the yard and studied it.

Because of the great fires that raged out of control, all round about and not far away, there was a heavy pall of smoke. But, even so, Halley's comet was plainly visible to the naked eye. It hung up there just above the top of the hill behind our house. It looked like a glowing tadpole and its presence added to the apprehension caused by the inferno that was devouring not only the forests, but people, farms, and towns as well. Papa was cooking for a crew of firefighters back in the wild country at the headwaters of the Clearwater River.

Papa wasn't a cook, you understand, but he was handy around a campfire, and the two or three hundred dollars he earned each summer was the lion's share of our entire year's cash income.

For many years Papa had been a preacher, and a good one, but he became disillusioned with the hypocrisy he encountered, gave up the ministry, and we moved to a rocky side hill homestead on the banks of the Clearwater River, three miles above the little town of Kooskia, Idaho, population four hundred. I was four years old at the time.

Papa supplemented his income with an occasional stint as an

auctioneer, but now he was back there in the mountains risking his life for two dollars and fifty cents a day. There had been no news of him for ten days.

Many men and even whole crews of firefighters had been burned to death when fires would jump from mountaintop to mountaintop and then incinerate everyting in between.

This afternoon the heavy pall of smoke which had been getting more dense each day was taking on a pinkish glow along the mountaintop across the river from our rocky acres.

The forest ended in a phalanx of tall pines at the top of the mountain like an army ordered to advance no farther. There were only a few lone trees scattered down the mountain face like scouts or sentries.

Mama was worried about "Mr. Taylor," and sister Lena was trying to reassure her that Papa was all right.

Lena was eleven. My brother Paul was only three, so young that this whole murky business left him completely unconcerned.

I must have been worried, though, or I wouldn't remember these events so vividly.

The glow over the mountain across the river grew brighter, and presently we could see the flames. The old familiar trees up there stood rigid as though paralyzed with fright, awaiting the executioner.

Through the years we had given many of those trees along that skyline descriptive names while the family sat on the porch on warm summer evenings and studied their distinctive features.

"The Man With the Cane" was the first to go. One moment a friendly old landmark, and then a pillar of flame.

"The Hunchback" writhed in agony as the relentless flames engulfed him, and "The Spear" grew twice as tall as the spire of flame shot skyward, and then there was just a skeleton.

We hid our faces when "Little Jim," the running boy, was overtaken in his rooted flight and consumed.

If this was happening so close to home, who could imagine what was going on back up in the mountains where dense cedar forests left very few open spaces where living things could hope to survive? Papa was back in there somewhere.

Mama had left the porch while our old familiar friends on top of the hill were still dying. She was listening in on the party telephone line. This single wire, strung on fences, trees, and occasional poles, was used by the dozen or so families along the river and on Harris Ridge. Ordinarily, Mama might have been listening for bits of news or gossip, as the conversations ran the gamut. But on that hot and smoky afternoon, as we children wiped away the tears caused by the sad end of our hilltop friends, Mama was not listening for gossip or frivolous news of personal happenings as she anxiously centered her attention on the old crank-type telephone. The Forest Service also used this line, and Mama was hoping to get some word of "Mr. Taylor."

Now, Papa was nobody's fool. He had been a Texas Ranger and fought Indians as a young man, not to mention the never-ending battle for survival in those days before social security and relief.

Calling on this reservoir of experience and hard-earned savvy, he managed to get to the river and the telephone line with no more damage than singed eyebrows and an occasional hotfoot for Bob, the little dapple-gray pony he was riding.

He was phoning in a report to the Forest Service at this very moment.

When Mama heard his voice she completely forgot her proper upbringing, one rule of which was that a married woman should address her husband as "Mr." She forgot that it was vulgar for a lady to display emotion in word or deed where a man was concerned, and right there on that party line, where she could be heard by the Forest Service and God knows who else, Mama suddenly burbled like an excited schoolgirl; "Hello Papa, Mr. Taylor, honey, darling!"

Lena and I were so surprised by Mama's unprecedented boldness that we couldn't even wait for her to report on what Papa had to say before we told her what she had said. And when we told her that we had never before heard her say such lovey-dovey words to Papa, she blushed.

Then, being careful to refer to him as "Mr. Taylor," Mama told us that Papa was at the river thirty miles up from Syringa, which was twelve miles upriver from our place, and where the road ended. Syringa was also where the forest began in earnest on this side of the river, and for anyone fleeing the fire it would be the first place with sufficient open ground to offer any degree of safety.

Papa had been surprised that the phone was still working because it indicated that the fire had not yet reached the river and that this only route of escape was still open. He hung up abruptly after saying he didn't have a minute to lose if he was to run that thirty-mile gauntlet before the fire closed in. In about four hours he would call from Syringa. So now, at this very moment, he was riding hell-bent-for-leather over trails that were in many places blasted out of the mountainside and just barely wide enough for a horse to travel. If the flames did not cut him off, and if Bob didn't stumble racing along some precipice, he could possibly make the thirty miles in four hours.

When Mama hung up the phone, she went out on the porch and stood looking up the river. She couldn't see very far or very clearly because of the smoke. After a few minutes she came back inside and started dusting aimlessly, but her heart wasn't in it. It was something to do to try and keep her mind off Papa up there in those fiery mountains. She had hardly gotten the dust stirred up when she discarded the duster, grabbed the broom, and went out and started busily sweeping the yard. Mama just couldn't stand to be idle at any time, and at a terrible moment like this it would have been unthinkable just to sit and wait.

Sweeping the yard was not a silly improvisation of the instant to relieve the tension. Whenever Mama ran out of something to do she always swept the yard.

"Sweeping the yard" may sound strange, but ours was a particular kind of yard.

It consisted of that area of hillside adjacent to our kitchen door extending no farther than a pan of greasy dishwater can be thrown. The greasy dishwater settled the dust, impregnated the ground, and eventually rendered the dirt waterproof and, to a certain degree, free from mud.

The constant tramping of feet packed the soil, and Mama's sweeping kept it free of extraneous dirt, pine needles, or chicken droppings. On this day she wasn't paying much attention to what she was doing, though. She hardly looked at the ground. Her eyes were gazing intently up the river like she was trying to look a hole in that curtain of smoke and see what it was hiding from her.

The yard sweeping hadn't lasted more than two or three minutes when she stopped, stood a moment, and then resolutely headed for the house. "Glen, son," she said, "go round up the team. We are going to meet Papa."

Between Mama and me and sister Lena we got the horses harnessed and hitched to the wagon. We headed upriver into that thick smoke that seemed to get thicker every time you looked.

We were never rich enough to afford a spring buggy, and it was a jolty twelve miles in that wagon, what with Mama urging "Old Hart" and "Old Babe" to an unwilling trot most of the time.

Syringa consisted of a farm and a store in what was more of a wide place in the river canyon than a valley. The mountains on either side of the river were not heavily timbered up to this point, but beginning a quarter mile upriver and visible through the smoke was a magnificent virgin forest.

We stopped on a sandy bar at the edge of the beautiful Clearwater to wait for Papa. He was already a half hour overdue. The river was a wide riffle at this point, perhaps a hundred yards or more across.

Upriver, the canyon became narrower and narrower as the mountains became more precipitous, more heavily covered with timber.

Up there at the head of the hole the river narrowed to a stone's throw. Just before it disappeared around a bend to the left white water was visible, obviously caused by rapids.

Instead of the smoky pall, motion was now visible above the hills, smoke actually moving skyward from a fire; an orange glow was beginning to tinge the gray blue of the smoke.

If Papa was up there round that bend he'd better hurry up and get out.

Mama stood biting her lip, and sister Lena, who was eleven, watched her for cues as to what her own reaction should be.

Flames broke over the top of the high ridge way up on the other side of the river.

Mama went over to the wagon and looked at the alarm clock she had brought along. She turned and announced firmly, "Papa should be here any minute now."

All of us strained our eyes on that last visible section of trail which entered the forest some two hundred feet up the mountainside above the white water at the head of the hole.

Flames sprouted up and then leaped high on top of the ridge on the left above the trail. Papa better be traveling—if he *was* still traveling.

Mama ducked her head quickly to meet halfway the handkerchief she had pulled from her apron pocket in a quick-draw motion she hoped we wouldn't see. She didn't even dab both eyes. Just one. Her hand went back to the pocket and she held her chin a little higher or she probably couldn't have kept it up at all.

As my eyes flicked back from poor Mama to the trail, I couldn't believe what I saw. The whole country up there broke into flames all at once. The fire didn't spread, it just flared like someone had thrown kerosene on it.

Mama made a little crying sound and just settled to her knees as though the fire had melted her down. Lena was holding Mama's head against her to comfort her as she cried. I'd seen this picture in reverse a thousand times, but to see Mama crying on Lena's breast left no doubt in my mind that the situation was pretty bad.

I started to cry too. Poor Papa. I guessed he was burned up all right.

A thousand pictures flashed through my mind. The first time I could remember seeing Papa, probably when I was about four, he had walked to town, and I remembered his return because he did something which caused me to remember.

He came walking up the road and he had on tight pants. I remember that. About twenty feet from the picket fence he started running with quick little steps and jumped right over that fence. Uphill, too. Funny how you'll remember some little thing like that.

And I remembered he had gone swimming with me just before he left to join the firefighting crew.

When he came up out of the water his hair hung way down on the left side. Papa was bald and let his hair grow long on the left so he could comb it across and hide the top of his head. Each time he came up out of the water he reached over with his right hand, and with a toss of the head and a flick of the wrist he flipped that long lock back into place. Every time he went down and came up he did that.

Very intriguing and impressive. Maybe someday, if I was lucky, I could do it too.

The last time I had seen Papa, and probably the last time I would ever see him, he had ridden away on Bob. Bob was a little white horse, lightly dappled. Only six hundred pounds, and when a grown man rode him the rider almost appeared to be walking with a horse between his legs.

I could feel the heat of the fire now although we were safe enough.

The forest came close to the water's edge up where you could see that white water at the head of the hole, but the timberline left the river at a forty-five-degree angle as it came downstream, and about halfway to us it disappeared over the mountaintop on either side.

Mama had gotten up and was holding on to the wagon wheel with one hand and wiping her eyes with the other. I guess she had given up because she was facing downriver. She wasn't even looking up there where Papa was supposed to come from.

Of course, it *was* kind of hopeless. Where the trail disappeared there was nothing but fire and smoke all jumping and boiling around.

Still, Papa was no ordinary man. He *was* my Papa—and anybody that could jump that fence, uphill, was a power to be reckoned with.

Mama started climbing into the wagon. She wasn't bustling like she usually did. She was moving very slowly, but I divined that the vigil was over and it was time to go.

I took one last look up where the trail entered the inferno. Nothing could live there certainly. I started to turn away but something caught the corner of my eye up where the white water entered the head of the hole. There was movement up there. It looked like a goose swimming downstream. Now you'd think a goose would just get up and fly and get out of there.

Whatever it was, it was getting closer, and maybe it wasn't a goose. In fact, there seemed to be two somethings bobbing along. Every few seconds the larger white object disappeared, and then the other smaller darker object disappeared for a second or two.

Maybe it was a goose and a duck coming downriver and diving every few seconds to keep from being burned up.

No, it was too big for a goose, and every time the duck came up there was a funny motion, a motion that was vaguely familiar.

The next time the duck came up I got it. That was no duck! That familiar motion was Papa flipping his hair across his head. You could see them now. The duck was Papa and the goose was Bob's head.

I yelled to Mama. She took one look and got out of that wagon faster than I had ever seen her move and started running toward the river, sort of cooing, "Mr. Taylor, oh Mr. Taylor."

Later, Papa told us that he had been only one hundred yards from where the trail left the timber when that big explosion-like thing we had seen took place, and he had to ride Bob on the run right off a ten-foot cliff into the river at the head of the rapids.

I guess it was awful hot up there where Papa was now but he had a system to beat it. He was hanging on to the saddle horn with one hand and he would put his other hand on top of Bob's head and raise himself half out of the water, which would push Bob's head under. Then as Papa came down, he would go under, and Bob's head would come up.

When Papa came up he would execute that old familiar gesture of flipping his crossover back in place. Then he would put his hand back on Bob's head, push him under, and repeat the cycle over and over. If he hadn't done that, the oven-like heat would have killed them in a few minutes.

The water was maybe fifty feet deep in that big hole at the bottom of the rapids, but Papa and Bob were coming on strong, and finally Bob's hooves hit bottom at the lower end of the pool out there.

As the water got shallower and shallower, Bob and Papa came slipping and sliding over the mossy, flattish round rocks on the river bottom, and there in knee-deep water we met Papa and Bob, and Papa and Mama embraced and kissed each other.

That was the only time I ever saw Mama kiss Papa, except for just a very proper peck, hello or goodbye, but this was a real long movie kiss. And right out there where everyone could see, too.

We couldn't see very plain, though, because Papa's hair had fallen down when he stooped to kiss Mama and he was so glad to see her that for the first and only time ever he forgot to flick his crossover back into place, and so it hung down on the side toward us kids, and Papa and Mama were pretty much hid from us until they finished that big, long kiss.

BUSINESSMAN   I had a brother E.K. (That was his name. Just E.K.) He was managing two movie theaters, one in Wallace and the other in Kellogg, Idaho. He decided to get going on his own.

He started two picture shows, one in Kooskia and the other in Stites, which was three miles up the south fork of the Clearwater River from Kooskia. Each town had four hundred people.

E.K. was not about to give up a good job and come to Kooskia to personally manage his new venture, so he hired me to act as manager of his new properties. E.K. would book the pictures. After that it was up to me.

I was janitor, I changed the meager lobby posters, and operated the machine. That's right, *the* machine. There would be just one. At the end of each reel there would be a "time out" while the operator changed reels. My pay was twelve dollars a week.

The "theaters" were not elaborate affairs, being simply vacant store buildings twenty-five-feet wide with four rows of backless benches down front for the kids and ordinary unpadded kitchen chairs for the grownups.

I had to take the five o'clock train to Stites because those films were heavy, and then I had to stay all night and come back on the train at five in the morning. That wasn't good because it cost me a dollar for a room besides train fare so I traded some show tickets to a kid for a beat-up little red wagon.

Then I could walk the three miles to Stites and pull the wagon-load of films. I wouldn't get home until after midnight. I was only twelve years old, but I got along just fine managing those theaters.

GRAVE ROBBER   When I was fifteen and in the ninth grade, my oldest brother, Ferris, came home at Christmas. He had his wife Nell with him. They were the leading man and leading lady with a tent repertoire show in California.

Everybody wanted to see Ferris and his wife in a show, so we decided to put on a play with just the family.

We advertised that the entire proceeds would go to the Red Cross, and the place was packed. We turned over better than fifty dollars to the Red Cross, thereby proving what great humanitarians we were, and the family's standing in the community as talented actors and singers was enhanced for all time.

After the success of our family presentation of *Arizona Rose,* and all the compliments paid me by the kids at school, my teacher, townspeople, and Ferris, I was hooked.

Running the picture shows and watching others do the acting was pretty tame stuff.

Not long after Ferris left to return to the McDonough Stock Company, I conceived a plan to get into show business.

There was a rather dilapidated metal suitcase back under the house that one of the older boys had brought home and left. In it there were more than twenty sets of slides. Each set was for illustrating a song. As the singer sang, different pictures were projected on the screen appropriate to the words being sung.

Without asking anyone's permission I appropriated this equipment, and illustrated songs became a regular feature between reels at the picture shows I ran in Stites and Kooskia. I had sung them all at least once or more and they went over big. Very few people in Kooskia had ever seen or heard an illustrated song.

I did not know that illustrated songs had become passé a good many years ago, and that was why the suitcase filled with the artistic ashes of a bygone time had been left under the house. It had not been stored there. Not really. Actually, I had robbed a grave. Not knowing this, I set out to make my fame and fortune singing illustrated songs. It is amazing what you can get away with if you are ambitious, intelligent, determined, and— ignorant.

I had heard the older brothers mention a man named Joe Stern in Lewiston who had gotten them a good many bookings for their quartet in such widely separated places as Spokane, Washington; Pocatello, Idaho; Butte, Montana—and points in between.

Although the family now lived in Kooskia, they would make occasional weekend trips to our rocky hillside homestead so Papa could plow and plant, repair fences, etc. I say "they" would make these trips, because I, being a big businessman running the theaters, had to stay in town.

The family left one Friday after school for the ranch. I left at five the next morning on the train for Lewiston to see Joe Stern.

Although he had never seen me, he recognized me as a Taylor the minute I walked into his office. Later I learned that out of this office he loaned money, bought and sold real estate, and ran numerous other more shadowy operations, including the placing of "girls" about the Northwest.

He was a sociable, cigar-chewing man, and he appeared genuinely pleased to meet another one of the Taylor boys. After telling me how talented the older brothers were, how much he thought of them, and how he would love to see them again, he finally got around to asking me why I had come to see him.

I didn't beat around the bush. I wanted to break into show business, I told him, and I asked if he could help me.

"Hadn't you better stay in school, kid?"

I explained that Papa had had the flu and wasn't too strong, and that I felt I should make my own way to lighten his burden a little.

"Well, let's see. What type of singing do you do?"

"I plan to sing illustrated songs."

He looked at me as if I were joking. "Why, kid, I haven't seen anybody sing an illustrated song for years. They were great, though. I'd like to hear Ferris sing 'Hello, Central, Give Me Heaven' again. He sure killed 'em with it. What a voice, and those slides were real pretty," he mused with a faraway look in his eye.

I told him that I planned to sing that very song, "and," I pointed out, "if you would like to see and hear illustrated songs again there probably are other people who would, too."

"Maybe you've got something there, kid," he admitted. "You're pretty young, though, for the place I have in mind."

I assured him that I had heard the brothers talk of the "places" where they had sung when they were younger than I, and I thought I could use good sense in taking care of myself.

He removed the cigar from his mouth and held it for a moment while he looked me right in the eye. Papa had told me about this.

"Never let anybody stare you down. Look 'em square in the eye. Don't let your eyes waver and never, never, duck your head." I looked him square in the eye and I didn't duck my head, although God knows it took an awful effort.

After a long look he seemed satisfied, replaced the cigar, and said, "I guess a kid who has managed two theaters successfully can take care of himself. I'll tell you what. I have a friend over in Pierce City, who runs a real high-class saloon, and he wants a singer. You go on home and I'll get in touch with him and let you know."

One week later I got a letter from Mr. Stern saying that I was to report to Mr. Jim Williams at the Bluebell in Pierce City the following Friday. Twenty dollars a week. Enclosed was a ticket and three dollars' expense money. Not a word about repayment or commission. If Joe Stern was a sharpie, he didn't take it out on me.

I wrote a letter to Papa. I told him that I felt guilty living at home when his health was so poor. A man had to make his own way. "I am sure you'll understand."

THE BLUEBELL I arrived in Pierce City at three a.m., and lugged my suitcase as well as the one containing the stereopticon slides to the hotel. The clerk eyed me in a rather puzzled and quizzical manner but permitted me to huff upstairs and to bed.

Despite the fact that I did not get to bed until four a.m., I was so excited I was up at seven. At eight I was at the Bluebell—I said at, not in.

I knew this was a den of iniquity and could not bring myself to go through those swinging doors. All day, at least once an hour, I would assume what I thought was a very nonchalant manner and saunter up to the gates of perdition, get a whiff of hellfire and brimstone, and very nonchalantly saunter away again. Finally, at eight p.m., I closed my mind to all thoughts except the overruling and transcendent importance of getting my career off the ground. With watery knees I pushed the doors open and stood there as tall as possible, as I had seen movie heroes do.

No one paid the slightest attention to me. I was a little disappointed but greatly relieved. I strode over to the bar. The bartender was busy.

The Bluebell was a big barn of a place, sixty feet wide by close to one hundred feet long. There were probably eight or ten tables in the back half near the stage where customers could sit and drink, watch the show, or play cards between shows. The bar was to the right as you entered. The rest of the place was filled with blackjack and poker tables, a crap table, and a roulette wheel.

I stood at the bar for what seemed an awfully long time. Finally there was a lull, and the bartender noticed me standing there. His eyebrows went up and the corners of his mouth went down as much as to say, "Well, look what we have here."

"What do you want, kid?" he inquired in a manner neither friendly nor unfriendly.

Trying desperately to be as grownup as possible I spoke in my deepest voice, determined to be suave and worldly. "I am the singer." Dammit, my voice cracked.

The bartender looked at me. He was having difficulty getting his wheels to mesh. Then the fog cleared from his eyes. "Oh," he said. "You're the new canary." It was half statement, half question. I was taken aback. I had never before heard the term "canary" used to identify a person as a singer.

While I hesitated he waited an instant for me to answer, and then he raised his shoulders and his eyebrows and drew down the corners of his mouth. I read his thoughts. "You look pretty young, but if that's what they want, what the hell?"

Putting the back of his right hand to the left side of his mouth to keep his message more or less private, he yelled toward a green-visored individual seated at a piano in the rear of the place, "Hey, Larry! Your canary is here."

Larry looked toward the bar, ran his eyes from one end to the other and then back to the bartender, who motioned back toward me and shrugged again, then directed me with his thumb to go on back to Larry.

As I approached him, Larry eyed me critically and greeted me with "The boss didn't tell me he was hirin' a kid." He hesitated. I made no effort to explain. "Oh, well," he sighed resignedly, as though he'd just have to make the best of it, and turned back to the piano. "What's your name, kid?"

That "kid" galled me. I wished they'd cut it out.

"My name is Glen. Glen Taylor."

Obviously, he liked Taylor better than Glen. "All right, Taylor, the first show goes on in ten minutes. The last show ends at two. You'll be on three times. Got your music?"

"It's out by the front door in my suitcase."

"What the hell you got in there?" he asked as I returned with the veins of my neck ballooning from the strain of carrying my future in the form of the heavy glass slides and the projector while trying to look relaxed when I was about to bust a gut.

I opened the suitcase and he seemed as surprised as if it were full of angleworms. "Illustrated songs!" he exclaimed, and looked at me as if waiting for an explanation. When I remained silent he said, "Why, kid, I haven't seen anything like this for five, maybe six years." I was beginning to feel like a boob, and I guess he could see it because he hastened on. "But who knows? Maybe they'll be glad to see an old friend. You don't need the machine. We got one. We show fight pictures and things. Better go up and explain the slides to the operator." He pointed toward the front and there to the left of the entrance door were apertures in the wall up near the ceiling, readily recognizable to an old pro like me as openings for the projection of motion pictures. I grabbed the heavy box of slides and handed my folio of music to Larry.

"Won't have time to rehearse this, Taylor. The show goes on in three minutes."

I said, "Okay. I'm doing 'Hello Central, Give me Heaven.' The others are in order."

THE LADIES? I rushed out front and climbed up to the booth. The operator was adjusting the machine. When it was working to his satisfaction he turned around and a puzzled look suggesting recognition, but incomplete recall, flickered across his face.

Time was short. The three-piece orchestra was tuning up. I dispensed with formalities.

"I'm the new singer. Here are my slides. I'm doing an illustrated song." And I handed him the slides.

He glanced at them, examined one or two, and said, "I have run these very same slides before." He thought a moment. "In Spokane, in 1914. Let me see," he mused, "that was the Taylor

Quartet." His eyes lit up. "You're a Taylor, aren't you?"

"Yes" I confirmed, "I am a younger brother. My name is Glen."

"Well, Glen, I'm glad to meet you. Those Taylor boys. Wonderful, wonderful." And he shook his head in disbelief at how wonderful they really were.

I started to explain how the slides were to be run. He raised his hand to stop me. "You don't need to tell me. I remember like it was yesterday. We'll make out okay, Glen. I want to talk to you more about your brothers. Good luck." And he held out his hand. I just barely made it up the four or five steps and through the door to the right of the stage when the orchestra struck up a lively tune. Once through the door I was brought up short. There just wasn't room to go any farther.

From the wings to the wall was no more than six feet, and from where I stood to the back wall was about ten feet.

Later, I discovered there were no dressing rooms. This was it, but who cared? This was show business and right there, so close I could have reached out and touched them, were four lovely ladies of the theater. They were ready to make their entrance.

My breathless intrusion startled them, and their collective attitude seemed to be, "Pardon *us!*" Then they all looked me up and down and their attitude underwent a definite change. They didn't voice it but if they had it probably would have been, "Well, well, look who's here!" They all gave me sexy looks, but one particularly caught my eye. She had hair so black it was bluish, high cheekbones, and slightly hollow cheeks. She gave me a smile. Very white, very even teeth. Ve-ry pretty! She looked me boldly square in the eye. Her eyes were gray-green and had depth. Something there struck a spark. My heart skipped at least part of a beat. There certainly was nothing demure here, but no open come-on either. Despite her slightly hollow cheeks she was adequately filled out elsewhere.

The four made their entrance kicking high, with big smiles, and the face of each one wearing her own conception of the seductive invitation with which they had just greeted me.

Now, lest you form the erroneous impression that these declassé damsels were unmitigated cradle snatchers, let me hasten to explain. I looked older than my fifteen years. My face was not round and babyish like most my age. My cheekbones were high, my nose somewhat angular. Some people had guessed my age as twenty or even twenty-one.

MONA The black-haired one who had aroused my interest was about five foot two, and she was the thinnest. Not too thin. The others were a little overweight. She just didn't carry any excess. Dancing, she gave the impression of being well muscled. Not lumpy, but sleek and sinewy. Probably twenty-two or -three. After their dance, which was more than just a little suggestive, they went back and sang in unison with gestures, a song that was shocking to me but at the same time exhilarating.

After all, a youth of fifteen who has suddenly bridged the gap to manhood by going out on his own must face up to life and learn the facts. This was it.

The girls finished with a few more high kicks and a swish of their skirts, which exposed their panty-clad bottoms for a tantalizing instant. Boy, this was really living! The snapshot finish brought the house down and there was loud applause, whistles, and raucous shouts.

The emcee-comic came bouncing on stage and regaled the receptive audience with five minutes of ribaldry. Rough stuff, but no four-letter words. Now he became the emcee and introduced Sandy, a redhead, and the oldest of the "girls."

Sandy sang a song in a rather coarse, throaty voice which was not unpleasant. For an encore she sang in French. While I did not understand French, I got the feeling she had learned the song by ear from a phonograph record. Understanding, though, wasn't important. There were wiggles, bumps, grinds, and gestures, and the audience was free to imagine what it was all about. Apparently those lusty customers out there were well pleased with their imaginings because Sandy got more of the "anything goes" applause.

Back came the emcee to gag it up for another generous interval, at the end of which he called the four hard-working girls back again. After that, the emcee again, with more humor calculated to appeal to the proven prurient tastes of the patrons. When he had reached the point of diminishing returns he introduced the busty strawberry blonde. Her name was Lil.

That's the way it went. The chorus, a girl, the chorus, a girl, with the emcee in between.

As he came offstage one time he stopped and peeked out at the audience through the peephole in the tormentor. When the emcee relinquished the peephole, I took a look at the audience and so began one of my favorite pastimes, audience watching.

Watching an audience watch a show is great fun. The most respectable and staid-looking sort of people will get the most way-out expressions imaginable on their faces.

This audience was at least two-thirds men, dressed in every imaginable garb. The women seemed to be pretty much alike, in that nearly all of them were made up as heavily as the girls onstage. Even I knew what this signified.

Between numbers, the girls had been changing costumes right down to their G-strings. At first I was embarrassed and looked away, then I stole a few furtive glances, and finally, when I realized that no one was paying any attention to me, I got in some good looks. Lil was on stage, and it seemed she went in for comedy. A song about a decrepit old codger who couldn't cut the mustard anymore, but liked to try, and he paid, and paid. Lil demonstrated by shoving a roll of bills into the gully between her and her brassiere. Lil got a good hand.

I was as tense as a Tennessee racehorse waiting for the gun. Surely I'd be on soon.

The emcee was out there again, but instead of introducing me or bringing the girls on again, as had been the order, now it was the juggler.

When the emcee came off he sat down, lit a cigarette, and picked up the *Police Gazette*.

I stepped over and asked him when I was going on. I didn't like to appear eager, but I could no longer contain myself. The waiting was bad enough without having to be on constant alert. Without even looking up, he said, "You're last."

I didn't know all there was to know about show business, but at least I knew that the star of the show came on last—or next to last. I could hardly believe my ears, but that's what the man said. The suspense had been a strain before but now, realizing that I was the star act, I got so tied up inside I felt sick to my stomach.

The juggler received the poorest hand of the evening. Apparently the mixed bag of customers were there to see girls, or at least hear jokes about girls, and this did not augur well for me.

Girls they wanted? Okay, girls they'd get! The emcee made some sort of crack about putting a dress on the juggler, and after a few more bids for belly laughs he called out the girls to take full advantage of the insatiable passion for pulchritude of the paying public.

After the girls, the emcee again with more murky merriment, then he brought out the bubbly blonde. Her name was Margarita, an unlikely Spanish name for one so fair.

Her voice had a childish quality that would not be unexpected, but surprisingly enough her song, instead of being "cute" to match her personality, was a tear-jerker about a poor girl who waited four years for her sailor to return and then, just as he started down the gangplank with his arms outstretched to enfold his loved one, her jealous former boyfriend shot him dead.

It went over well. I looked out through the peephole. Big strong men were applauding, I'd say, because she was such a beautiful blonde doll, soft and cuddly. The very idea of one so ripe for love being without a lover was unthinkable. Each of the preheated males was probably thinking he would like to substitute for the defunct sailor, and this excitement resulted in more vigorous applause. To make it unanimous, the overly painted ladies, being the notorious suckers for sentimentality which they are, were dabbing their eyes while they applauded more enthusiastically than they had all evening. If they liked that song, these ladies should go for "Hello Central, Give Me Heaven." It was the tear-jerker to end all tear-jerkers.

For an encore, Margarita sang a song in Spanish. Maybe that name "Margarita" wasn't completely misleading, after all. While this song called for some fancy eye rolling and sideways bumps, it was quite refined when compared to the other girls'.

To wind up, she did a little Spanish dance.

Now without bringing all the girls out, as had been the invariable order up till now, the emcee introduced the sinewy girl with the black hair. Her name was Mona. She seemed to be something special because he devoted more time to extolling her fantastic talents and accomplishments. To boil it all down, she was going to do an acrobatic dance.

She was certainly limber. No wonder she was sinewy. Anyone

tying themselves in knots like this three times a night had to be in the best possible physical condition.

She was good. Of course, in order to please this type of audience, she had to impart sexy overtones to her performance. With her shoulders on the floor and her feet back under her waist, she did bumps and grinds with her elevated hips. She did unbelievable splits on the floor and in the air with her shoulders on the floor. As the climax to her act, she placed on a water glass what I later learned was an imitation celluloid cucumber about five inches long. Then she bent over backward and put her head between her legs and took the cucumber in her mouth and proceeded to swallow it until just the tip was showing.

This brought down the house.

She reproduced the vegetable, replaced it on the glass, and straightened up to terrific applause.

As Mona came by me I said, "You were best of all."

Chorus girls are generally a jealous, bitchy, back-biting lot of lovelies whose greatest desire is to be more popular than those others, whether it be with the paying customers on the other side of the footlights, or in the romantic arts. This is not invariably true, by any means. I have known chorus girls whose mothers traveled with them as chaperones. I have know others strictly on their own who couldn't be touched with a ten-foot pole.

If I had said to Mona, "I thought you were very good," that would have been very good, but to tell her she was "best of all" not only elevated her to her proper eminence, but it put those others who thought they were so cute and pretty and smart right down there below her where they belonged.

Mona stopped, looked up at me, gave me an odd, square-cornered smile, and reached up and put her hand on my arm. As she said "Thank you" she gave a squeeze, and she squeezed in just the right place for the most erotic effect, right where every male has been felt a thousand times to test how his manhood is coming along. Right on the muscle.

If the top of my head had been of balloon rubber with a tube running to the muscle of my good right arm, it couldn't have worked better. When she pressed my arm, the top of my head went up two inches and settled back down only when she removed her electrified little hand.

Now I *had* to make good. I just *had* to stick around this place and that sweet, lovely, friendly, high-voltage girl.

The emcee had taken over again while I was preoccupied with our little romantic interlude. Shortly, he called the girls out again. As they started to exit I cleared my throat and got ready. This had to be me. There wasn't anyone else.

When the girls exited they came back for a bow, and the juggler was with them. He stood in the center, and they all put their arms around the waists of those next to them and swayed in unison. The emcee stepped out front while the others sang something about "We've Had a Wonderful Time." As he spoke they softened their singing so he could be heard. What was this? It was obvious to anyone that this was the finale. My heart sank. When would I go on? Or would I?

"Ladies and gentlemen," he was saying. "This concludes our first show of the evening, but we have a special treat in store for you. We have a lad who is a very talented singer. Tonight he is making his first appearance as a professional here on the stage of the Bluebell. If you like him, he will be with us as a regular feature."

This is a hell of a thing, I was thinking. *I'm not the star. I'm not even part of the show. They have refused to accept any responsibility for me at all and downgraded me as an amateur. If I'm good they've got themselves a singer, and if I'm not, no one has any kick coming because I'm thrown in free and extra.*

The emcee wound up as the girls and the juggler faded into the wings. "Ladies and gentlemen, a nice round of applause for this handsome young man, Glen Taylor!"

By God, I'd show 'em! My temples were pounding as I walked into the spotlight.

"SING, CANARY"   With illustrated songs the singer had to stand to one side in a separate spotlight so the slides could be projected on the screen, which was being lowered into place as I came onstage.

Everything went off without a hitch. The orchestra, violin, piano, and drums were pros and the projectionist timed the slides perfectly. I didn't have the best voice in the world but it was good and young and clear, unclouded by liquor or smoking or overuse. I was no amateur. I had been singing at the picture show for nearly two years, so I had good stage presence and I was pretty damn good looking. In Lewiston I had bought a black suit and shoes and a black-and-white diagonal striped tie. I knew I looked my best.

My hair was a peculiar shade of brown, sort of light milk chocolate. I kept it combed loosely, with no dressing of any kind. Once a dear lady in Kooskia had said to me after the show, "You looked like an innocent angel when you sang tonight. The spotlight made your lovely hair look like a beautiful halo." The orchestra played my introduction and waited for me. I was in no hurry to start. I looked around the hall, opened and closed my hands. I wanted to give the impression that I was uneasy, pulling myself together. If they wanted to class me as an amateur I'd make the most of it. I had been studying the audience through that peephole. Those men were regular guys. They'd like a kid who wasn't too cocksure. Those hard-faced women were really sentimental softies. Some of them may have had husbands and possibly even a child at one time. Those who hadn't were hiding a great emotional void within them. Some of them might have had a teenage son if things had gone differently. Maybe they did—somewhere.

I put my closed hand to my mouth as I turned from the audience a quarter turn as though clearing my throat.

I turned back, raised my chin, and looked up toward the source of the spotlight and sang. Before I was halfway through the song, handkerchiefs were dabbing wherever there was a feminine heartbeat. I put every bit of pathos into my notes that I could summon and, as I sang the last few bars, sobs were plainly audible from every hustler in the saloon. My cheeks were tear-stained when I finished.

Would they go for this outdated offering? This was the payoff. As the last note was ending I bowed from the waist till my head hung straight down and was even with my knees, my arms hanging loosely nearly to the floor and my hair falling in profuse disarray. I held the pose as the applause started and grew and swelled, louder and louder. No whistling, no shouting, no foot stomping, just good solid applause.

After six seconds (I know it was six seconds because I had practiced this while singing in the picture show) I straightened up and stood there unsmiling without making any effort to straighten my wayward locks, or wipe away the tears, plainly visible on my cheeks. After another six seconds I repeated my bow and held it for five seconds. The applause was continuing. I stood erect, took my breast pocket handkerchief, and pressed it to each cheek to dry the tears. After a few seconds I tried to manage a slight, compressed smile to give the impression that I was pleased with their applause but too emotionally upset to relax and really smile. This act (let's admit it, that's what it was) stripped the veneer of cynicism from those poor, overly painted, pitiful pretenders and drove them to the verge of hysteria. Some were sobbing, all were dabbing their eyes and applauding frantically, while at the same time urging their heavy-handed escorts to greater efforts.

I bowed once more and this time came up smiling, and there was plenty of equipment there to smile with. My teeth were even and white. That did it.

The applause became bedlam; shouts of "More!" frantic whistling and stomping. I smiled and bowed, bowed and smiled.

After at least a minute and a half, the emcee came out. As he passed me, he whispered out of the corner of his mouth, "You're great, kid."

I have on occasion taken as many as seven legitimate encores during my career on the stage without changing the song, simply singing another chorus, but no other triumph could ever be as sweet as that night in that rough town. I took five encores singing a different song each time with many bows in between. When you have been thrown to the wolves as I was and then come through, it is the most soul-satisfying experience imaginable.

It was nearly time for the second show to start when the emcee called everyone on stage again for another finale in which I was not only included but was in fact the star. The emcee said, "Ladies and gentlemen, I wish to thank you on behalf of our new young singing star, Glen Taylor, for the wonderful reception you have given him tonight. He will be featured in our two shows yet to be presented this evening."

As the curtain descended, the applause started and grew and became louder until the emcee, who was finally getting around to introducing himself to me, stopped to listen and then told the girls and the juggler, who were waiting to congratulate me, to get in position for a curtain call.

For one who had never been party to this most rewarding of show business experiences, I did pretty well. I had seen this happen in the movies so I had a general idea of what to expect. We took six curtain calls, with the emcee frantically rearranging his cast for each one. This was something that had not happened since Lillian Russell was here, and no one could remember when that was.

As the curtain fell for the sixth and final time, I noticed the four girls. Each had the most unsightly black smears under her eyes. Obviously, they had been as emotionally involved as the painted ladies out front. Having no claim to star status, they respectfully stood back while the juggler and Al, the emcee, congratulated me. Then they each approached me again in the same order in which they had made their entrances and told me how wonderful I was. Lil, the busty one, broke down sobbing and completely enfolded me to her heaving, overblown breasts. She had to be literally dragged away by the juggler and Al.

When the others had gone to relax in their chairs offstage Margarita, the blonde, came back for a few seconds. She put her arms around my neck while she half whispered exaggerated paeans of adulation and gave me a sexy massage with her plump tummy. Mona spotted her and dashed to my rescue in a fury. She grabbed my seducer by the shoulder, spun her around, and hissed between clenched teeth, "Listen, you tramp, you keep your hands off this boy. He's not for your kind. Beat it!"

I don't know by what right Mona presumed to give orders, but poor thwarted Margarita didn't argue. She shrugged and flipped her fanny from side to side as she walked away.

Mona squeezed my arm reassuringly with the same effect previously noted.

Just as the top of my head had settled back down, a buxom lady came bursting through the stage door. She rushed over and hugged me. She was followed by a tall, gangly, farmerish-looking man whom the emcee introduced as the owner of the Bluebell. He shook my hand and congratulated me and then introduced me, I'd say a little belatedly, to his wife who had been squeezing me and pinching my cheeks.

LOUNGE LIZARD During the thirty-minute interval between the second and third shows, Mona asked me *sotto voce* if I would like a sandwich. I certainly would. I hadn't eaten since breakfast, and it was midnight. That's a long time for a healthy, nearly sixteen-year-old boy to go without nourishment. I had been too nervous and tense all day trying to work up courage to enter the Bluebell to even think of eating, and after I got inside there had been no time. The first show had run overtime because Al had expected no more than a song or two from me and the five encores had used up practically the whole intermission between the first and second shows. The second show had been trimmed and tightened and even though I had again sung five numbers, we were now back on schedule.

"I'll see you in the rear booth in the restaurant through the door over there," she directed me. The management frowned on the performers being together while on the premises. You were supposed to get around individually and let the customers have the thrill of meeting you and basking in your glamorous presence. This was particularly true where the girls were concerned. They were supposed to take no more than fifteen minutes to eat and spend the other fifteen circulating.

Mona ordered a fruit salad and a dry roast beef sandwich and did not eat the bread. This was the first time I had ever seen anyone attempting to control their weight by eating selectively. I had never heard of the idea of not eating certain foods because they were more fattening. This was the penalty she had to pay for that supple, lean body of hers.

As I sat down beside her she said, "Glen, you were simply magnificent tonight."

This girl must be pretty well educated to use a word like "magnificent" flashed through my mind. She put that electrified instrument of exquisite pleasure—namely, her long-fingered hand—on my arm again. This time she did not squeeze my muscle, she just laid it on my forearm, but the effect was the same. There went my scalp up in the air again. She must have noticed something wrong with me because a perplexed expression flitted across her face as she broke contact by removing her hand from my arm. I returned to normal, "Phew," and ordered ham and eggs.

She asked questions about where I was from, my family, and how I happened to come to the Bluebell.

I was only fifteen years old and had not yet learned that silence is golden. I was happy to talk, particularly about myself.

When thirteen of our fifteen minutes were gone and I was bolting my ham and eggs, she asked me where I was staying. Fact of the matter was I wasn't staying anyplace. I had checked out of the hotel that morning and left my other suitcase with the clerk, because I was unsure as to what the order of my new life might me. Perhaps a room went with the job. Mona assured me it did not.

"But," she said, "you can't afford to pay seven dollars a week at the hotel. You can get a room in a private home for two and a half or three dollars."

"Do you know anyone with a room to rent?" I asked.

"N-n-no," she admitted slowly, and brightened as a solution to my problem occurred to her. "I have an extra room at my place and you can stay there if you want to. You wouldn't have any rent to pay that way, and I could fix you a home-cooked meal once in a while. You'll get awfully tired of eating in the restaurant all the time."

If you had been me, what would you have said to such a neighborly invitation? That's exactly what I said.

I hadn't asked her about her marital status, but if she had a house and was inviting a young man to occupy the vacant room, it followed that she had a husband. There is no blinking the fact that I was more than a little let down by this deduction but, after all, she had done nothing to lead me to believe she was single. To be sure, she had put her hand on my arm three times with results that had gone beyond the bounds of friendship, but that wasn't necessarily her intention.

She gave me detailed directions to her house. After the last show I was to get my suitcase and go there. There would be a light in the window.

Inasmuch as Mona was married, I might as well forget it and start looking around. During the last show I took advantage of a couple of opportunities to start conversations with the blonde, Margarita. Mona kept a close watch on these goings on, and Margarita was careful not to touch me.

After the last show I went to the hotel, got my suitcase, and made my way to Mona's place. It was a small frame house in what was hardly the best part of town. Mona let me in. She was dressed in a robe with a nightgown showing top and bottom.

She showed me to my room and helped me unpack my things. There wasn't much: one suit, four or five shirts, as many neckties. Two pairs of BVDs, some handkerchiefs, and three pairs of cotton socks. I had another suit, and another shirt and tie, and another pair of BVDs. These were the clothes I was wearing. I also had a straight razor, mug and soap, and toothbrush and paste. That was it.

I got the impression that Mona's attitude was quite motherly. "I am heating up some homemade soup," she told me.

By now I had finished unpacking and she had been helping, taking the things and placing them in drawers.

"Don't you have any pajamas?" she asked after none had shown up. A little sheepishly and perhaps a little irritated that she had put me in an embarrassing position, I had to admit that I didn't.

"Here," she said, bustling over to the closet, "here is a pair that should just about fit you," and she handed them back to me without turning while she stooped over and rummaged further. "And here is a pair of slippers and a robe."

This was a nice robe. Satin? I had seen suave villains in the movies wearing robes tied at the waist with the long-tasseled cord or narrow sash. I had often thought that some day I would have one, and here I was, only one day in show business, preparing to spend the evening in this villainous raiment.

"Now," she was saying, "you get into these things so you can relax. You've been under a terrific strain. Your first day as a professional and all. You must have had a hard day. When you're not used to such things, being cooped up with four girls having to change practically right in your lap must have made it real hard. Hard—and long, too, I'll bet."

Unless I just had a dirty mind, she had put undue emphasis on those two words, "hard" and "long." She hesitated just long enough for me, had I been quick on the uptake, to have leered recognition of the innuendo, but being such an unsophisticated dolt I was taken aback and stood there slack-jawed at such brazenness—if that was the way she meant it.

For the brief instant it had taken her to enunciate those words there had been the same bold manner, the same challenging gaze that I had noticed at our first encounter. It lasted a fleeting moment and was gone. Then she smiled sweetly, gave her shoulders a cute, quick little hunch, and favored me with a flash of an innocent wink as she tacked a questioning, short spoken "Huh?" on the end of the sentence as if asking, "Are those plans okay?"

"Now you get changed and I'll go dish up the soup," and she patted me on the shoulder. There it was again, that motherly attitude.

I never felt so grownup in my life as I did in that outfit. I was in the same class with Bert Lytell, Thomas Meighan, and William Farnum. It was a feast of self-satisfaction, admiring my lounge-lizard self in the slightly wavy full-length mirror on the closet door. Even the curve in the mirror was a plus. It made me look taller. I could hardly restrain myself. I was so thrilled with what I saw, I wanted to jump up in the air and holler "Yow!"

I couldn't wait for Mona to return, so I went to the kitchen and stood leaning carelessly against the doorframe.

She was stirring the soup, and when she turned around she was so startled she inhaled a surprised "oh" and nearly dropped her spoon. She quickly recovered and did what was expected of her. She caught her lower lip between her teeth, opened her eyes wide, spread her arms full length, and admired me.

"Oh, Glen, you're even more handsome than you are in your black suit."

I was convinced of that, but it was good to hear her say it.

On her way to the cupboard for soup bowls, she hesitated long enough to pat my cheek. Mama had done that thousands of times.

The soup was good. In addition to her more exotic talents, she could cook.

Somehow the conversation got around to her family. She had none. The last relative she knew of had died two years ago. A brother. "If he had lived he would be just about your age," she said.

They had been very close. "You remind me of him so much." As she said it she stopped eating, leaned back, and with both hands on the table gazed reflectively at a spot occupied by the sugar bowl. It was plain that she was seeing a face and not the object.

So! She doesn't have a motherly feeling toward me. I'm her brother. This thought did not help to enliven things or make the cozy snack more romantic.

What difference does it make anyway, I asked myself, *if she is married? I wonder where he is. Maybe he is a traveling man. He might even be asleep in their room.* No matter where her husband was, it was clear where I stood. Her brother. One thing was sure. I'd been way off base reading an unwarranted suggestion into her remark about the long hard day.

"Now let's get right to bed," she was saying. "I'll clean up the dishes in the morning." That "Let's get right to bed" wasn't lost on me, but I let it pass and complimented her on the soup, doing my best to spread it on like Papa would have done.

I had been somewhat embarrassed about calling her Mona after I decided she was married. Concluding she had a motherly interest in me had added to my conflict, but now that I was her brother, Mona would certainly be in order.

While she was still puttering with the dishes I said "Goodnight, Mona" from the door to the parlor, went to my room and to bed. The pajamas were irksome. For the last three or four years I had slept naked, but I was going to wear these things and learn to be a gentleman if it killed me.

I was reaching for the switch on the lamp when there was a knock on the door. *What now?* Unspoken. "Come in," I called.

She opened the door and smiled sweetly as she came over and sat on the edge of the bed. "I just wanted to say goodnight," she explained.

MONA'S STORY   For want of something better to say, and to satisfy my curiosity, I asked, "Do these pajamas and the robe and slippers belong to your husband?"

She looked at me for several seconds before answering. "Yes—they do—or did," she confirmed in a manner that left no doubt that there was something not too happy about the situation.

"Is—he dead?" I did not want to stir unhappy memories, but she appeared to be waiting for me to say something, and that question seemed to be the logical one.

"He might as well be," she sighed, and after a pause while she looked at the floor, she launched into a story of how her husband had worked in a place similar to the Bluebell. He got to gambling, stole money from this fellow Norcus, his boss, and was now doing ten to twenty in state prison, right here in Pierce City. Not a half mile from where we were at this very instant. "It has ruined both our lives and I would have been perfectly justified to have divorced him long ago. He started me on the road to where I am."

I had a pretty good idea where she was, but I didn't want to hear her say it. It is much more agreeable to close one's mind to the faults and foibles of those we like than to be apprised of bitter, degrading truths. If denouement comes in the form of a confession, it is even more unpleasant, so I kept still. I didn't encourage her, but she was hurrying on.

"He begged and pleaded with me to give myself to Rafe Norcus in exchange for a promise that he would not be prosecuted and be allowed to repay the money over a period of years." She paused and bit her lip. "Finally I consented."

I had heard my older brothers talk about dancehall girls when they had thought I wasn't listening or didn't understand. Invariably, it seemed "the girls" always had a sad story to justify their downfall and their way of life. Generally, they were very convincing. Was Mona's story true, or was it just a story? She was intelligent. If she made up a story it would be a good one.

It made me feel very adult to be listening to this confession by a grown woman, but embarrassment tied my tongue, and I just lay there with my hands clasped behind my head.

She remained silent for some time after admitting she had surrendered herself.

"I don't know how Rafe Norcus ever accumulated his fortune," she finally went on, "because I never knew him to talk of anything but women and what could be done with them. It was an obsession with him." She got up and started pacing back and forth, clasping and unclasping her hands. After a bit she started in again. "In order that I should be handy when the whim struck him, and to rob me of my respectability as a housewife so that anything I might say against him would be worthless in any court, he made me go to work at his saloon. He had living quarters upstairs where no one dared disturb him." She stopped pacing and stood with her hands on the foot of the maple bedstead before continuing.

"I was a dancing teacher before I married. I was forced by

Rafe Norcus to do the sort of thing you saw tonight. For six months I was compelled to do anything he demanded of me," she was almost snarling now. "Not only that, but he demanded my passionate cooperation. Finally, when I found it impossible to satisfy him, he sent Bob to the pen."

Truth or fiction? I was convinced and told her, "You certainly did more than could be expected of you."

"I have never been able to convince myself of that," she said with a slow shake of her head, "so I have kept trying. I came here and got this job to be near Bob. I have had three lawyers. They have made promises that they could get him released, but they wanted money. One I paid the same way I paid Rafe. The second one wanted cash. I paid him, and paid him, with money given me by three men who had money and were willing and anxious to give it to me." She became quite agitated and her voice rose. "I am not like those others," she breathed heavily, pointing her finger at me. "I am not a common hustler. They deal on a volume basis and before long they lose their womanhood and become passionless. I am not like that. I am an expert and an artist, thanks to Rafe Norcus, and I get paid accordingly, but what good does it do me? Every cent to shysters. Damn them! I am intimate with men more seldom than most married women. I am not common. You understand?"

She was getting so worked up I was a little uneasy. I got up and put my arms around her as I would have had she been my own sister. I held her head to my chest and patted her hair. She broke down and sobbed.

At length she regained control of herself. "I have been a fool to act like this, Glen," she murmured, "but I just had to let it out. There is no one else. No one. I have been so lonely. So lonely." She relaxed in my arms a moment and then she saw the pendulum clock on the wall.

"My God, it's four o'clock! I'm sorry. I'm sorry," she apologized. "Here, get in bed," and she led me like I was a child and tucked me in and then stooped down and kissed me. There it was, that electrifying effect again and I felt ashamed that it could happen at a moment like this, but I could not control the wave of desire that engulfed me.

You're as mercilessly horny as an old turkey gobbler, I reproached myself, but at the same time I reached up to pull her down to me.

I'd swear she discerned what I had in mind before I had even moved because she straightened up quickly, said "Goodnight, Glen" as she patted my cheek, and walked to the door. She hesitated, then turned, and her breast was noticeably rising and falling. I thought she was about to rush back to share my bed but after a moment she smiled a strained smile, said "goodnight" with an obvious effort to keep her voice normal, and as she softly closed the door I could hear her passionate breathing.

Despite the fact that it was four-thirty, I lay awake for some time. What goes on here? Why tell me all this? How did she feel toward me? Was that a sisterly pat on the cheek? Then why the heavy breathing? That's the way Lil back in Stites had breathed after we had fooled around a while and she was all worked up.

I didn't sleep too well. I wasn't used to the striking clock. It would wake me up and then I'd lie awake and think of Mona and all she had said. I had a hard night. I was awakened by Mama stroking my brow and hair as she always did when she had to wake me up and disliked having to do it. As I emerged from unconsciousness and before recollections of the night began to take shape, I thought, *How can this be Mama?*

I opened my eyes. It wasn't Mama. It was Mona. Sitting on the edge of the bed tenderly caressing my brow.

"I thought you'd never wake up," she laughed. "Do you know it's afternoon and we have to rehearse at one-thirty?

"We'll have ham and eggs. This is the first time I've cooked ham and eggs for years," she exclaimed delightedly. "I've been to the store already to get them," saying which she threw the covers off me and held out both hands to help me rise. She gave a husky yank and I wound up standing against her. After the frustrating night I had had, coupled with the fact that I was rested, I had a mad desire to crush her to me.

Before I could, she stepped back and looked me in the eye like a lion tamer and said, "Hurry now. Everything is here. Hot water, razor, mug, towel. I even got you some lilac shaving lotion." She pointed to each item as she mentioned it, all neatly arranged on a marbletop dresser.

Boy, what service! It was something foreign to my experience.

Lilac shaving lotion! Shaving lotion had never touched my smooth, virgin cheeks.

"Well, thanks. Thanks for the lotion, too," I stammered, almost bashfully. I was overcome by such solicitude.

Plainly, she was completely captivated by my boyish behavior. She laughed and did an out-of-character hopscotch step as she left the room.

The little room where I shaved had hot running water but no bathtub or toilet. I needed a toilet, and I needed it bad. I managed to keep things under control until I had shaved and dressed. I was too bashful to ask this "strange woman" where her toilet was. All the talk about intercourse and all that was bad enough, but to ask—forget it.

My room was on a back corner of the house. That shade hadn't been opened since I moved in. I went over and peeked out. There it was, so near and yet so far. The only way to get there was through the kitchen where she stood guard, or out the front door and around the house. I tiptoed out the front door and hurried so fast I would have been disqualified in any walking race.

I made it! Boy! Relaxing there, I pondered the momentous question, *Which is best, a drink of clear cold water when you are nearly dying of thirst, or a good old two-holer when you really need it?*

Say, this lady has class. Roll paper! I had to admit, though, that a Sears Roebuck catalogue had advantages. Something to read and look at. Particularly those pictures of females in panties and union suits, but then the realization dawned on me. Those mail-order pictures were pretty tame after what I had seen last night when the girls at the Bluebell had stripped to practically nothing.

Like a stupid oaf, I didn't have sense enough to return to the house the way I had come. I used the back door into the kitchen. Mona was watching the other door where, by all that's right and holy, I should have made my entrance. My hostess was in the act of turning a pancake when I, with youthful exuberance and hurrying to escape the cold, burst through the door. She jumped and the pancake flew up in the air and lit in a gooey mess on the stove. I was mortified and she was petrified, but not for long. She laughed so hard she doubled over until there was another near

calamity. She nearly got her nose in one of the remaining un-
turned pancakes. That tickled her more, and we both laughed.

"Where in the world have you been?" she giggled. Later, she
told me I blushed. She needn't have. I knew it. If she had any
doubts about my countrified innocence that certainly must have
dispelled them.

"Oh-h-h," she apologized, "I am sorry. I don't have a bathroom. But," she hastened to inform me, "not too many people do
here in Pierce City."

"Nobody in Kooskia does," I admitted shamefacedly.

I pitched in and helped her get the pancake mess cleaned up
and we sat down to breakfast. Before it was over I realized that,
aside from any boy and girl attraction, I liked her a lot. An awful
lot.

LOVE NEST   At rehearsal Margarita kept making eyes at
me, but she didn't try to make physical contact in any way. I
could see that Mona was burned up clear down to her trim little
feet.

Both Larry, the pianist, and Al, the emcee, suggested that I
start getting away from illustrated songs. They said it was my
voice and delivery that went over, not the illustrations. They had
a lot of popular music. I ran through a song Larry suggested,
sang it to myself several times during the afternoon, and did it
that night. It went over as well as or better than the illustrated
songs. We decided that I should learn one song a day until just
one illustrated number was left, and keep that as a novelty.

The juggler had nothing to rehearse. They called his the
"floating act." That is, the rest of us were more or less permanent, but the one act changed every week. Starting Monday a
trick roper, who was also a fancy dan with a sixgun, would
replace the juggler.

As soon as we got to the Bluebell, Mona went out the front
door and came back just in time to rehearse the chorus dance
routines for the following week. She seemed quite breathless and
excited.

The girls didn't have any new steps to learn. There seemed to
be only a certain number which they already knew, and it was
simply a matter of rearranging them. As individuals, the girls

were constantly rehearsing new material. They seldom made any suggestions as to what they felt they would like to do. They seemed to have no ideas whatever. Al and Larry did their thinking for them. Mona was the exception. She simply told Larry what music she wanted and was left free to ad lib her dance routine.

After rehearsal, I was free to do as I pleased, so I roamed around and watched the gambling games, which were absolutely new and strange to me, of course.

It was a strange phenomenon that no one paid any attention to the rehearsing, yet at show time it became a big deal, and these very same guys would applaud and stomp and whistle.

The rehearsal was over by three. Mona got me aside and said she had an appointment with the lawyer. If I wanted to wait until six we could have dinner together.

"Of course I'll wait. I'd wait a lot longer than that for you." I tried to make it a pointed hint. I'm sure it wasn't lost on her, but she pretended to take it as a compliment and smiled. I had a feeling she wasn't telling the truth about the lawyer. She said, "I'll see you at six in the restaurant," patted my arm, and hurried out.

I walked around town and by chance strayed into the red-light district. There wasn't much activity this time of day, but some of the poor damn women were out sunning themselves and getting a little fresh air. I was invited in several times and my awkward answer of "maybe tonight" elicited knowing smiles which said as plainly as words, "Here's another young buck doing a little scouting and working up the nerve."

The posted sign advertised prices from one dollar to two and a half. One or two of the better places had no price advertised. I kept the thought out of my mind that the girls at the Bluebell were only a degree removed from what I saw about me. Each had a crummy little house in the area around the Bluebell and entertained just one customer each night.

At dinner Mona was unmistakably excited. I didn't ask her what had happened at the lawyer's. If she wanted to tell me that was her business, but no matter how curious I might be I would not ask her.

I *was* curious, and there was an element of jealousy here, too.

It's none of my busines what she does, I told myself, but that didn't change the fact that I felt a proprietary interest.

Mona picked at her meal. She pressed some money in my hand as we were getting up from the table. I'm sure I flushed with anger, and I handed it back a little brusquely. It was bad enough living at her house without paying. Incidentally, we'd have to make some arrangement about that.

I had less than five dollars, but the check was only seventy-five cents plus a dime tip.

She walked out the door while I stopped to pay the check and stood there looking like a reprimanded child. As we started down the street she said, "You're not angry, are you?"

"Well—no, but it wasn't very flattering." There was still a little bristle in my denial, and she demonstrated her good sense by remaining silent a little while and giving me more time to cool off.

Then very brightly, as though the idea had just popped into her mind, she suggested, "Let's go to our house." The "our" was not lost on me, but if it made her happy to call it "our house," what the heck. So I agreed, and as we strolled along she put her arm through mine. Despite all the reasons why I should not let her get under my skin, my pulse rate increased measurably, but I resisted the urge to tighten my arm around hers. We should turn here, but she steered me straight ahead. I could see a corner of the house a block up the side street. Oh well, she just wanted to take the long way home. Stroll a little. At the next corner she turned.

"Where are we going?"

"To our house," she answered matter of factly.

I was positive she was mistaken and said so. "We are a block past where we should have turned."

"Oh no we're not," she contradicted.

"Well, this isn't the shortest way," I insisted.

"Yes, it's the shortest way," she stated flatly.

"Well, either I'm dreaming or you are out of your mind," I protested.

She seemed to be enjoying all this. "No, you are not dreaming and I am definitely not out of my mind. This is the shortest way to our house."

She emphasized that "our" a little heavier. "Well," I said, "I

would have bet anything we should have turned a block back."
"How much do you want to bet?" she challenged. Something
was going on here but I played along.

"I'll bet a dime this is not the shortest way to the house."

"All right," she accepted, "we have a dime bet. I say this is
the shortest way to our house."

At the first house off Main Street she turned in through the
gate, up the walk, up the three steps, across the porch, and then
took a key from her purse and unlocked the door. Once inside, I
was astonished. Here was the same furniture arranged in almost
the same manner, but this was not the same house.

The joke was on me, it seemed, so I laughed. "What goes on
here anyhow?"

"Do you like it?" she asked as she maneuvered me from room
to room.

"Sure I like it." It was the same number of rooms, but definitely newer and more spacious. "This is real nice," I conceded,
"but what's the idea?" We had now inspected all the rooms, but
there was one door off the little hallway which we had not yet
opened. We stopped in front of it. She smiled her very attractive
smile, patted my cheek with a quick one, two, three, so hard it
hurt. It reminded me of Mama. She would do that to show
affection, and always it would make my dander rise at the very
same instant I was being ashamed of myself.

Mona opened the door, and there was a very pretty bathroom.
Tile and everything.

"Like it?" she inquired, again a little anxiously.

Everything fell into place. Because of that stupid, embarrassing situation this morning she had somehow managed to move
here in the four or five hours since.

"Mona, goddamn it, you shouldn't have done this," I protested, wagging my head. I felt terribly guilty. It was an outlandish imposition to cause her to go to all this trouble and expense.
How in the hell had she done it? I was overcome. Tears came to
my eyes and I gathered her to me, her head on my chest as I
patted her hair. I held her tenderly for at least a full minute and
then released her and pulled my handkerchief from my hip pocket
and wiped my eyes.

I grinned at her apologetically and noticed tears brimming in
her own eyes. I threw my head back and laughed as I took my

nice linen breast pocket handkerchief and tried to dab her eyes dry. My farmer touch wasn't sufficiently gentle, and she took over in self-defense. I held her again and then, with my arm about her shoulders, we went over the house once more. "But how did you ever do it?" I asked incredulously.

She explained briefly what had had to be an all-out effort.

"I knew this house was for rent and I had thought of moving before. When I went out while you were rehearsing I rented the house, then called the dray company and told them to move everything and arrange it as nearly like it was as possible. After rehearsal I came over and worked until six getting things straightened around." I could no more have resisted the innocent urge to take her in my arms than I could have flown to a star.

"You darn nut," I said affectionately, "I could have helped you."

"Yes, but it wouldn't have been a surprise," and she was half laughing and half crying for joy as she said it. We stood there, each secure in the protective embrace of the other. Then we had another tear drying and laughed foolishly at what sentimental softies we were.

Nothing was said for some time, so I suggested that we go outside and reconnoiter the surroundings.

We had come out the front door. The porch was effectively screened from the street with climbing vines that continued in the form of an arcade clear to the front gate. Anyone entering here could be walking along the street and instantly vanish. To the right of the house was a vacated lumberyard.

On the left and also across the alley in the rear were vacant weed-grown lots. This was not much better—if at all—than the part of town from which she had moved. It occurred to even my uncynical mind, that a lady who worked at the Bluebell might not be welcome, and probably not even allowed to move in, among those who considered themselves to be "respectable" people.

Surveying the uninviting surroundings I observed, "We are almost in the country."

"I like privacy," said Mona.

DON'T TUCK ME IN   During the show Margarita became a little bolder. She brushed against me and placed her hand on my arm, being careful that Mona wasn't in sight.

This was a dilemma. I knew Mona frowned on my having anything to do with Margarita, but what the hell? I was a man—a young man, at any rate—and I had a man's passions and, aside from that compelling biological fact, I was anxious to complete my transition to manhood. I was sure that I could because now I was on my own. I was no longer under my father's roof so I would not be obligated to honor the standards he had set for my behavior as a boy.

I did not want to be sneaky about it, though. I'd have to talk to Mona. I'd rather be more than a brother to her, but if that was what she wanted, then she must realize that even her own brother would have been involved romantically long before now, and she would have had to reconcile herself to sharing him with some other woman or women. Yes, I'd have to talk to her about it tonight.

By bedtime I still hadn't talked to Mona. I figured she must be exhausted after all she had accomplished this day, and I couldn't bring myself to open a subject that might prove emotionally upsetting to her. I had no idea how she would react.

I reached for the switch just as she knocked. "Come in, Mona." She was beautiful. Beautiful as hell, dammit. I wished she hadn't cast me in this stupid role of her brother. There was something strange about her smile. It was strained and unnatural.

"I just came to say goodnight," she said as she came toward me, "and to tuck you in." My dander rose. Tuck me in, my ass. I didn't need her or anybody else to tuck me in. I needed something, all right, but I didn't need to be tucked in. I needed something and needed it bad, and here it was, but I had to keep up this silly masquerade.

She was sitting on the edge of the bed as she had the night before. She pulled the covers up and there my arms were pinned to my sides again. How stupid can you get. Now she leaned over to repeat that sisterly goodnight kiss. Her left hand rested on the bed, effectively straight-jacketing my right arm, and she was practically sitting on my left arm.

As her lips brushed mine I made a heroic effort to extricate my arms and grab her in one continuous motion. My left arm came out the side of the bed and I succeeded in getting a precarious hold on her right arm, but in concentrating on freeing my right arm I loosened my grip and she was gone. She was really gone. She didn't even say goodnight. She didn't stop at all. Not even to close the door.

I heard the door to her room close, and not too gently. I lay there, my heart pounding as a result of my passionate intentions and physical exertion. When my temples quit throbbing and my breathing became less labored, I could hear her sobbing convulsively.

A wave of remorse swept over me. What an ungrateful heel I was. Here she had been enjoying her first happiness in years, and now I had changed from being the source of that happiness into an additional emotional problem.

When I finally went to sleep my rest was disturbed by dreams compounded of Mona, Margarita, and the fact that I was a healthy young male, not yet sixteen years of age.

When I woke up the old pendulum clock seemed to have been waiting for me. It started its gong-like toll. Eleven o'clock. I could hear Mona moving about in the kitchen. I took my razor and toothbrush and went to the bathroom.

As I passed the closed kitchen door the rustling of pans stopped. Well, it was just too damn bad. This poor girl who had been victimized by every man she met was now so afraid of me that she acted like a frightened mouse. "Hell!"

In my careless anger, I cut my chin quite badly while shaving. I started bleeding, really bleeding. I held a washrag to the wound and searched through the medicine cabinet for a styptic pencil, adhesive tape, anything. Nothing. At least it took my mind off the gulf I had opened between Mona and me.

I stuck my head in the kitchen and asked if there was a styptic pencil around. When she first turned there was not the expected fear I anticipated, but an air of tired resignation as though she had said in so many words, "Here I am, do what you will with me."

If there is anything which will take the mind of a fifteen-year-old Romeo off the subject of sex, it's the sight of his own blood. The whole washcloth was red, and when Mona saw it her first thought was that I had deliberately tried to commit suicide, or at least made a bluff of it. She later admitted as much.

Her eyes widened in terror and she flew to me, whispering, "Glen, oh Glen," and with trembling hands she raised the blood-soaked cloth to expose the quarter-size piece of flesh that was three-fourths severed and hanging down. She put the back of her hand to her face to shut out the sight of my bloody chin, and turned her head away, but just for a few seconds. Then she pulled herself together, took me by the arms, and authoritatively pushed me into a chair by the breakfast table. She hurriedly produced some bandage and adhesive tape and bandaged the wound. The fact that I had only shaved half my face made little difference. A microscope might not have detected which side was which.

As she worked she kept repeating, "Glen, oh Glen," and when she finished, she added to my bewilderment about her feelings toward me by emotionally cooing, "Glen, sweetheart." If I hadn't been so shaken up by my more-blood-than-injury fool trick, that "sweetheart" might have started me all over again where I left off the night before. As it was, I made a mental note of it to be mulled over when my continued breathing was assured.

SWEET ROSIE O'MOOZY   We had breakfast with no word of last night. Small talk about "the new house" from me and "*our* new house" from her. She was dressed, but I had breakfast in my—"my?"—pajamas.

As the meal progressed she asked me questions about Kooskia, my home, my parents.

Without being too obvious and in a half-teasing sort of way, she asked me how many girls I had left brokenhearted back in Kooskia.

"Oh, I don't think anyone was brokenhearted. There wasn't anything serious," I admitted, perhaps a little ruefully.

"Do you mean to say," she probed further, "that a handsome guy like you never went all the way with any girl?"

If I had any feelings of resentment over her personal questions they were more than outweighed by the sexy pleasure of discussing the subject. "No, I didn't," I had to confess, but I hastened to explain. "That's the way I was trained. Respect and chivalry toward girls, and when I would get right to the that point I couldn't go on. I've been thinking about it though, and I know that men have to do things like that just like they have to eat," I expounded eruditely. "What Papa really meant, I believe, was that I should not get in a mess and have to marry some girl, and—well, you know," I ended aimlessly.

"Yes, I know," she said.

"Now that I am out on my own I don't believe that I am bound by those old rules anymore," I argued, and rested my case by declaring, "I'm sure I can be like other men."

She picked up the loose ends and summarized for me, "And you are anxious and determined to find out."

"Well, yes," I agreed, not too positively. The prospect was a little overwhelming. It would be the biggest event in my life. At least in my life to date, and while I was anxious for it to happen, I was also anxious about what *would* happen. I took a bite of hotcakes. A mouthful of food is always an excellent out when you are at a loss as to what to say.

Mona sat studying me. I knew she was, but I did not look up, pretending to concentrate all my attention on eating. The silence was becoming a little bothersome when she finally spoke. It was just a barely audible murmur as she mused incredulously, "Never? Not once?"

"Now wait a minute," I interjected. "Maybe that's not quite true." She looked at me as if to say "Oh?" I had a secret I had never told anyone. She had treated me so adultly by discussing this intimate subject that I decided to make a clean breast of the whole business. It's a strain to keep a secret, particularly if the secret causes you to have feelings of guilt. "I can't say I have 'never' done it," I hedged. "I have."

At that Mona raised one eyebrow, slightly puzzled, I imagine, by my contradictions.

"I have done it, but not with girls."

Her other brow went up and a hurt expression of disappointment and disbelief appeared on her face. I read her thoughts. *Oh oh, what have we here?*

I hastened on to dispel this obviously painful misapprehension. "Now, I've never told this to anybody." I anxiously pledged her to secrecy. "I have done it with Rosie."

An "I thought so" expression crossed her face, but she did not say it.

"I didn't think it would hurt anything. All the other farm boys were doing it." I hurried on, and further excused my action by stating positively, "She wouldn't get pregnant or anything."

Mona was plainly puzzled and asked, "How can you be certain that Rosie couldn't get pregnant?"

"I was only ten years old, for one thing."

"How old was she?" Mona asked.

"Oh, about six months old," I said blandly.

"Six months?" she blurted, astonished.

"Yes, but she was almost as big as her mother," I assured her.

"Six months old and almost as big as her mother?" she repeated with a "now, come on" in her voice. Then she asked, pointblank, "What in the world are you talking about?"

"Old Brownie's calf."

Without actually formulating any thoughts on the matter, I had expected such an experienced hand in these things to take in stride this confession of my most shame-ridden, worrisome, and inviolate secret. I was, to say the least, totally unprepared for her reaction. As I approached the climax of my rustic recitation, Mona was draining her cup of coffee and taking advantage of the concealment the raised cup afforded to mask her thoughts and emotions while peering at me over its rim.

When I blurted out "Old Brownie's calf" Mona exploded. Coffee all over the place. The table, the last bite or two of breakfast, her, me. What a mess!

While I was angrily disappointed at her response I realized how terribly embarrassed she must be.

There was no purpose to be served by venting my indignation vocally because she was too busy to listen. Too busy wiping her eyes, blowing her nose, and wiping her face as extravagantly as a slapstick comedian after being hit in the face with a pie.

I know she exerted a superhuman effort to control her hysterical mirth and she did manage to present some semblance of a straight face in a surprisingly short time. She got a dishtowel and walked sidewise to the table in order to keep her face averted so she would not have to look at me, and as she started to clean the table by touch instead of sight she had regained sufficient control to say tremulously, "Glen darling, I'm so—" Powie! She exploded again with the most unladylike snort you ever heard. After a full thirty seconds she controlled herself sufficiently to start all over again, wiping her eyes, blowing her nose, and wiping her eyes. All the while she was tittering and giggling, red in the face from her efforts to stop. Gradually the tittering and giggling turned to a mixture of tittering, giggling, and crying. I could see that she was becoming unstrung and, despite my indignation, I got up and put my arm around her and in my deepest, most masculine, and authoritative tone of voice I commanded her: "Cut it out now. Get hold of yourself."

She tried with no great success and when she started to become more emotional again I did the only thing I knew to do. I had heard that it worked. In fact, I had seen it work, like magic, one time when my sister Lena had become hysterical under somewhat similar circumstances, and Papa had been obliged, much as he may have wished for some alternative, to use the age-old remedy as a last resort.

CAVEMAN STUFF   I slapped her face. I didn't slap her daintily, either. The secret of success, I had been told, was to do it right, not be halfhearted about the matter, or it could actually make them more hysterical.

I slapped her hard. A resounding "whack" with my right hand on her left cheek. The clear imprint of my hand was left in red on her extraordinarily white skin.

It worked. She stopped instantly, an expression of injured disbelief on her face. I didn't relent or show any sign of sympathy or compassion. I had been told that could start them all over again. I just stood there sternly looking her straight in the eye and holding her by her upper arms so tightly my fingers bit into her firm flesh. Apparently she was not unaware of this caveman therapy, because gradually the hurt expression left her eyes and by degrees her breathing returned to normal.

You have no idea how masculine I felt at that moment. The Lord and master.

After perhaps thirty seconds I released my grip on the sufferer whom I had made whole, seated her in a chair, picked up the dishtowel which she had dropped at the onset of her womanly manifestation, sopped up the coffee on the table, and started carrying the dishes to the sink.

After a number of jerky sighs that reminded me of a child

trying to stop sobbing, she recovered to the point where she trusted herself to speak. "Please, Glen, I'll do that."

"Okay," I said, and I am sure I sounded miffed. I got up, stalked off to my room, and flopped myself down on my bed. Mona followed me and sat down on the edge of the bed. After a few seconds of silence, she said, "Glen, I really did not laugh at what you said so much as the way you said it. Who else would be so frank and honest? I was really heartsick when I thought you were partial to boys and then you cut the ground out from under me so unexpectedly, I was actually laughing at how mistaken I was. I am flattered that you should confide in me. It was the most precious thing I ever heard. You are so honest, so frank, so ingenuous, so—so—what you are. You restore one's faith in truth and goodness." She was beginning to cloud up again, and I was apprehensive lest she get started all over. Besides, she had spread generous flattery on my wounds, although I wasn't certain what she had said because one or two of those words I had never heard before.

I rolled over and came to a sitting position beside her. She was starting to dab at her eyes so I put one arm around her and with the other I pressed her head to my shoulder. Now it is a well known fact that an emotional crisis can result in a woman being ready for love. Making love relaxes tension and is an emotional release. This was the day. This was the hour. This was the moment, for our romance to be consummated.

"Glen," she breathed, "you are the most darling thing I ever saw." I am sure she would not have used that wording if I had been older, but at a time like this, who cares?

She put her arm around my neck and kissed me. It started as just a kiss. A sisterly kiss, I am sure, and then it lingered. Her breast started rising and falling against my chest, where my heart was accelerating at a frantic rate, trying gallantly to pump sufficient blood wherever it might be needed to prepare me for any eventuality.

Her hand moved up the back of my neck and stopped to entwine itself in my hair. I crushed her to me as I leaned back, taking her with me until each of us had an elbow on the silk coverlet.

At that instant she seemed to freeze, and then with all the

strength she would have needed to resist a rapist she pushed me violently from her, scrambled from the bed, and ran for the door. There was a small throw rug on the varnished pine floor. It flew out from under her and she fell. She was in such amazing physical condition that she turned her body even as she was falling and lit on her hands and feet as gracefully as a cat, but her recovery was not quick enough to save her. I scooped her up in my arms and unceremoniously threw her on the bed and flung myself on her like a football player determined to recover a fumble. She strained and struggled but she did not fight dirty. No kneeing, biting, scratching, or hitting. What the hell was the matter with this unpredictable woman, anyway?

Suddenly she went limp. Was this surrender, or just a moment's respite for that beautifully conditioned, beautiful body to recoup for another effort?

As if to answer my question, she flung both arms about me and nuzzled frantically to find my lips. We lay there panting, locked in a savage embrace. *Surely there can be no pulling back now,* I thought, but I was prepared for anything. Anything except what happened. There was a knock on the door.

BIG MAN   What an outrageous violation of all the rules of chance this was. That it should come at this climactic moment.

We froze in each other's arms, making no move to disengage ourselves from our wild embrace, hoping that the intruder would depart and leave us to complete the act of love which has been the passport to manhood since the beginning of time.

The knock was repeated. Louder, more insistent. By now the intoxicating effects of passion had cleared enough to permit some action other than that on which our minds had been wholly intent. We sat up. Mona had left the bedroom door open when she came in. Our feet had barely touched the floor when the front door slowly opened and a tall, quite good-looking man of perhaps fifty stood framed in the doorway.

He was wearing tailored western clothes. Not flamboyant drugstore cowboy regalia, but the accepted garb of the well-to-do rancher. Expensive boots, cream-colored trousers, tapered but not too tight, tailored brown-tone coat, tastefully trimmed with a dash of braid which matched the pants, a black shirt, a gray-and-black narrow string tie, and the whole thing topped off with a light gray four-inch brim Stetson creased down the middle. His hair was crisp, curly, salt and pepper.

As he slowly opened the door the intruder was calling, "Mona—Mona—Are you here?" He was removing his hat when he saw us sitting on the edge of the bed. He was embarrassed at what he saw and stammered, "I b-beg your pardon" and started to back out.

Mona was quite an actress. She arose as though nothing had happened and when she spoke, her voice was amazingly free of the passion she had shown just a few seconds before.

"Why, hello, Mr. Bradley," she said cordially as she walked toward him holding out her hand. He looked at it as though he was uncertain what to do with it, and then caught himself and awkwardly took hold of it between his thumb and fingers like it might have been a raw fish. Obviously, he was not used to being greeted in this formal manner.

"I'm so glad to see you," Mona continued.

Mr. Bradley was looking at me sitting on the edge of the bed in (my?) pajamas. "Well, now, Mona, I'm sorry if I interrup——I mean I'm sorry if—" and the big man just fizzled out.

Mona broke in and took him off the hook. She was saying with all the positive assurance in the world, "Mr. Bradley, I want you to meet my brother, Glen. He's here visiting me for a couple of weeks. Glen, dear, this is Mr. Jim Bradley."

My scalp was crawling. Did she really think I was her brother? Could it be that she was mentally unbalanced?

Apparently I was expected to advance and be recognized. I was most reluctant to stand up, much less advance and stand inspection. A man cannot instantaneously erase all signs of sexual excitement simply by being a good actor. There are physical factors to be considered, and I had not had enough time to return to a dispassionate silhouette. Thank goodness, these pajamas were full cut. I left the protecting gloom of our unused love nest and emerged into the comparatively well lighted parlor. By walking a little stooped like I was, say, eighty-seven years old, I presented a more or less normal facade. I imagine our stalwart visitor must have felt a measure of pity for such a young fellow so afflicted with arthritis, or whatever it was, that he could not walk erect.

It did appear, though, that my extreme youth convinced him that everything was on the up and up, and that he had not interrupted anything.

As soon as I came full into the light and he had had a good look at me, his suspicions seemed to vanish and his uneasy attitude changed. He became the hale and hearty big man of the wide open spaces.

"Well! Hel-lo, Glen. I'm glad to meet you, son," he boomed in a cordial greeting loud enough to be heard at least two houses away. If all Mona's guests were this robust, no wonder she needed vacant lots right and rear and an abandoned lumberyard on her left to give her privacy. Mr. Hale and Hearty grabbed my outstretched hand in a grip that could have crushed a coconut and pumped it enthusiastically. Much as my encounter with Mr. Bradley's flesh-and-bone version of the Iron Maiden hurt, it did accomplish one thing. My mind was purged of all lascivious thoughts and any physical evidence thereof vanished instantaneously. My good friend, by banishing the horizontal, enabled me to resume the vertical.

I had more than a sneaking hunch who this walking fashion plate of western affluence might be, and the jealousy-inspiring nature of his mission.

I wanted desperately to meet him on an equal footing and call him Jim, particularly after he had so downgraded me by calling me "son." He had left the door open for me to call him by his first name and thereby breathe a little life back into my shriveling ego, which was as withered and wrinkled as varnish on wet wood.

When I opened my mouth I had every intention of saying, "I'm glad to meet you, Jim," but long years of being trained to respect my elders and possibly the devastating effect of that John L. Sullivan handshake prevailed, and my salutation came out, "I am glad to meet you, sir." Dammit all, I had intended to say "Jim" right up until I heard myself saying "sir." My humiliation and resentment grew.

Having formalized the amenities, Big Jim turned to the lady of the house and, in view of the fact that we had, like the proverbial Arabs, "silently folded our tents and stolen away" from her previous abode only yesterday, voiced an understandable complaint. "I had quite a time finding you, Mona." Without waiting for an explanation he went on, "Pretty nice place you have here."

"Thank you," Mona said, bowing slightly. "I'm sorry you had trouble finding me," she apologized, "but in the excitement of moving and my brother's visit, I completely forgot. . . . I hope you will forgive me." It was a statement, not a question. "If you can come back in a couple of weeks we can discuss the matter about which I called you," she said sweetly, taking him by the arm and urging him toward the door. "Oh, sure, sure," the unwanted caller was agreeing, "that'll be fine, just fine. I'll see you in a couple of weeks then, Mona." It must have occurred to him that he was out of character calling her Mona inasmuch as she had been calling him Mr. Bradley, because he hastened to get back in the spirit of things by adding, "Miss—Mona."

"Glad to meet you, Glen," he called from the door and held his hand at the ready, like a gunfighter prepared to draw. Quite clearly, he expected me to come to the door so he could have the pleasure of breaking the rest of my fingers, if any had escaped the excruciating pleasure of our introduction. I wouldn't have taken those three foolhardy steps for a week's wages.

I held my defensive position well behind Mona. Ungentlemanly, to say the least? Perhaps even cowardly? Well, what good is a gentleman hero running around with a handful of fingers so busted up he can't even pick up a piece of flypaper?

Mona shut the door and turned to face me. We both stood there for at least five seconds waiting for the other to speak. She outlasted me in this eye-to-eye confrontation. She was showing no particular emotion.

"Who is he?" I asked bluntly, turning away. I had told her I knew she was lying when she told me she had to see her lawyer and instead spent the time arranging things in the new house, so I guess she figured she had better tell the truth now. Perhaps she would have anyhow. I don't know.

There was a note of sadness as she answered. She may have thought that this face-to-face confrontation with reality would be more than our stormy relationship could stand.

Her eyes fell and then she raised her gaze to stare out through the big side window. "He is one of the men who have helped me." Quickly, as if to remind me again that she was not a common person, she added, "One of the three." I felt a great compassion for her.

As gently as possible, I asked, "Why did you introduce me as your brother?"

She hesitated and then gave a little shrug of her shoulders, spread her hands slightly, and let them fall limply to her sides. Almost imperceptibly shaking her head in a combined gesture of hopelessness and resignation, she spoke so softly I could scarcely hear. "What else was I to do?"

I didn't say anything. What the hell *was* I to say? Perhaps she expected an answer, or hoped for one. When it didn't come she continued, "Jim had an appointment for today. In all the excitement," there was a catch in her voice, "our new home and all, I forgot."

She clasped her hands loosely as they hung in front of her and just stood there, a picture of dejection and misery. I wanted desperately to take her in my arms and tell her to forget the whole goddamn business, but this "brother" thing had to be settled some time. I had felt sure it was about to be resolved when Mr. Big had knocked on the door, but here we were in deeper than ever. Now she was *introducing* me as her brother.

"But, surely, you could have said something besides introducing me as your brother," I said lamely.

"He had an appointment, I had moved without letting him know," she pointed out, and then explained, "He is a proud man, a big man. What do you suppose he would have thought," she asked, "when he saw a handsome b—— young man in the bedroom?"

She had almost said "boy." That was, in the words of Bill Shakespeare, "the most unkindest cut of all." Nothing can more completely deflate a boy who imagines himself a man than to be called a boy, particularly by a woman with whom he aspires to assume the role of a man.

HER BROTHER I was boiling! *So that's it,* I angrily thought, *to her I am a boy. A boy* brother, *no less.* She had hurt me. All right, I'd hurt her. "He sure as hell didn't have any reason to be jealous of a 'boy' like me." I emphasized the "boy."

"I haven't been to bed with you," I reminded her, "and after seeing that hulk I doubt if I could follow him anyhow. I'd feel like David trying to follow Goliath."

I was doing great! At one fell swoop I had deeply hurt us both and then proceeded to rub salt in the wounds. About the worst thing one can do to injure a man's ego is to even intimate that he is poorly equipped. The reverse is true of a woman. To be young and firm and dainty is the cherished ideal, and I had practically put her in the same category as a cow. I rambled on, intent on hoisting myself on my own petard.

"I'll bet he's twice as big as me," I complained bitterly, and the only thing that held back tears of self-pity was my obsessive determination to behave like a man.

Mona shook her head from side to side and, still looking toward the window, she spoke slowly and matter of factly, like a tired teacher trying once more to enlighten a class of stupid kids.

"Strangely enough, the size of the man has little to do with it," she said. "In stature, Rafe Norcus, for example, was not as big a man as you, but in that one respect he was twice the man Jim Bradley is," she divulged. "You are probably much better off than he is, too." She said it calmly but with a certain conviction, as though her womanly intuition told her it was so.

Now, any woman who achieves more than average success with men must know what to say as well as what to do and how to do it. Perhaps what Mona had just said was a chance remark made with no thought of what effect it might have, or it could have been a brilliant ad lib calculated to defuse my wrathful pique.

Practically every male of the species homo sapiens craves to be well rated as to his manhood. The yardstick to determine the relative degree of manhood is based on a fundamental rule. The rule is divided into inches.

While Mona's lesson in physiology exposed my ignorance, that was of small consequence compared to the possible compliment she had paid me and the lift she had given me. The titillative thought that I might be more of a man than this big rich smart alec so restored my ego that I was hard put to refrain from committing rape on the spot. At any rate, it ill behooved one so generously endowed to be petty and small. A he-man so favored could afford to be magnanimous. I stepped over and patted her condescendingly on the shoulder.

If she never did find out what a treat she had missed, that was her fault. Not mine. "Forget it," I generously advised her, and retired to my lonely bower where I remained for some time, brooding over my frustrations. After a while I stalked out of the house. As I passed through the living room, I could hear water sloshing in the bathroom. I had heard of people who felt guilty washing to excess. Poor girl. She was no doubt trying to wash away the feeling of guilt she probably felt as a result of my having to meet her paramour face to face.

MARGARITA   I headed toward the Bluebell for no particular reason. Near the end of the first block, who should I come upon but Margarita, out picking up sticks and leaves in the yard of her house. I stopped and started a flirtation. I was sore and fed up over that "brother" business.

We had been moving right along for perhaps five minutes and I had just jumped over the fence, even as I remembered Papa doing, and thereby implanting in my four-year-old mind that first recollection of him. I could have used the gate, but in jumping the fence I had instinctively resorted to that primeval compulsion of the young male to impress the female with his physical prowess. I am quite sure that Margarita just as instinctively recognized my act as the courting gesture that it was.

Being a young female in the business of attracting males, Margarita showed the proper admiration and appreciation for my show of muscle by squealing delightedly with her hands up high. Not ungracefully high. More as if she were being pleasurably robbed at gunpoint by a handsome stickup man with a water pistol. We both laughed. I held out my hands and she eagerly placed hers in mine.

"Won't you come in?" she was saying, but I impolitely ignored her. I was facing in the direction from which I had come and my attention was fixed on a woman who had just appeared rounding the corner on to Main Street. She was running full tilt as though fleeing imminent danger. As she made the turn she lost her footing and fell headlong, but there wasn't an instant's hesitation in her movement. Even before she hit the ground, she was scratching her way forward and scrambling frantically to regain her feet. Before she was more than half erect, she was running again like a sprinter at the gun. A half block away I recognized her. "Mona!" I exclaimed involuntarily. Her hair was not done up, and it was flying wildly about her face. She did not see us until she was no more than thirty feet away. She stopped even with us and leaned on the fence gasping for breath. I had noticed yesterday that she had used much less makeup, but now she wore none at all and her face was white, as if she had been terribly frightened.

I met her at the fence. I was deeply concerned, and I am sure my voice reflected it. "What's the matter, Mona?" I asked, half under my breath, as I held her head against my chest. She could not speak for some time and her gasps for breath gradually turned into sobs. Even though she had been unable to speak, the obvious facts were falling into place.

She had heard me leave the house and fearing exactly what had happened she had come running in hot pursuit, giving no thought to her appearance. "Dammit all." I didn't want to hurt anyone like this, but when she regarded me as a brother, even introduced me as her brother, it was unreasonable of her to be so possessive and jealous.

Her breathing was becoming nearly normal. Margarita waggled her fanny over to within a step or two and said pointedly, "She's okay now," and then asked invitingly, "Are you coming in, Glen?" Luckily the fence was between them or, I am convinced, these two would have been at each other fang and claw.

Mona tensed. Her eyes narrowed to slits and they were spitting hatred. Her black, black hair hanging about her face, she reminded me of a black cat. A black cat about to spring.

"You keep your filthy hands off this kid or I'll kill you," she hissed. "He's too good for you."

"Look who's talking," Margarita taunted. "Just because you can swallow a cucumber don't make you so muckin fuch. How are you in bed?" she jeered with one hand on her hip, which she had been raising and lowering in rhythm with her premeditated provocations.

"Why, you—" and Mona would have been over the fence if I hadn't restrained her.

"Come on, Mona," I said firmly, "I'll take you home." The two diametrically opposed types glared at each other, and Mona favored her rival with a closed-mouth grin as much as to say, "See, smartie?"

I climbed over the fence and offered her my arm. At that, she could not resist one last look of triumph at Margarita.

I felt sorry for Margarita because she had been humiliated. I had, in part at least, been responsible, and I had not intended it that way. The final humiliation was when I refused her invitation and walked home with Mona. Actually, I would have preferred to stay with Margarita. My guess was that she would not fly the coop at the crucial moment. First, I would have a talk with Mona. Plenty of time after that to see Margarita.

There was no rehearsal today. It was now one o'clock. We had until seven to get to the Bluebell. I had the whole afternoon. We walked home in silence, Mona clinging firmly to my arm like a little girl who had just recovered a lost pooch. There was not a word spoken until we were in the house.

In the center of the living room she stopped, turned me until I faced her, and gripped my other arm. She looked me in the eyes and then dropped her gaze. Shame? What? I didn't know.

"Glen," she began softly, "will you do something for me?"

"Now, Mona, you know better than to even ask that," I rebuked her. "You know there is nothing I wouldn't do for you. I think you are the nicest person I ever knew. I enjoy just being in your company more than anyone I can think of. The too-bad part of it is that every time I'm near you I get all steamed up. Right now I feel like I had a battery wired to each arm where you are holding me. This just doesn't go with you treating me like a brother."

"I know, I know," she interrupted. "It's been difficult, very difficult for me, too." Then she got back to her original question. "Will you do something for me?"

"Sure, I will," I promised irritably. "What is it?"

"I am going to bathe. I am a mess," and she showed me the palms of her hands and her knees, which were grimy from her fall. "While I am bathing I want you to go in and put on your pajamas and wait for me, will you?" and she looked into my eyes beseechingly. My heart did a flip-flop and started right in pumping me up. For what? The memory of all the nutty events of the last two or three days had me gun-shy.

"Now, look," I said, "if this is more of the same kind of monkey business, please don't. Let's not play any more games. If you want me to behave like a brother, I can do it better with my clothes on. If that's what you want, then treat me like a brother. Let me go my way and I'll be home for meals and to sleep at night, but the first place I'll go is to Margarita and find out what it's like to be a man."

She had listened, displaying no emotion, until I mentioned Margarita, then her eyes filled with apprehension approaching terror. "Please, Glen, please, don't." This was not meant as a request not to carry out my threat but not to talk that way.

"I know you will, I know you will," she repeated. "That's why I have decided to do what you want," she said nervously, wringing her hands. "Anything you want. Anything. Margarita is not good enough for you. You should go home. You should find a nice girl and some day get married and have a nice family." She kept repeating the word "nice." It was an important word to her. She was starting to get hysterical again.

I took her by the arms and said, "Now, cut this out." Then I asked, "How the hell am I going to meet what you call a nice girl? Have you seen any girls you thought were virgins at the Bluebell lately? Forget it. I know some nice girls in Kooskia, but if I was back there right now I'd go straight to Lil and she's not a nice girl, and when I got to Lil I would keep on going and I'd go all the way and I'd keep on going as many times as I could. I'm tired of being considered a kid and I don't want to be kidded. Now, if you still want me to put on the pajamas, okay."

Her breathing was noticeably faster than normal as she took my face between her hands and kissed me. It wasn't a passionate kiss, but it seemed to be filled with promise.

"Please do," she whispered, and hurried away.

I turned and went to my room but first I locked that goddamn front door. The next son of a bitch who knocked could knock his brains out. This was for real or else, and she knew it, so we'd see. I removed the silk spread on the bed, folded it, and placed it on the chair as she did. I turned the covers down and then I put on my pajamas and got in bed to wait. It was no more than five minutes until I heard the bathroom doorknob turn. My heart jumped and almost choked me. I had to cough a little cough to keep my throat from closing.

I was waiting for her to appear, but instead I heard another door open—and close. Of course, why hadn't I thought of that, she would have to go to her room to get at least something on, and that was probably where she kept her makeup.

I AM A MAN   This waiting was torture, but exquisite torture. My heart had things under control so well it had even slowed down a little like a motor that had to labor to get all the wheels turning, and then settled down for the job ahead.

The wall clock struck two. Thank God *that* was out of its system. We wouldn't have *that* for a distraction. The last lingering note of the old clock's mellow "bong" died, and there was the sound of her bedroom door opening. My heart started up again.

My temples were pounding so hard I was worried I might have a stroke and die right then and there. Wouldn't that be some joke! Before I ever—There she stood! I had not been at all certain. But there she was. Not relaxed and pretty as I had pictured her. Instead, she called to mind pictures I had seen depicting Joan of Arc going to the stake.

It was plain, even to my inexperienced young eyes, that she was torn by some terrible emotional conflict. I felt a twinge of conscience that I should be the vortex of the inner storm that was reflected in her eyes and the tense lines of her face. Why couldn't there be simple solutions to things so people wouldn't have to suffer like this?

Immature and new in the world as I was, I had a pretty good idea of her problem. I believed she wanted me but felt guilty because of what she was. She felt shame that one so stained should covet one so young and inexperienced. The fact that I reminded her of her brother further complicated her maze of difficulties. The ultimate feeling of guilt might be because this was the first time she would actually be unfaithful to her husband, and give herself in an act of love because she needed and wanted to do so.

I was not the only one for whom this would be the first time. It would be the first time for her also. A first time that would not be unadulterated pleasure.

Lastly, she knew that if she did not, then Margarita, whom she loathed as a common whore, surely would.

She stood unseeing, looking inward, watching the life-and-death struggle between her opposing selves. She appeared as though in a trance, and even when she moved nearer there still seemed to be that unreal aura about her as though she were sleepwalking.

I noticed that there was no nightgown showing above her robe or below it. My mind removed this covering and my heart tried to leap with ecstasy, but it was constricted by pity and the conflicting commands produced only pain.

She spoke. "Glen," she said, "Glen darling." She was not looking at me. She was looking straight ahead as though she saw me there. "These days with you have been an eternity. I feel like you have been close to me always. I cannot conceive of what it would be like without you near me." She gently shook her head. "Glen, I love you," she whispered softly. "These days with you have been the happiest days of my life." And there was so much feeling there that no one could have doubted her, but she qualified that statement with—"They have also been the most sad. A hopeless old love is not dying easily.

"I know you have been puzzled at my behavior but no more than I, believe me. The first night you were here, before I knew how truly unworldly you were, I extended you an invitation, but you did not recognize it as such. If you had I would probably have been satisfied to leave you to Margarita, but when you gave not the faintest sign, I recognized what an innocent dear you were and I was ashamed. I wanted to protect you, and at the same time I wanted you. That is part of the conflict which has caused me to act like a tease and a fool."

So that was it! I knew those two words "hard" and "long" that she had spoken two nights ago had been said with special meaning. Perhaps if I had been a little quicker in my realization I would now be in Margarita's arms. I was glad! Glad that I had been caught off guard and had given no sign.

She had more to say. I could wait if only this didn't turn out like the other times. "Glen," she was saying, "I wish with all my heart that we could have met under other circumstances. I wish more than I ever wished for anything that we were more nearly the same age. I wish that I was fresh and new like you are. I want you so and I feel so unworthy. Darling—Glen—you are too good for me." She was getting emotional again. At any moment she might convince herself that what she had just said was true, and this interlude would end like the others.

I had to reassure her or this would probably be the end between us. I put all the conviction in my voice that I could command. It wasn't difficult because I believed what I said. I believed it with every fiber of my being.

"Mona—sweetheart," I said, "I do not believe there is a man on earth too good for you." I hesitated an instant. There was a catch in her breath, and the long row of pearly teeth bit her lower lip. I had at least lessened her despair. "I do believe," I added, "that there are few men who could possibly be worthy of you." I had said the right thing. That was what she had wanted to hear from my lips. She closed her eyes in thanksgiving.

Taking her as she was then, transgressions and all, she was a saint to go through the hell she had endured for a weak and unworthy man. Yes—she was a saint. She released the robe she had been holding about her, and as she reached up and gracefully moved it off her shoulders I was spellbound. Onstage her partly clothed body had been alluring but now, as she slowly parted the garment; her nudity became a thing of beauty which dispelled completely any realization of her nakedness.

The robe fell to the floor and she started to tremble from head to foot. Her breathing became more audible. Her breasts stood out firm and unashamed and rose and fell more vehemently with each breath she drew.

I do not believe that she had really made her decision until this very moment. Her breathing and the trembling of her body were manifestations of the final struggle between passion, desire, and love as opposed to her feelings of guilt and unworthiness.

Her breathing stopped. The trembling ceased. I knew the decision had been made. Would she come to me or would the inhibitions that had so far kept us apart prevail? With a cry that could have issued from the throat of some wild thing she threw herself upon me.

Her fury and abandon were almost frightening. She started tearing at my beautiful silk pajamas. Much as I would have liked to see them spared, the frantic intensity of her passion warned me not to protest. Paying no heed to buttons or logical procedures, she tore them to shreds and threw them wildly in all directions.

I had an urge to giggle like a child being tickled, but again the awesome release of emotions I was witnessing saved me from a juvenile reaction that could have been disastrous. She was whining and whimpering as she frantically tore at the last few fragments of my proudly cherished garment. When my pajamas were ripped away, she fell beside me and I was bathed with kisses. Deferring to her expertise in the matter, I was not what one would call a masterful lover on this first occasion. Willingly, I allowed her to maneuver me like a grand dame waltzing with a cub scout.

The consummation was tumultuous and brief. I was grateful for the fact that there were no close neighbors. Her cries of ecstasy would surely have been heard beyond these walls and I could not have suppressed my own loud, hoarse gasps of exquisite agony had I known my life depended upon it.

As I fell limp beside her, I uttered Papa's favorite sterilized blasphemy, "Hot all mighty!" When the gates of ecstatic bliss have just been unlocked and no one knows how long you may have access to the forbidden fruit, time is indeed fleeting. We made the most of it. Each foray into the wondrous garden of love took a little longer, and a little longer, and a little longer, as the first heat of explosive passion cooled to the point where some degree of control was possible.

I think we both had a vague feeling that this was "too good to be true," that the pleasure we were sharing was impermanent, although we blindly refused to look into the future. Youth is like that, "Sufficient unto the day."

Realizing that I was determined to learn and that Margarita was waiting to teach me if she didn't, Mona pressed my education without qualms of conscience or reservation. There were no sheepskins at the end of the course, but if there had been, I surely would have graduated cum laude. Between two-thirty and six, three rapturous lessons were crammed into the three and one half hours. School was never like this.

THE WRISTWATCH   At six o'clock, for the first time during that unreal afternoon, Mona changed the topic of our murmured exchanges from lovemaking to the more prosaic subject of food. She reminded me of the time, and of the fact that we were due at the Bluebell in a couple of hours. She insisted on cooking my dinner. This long-denied outlet for her domestic instincts was probably as great a fulfillment for her as our passionate lovemaking. Mona arose and swirled her robe about her, bullfighter fashion, as she hurried from the room.

Never in all my life had I felt so relaxed, so at peace with myself and the world.

Not until I got up and started to dress did I realize the full extent of the catastrope that had befallen my proudly cherished pajamas. Strips and shreds and bits and pieces were scattered over an area six or eight feet from the epicenter of the passionate storm. Remnants were draped on lamps and chairs and dressers and bedposts. However, I could now take the loss philosophically. Who wanted pajamas?

Between shows, I went out front to shower the customers with my personality and gracious presence. I was now a man entitled to all privileges and rewards. I sauntered over to the bar.

The bartender, who seemed to be a person of considerable importance around there, ignored me except for a friendly "Hello, kid." At length, after he had served customers to my right and to my left and skipped over me at least twice, he looked at me questioningly and inquired, "Do you want something, kid?"

"Give me a nit," I ordered in my deepest bass voice, loud enough for the "other" men standing nearby to hear.

Now, I had no more idea of what a "nit" was than the man in the moon, and I still don't, for that matter, but I had just heard a man, obviously a real drinking man, order a "nit." At least that's the way I understood it. "Give you a nit?" bellowed the bartender. "You get the hell away from this bar before I hit you in the ass with a bungstarter." I don't imagine I could have looked more flabbergasted if he had hit me on the head with that bung-starter at the same time he delivered his massive verbal insult to my emergent manhood. I was never so humiliated in my life. Thank God only one or two customers were close enough to hear.

The rebuff was made more galling by the fact of my recent graduation to manhood. The higher you are, the farther you have to fall, you know. If I could have fallen right on through the floor that would have been just fine. As it was, I summoned my last ounce of dignity and casually sauntered backstage, managing to keep my chin high and my cheeks dry despite the tears of rage that blurred my vision.

I found a secluded corner and set about trying to reglue my shattered ego. Surely there must be some pluses in any situation. Yes, there was one thing to be grateful for. None of the performers had witnessed the scrambling of my pride. It was unthinkable to contemplate my loss of face if Mona had been with me.

Thinking of Mona was the best thing that could have happened at this moment because to think of Mona was to think of her in bed. I forgot about my disastrous encounter with old loudmouth. I was chomping at the bit to get the show over and get home. More specifically, to get home and to bed. The recuperative powers of a fifteen-year-old are amazing.

We made love upon retiring and again upon awakening at eleven in the morning. As we lay there resting, Mona tactfully brought up the subject of what a man can and cannot do without weakening himself and losing his snap, verve, and ambition. "There *is* a limit," she said.

I had heard this subject discussed among boys my own age, but the figure on "how many times" had varied so greatly I really had no idea.

She suggested no more than twice a day. I would have preferred to double or triple the figure but agreed reluctantly. Generally, we stretched a point and had a matinee around five o'clock. I am quite certain that she had made allowance for that by setting the goal a little low so we could stay within limits and still leave room for me to have my way. That night I sang a song I had just learned—"She's Only a Bird in a Gilded Cage." It was all about a girl who became a rich man's plaything. It was taking an unfair advantage of those poor women who worked in the Bluebell.

They seemed to love songs they could take to heart as reflecting their own unfortunate circumstances. They also seemed to love to be sad and to cry.

When I came offstage, Lil, the busty blonde, was standing in the wings sobbing her heart out. She folded me to her ample bosom and blubbered, "Oh Glen, you dear sweet boy. You're so wonderful," and on and on. I couldn't free myself to take a bow. The other two girls were almost as maudlin as poor Lil.

Mona was dry-eyed and unaffected. I believe Mona now considered herself a respectable one-man woman and saw no reason to join in the orgy of self-pity. She stepped over and laid her hand on Lil's arm and with almost motherly kindness said, "That's enough, Lil dear. Let the man take his bow." Lil desisted forthwith and, believe me, that "man" wasn't lost on me. If there were psychiatrists in those days Mona would have made a good one. She understood people and words. Even at that young age, I was beginning to realize if you understood people and words you had it more than half made.

That evening—or, rather, that morning—while we were having our after-the-show snack, I noticed a small leather-covered box on the table. I just noticed it and then forgot it. When we had finished eating Mona reached over, put her hand on mine, and said, "I have a present for you, mister." She shoved the black box over to me and explained, "I got it for you today."

Presents of any kind were something I had had very few of in my young life. I opened it eagerly. A watch. A beautiful watch, *but*—IT WAS A WRISTWATCH! Now, this may be difficult to believe, but wristwatches were quite new on the market. Two had been seen on the wrists of dandified sissies passing through Kooskia, and one of those two had gotten into a fight with one of our red-blooded boys who had intimated what everyone knew—only sissies wear bracelets. That's the way it was, really.

It was a beautiful watch, though, and what was I to say? I was no sissy. That was the last thing in the world I wanted. A badge to identify me as a sissy.

Mona perceived my hesitancy. She couldn't have missed it. This was a big deal. Under her questioning, I had to tell her what she was trying to do to me. The corners of her mouth twitched, but she managed to suppress the outright laughter which bubbled within her. She kept a straight face and explained that this was the way it was with anything new and different. Look how people had laughed at automobiles just a few years ago, and now lots of people had them and all those who didn't wanted one.

I had to admit that was a fact but "you don't want me getting into fights all the time, do you?" She didn't think there would be any fights. Pierce City was a little bigger than Kooskia and, really, there were quite a few wristwatches around.

Come to think of it, I had seen a few, and it surely was a beautiful watch. I had owned a dollar Ingersoll once, but it wasn't anywhere near this beautiful. After more cajoling and coaxing, I accepted it and agreed to wear it. It was so attractive that I put in on right then and wore it to bed. Wearing it to bed was one thing. Wearing it to rehearsal the next day was something else.

I couldn't have felt more conspicuous and out of place. In fact, I couldn't have felt more like a sissy if she had presented me with a lace-trimmed purse and asked that I carry it with two fingers. I kept it well up on my arm so my coat sleeve would hide my badge of shame. Occasionally, I would find some pretext to flash it for an instant. Accidentally, I jiggled it down so it would show a little. When that didn't work, I kept getting more daring, and finally it happened.

I reached over to turn a page of the song I was rehearsing and Larry spotted it. "Say-ay! Watcha got there, kid?" he asked with what must surely be pretended admiration. I had thought Larry was a he-man. He must be pretending admiration just to set me up for a good ribbing.

I'm sure I blushed, I was so flustered. I stammered apologetically, "Well I—well you see—" He had hold of my arm and he wouldn't let go. "Say, that's a beaut, kid. I wish I had one. Where'd you get it, kid?"

"Well I—that is—Mona—"

"Mona, huh?" he grinned meaningfully, and jabbed me in the ribs with his thumb. "Atta boy, kid. You're learning fast. Let 'em pay *you* for it, huh, kid?" I hadn't meant to get Mona involved, not that everybody didn't know, but—aw nuts!

After Larry's envious admiration I was sold. That night I wore it practically just above my thumb. It sparkled real pretty in the spotlight. Boy, if the folks back in Kooskia could see me now!

TOUGH GUY TAYLOR   The new watch gave me another shot in the arm. I was Mr. Jesus again, and it got me into trouble again.

After the first show I went out to be seen. I stopped at a blackjack table and stood watching. I was spending more and more time watching blackjack lately. It intrigued me, and I was getting to be quite an expert. I decided to sit in. I started with a dollar, and after about ten minutes I had ten dollars. Half a week's pay! I was beginning to realize how stupid I had been not to get in on this easy money before.

I was playing third base. I didn't know that the last man on the left facing the dealer was called the "third baseman," but in a few days as a spectator I had perceived that the man sitting here had the benefit of seeing what everyone else drew before having to make his decision as to whether or not he should draw. The other players seemed to be unable to resist the temptation to excuse their own wrong guesses by blaming the third baseman. If things go wrong for them they will quite often react as though he had deliberately, or at least very stupidly, betrayed them. It takes a thick skin to ignore their sarcastic remarks.

Eventually, a gangly young sheepherder sitting to my right said, "I don't think they ought to let people who don't know how to play sit in and mess everybody up."

I am slow about taking exception to jibes like that. The fact is, I expect everyone to be as considerate of other people's feelings as I was taught to be. I am caught off balance by such inconsiderate, unfair remarks. By the time I had fully grasped the barefaced nature of his insult the fast-moving game was well into the next hand. The more I thought of it, though, the madder I got. I determined to be ready next time. The "next time" wasn't long in coming. This time the pimply-faced young wise-off said, "Listen, kid, if you don't know what you're doing would you like to trade places with me?" And he said it loud enough for everyone at the table to hear.

I sneered, "No, you can't have my place, sheepherder, but if you want to move to another table it'll be okay with me. You smell bad." After taking his first jibe with no return, it felt damn good to slap his face with that one.

It took a second for it to soak in, and then he awkwardly and angrily unwound himself from around his stool and stood up. I was just sitting there trying to act as though I insulted people five inches taller than me all the time.

He grabbed me by the shirt and tie and rather forcefully helped me get to my feet. It was only a matter of helping because at his first overt move, that is, when his hand started toward me, I had started to get up. As I came erect and before I could get set he let fly. It was a glancing blow off my chin, but that slightly healed quarter-sized piece of flesh which Mona had pasted back after my shaving accident was knocked off, clean as a whistle, and the blood flew. As his fist went on by and his chin followed through, I hit him a short, stiff punch right on the button. It wasn't a knockout punch by any means, but it set him back on his heels just enough to make him take one step backward to catch his balance. Ordinarily this would hardly have caused any perceptible pause in the action, but Lady Luck had her arm around me. This guy had evidently been in such a hurry to lose his wages he hadn't even stopped to rent a place to leave his bedroll. He had put it on the floor to his right, and when he stepped back to recover his balance his heel hit his bedroll. He fell over backward and hit his head on the floor. He was out like a light. That ended the altercation. With only two blows having been struck, my larger opponent was lying flat on his back unconscious and I was standing there the one-punch victor, but bleeding as much as I had when I first cut myself.

Mona must have been only one or two tables away because she was at my side trying to stem the flow of blood with a lace-trimmed hankie. "Boy, you sure cold-cocked him with one punch," she proclaimed proudly in the dancehall vernacular.

If it had been a satisfaction to clout that stupid oaf and teach him a lesson, and believe me it had, the thrill of the successful combat was as nothing compared to the fact that my woman had witnessed the decisive display of my manly maturity. The admiration she voiced was the sweetest music my eager ears had ever heard.

I stood there for a moment trying to conceal the elation I felt and looked around, presenting as calm a demeanor as possible, as much as to say, "It's nothing, folks. No cause for concern at all. I can take care of myself," and after doing my histrionic best to silently project my new image, I allowed Mona to lead me backstage where she lavishly proved her love by tearing up a perfectly good petticoat to stanch the flow of blood. The bandage she applied was at least an inch and a half square and, of course, would be with me at the next show and for several days thereafter.

Mona told me, and the other girls who were clustered about confirmed the fact, that Shavely Stokes, the tall young gentleman whom I had so expeditiously dispatched, was known as a troublemaker, and that it would generally be felt that he had probably gotten his comeuppance.

Even Larry, the piano player, who was a pretty blasé guy, came backstage and congratulated me for the way I had handled myself, and the no-sweat manner in which I had punctured Shavely's reputation as a saloon brawler.

When I appeared on stage for my number during the next show with my gauze-and-tape purple heart plainly visible on my chin, I received a boisterous hand from the rough men and painted ladies.

I learned that the unanimous reaction from the male patrons had been something like "The kid's okay. He sings purty and hits hard" and my lady admirers' feelings were summed up in the words Larry overheard and ribbingly relayed to me, "Bless his little heart. That dear, sweet boy taught that smelly son of a bitch a lesson."

"HELLO, PAPA"   Between the second and third shows I hastened out to the floor to resume my get-rich-quick career at the blackjack table. It was gratifying to notice and acknowledge the friendly man-to-man grins from the gents and the adoring glances and smiles from the ladies.

When I found a vacant third baseman's seat and sat down, my ego was further inflated by the nudges and whispers around the table. I was no longer the singer, an abstraction from another world, I was a flesh-and-blood young buck who had been accepted by the community, at least the seamy side of the community, which made the Bluebell its headquarters.

I had been playing for perhaps ten minutes and was doing real well. My dollar had grown to fifteen this time, and I was beginning to increase the size of my bets. I had a third of my stack out there when a voice at my elbow said, "Young fellow, I'd like to have a talk with you." It was Big Jim Williams, the owner of the Bluebell. The dealer raked in my five dollars, and I followed my seldom-seen boss to his office under the projection booth.

He stopped with his hand on the doorknob and, looking me sternly in the eye, he spoke to me in a rather sarcastic tone, "What the hell are you doing at the blackjack table?" and without waiting for an answer he gave me to understand that he was not happy about my addiction. "Don't you know those are house games? You can't win. If I see you around there again I'll kick your rump up between your shoulders." And with that blunt warning he roughly opened the door and went in. He sat down behind his desk, motioned me to a seat facing him, and let me cool it while he took his own sweet time lighting a cigar.

After making the air blue with several prodigious puffs on his stogy, he leaned back, put his number tens on the desk, and said, "I hear you had a little set-to with Shavely Stokes." I admitted I had and explained how it had come about. When I repeated the verbal exchange that had preceded the fisticuffs, he tried to smother a grin, which in spite of himself turned out to be a plainly visible, puckery, humorous grimace.

"I guess you know we don't like for our people to fight with customers," he said matter of factly, and added, "we have Big Mac to take care of things when necessary."

I tried to excuse myself by saying, "I never thought about that. I was sore, but it won't happen again."

He adopted a more fatherly attitude. "Where do you live, Glen?" he inquired. I told him and he continued his probing. "What does your father do?"

I explained that he was presently the justice of the peace, but that he used to be a preacher.

"A preacher and his name is Taylor." He said it more as if he was talking to himself than to me. "What's your father's first name?"

"Pleasant John. Most people call him P.J.," I explained.

"Was he ever in Gunnison, Colorado?" he asked, obviously trying to nail something down.

"He might have been," I conceded. "The family came up through Colorado on the way to Oregon from Texas. That was about twenty years ago."

His chin came up quickly as much as to say, *Would you believe this?* and looking at me through half-closed eyes he stated, "I met your father, Glen. I heard him preach in Gunnison. Had a little talk with him afterward. That's the closest I ever came to being saved," he recalled with a half grin. "He was quite a preacher," he said, half to himself, shaking his head. He ended our conversation by saying, "You've got a good voice, young fellow, but what's more important, you've got personality or whatever it takes to get through to people. Another guy could sing just as good as you and maybe better, and yet not go over anywhere near as good. You've got it, Glen, and I'd say you'll do okay in any business where you can work with people. Don't ever get yourself fenced in where your main business is not working with people. Maybe I should say 'working *on* people.' You've sure got it. Good luck." What he said was very flattering, pleasing to my eager young ears. The "good luck" seemed a little final, as if he had said "goodbye" or "Godspeed." Perhaps, I thought, it was just my imagination.

Two uneventful days flitted by—uneventful insofar as there were no Shavely Stokes episodes or command appearances with Big Jim. They were completely happy days filled with the ecstasy that only young love can know. There was one fly in the ointment. I couldn't play blackjack anymore. Hell! I could have gotten rich at the damn game.

My wristwatch still loomed large on the horizons of my world, but my enjoyment of the precious timepiece was not an unadulterated source of pride and pleasure. The more I thought about it the more it ate on me. I shouldn't be taking expensive gifts from a girl. I recalled Larry's leering advice to "make 'em pay for it," and I felt like a pimp.

On the third morning after my talking to by Big Jim, I brought up the subject of the wristwatch at the breakfast table. I told Mona that I did not feel right about the matter and that I did not want her to do anything like that again. I sensed that she was surprised, almost amazed to know that there was at least one male who had too much pride to accept anything and everything a woman might offer him.

She had to fight back tears. It wasn't because she was hurt. I got the idea it was pride in her man that choked her voice a little as she said, "I'm sorry. I didn't know."

"It will be all right after we are married," I hastened to add in an effort to reassure her that my displeasure wasn't because she had given me the watch, but because of our unmarried status. It never occurred to me that this was not a very romantic proposal. In fact, it was not meant as a proposal. Just a statement of something that would naturally follow when two people were in love and living together as we were.

When I spoke the unpremeditated words, her face and her beautiful, expressive gray-green eyes lit up with a happiness that made me feel like a king who had bestowed a royal title on a scullery maid. The expression of happiness lasted no more than a fleeting second, to be replaced with a look so profoundly sad and agonized that I knew instantly some great emotional upheaval had rent her soul in those few seconds. I hesitated even to ask what the trouble was. I waited until the storm seemed to have subsided. I reached over and put my hand on hers. "What's the matter?" I asked with all the tenderness of my love for her.

She looked for a moment as though she might break down. I got the impression that she wanted to run and hide but she controlled herself. She picked at her food and shoved it around with her fork before answering.

"Glen, we can never get married," she whispered, and the whisper was as strained and hoarse as if she were being strangled and these were her last words.

I was amazed at what she said. I am sure I sounded more astonished and impatient than concerned at her foolish statement. "What do you mean 'we can't get married'?" I demanded. "What's to stop us?"

She carefully arranged two bite-sized pieces of hotcake, one on top of the other, before she answered. "I am so much older than you are." Her voice sounded hollow and dead. No emotion. No feeling.

"What do you mean too old?" I rebuked her. "Maybe seven or eight years. Why, I'll bet there are millions of couples like that," I ventured confidently.

"Glen, I am twenty-five years old." She uttered the words with such resigned finality that one could imagine she had just made a confession dooming her to the gallows.

I'll admit I was taken aback. So I had made a mistake of a couple of years. So what? What's two years? "Well, what's the difference?" I wanted to know. "I thought you were about twenty-three, but two more years don't make any difference."

"I am ten years older than you are." She said it like she was telling me she had leprosy or something. I was getting impatient. When you aspire to be grown up and crave to be treated like a grownup, it is not the most pleasant thing to be reminded of how young you are. Now she put it in the bluntest form possible. "I am nearly twice as old as you are."

"Now, what started all this?" I said. I was getting irritated and a little angry. "Let's forget it. Live our lives and let the future take care of itself." I said this with the proper emphasis to suggest that this should settle the matter, but she insisted on beating what I thought was a dead horse.

"The gap in years between us is not all. The life I have lived—" She trailed off as if her last half-finished statement was the coup de grâce to our hopes and there was no need to go further.

"There you go on that again." I was getting louder. "So you've been around. So you're the teacher and I am being taught. What of it? Did you ever make love to a calf? Well, I did!" She burst out laughing through her tears and, to head off another bad time like she had had the other day, I got up and quickly scooped her off the chair, carried her to the bedroom, and we worked off our tensions in bed in the most emotional and passionate embrace of all. And that is saying a lot.

Between the first and second shows that same evening, I was standing itchily watching a blackjack game when I felt a hand on my shoulder. I had felt that hand with just the same touch in the very same place before. I didn't have to look around to see who it was. I realized that this was the end of a glorious, wonderful, happy dream. Without moving, and certainly without the gladness that would ordinarily have been in my voice under other circumstances, I said, "Hello, Papa."

"GOODBYE, MONA"   "I've come to take you home, son." Papa spoke the words sadly. There was pity and regret there, too. Papa was an understanding man. He had been young once. I stood for a few seconds while the full significance of what was happening soaked in, then I turned and taking hold of his arm guided Papa toward a place near the door to the restaurant where we could talk without being overheard.

On the way we had to pass the table where Mona was sitting. She was facing us and when she saw us she recognized Papa as my father before I even introduced them and her eyes filled with a terror that could not have been more apparent had she been facing a firing squad.

"Papa, I want you to meet Mona. She works here. She has been very good to me. She is the most wonderful person I ever met. Mona, this is my father."

Mona was visibly trembling. Papa realized that this moment was no time for his usual hearty greeting and he played it with reserve and restraint. He took her weakly proffered hand and put his free arm about her shoulders. "I am glad to meet you, daughter," he said. This was Papa's usual way, to call a younger woman "daughter." Whether it raised hopes in Mona's fluttering breast I do not know.

"I am pleased and honored to meet you, sir," she said very softly and bowed her head, either as a sign of respect or to hide the fear and dread her face might reveal.

After a moment she looked up. Her eyes were swimming as she said, "Sir, you have a wonderful, talented, and lovable son. You can be very proud of him."

"I am proud of him," Papa stated, getting a little louder. "He takes after my father. He was a very smart man. Some day Glen will be a great man. A governor or a senator or maybe even president."

Papa was getting carried away. If I hadn't gotten him moving, he could very well have made a speech extolling my virtues to the whole damn place. He was sincere about it though. He had on more than one occasion told me in confidence that of all the boys he expected great things of me. As I left Mona I pressed her arm reassuringly and whispered, "I'll see you in a few minutes."

My *sotto voce* confab with Papa confirmed what had flashed through my mind when I felt his hand on my shoulder. Big Jim was evidently a man of some principle and had decided that the Bluebell was hardly the place for a fifteen-year-old. That is why he had pumped me about where I lived. He had written Papa, and Papa was here to take me home. I could have rebelled, but what would I gain? No job. My only alternative would have been to become a sponge living off Mona. A gigolo.

I was not prepared for the speed with which the end was to come. The train was due in at two-thirty. It was now a quarter to ten. The second show would go on at ten. The last show at one a.m., and finish at two. I explained this to Papa, and he readily agreed that I should finish out the evening. It would be cutting things a little thin, but we could make it. I also told him I would have to go to my room and pack my suitcases. I didn't tell him where my room was.

It was amazing how fast word could get around the Bluebell. In a gambling casino in a large city, a man could drop dead and people two tables away might never know it. That wasn't true about the Bluebell. In a small town like Pierce City, where everybody knew everybody else, word of some recent or pending event would spread like someone had kicked over a forty-gallon mop bucket.

By the time the second show went on, the word had pretty well been passed around that the kid singer's dad had come for him and that tonight would be his last.

Papa and I finished our talk just in time for me to get backstage before the curtain went up. Mona was in line with the other girls. Her eyes were looking through the solid floor at a spot seven or eight feet away. When I came close enough for my legs to enter her vision she looked up and smiled, but it was strictly a muscular affair. There was no expression in her eyes.

Each time we were offstage we huddled in a corner holding hands, holding each other, holding on to the precious moments left us. She didn't ask, but I promised her that I would be back just as soon as I could. First I would have to save some money and figure out some scheme to make a living here. The general atmosphere backstage was as cheerful as the death scene in *Hamlet*. The girls would look at Mona and me and dab their eyes. Even Margarita seemed to have compassion for her rival.

Mona did not put the usual finish on her act. I understood why.

The audience was particularly kind to me at the second show. Handkerchiefs were more in evidence among the ladies of the evening. Ordinarily I would have been bursting with pride to have Papa see me taking all these bows and encores, but my heart was so heavy I couldn't feel much satisfaction. Mona and I hurried home immediately after the second show. Not a word was spoken during the three-block walk. We simply clung to each other. Arm in arm. Tight. Tight. Our free hands clasped over the interlocked elbows trying to fend off the inevitable approach of the moment that would tear us apart.

The packing was done in silence. Neither of us dared trust ourselves to speak. My own throat was so tight it hurt.

The job was done in no more than five minutes. I picked up the suitcase and we walked to the door. I stopped for a last look around. My eyes made the circuit of the room and then met hers for the first time since leaving the Bluebell. It was more than we could bear. I dropped the suitcase and we held each other close, making no effort to control the wrenching sobs that filled our new home where we had known such happiness.

We cried till we were spent, and even then we made three or four false starts toward regaining our composure, only to break down again. At long last we were drained of emotion. Our eyes were finally dried. I picked up the suitcase. We stepped out the door. When we approached the lighted area in front of the Bluebell, Mona ducked her head to hide the devastation wrought by our emotional crisis, and hurried in and on backatage. I looked around for Papa. The door to Big Jim's office was ajar. Papa was in there. He and Big Jim were laughing uproariously, having a great time together.

Without raising my head I shoved the suitcase inside, saying: "Here's my suitcase, Papa." He barely glanced around, for which I was grateful. I pulled the brim of the new hat, my first, which I had bought only yesterday, down low to conceal the evidence of my own tears, and hurried backstage. I kept my face toward the wall as much as possible as I made my way down the right side of the big room.

The last show was a reptition of the second, only more emotional. The emcee told the audience that this was my last performance, but he needn't have bothered. The grapevine had long since done the job. He really laid it on. I had a "great future." Everyone was "sorry to see me go," but I was "preparing to enter college," etc., etc. All marlarkey. If there had been the faintest glimmer of hope that I could go to college, or even finish high school, I never would have left home.

Finally, when I did come on, I got a really wonderful reception. Applause, cheers, foot stomping, and finally a standing ovation. The place was aflutter with lacy handkerchiefs held in the hands of "the girls" waving goodbye. God bless 'em, I loved every one of them.

I sang six songs. It was two o'clock. The train was due in at two-thirty.

The applause would not stop. After futile efforts to stop the demonstration, which had assumed the proportions of hysteria among the ladies, the emcee held up one finger designating just once more.

I had no idea what Larry would play. That sixth song had been one more than we had planned for.

The band was playing. I didn't immediately recognize the tune. It sounded sad, but then most of my songs were tearjerkers. Then I recognized it! "God damn him! God damn that son of a bitch Larry! Why would he do this to me? He knew better than that. He must like to torture people."

I was in the spotlight. The introduction was ended and they were vamping till I was ready to sing. I almost broke down before I ever sang a note. I had to swallow hard. With a great effort I pulled myself together, lifted my chin, and sang, "I Wonder Who's Kissing Her Now."

Before I was halfway through the audience was in a shambles. The hardened women with their soft hearts were sobbing so loudly I could not possibly have been heard. The backstage sobbing had become anguished wails. I broke down and left the stage sobbing.

I went on out the stage door and down the steps.I could not see. I had to stop to wipe away at least some tears before I could go on.

Mona came running down the steps from the stage and laid her hand on my arm. "Goodbye, Glen," she managed to quaver between sobs. I realized then that I had nearly gone without even saying goodbye. I was excited, ashamed, confused, and angry at myself. I grabbed her violently and crushed her lips to mine in a short savage farewell. I managed to pull myself together. I couldn't leave them thinking I was a crybaby. I looked out over the audience and managed a smile. The scene fixed itself in my mind forever.

There was never such an emotional madhouse. Every woman in the place was in the grip of mass hysteria. All of them were sobbing; some were crying on the chests of their escorts of the evening. Others had their faces buried in both hands. One older woman, with makeup piled on to hide her years, was frantically but absentmindedly tearing her dress at the neck.

Some men were just standing, embarrassed. Some were patting their girls to soothe them. I literally shoved Mona from me and held my right lapel up to hide my childish bawling as I dashed from the place. Papa was waiting near the door with my suitcase. Tears were running down his cheeks, too. As he reached out and grasped my arm, a big rough-looking man, the last in the world you would expect to be sentimental, interposed himself between us and the door. He put his outsized hand on Papa's chest to stop him and asked in a manner more suggesting a command than a question, "Can't you let the kid stay here with his girl, mister? We'll look after him."

Papa slipped around my unknown, sentimental friend, pulling me by the arm, and we were out in the calm cool night. As we hurried toward the depot the hubbub inside the Bluebell gradually grew less audible and the clomp-clomp of our hurrying heels was the only sound on the deserted street.

Suddenly I remembered. I had left my slides for illustrated songs. My impulse was to run back, and then I realized that Larry had weaned me. I had not sung a single illustrated song. Last night I had probably given voice to my last illustrated song.

On the trip home I did a lot of thinking. I wanted to hurry back to Pierce City and Mona but a realistic appraisal of the situation told me it would be quite a while before I could save enough money on the twelve dollars a week I would earn managing the theaters.

In order to make my twelve dollars a week go farther I put a cot in each of the "theaters," where I slept. Now that I was no longer a bashful country boy I made good use of these accommodations.

I lived this "gay dog" life for six otherwise uneventful months. I did not forget Mona. Not for one day. I would gladly have traded my youthful harem for the bliss of holding Mona in my arms once more. Then, out of a clear blue sky I received a letter from E.K. saying that in two weeks he was closing down the theaters. The towns were just too small. I was utterly despondent. What would I do in Kooskia with no job?

Then, on the very same day that I had been plunged into complete despair by E.K.'s letter, a miracle happened. I received a wire from Ferris, my oldest brother, who had staged our family home-talent production.

The wire was brief and to the point: HAVE JOB FOR YOU WITH MCDONOUGH STOCK CO. OPENING MAY 1ST. ANSWER. LOVE. FERRIS.

Here it was! Here it was! My chance to be a real actor! My elation was compounded because the wire had come at the moment I needed it so desperately. Wowee, whoopee, and hooray! I would have had to quit school and find some sort of job in any event, so it was agreed that I should accept the job Ferris had promoted for me.

I wired, OKAY. WILL BE THERE.

The McDonough Stock Company wired me a ticket to San Francisco as an advance against my salary. They did not pay my fare. It was not customary.

I left four days before it was necessary. It would be a long trip to San Francisco via Pierce City.

LOST LOVE I arrived there at three p.m. It had been six months since that night Papa took me home to Kooskia.

I had to pass the Bluebell on the way to *our* house. As I hurried up the street something about the scene seemed unfamiliar. A half block from the Bluebell it dawned on me. The Bluebell sign was gone! In its place was another sign that said "Ritz." I hurried to see why the Bluebell had changed its name to Ritz. The Bluebell had been remodeled into a movie theater. The lobby display was for a picture starring William Farnum.

But what about the people who had worked here? Lil and

Margarita, Sandy and Al and Larry. And what about Mona? Yes, what about Mona? The constricting hand of vague apprehension reached inside my chest and squeezed my heart until I could hardly breathe.

I hurried on two blocks up the street and to the left. There was our house. That was a relief, just to see it there. Through the gate, up the walk, across the porch. The door was locked. I knocked gently at first, then I noticed that the blinds were drawn clear down and there were no curtains on the windows. I knocked louder. No answer. The blind was probably two inches up at the bottom. I got on my knees and peered under the curtain. It was dark inside and difficult to make out anything. Gradually my eyes pierced the gloom. Nothing. Nothing at all. The place was empty. *Our* house was deserted.

Mona! Where was Mona! The walls of my chest were pressing harder against my heart. My breathing became more labored. I picked up my suitcase and hurried back to the Bluebell.

No one was around there. It was locked up tight. I went into the restaurant next door. No one I remembered in here. I stood by the cash register, undecided what to do. The oldish waitress noticed me and signaled she'd be right with me. When she had finished pouring coffee for the couple she was waiting on, she came up front and said, "What can I do for you?"

"Uh—what happened to the Bluebell?" I foolishly inquired and got the obvious answer.

"They made a movie theater out of it. Didn't you see?" I guess my blank look of dismay softened her up a little and she elaborated. "Big Jim Williams died about six months ago, and what with Prohibition being voted in, the new people just decided to turn it into a movie show."

"B-but what about the people who used to work there?" I stammered.

"Gone, all gone," she said matter of factly, shifting her gaze to squint through the window as though looking for the ghosts of the departed. Then her eyes came back to me and a flicker of recognition appeared in their rheumy opaqueness.

"Say, aren't you the kid that sang in there for a while?" she inquired, her interest kindled by the realization that she was talking to one of those mysterious, glamorous creatures, an entertainer.

"Yes. Yes, I am Glen Taylor. Do you remember me?" I asked, hopeful that she would open up and help me.

"Yeah, I do remember you, kid. I was watching that last night you sang. I was watching from the door there that used to go into the Bluebell. I saw your old man take you away. What'd you come back for, kid?"

I was sure she knew and just wanted confirmation. "Well, I—that is, I—well, I was looking for someone," I lamely explained.

"Mona?" She put the one-word question, eyeing me intently like a prosecutor trying to pin down his point.

"Well—yes," I admitted.

She looked at me pityingly for several seconds and then in a rather maternal sort of way advised me: "You look like a nice young kid. Why don't you just forget it and go on home? Huh?"

She just didn't understand and I had to explain. "Well, you see, I can't go home. That is, I have come a long ways and I promised Mona—"

She put the coffeepot down and rested her elbows on the cracked-glass top of the scantily stocked two-by-four display of cheap cigars. "Kid—you don't want to see Mona," she insisted. "Be smart and forget it."

"Well, what makes you say I don't want to see Mona?" I had to ask the question. I had to know but I was afraid. There was something about the way she spoke. Something was the matter. Something pretty serious. I put my hands on the cigar case, facing her, and when she just stood there I repeated my question. "Why don't I want to see Mona?" I'm afraid I sounded pretty much like an immature sixteen-year-old then. I forgot to use the grownup voice I was so assiduously cultivating.

She reached over and put her hand on mine. The gesture was gentle and sympathetic but the hand was rough, as was her voice. "Kid," she said, "Mona's not like she was when you saw her. She had a rough time. After the Bluebell closed she just locked herself up in her house. She never came out. Never. She had a delivery boy bring what groceries she needed to the house and that wasn't much. Mostly it was liquor. She drank a lot in the last six months. She don't look like she did when you was here, Kid. I guess her money ran out because yesterday she left for Silverton. She's got a job over there," she said, looking down at her blurred reflection in the fly-specked cigar case and shaking her head from side to side, slowly, as might a gypsy seeing unpleasant things in a crystal ball.

"Where?" I asked hurriedly. The trail was getting warm. I had to be moving along. "Where?" I repeated. "What's her address? Where does she work?"

Tears made the perpetual wateriness of her eyes overflow as she begged me, "Kid, for God's sake, forget it. You don't want to see her. It'll hurt you. You don't want to be hurt, do you, kid? Please forget it. Mona told me that the only thing that could help her now would be to get her husband paroled, and that ain't about to happen." I heard what she said but it didn't sink in.

Mona was in trouble. I had to find her. I had to help her. My voice wasn't childlike now. I was serious. Time was wasting. I leaned over and spoke through clenched teeth, "Where can I find her?"

She looked me in the eye for what seemed a long time. Then she pulled her hand off mine, sighed, picked up the coffeepot, and turned to go. She wasn't going to tell me! I was opening my mouth to stop her when she spoke over her shoulder. "Geraldine's—in the district," she said without stopping.

In the district? I knew what that meant and for a moment I felt sick to my stomach, but then I realized how stupid I was. There could very well be places like the Bluebell in "the district." Of course. That was it.

I grabbed my suitcase and, as fast as I could go without breaking into a run, I hurried to the depot. I must catch the first train. If I lost one minute I might miss it.

There was no train until three the next afternoon. I went over and slumped on the hard wooden bench that was along two sides of the waiting room. I had not gone to bed for two nights. I had gotten some sleep on the train but I felt crummy, unwashed, unshaven, dog-tired. I had better go to the hotel. I wanted at least to clean up and look my best when I saw Mona. I'd try to sleep, too. I wanted to be rested when I saw Mona. Yeah, I wanted to be *well* rested when, in just a few hours from now, I would hold Mona in my arms again.

I went to the hotel and for the first time in my life I signed up for a room *with bath*. Two-fifty. What extravagance!

"PARDON ME, GOVERNOR"   I bathed and shaved, put on my black suit, and took the one I had worn on the train down to be pressed. I barely made it before the tailor shop closed. I waited ten minutes for the suit and took it back up to the room. It was after five. The dining room would be open. I went down for dinner. In the lobby I picked up a newspaper someone had abandoned. The dining room wasn't crowded, so when I finished eating I continued to sit at my table and read.

A little before six a party of fifteen men came in. I was no more than four feet from the closest end of their table, and by straining my ears a little I could make out nearly everything that was said. This was no ordinary group. These men were staff members and officials of the State Parole Board. The distinguished looking man at the head of the table nearest me was the governor. Boy, was I in classy company!

As I listened, something vaguely bothered me. What was it? Something was trying to get through to me.

A plump busty lady of perhaps fifty came hurrying into the dining room and hustled toward the governor, holding both hands in front of her ample bosom, palms out, like babies do when learning to walk. "Oh, Charles," she began excitedly while she was still fifteen feet away. "Something terrible has happened." The governor got up, but in no excited hurry. Evidently "terrible" things happened quite frequently to this excitable lady who obviously was the *first* lady. "That terrible man! How could he do this to me?"

The governor was calm, cool, and collected. "Now, Marion, control yourself." She was dabbing her eyes and sniffing as he put her recently coiffed head on his chest and patted it gingerly so as not to disturb the fresh hairdo.

He held her at three-quarter-arm's length and inquired, "Now, what's the trouble?"

"Oh, that horrible violinist from Silverton," the governor's wife exclaimed. "He just called and said he won't be here. His wife is ill or something," she wailed. "The ladies are due to sit down in fifteen minutes and I have no entertainment for them. What *am* I going to do?" The wail was a little louder, a little higher pitched.

"Now, Marion, we'll find somebody. Surely there is someone

with talent of some sort in Pierce City," he ventured.

"Not in Pierce City," the lady stated with finality, shaking her head for emphasis.

"Clyde," said the governor, crooking his finger at a young man who was seated at a separate table.

The man jumped to his feet with an eager "Yes, Governor?" and took a step or two forward.

"Clyde, do a little calling around and see if you can locate someone to entertain the ladies for Marion," the governor suggested glibly. Apparently he had a higher opinion of the cultural level of Pierce City than did his wife, or perhaps he had confidence that his helper could do the impossible.

The governor's wife seemed quite pleased with this turn of events. She gazed upon the rather good-looking young man as though she were happily receiving another diamond ring to add to the assortment which already covered her hands like barnacles on a boat bottom. She slipped her arm through Clyde's and exited almost gaily.

I had an idea. They were desperate for an entertainer. I was an entertainer. I stepped over to the governor, who was shaking his head slightly and was just ready to resume his seat. "Pardon me, Governor," I said in my deepest, most cultured voice. "I didn't mean to listen, sir, but I could not help hearing. Perhaps I can help out. I am a professional entertainer. I am a singer."

When I first started to speak I know the governor was all ready to cut me down, but I managed to get to the crux of the situation before he could get going. He looked at me for a moment, trying to reorient his attitude. "You are?" he asked skeptically.

"Yes, sir, I am. You don't need to take my word for it. I would be glad to try out for your wife and let her be the judge."

Listening to the scuttlebutt that flowed as freely as the hard liquor around the Bluebell, I had heard the governor called "an old tightwad" and several other things that indicated he was something of a nut on the subject of keeping the purse strings tight. Not only the state's, but his own as well. The Bluebell political pundits had evidently known their man. "How much do you want?" he asked bluntly.

"I would be very happy, sir, to do what I can without thought of remuneration. I would consider it a privilege," I proclaimed rather grandiloquently. Now, if you think this language and phraseology is a little unusual for the average sixteen-year-old to be spouting, let me explain that I was an unusual sixteen-year-old. I had, as far back as I could remember, had an affinity for words. I had heard Papa deliver a good many sermons in his flowery style, and I had been reading pulp magazines for years. Before I could read, our favorite family pastime had been listening to Papa read novels in *Adventure* and *Argosy* magazines, sometimes until two or three in the morning.

Papa had suggested to me that I should never let a word that I did not understand, or could not pronounce and spell, go by without looking it up in the dictionary. I had always had the highest grade when it came to writing essays or stories in school, and one of the poorest grades when it came to diagramming sentences or explaining how I had written with such command of the language. My offer to perform for the honor of the thing hit the parsimonious governor right where he lived.

"Come with me, young man," he commanded. It was plain that he was accustomed to using the power and prestige of his office to short-circuit formalities.

I followed the governor to the lobby, where we found his wife and Clyde earnestly and a little desperately talking to the clerk. It was clear they had not been able to find a budding Heifetz or Caruso in Pierce City.

"Marion, I believe I have solved your problem. This young man is a professional singer and he has offered his services *free* to entertain your friends," he proudly announced, as though he had miraculously dug me out of a sandbank. She looked at me, and it was plain that she liked what she saw. She threw her hands up into her walking-baby position and exclaimed happily, "Oh, that's wonderful. Governor, you *are* just wonderful." The governor asked my name and introduced me to his wife and Clyde.

"Now, Mr. Taylor, if you will excuse me, I am here for a meeting of the Parole Board."

"The Parole Board?" The words that the old waitress had spoken when she told me, "Mona said that all that could help her would be to have her husband paroled," came back to me.

If Mona had said that, and I had no reason to doubt the waitress, then I was not the most important thing in her life as I had conceitedly imagined. Then again there was every likelihood that Mona felt that with a young guy like me, it would be "out of sight, out of mind" as far as she was concerned. That would be up to her. Whether she wanted me or him. At any rate, I had a golden opportunity here to put in a good word for the poor son of a bitch she was married to and I could, in good conscience, do no less.

THE BARGAIN "So you are a singer?" the governor's wife was saying. "Well, you will have to have an accompanist, won't you? Do you have one?"

"No," I admitted, "I don't, but surely there is someone in Deerlodge who can play a piano."

"I am a very good pianist, Glen, I will play for you," she stated positively.

God help us and save us from home-talent piano players. Why hadn't I kept my mouth shut and scouted around on my own. But I was hooked. When the governor's wife states that she *will* play piano for you, what can you do? Particularly when you want to ingratiate yourself for an ulterior purpose. I'm sure my jaw fell, but I recovered and, taking a page from Papa's gracious manner and flattering vocabulary when he was buttering up the ladies, I pretended to be overwhelmed at my good fortune. "Young lady," I exclaimed delightedly, "I'll be thrilled, but I'm afraid I'll have stage fright with the governor's wife as my accompanist." That got the affected lady atwitter so I decided to spread it on thicker.

"I knew when I first saw you—I could tell by your manner, something about you, that you were an artist," I said, with all the insincere sincerity that I could manage. Bless her vain heart, she nearly took off, fluttering her hands up and down so, and she giggled like a schoolgirl.

"Excuse me, and I'll run up and get my music," I said, and took the stairs three at a time. I came down the same way, forgetting my newly assumed maturity and dignity, and we went in the banquet room where the First Lady was to entertain the wives of the Parole Board members. We had the room to ourselves except for the two waitresses who came and went.

What about that? This woman could really play the piano. She was a regular pro. I complimented her and in the ensuing exchange it came out that she had indeed played piano in the orchestra at the Pantages Theater in Seattle, and not too many years ago. She had to be good to have done that. We ran through five numbers quickly. Her praise for my voice was as effusive as my now-genuine compliments on her playing.

The governor came in to see how his lady was doing. She smothered him with hugs and kisses and pats for finding this wonderfully talented, handsome young man. The governor was somewhat embarrassed at this show of affection in front of a stranger. He straightened his tie, harrumphed a couple of times, and stiffly said to me, "Now, young man, we appreciate what you're doing. If there is anything I can ever do for you, let me know." He expected that would end it and turned to go.

"There *is* something you can do, sir," I said, possibly a little louder and more forcefully than was necessary because I was scared.

He stopped dead in his tracks, one foot a full step ahead of the other, as though you had stopped a movie film.

He stood there for a good three seconds, and I imagined I could read his thoughts. *Oh-oh, I said the wrong thing* was going through his mind, I'd swear. He relaxed from his awkward frozen position and turned around with a resigned sigh.

"What did you say?" he inquired, in a brusque manner calculated to scare me into saying, "Oh, nothing, sir."

But I repeated my statement just as firmly and positively as before, and with more assurance because I had broken the ice. "There is something you can do for me, sir."

He looked at me and I'd guess he was saying to himself, *Now, what the hell can this kid want?* Aloud, he asked, "All right, what is it I can do for you, young man?" He didn't make it easy for me. He just stared at me.

I had been thinking over what I was to say when this moment came. "Sir, there is a man serving time in the prison here at Pierce City," and I handed him the name of Robert McComber, which I had written on a piece of hotel stationery when I had gone up to get my music. "He is not a bad man, sir. He did not kill anybody or anything like that. He just gave in to temptation and took some money. I know he would be willing, and if he were freed, he would be able, to repay the money over a period of time because he is an educated man. An accountant. He has already served more than the minimum number of years to which he was sentenced. Aside from this one transgression, he has lived an upright and honorable life. He has been a model prisoner. Sir, his wife still loves him, and she is very sick and needs him terribly. She is a very fine woman. She is a most gracious lady, like your own wife is, sir. I would appreciate it and consider it a great favor if you could prevail upon the board to free him, and I am sure that Heaven would look with favor upon you if you can, in good conscience, grant my request and answer the prayers of his sick wife.'' This was quite an emotional appeal, and I did not try to hold back the tears, but let them run down my cheeks. If they would help, then by all means let them run.

I stood absolutely still when I had finished. I had pulled out all the stops and touched every base to the best of my sixteen-year-old ability. I could see that he was impressed. I didn't move. I hardly breathed.

He raised his head and, looking me square in the eye, promised, "I will see what I can do. You stated your case well, young man. You made an excellent appeal. Some day you could be a great lawyer." Having delivered himself of the promise and the compliments, he turned on his heel and stiffly left the room.

When he was gone, I turned back to the piano, wiping my eyes. The dear woman whose misfortune had made my opportunity possible was sitting there on the piano bench crying in her handkerchief. Instinctively, and without thinking about her being the governor's wife, I sat down beside her and put my arm around her comfortingly. Instead of soothing her it had the opposite effect, and she broke into uncontrolled sobs. I was thankful that she did her best to make as little noise as possible. After a minute or two, she regained her composure and said, "I'm sorry, but you are so young and so brave and—" she left it unfinished and, knuckling a tear from her eye, started playing the song we had just put up before her husband came in.

It was eight o'clock before dinner was served. Although I had eaten at five, I hadn't had much for two days before that, and I managed to do at least as well as any of the ladies.

My sponsor gave me a nice sendoff. She told the ladies that I had sung at the Davenport Hotel in Spokane. I hadn't, of course, but my sister had, and I had to tell her something—I couldn't say that I had sung at the Bluebell. I got considerably more than a polite hand. Older women are generally kind to a very young man, particularly if he is a good-looking young man, and more particularly if he is an innocent-looking, good-looking young man.

After I had resumed my seat, my accompanist added modestly, "I am going to accompany our young virtuoso." She got a much better hand than I had. These girls knew on which side their bread was buttered. Incidentally, that was the first and last time I was ever called a "virtuoso." I could hardly wait to look up the word. I thought this was possibly the word for a male virgin, and I snickered a little cynical, wise-guy snicker.

For some reason I cannot explain, I was impelled to sing "I Wonder Who's Kissing Her Now" for my first song, and I almost ended up as shaken as I was that last night at the Bluebell. My fresh, young good looks and the emotional delivery had these upper-crust gentlewomen just as sentimentally maudlin as their fallen sisters ever were at the Bluebell. They applauded and cooed and whispered among themselves and one or two rolled their eyes like, "My God, isn't he something?"

After I had bowed twice, I held out my hand to my proud pianist and we bowed together. While we were standing there hand in hand, the door opened and there stood the governor. He came in and sat down. In fact, the entire Parole Board came in and sat down.

Someone had evidently told them they were missing something and rousted them out of the bar. I'm sure they were puzzled to see every last one of their wives crying like I had sprayed them with onion juice. We sang and bowed and bowed in tandem and sang and bowed for an hour and thirty minutes, and the dear ladies at the tables smiled and cooed and "oh'd" and "ah'd" and cried and cried. After it was over the ladies, the Parole Board, and the governor came up and shook my hand, congratulated me, and thanked me for the wonderful evening.

I was careful to keep the First Lady close at hand to share the kudos. If the governor forgot his promise, I wanted an ace in the hole.

As she was helping me put my music away she whispered,

"Now, don't you worry, Glen, that poor husband will be pardoned so he can go to his dear sick wife, and he won't have to pay back that dirty old money either," and she shook her head real fast in the affirmative. I got the message.

Something close to a hundred years passed before the train left the next afternoon for Silverton.

GERALDINE'S   The train was quite crowded. Shortly before we pulled out a man, maybe thirty years old, came down the aisle looking for a seat. He wore a brand new but sloppy fitting blue serge suit. I had a vague notion I had seen him before somewhere. *At the Bluebell, probably,* I thought. He went on by and out of my mind. We arrived in Silverton at eight o'clock in the evening. I headed uptown carrying my suitcase. I finally came to a hotel. It wasn't exactly fancy, but it looked fairly decent so I went in, walked up to the desk, and from his startled look I guess I caught the clerk a little off balance by asking, "How far is it from here to the district?"

After being startled, he grinned wisely and said, "It's just three blocks down the hill and turn left. Go down that street right out there," and he pointed out the side window.

This was lucky, getting so close just by accident. I got a room for a dollar and a quarter. By the time I got to my room and washed up a little, it was dark.

I had eaten on the train so I hurried to find Mona. My heart was pounding as I went clompity-clomping down the board sidewalk. When I turned onto the side street my guts tightened up. The scene reminded me of the red-light district in Pierce City. Two-story frame houses, some unpainted and all with a red electric light bulb over the door. Some were more prententious than others. Some had display windows like converted drygoods stores. Instead of articles of clothing or bolts of cloth being displayed in each window, there would be one or sometimes two girls wearing filmy dressing gowns, sitting in red upholstered chairs. To light the scene there would be three or four incandescent globes strung across overhead.

Surely there must be something better than this in a big town like Silverton. These girls were even older looking and more saggy than the ones I had seen in Pierce City. A man came out of the "house" just ahead of me, the first man I had seen since I left the hotel. He staggered slightly. I accosted him and asked if he could direct me to Geraldine's.

"Sright tair," he said, waving his hand drunkenly toward the next building down the street, which was probably a hundred and fifty feet away past a vacant lot.

I thanked the man and turned, but before I could start running that last short sprint he said, "Hey, kid!" I was off balance, leaning in the direction in which I had intended to run, but I caught myself and stopped. "Whaddya want Geraldine's for? It's a crummy joint. Now, why dontcha go in here? There's a cute new one in there ain't no older'n you, I betcha. I just rode her and she's young and tight."

I wanted to get going but the guy, while quite drunk, was friendly and wanted to be helpful, so I didn't feel like just walking away and leaving him talking to himself.

I opened my mouth, though I had no idea what I was going to say. He saved me the trouble by offering more advice.

" 'Course, they got a new one at Geraldine's. I heard the girls talking in the Purple Pillow here and they said Geraldine has a new girl startin' to work tonight. A little lady from Pierce City." As I turned and hurried away he was saying, "I guess I'll try her *tomorrow* night."

As I drew near I could see that Geraldine's was no better and no worse than the other places I had passed. There was a difference, though. The window was soaped with Bon Ami.

I rubbed this coating off to make a small peephole so I could see in. It was furnished pretty much like the others. Gold-colored wallpaper on the wall which separated the display window from the room beyond and, of course, there was the upholstered chair.

The door in the partition was being held open by a woman whose back was to me. She was talking to another woman who was facing me. Boy, was she a hard-looking customer! Too old to be working. She must be Geraldine. She seemed to be giving instructions to the woman whose back was to me.

At this point, someone came out of the place and started washing the Bon Ami off the window.

I looked, and I couldn't believe what I saw. The window washer was a woman, but with the ugliest, coarsest face I ever saw. Thick lips, a deep wrinkle down each side of her face, heavy eyebrows, and a forehead as corrugated as a washboard. She wasn't old, not over thirty-five. I'd say she was at least six feet tall, probably weighed two-twenty, and had shoulders like a wrestler. I was staring in such open-mouthed awe that I was embarrassed when I realized what I was doing.

I took one last look through the peephole. Geraldine was gone and the woman she had been talking to was climbing the two steps to the cubicle behind the glass. She was looking down to be sure she did not stumble on the steps. When she gained the firm footing of the display chamber, she looked up.

G–O–D   A–L–M–I–G–H–T–Y ———

It was Mona! Or was it? Just a few months ago she had been young and beautiful. Now her face sagged. The corners of her mouth were now two deep wrinkles that angled downward and gave her a bitter, even hateful, expression. Her stomach, which had been so flat and muscular, was decidedly paunchy and those beautifully rounded hips bulged under her diaphanous garment. The once beautiful eyes so full of sparkle were watery, rheumy, and opaque. My God! She was—old.

I wanted to hide my face to shut off this apparition. Hide my face and cry, but I couldn't do that.

Anyhow, this wasn't Mona. That woman in the resturant in Pierce City had said she had been drinking heavily. That was it. She had gone to pieces because she loved me and thought she had lost me. I should be horsewhipped for not writing to her. Now I would make up for that. I would save her. In the shelter of my arms she would soon be herself again.

I turned to go to her and ran into the window washer. I might as well have run into a cement post. I was jolted from head to foot. As I mumbled "Pardon me," the creature grinned a vacuous grin and returned to the chore at hand.

I stepped inside. Geraldine sat just inside the door—knitting. She placed the ball of thread and the needle on a small stand and rose to greet me. Her face fell. Obviously, she felt I was too young to enjoy the service her establishment offered—that is, without an escort. It was a common practice for fathers to bring their young sons in, either to be taught the facts of life or just to be serviced, but the place could get into trouble by catering to boys.

"What do you want?" she demanded, not too pleasantly.

"The girl—the woman in the window, I want to see her," I said as ungently as she had spoken to me.

"I'm sorry, son, but you are a little too young."

"I want to talk to her. She's my—I've got to talk to her."

Geraldine stared at me for a moment, then stepped to the street door and said something to the Amazon who was washing the window. She put down her rag and came in, drying her hands on the towel she had thrown over her shoulder. She walked about four feet past me, turned, and looked me over as though I were a beef being sold on the hoof.

Geraldine asked, "Do you know the girl in the window?"

"Yes, I do. Her name is Mona."

"And what is your name?"

"Taylor. Glen Taylor."

Geraldine stepped over to the door of the window enclosure, opened it a crack and spoke to Mona in such a low voice that I could not hear what she said. Mona must have been whispering, because I could hear nothing.

Geraldine glanced back at me over her shoulder, and then quickly stepped through the door and closed it behind her.

As she opened and closed the door I caught a glimpse of Mona. She was seated, her head was turned away from me, and she was holding her face with both hands.

Geraldine was in there for at least one minute, perhaps two, then she came out, and even before she was down the two steps she said, "She says she never heard of you!"

I was astonished—thunderstruck. I opened my mouth and nothing came out. Finally I managed to get my voice back, and although I was still pretty shaken I said rather weakly, "There's some mistake. She—she knows me." And I started for the door leading to the window.

Before I had taken more than one step, Geraldine's eyes had flashed a signal and I felt a strong hand grasp my collar. The other hand came up under my overcoat and grabbed the seat of my pants. Geraldine had moved to the door and held it open, and

I was given the bum's rush out the door with sufficient impetus to send me sprawling across the sidewalk and into the street.

I was bruised and skinned up a little, but that was as nothing compared to my mortification at having been handled so easily by—a woman.

I picked myself up and made a charge for the door, but I caught my toe on the edge of the sidewalk and dove headlong just in time to strike the legs of a man who came into my line of vision only after I had stubbed my toe and was already airborne. The two of us were on the sidewalk. We both scrambled up muttering apologies while brushing the dirt off our clothes. Then we straightened up and looked at each other, and I'll be damned if it wasn't the guy I had seen coming down the aisle as the train pulled out of Pierce City. I had that feeling again. I had seen this guy someplace.

He turned and stepped to the door through which I had so recently come head first. As he grasped the doorknob he caught sight of Mona and froze. I looked from him to her. She was standing still, clutching her cheeks, and with so much emotion on her face that she reminded me of pictures I had seen of agonized victims in an illustrated version of Dante's Inferno.

Her eyes caught mine, and she slowly moved her head from side to side as though she was mystified. The man's eyes followed hers, and he looked at me and flung open the door. I looked back at Mona and she pointed to the man, and her lips elaborately formed a word or phrase that I did not catch.

Then she motioned with outstretched arm and pointing finger like a stern New England father in an 1890 melodrama sending his wayward daughter out into the cold, cruel world, saying "Go" with more emphasis and urgency. There was no mistaking it. I understood the command and the gesture but the entire situation was beyond me. The man. Her obvious recognition of him. Her frantic motioning for me to go. I stood there, uncomprehending.

Geraldine appeared at the door of the display window and motioned for Mona to come. As she reached the door, Mona hesitated with a hand holding the door frame on each side to steady her as she prepared to descend the rickety steps, and again she formed the words, *"Please go."*

My confusion began to give way to anger. She was sending me away, refusing to admit she ever knew me because of this "john." Well, by God, I'd at least give her a piece of my mind. I stepped to the door and yanked it open.

The window washer stood there with what looked like a policeman's billy club. Remembering what she had done to me *without* any club, I took a step backward. I could see into the reception room, and just then Mona and her john came together. Boy, were they gone on each other!

He held out his arms and said "Mona" and, believe me, there was a lot of feeling there, I had to admit. She was crying and grabbed him around the neck and between the kisses she kept saying, "Bob, oh Bob!"

I didn't know what the hell was going on and I couldn't even get in to find out, with that female Jess Willard standing guard with that billy club.

I was just about ready to go out in the street and start throwing rocks at the goddamned place when Geraldine stuck her painted old face around the doorjamb and whispered, "Sonny, I don't know what this is all about but I think, if I was you, I'd git while the gittin's good. That man is her husband."

If that female bouncer had hit me over the head with her billy club I couldn't have been more dazed and chagrined. Of course! That's why he looked familiar. Mona had shown me his picture once. Everything fell into place. The governor, bless his heart, had kept his promise.

THE SUITCASE   *Well,* I thought, *that about winds up this episode,* and I made my exit from the scene, walking backward till I was well out of range of that billy club and the only woman that ever got the best of me in a fight, fair or foul.

By the time I got back to the hotel, I had begun to remember Mona as I had last seen her on that memorable night of high drama when we had parted in the hubbub and histrionics caused by Papa showing up to save me from a life of sin and shame.

Probably not more than twenty minutes after leaving Geraldine's I came down the hotel stairs carrying my suitcase. Halfway down, there was a landing and the stairs turned sharp right and headed toward the street. As I started down this last flight, the front door opened, and a man held it for a woman. It was Mona!

I didn't know what to do. I couldn't turn and run, although I had a strong impulse to do so. I steeled myself and determined to go straight ahead and pretend not to see them. If she chose to recognize me, that would be up to her.

Beads of sweat broke out on my forehead. A couple of times my suitcase, which wasn't the most expensive, had come open accidentally, allowing the contents to fall out. I prayed devoutly that it wouldn't happen now. Mona's husband's fancy robe, the slippers, God knows what all. They were in there. I was almost even with them now. Two more steps, and I'd have it made.

"Glen! Glen!" Mona cried out, loud enough for everyone in the lobby to hear. Thank goodness, there was no one in the lobby. Her arms were around me and she was kissing me, not once but several times, on my cheeks, my forehead, my mouth, with loud "m-mms" as though I tasted good.

Her husband, the man whose belongings practically filled my suitcase, just stood there. What else could he do? Obviously, these were not passionate kisses, but kisses of joy at seeing a teenage boy. I looked as young and innocent as I possibly could, hoping that she could explain this, and that my suitcase wouldn't come open.

Finally, she desisted and said, "Oh, Glen, I'm so glad to see you. I was afraid I might not get an opportunity to thank you." She paused to get her breath and I laid my suitcase down. I didn't set it down. I laid it down—flat. This bit of action gave her time to catch her breath and she continued, "Bob, this is Glen Taylor, the boy [I think she bore down a little on the 'boy'; ordinarily my ego might have been offended, but at this moment I was in full accord, not only with the word but the inflection]." She repeated, "The boy I used to work with at the Bluebell, and whom I told you so much about and the dear friend who has done so much for us." Then she turned to me, and what she said was really enlightening.

"Glen," she said, "Bob has told me about what you did. The warden told him that he was getting him a pardon because a young man who had sung so beautifully for the governor's guests had requested it. The minute he told me that I knew it could be no one else but you."

I explained how I had come back to say hello to the old Bluebell gang, but found that most of them had moved to Silverton so I had come on over here.

"My brother in San Francisco," I said, "has gotten me a job with the McDonough Stock Company," and I proudly showed her his telegram but kept my thumb over the Kooskia address. Boy! Did it do my heart good to be able to show her that telegram. Bob was glad. Mona was delighted and kissed me a few more times, and then Bob reached down and picked up my suitcase and handed it to me.

My heart stopped beating and I was so weak and trembly that I fumbled the pass. The metal corner hit the tile with a sharp sound like a metal corner hitting tile and—the suitcase popped open. I saw the suitcase falling, falling, falling, and I tried to catch it. After it hit the floor I commanded myself to fall on it before it could come open, but the lawful owner of most of the contents beat me to it. The suitcase lit on a corner and then fell over on its bottom with the lid open three or four inches, but not enough for Mr. Mona to see in because the open side was toward me. He reached down, pushed the lid down, and the fasteners clicked shut. He handed it to me and I put my arms around it and beat a hasty retreat.

The last I saw of Mona she was laughing. She had her hand over her mouth, but I could still tell she was laughing. It showed past the edges of her hand and in her eyes. Besides, her shoulders were shaking. She was laughing because when my suitcase flew open, she had been standing where she got a glimpse of a silk smoking jacket, and after I got the suitcase shut and the danger was past, she couldn't help but laugh at the way I had bungled things and was holding my suitcase clutched to my manly chest like a fireman rescuing a chee-ild.

The outside air seemed much colder than when I came in, but that was because I was wringing wet with perspiration. All the way to the depot I carried my suitcase full of contraband like one would carry an infant. While I purchased my ticket to San Francisco, I laid my suitcase flat on the floor by the ticket window and kept my foot on the lid while I occasionally cast an apprehensive glance at the door to see if pursuit had yet been organized.

As I sat in my red plush seat with my securely tied keister stowed safely overhead, I had time to reflect on the recent happenings and a comforting realization came to me. Mona had not looked nearly as bad in the hotel as she had in that window. Not as good as she had during those romantic days at the Bluebell perhaps, but not bad, not bad at all.

One thing was certain. I'd never, *ever* forget Mona.

II

Show

Business

"TAB" SHOWS   I had no trouble breaking into show business. I was a good study and I imagine it would be fair to say that I was a natural-born actor.

That fall at the end of the tent season the McDonough Stock Company closed and would remain closed until the next spring.

Instead of looking for another job, as the other actors were doing, Ferris decided to start his own show. He hired me, and I stayed with him for seven years.

During that period I also married—briefly. It's the old familiar story: We thought we were in love and married in haste. Before very long, we split up, and later I read in *Billboard* that she had been granted a divorce.

At the end of the tent season in September of 1927, Ferris closed his show because he didn't want to buck the snows of winter. He would open again in the spring, but I was not financially able to sit out that long wait. I got in touch with another brother, Slade, who had a show, and I got a job with him. Ferris had been paying me fifty dollars a week. Slade offered me seventy-five dollars. I joined him at Great Falls, Montana.

Slade's modus operandi was very different from what I had known before. The Slade Mike Taylor Musical Comedy Company was what was known as a "tab" show, the "tab" denoting "abbreviated" or "shortened." Instead of being a full evening's entertainment, a tab show ran only forty-five minutes to an hour and was presented in conjunction with a movie.

There were eight principals and a chorus of sixteen girls.

The plot of these productions was tenuous or nonexistent. Quite often the entire show would be composed of brief comedy skits known as "blackouts," the name deriving from the fact that when you came to the "snapper" or "tag line" the lights blacked out to give greater impact to the belly-laugh ending, with no possibility that attention would be distracted by some actor moving or, for that matter, the motion of the curtain closing. With just one day's rehearsal before opening, I became the second comic. Tab was really burlesque cleaned up sufficiently to be acceptable to the family trade.

The comedy was risqué and double entendre, but not outright dirty. No strippers, no bumps or grinds.

There were scripts and parts for a few of Slade's shows which had been cut down by someone from Broadway shows or other sources, but most were bits and blackouts. All these skits had names but no scripts or parts. They were just passed along and a good tab comedian or straight man could join a show and go on with only a perfunctory running through of the bits to be used. Slade played an exaggerated Irish character called "Mike Casey" and I was an effeminate tramp with a sponge nose, black grease paint whiskers and eyebrows, and a white minstrel-type mouth.

Actually, it was a black-and-white clown effect. The "fairy" lisps and gestures were completely incongruous with the makeup.

It took me a week or so to get used to the idea of just talking things over and ad libbing it, but then it became great fun. It afforded endless opportunities if you had a sense of humor. Shortly, I was making Slade get in and dig to keep from being overshadowed.

My costume consisted of an old full dress coat so large that the tails hung down to mid-calf. The pants were so big they could have accommodated a small pillow in front. They were cut off at high ankle's length and held up with a loud pair of two-inch-wide suspenders. I wore a beat-up old silk opera hat and my heelless, high-top shoes were size twelve with a sole that stuck out an inch all around, giving the illusion of duck's feet.

For most "bit" shows we had a center entrance with four steps up, then a landing and four steps up and off to the right. One night I discovered that my shoes were long enough to bridge the distance from one step to the next and I could ski down the steps. I broke up everybody, including Slade. From then on, that was the way I made my entrance. Slade just couldn't compete with that, and I have a hunch he would just as soon I had never discovered it.

When I joined the show two of my brothers, Jack and Paul, were there ahead of me. Don't get the idea that this was an eleemosynary institution run as a refuge of last resort for members of the family. Slade hired brothers because they were good, the best to be had.

Jack had been with Slade for years and was probably the best straight man in the business. Paul was just twenty. The baby of the family, the tallest (six feet), the best looking, and with the most melodious singing voice I have ever heard.

When I first hit the show and looked over that sixteen-girl chorus of really attractive girls I thought, *My God, this is heaven,* but it wasn't that way at all, really.

Instead of thinking of those girls as glamorous love objects, I believe I regarded them more as part of the show equipment, like the scenery and wardrobe.

I was really enjoying myself in Slade's show. Everything was roses, and I had no way of knowing that a very dramatic turning point in my life was sneaking up on me.

DORA   It was a weekday and we had no matinee at the Rainbow Theater where we were playing. I decided to go see an Abbott and Costello film at the Liberty Theater three blocks down the street. As I entered the lobby an usher came forward to meet me.

I wouldn't say she was pretty because that brings to mind a rosy-cheeked young thing, and she wasn't that type at all. Her face was more angular. High cheekbones. Her skin was ivory with a blush of color and absolutely flawless. Not a blemish. Like a marble statue. *Her name was Dora.* Next year (1980) we will celebrate our Golden Wedding Anniversary.

During our stay in Great Falls my brother Slade, who owned the show, and his wife divorced. Slade got so POed at his wife for sticking around and taking half the profits that he posted a closing notice. Sort of cutting off *his* nose to spite *her* face.

I had a few hundred bucks saved and I decided to take over the show rather than letting all these people, including me, lose their jobs. I told Dora what I planned to do. She wanted in on the deal;

she had some money saved, too. We took what we had, and borrowed a few dollars here and there. I couldn't get away so Dora took off to find us a town to go to. I told her where to go and what to look for, etc., but that's still quite a responsibility for a young girl.

In Pocatello, Idaho, she found an old theater that was a relic of the Gay Nineties. It was small (about five hundred seats), run-down, and shabby. It had facilities, machines, etc., for showing motion pictures. We would have to assume responsibility for the whole deal, the show *and* the picture.

Ordinarily Slade had played on a percentage basis, with the theater owner furnishing the picture, so all he had to worry about was the show. In this deal we paid thirty-five dollars a night rent, and the rest was up to us.

Time was short. We couldn't pay salaries during any kind of layoff so we had to work fast.

I ordered our advertising, window cards, and handbills without discussing the matter with Dora.

When she saw the name I had selected for our enterprise she was so overcome with pride and happiness she cried. That was one of the high points of my life—and hers. The name I had chosen was "The Glendora Players."

We had to have motion pictures and I didn't have the first idea about that end of the business. Dora did. Her manager at the Liberty Theater in Great Falls had put a desk for her in his office where she could do occasional typing chores. That was a lucky break for us now. She had heard her boss haggling with salesmen over terms, etc., as he booked his pictures.

So, after she had made arrangements for the theater, instead of coming back to Butte, she had taken the bull by the horns and gone on to Salt Lake, which was the film distribution center for the Pocatello area.

She did a fantastic job.

One party owned the three picture theaters in Pocatello, and they had given the distributors a bad time. They had been show-ing a lot of second-rate stuff so there were many top pictures available and Dora booked them. Being a beautiful, as well as a very smart, girl didn't hurt matters either. The only trouble was she haggled and bargained so hard and shrewdly with one assistant manager, and got such a fantastic deal out of him, that when his boss came back he fired the assistant and insisted on renegotiating the agreement.

Unfortunately, the agreement had been signed subject to the approval of the big boss. He came up to see this smart dame who had razzle-dazzled his boy out of his eyeteeth. This big shot was so impressed he offered her a fantastic salary and all sorts of special inducements if she would come to work for him. I haven't the slightest doubt that if she had decided to accept she would long since have been a millionaire on her own.

The scenic artist, who was really the heart of the show and the most important and necessary of all, was supposed to come straight down and start painting scenery and touching up the old theater here and there. We had given him the fare and a substantial advance. He never showed. He took the money and went back east without even bothering to let us know, so we could try to get someone else.

We couldn't have, though. We didn't have money to bring a scenic artist from the East. We could have starved before the show opened, but fortunately the old boy who owned the theater also owned a second-rate hotel and restaurant across the street and I induced him to let our room rent and meals go until we opened.

We would have had our hands full even if the scenic artist had shown. Now it was almost hopeless. We'd just have to do the best we could and let it go at that. We had no scenery or costumes. We had no money to buy either ready-made, so we set about making them. We rented an old foot-pedal sewing machine and Dora started sewing. We bought yard goods and she made two "oleos" and a "close in." They measured eighteen feet high by thirty-six feet wide. Imagine what a job that was! Using fabric thirty-six inches wide and having to sew each seam twice, plus the task of keeping the great pile of cloth moving through the sewing machine. A foot-pedal sewing machine!

In addition to the curtains, there were three sets of wardrobes to be designed and sewed for the chorus. Impossible? She did it.

I couldn't help her except in emergencies because I had my work cut out for me, building and painting scenery. I had closely observed the work of the scenic artist who had left us in the lurch like this and felt I could do a pretty good job.

But all this takes time. Dora and I would go to work at eight each morning and stagger across the street to bed at five the next morning. Just three hours sleep. We won't deduct any time for going to sleep because we were asleep when our heads hit the pillow.

The Glendora Players opened on June 13, 1928, on schedule and to a packed house.

GOOD AND BAD   My scenic effort got a nice hand. Not the oohs and aahs that Jack Marlowe's breathtaking creations had, but at least it got a hand.

Dora's costumes, which she designed as well as made, also got applause when the girls made their first entrance.

The show went over with a bang. And well it might! Thirty people on the payroll, each one of the performers a talented professional. We were off and running, but at a terrible price. I had survived the fearsome ordeal with no obvious physical effects, but working that old foot-pedal sewing machine twenty hours a day had broken the blood vessels in Dora's legs until they were an unsightly purple network.

The condition was permanent, and I have always felt a sense of guilt about the tragedy, although I could have had no idea what the consequences of our desperate struggle would be.

Slade had let me copy his shows but Dora had only finished typing his opening show when time ran out, so after our opening we had nothing to offer except bits and blackouts with no plot, and while they were funny they had no substance.

Our first four nights the house was packed. The first night of our second presentation was also packed, but we had to repeat two of the three sets of wardrobes the girls had worn in the first show and we had to use a makeshift setting thrown together with the house stuff. The second night of our second offering the house was only half full.

Despite our dogged efforts, we were falling behind in salaries. I warned everyone that we hoped but could not guarantee that things would get better. I told them that if they wanted to leave we would give them whatever we could without leaving the rest of us so strapped that we could not keep going.

People started leaving one by one, and all accepted the pittance we could scrape up as a farewell offering. We would part as friends with mutual good wishes.

We cut our appearances in Pocatello to two nights a week and filled in with five smaller towns.

Brother Ferris sent me thirty good plays and, with a half-dozen fewer salaries, business stabilized at about a break-even point.

Some of our plays had dandy comedy roles for females. A number were foils for the comedian.

I cast Dora in a small role in one show and she showed promise. I rapidly brought her along and, after she had played three or four bit parts, I cast her in a very important comedy role. She was an old maid and wore a gray wig with coy ringlets in front of her ears. She owned the ranch and I was a raunchy old cowpoke with a handlebar mustache who was dead gone on the old gal. There were some great comedy love scenes between these two characters. We were sensational. I never saw an audience laugh so. When she came off after the first scene and the audience laughed and laughed and then applauded, she almost fainted. She had arrived!

With that encouragement, she was like a hungry lioness that has just tasted blood. She stood in the wings waiting for her next cue as tense and eager as a runner waiting for the starting gun.

Now comes the sad part. Dora is simple-minded about one thing. When she is watching a play or a movie, she hates the villain and can scarcely restrain herself from hollering to the leading lady, "Look out, he's over there behind the bushes!"

You can imagine how she felt when in our very next play I handed her the part of a gossipy old biddy who was so downright obnoxious that the audience really got to hate her.

When Dora made her entrance in this part, looking not too different from the way she had in the previous show, the audience remembered and gave her a genuine ovation. Thirty minutes later she was playing the role so well that she was being booed.

She came offstage followed by derisive laughter because she had just been put down and in her place by Toby, namely me. She was distraught and sank to the floor in her ugly old black dress sobbing great sobs of anguish. "Ohhh," she wailed, "they loved me so I got a big hand and now they hate me. Boo-hoo-hoo-hoo-hoo!"

I had to get cross and threaten to end her acting career before she would go back onstage and face the disfavor of the audience.

She never did get so she enjoyed playing roles like that, but she did get so she could do them without letting it tear her apart. We started trouping, playing three- and four-day stands in small towns, but business was poor and our thirty people had dwindled to thirteen. Then we hit the Big Horn Basin in Wyoming. It was a gold mine. Seven towns and seven weeks of land-office business.

We thought we had it made. We bought a truck, a car, scenery, and wardrobe.

Things were rocking along beautifully when something happened that scared the hell out of me and changed our lives immeasurably, for the worse.

When we arrived in Lovell and started unloading our stuff we were thunderstruck. The stage was filled with massive horns. They had installed equipment for talking pictures. With less than ten feet from the horns to the footlights, we could not use the framework from which we hung our scenery. We had to improvise and, in spite of all we could do, it looked amateurish and shoddy. The other towns quickly followed the new trend. We had to move on. But where to? Talkies would be everywhere.

LANDER *POST*   On our farewell trip around the Wyoming circuit a most amazing thing happened in the town of Lander. Never, in all my years in show business, have I seen anything like it at all. I have been bragging about what a good show we had. I am most grateful to have some proof. Namely, the front page of the *Lander Post,* which appeared on the same day as our farewell appearance.

To begin with, there was our customary ten-inch, two-column ad. That's a fair-sized ad and over the fourteen weeks of our stay in the Big Horn Basin it had amounted to a considerable sum of additional revenue for the *Post*.

It has hardly enough, however, to account for what follows. Our ad, which had heretofore appeared on page three, was in the top center of page one. That was pretty damn nice of that editor, wasn't it? But wait! That wasn't all.

To the right of the ad is a one-column, twelve-inch article written by the editor, using exactly the same type and size heading as the other articles on the page. It appears right under the masthead, as does the ad.

The heading reads GLENDORA CO. TO CLOSE SEASON HERE THURSDAY. The subheading, in smaller type, says, THIS COMPANY HAS MADE A BIG HIT HERE AND HAS PACKED THE GRAND ONE NIGHT A WEEK FOR FOURTEEN WEEKS. After the above heading the article goes on to say,

> Today, matinee and night, will be the last appearance of The Glendora Players in Lander this season. They are without doubt the most popular company that has ever played in this city. This popular company of singers, dancers and actors has been appearing at the Grand Theater one night a week for fourteen weeks and many nights hundreds were turned away. The reason is plain. Their plays are all clean and full of fun. The singing and dancing numbers are not just fill-ins between acts, but of a calibre on a par with the vaudeville acts seen on the large circuits.
>
> The male quartette draws many patrons who consider it worth the price of admission alone and Glen Taylor is a comedian who can get more laughs from old and young than any comedian we have ever seen, and all without resort to smut or dirt.
>
> Off stage the reputation of this company is just as good, each member of the cast carrying themselves like ladies and gentlemen. And in all the time they have been coming to Lander we have never heard one word against their deportment or personal conduct in any way.
>
> There is just one more thing I wish to mention in closing, and that is the way this company pays all their bills without any wrangling or running after them.
>
> Since they have been appearing here this paper has had a lot of dealings with Mr. Taylor and we want to say that they have been more than satisfactory. He wants what is right and he pays for everything he agrees to pay for. We are really sorry to see this company leave, but they must because they are booked up solid until spring in Arizona and California.

I wished that last sentence were true.

The encomium ends with the editor going way out on a limb with a flat prediction by saying, "Their farewell presentation will be 'Michael in Society.' It will be good."

Dora and I always had a pleasing show. Even when we got

down to four people. Three? Yes, even when we got down to three people, we still had a good show. And we put on a pleasing show with more belly laughs than ever that night when our fortunes reached rock-bottom and just Dora and I were the entire cast.

But wait a minute. To the left of the ad was another four-inch mention, again reminding the reader that tonight was the farewell appearance of The Glendora Players and urging all and sundry to attend. Amazing! All that on the front page? I was overwhelmed. But there was more.

Across the very top of the page—the front page—above the masthead—above everything—is a banner headline reading THE GLENDORA PLAYERS FOR THE LAST TIME TONIGHT—IN "MICHAEL IN SOCIETY"—PRICES 25¢ AND 50¢—A BIG SHOW. I have never, ever, seen any newspaper go so all out to show their appreciation to a show company.

STAR VALLEY   Desperately fleeing the onslaught of the talkies, we straggled into Afton, Wyoming, a town of some twelve hundred people and about as remote a place as there was in the United States. Fifty-four miles from a railroad. The "talkies" were there ahead of us. When we opened, we were down to one hundred dollars.

Afton was a flop. After our second night we were feeling low as a snake's belly. The old man who was the janitor suggested that we try Freedom. "It's twenty miles north of here, over in the lower Star Valley," he said.

I had been studying the map and had seen the name Freedom on it, but when I looked at the population chart on the back of the road map, there was nothing listed for Freedom. I pointed this out to the janitor and he said, "Don't let that fool you. There's nothing in Freedom but a store and a hall, but it's a big valley and twelve or fifteen hundred people live there. It's a dairy country and those folks always seem to have a little money." He pointed out one other advantage which would soon come to be the decisive factor in considering whether or not we would play a town. "There ain't no picture show in Freedom," he said, "so those folks ought to be ready for a little entertainment."

The next morning Dora and I drove to Freedom and booked the Mormon hall for the following Monday.

Star Valley is tucked away between moutain ranges on the border between Idaho and Wyoming. This choice example of creation's handiwork is one of the loveliest spots on earth. People who are so fortunate as to live in Star Valley should consider themselves blessed far more than most.

Shaped like a saucer some ten miles in diameter, green and fertile, this is a place to bring joy and gladness to the heart of anyone who loves and appreciates the grandeur of nature.

Through the middle of Star Valley a beautiful stream winds its way to join the famous Snake River twenty miles or so to the north. In the center of this idyllic setting is the little community of Freedom. To look at Freedom was not reassuring. A store with a gasoline pump and the Mormon amusement hall, which also served as the church, plus half a dozen houses scattered about. There was no street.

The storekeeper, who was also the bishop, was quite optimistic. "You ought to do all right," he prophesied. "We haven't had a show here for years."

Monday night came and Dora was ready to start selling tickets at seven-thirty; but the bishop was not there to take tickets. Eight o'clock came, and still no bishop. At eight-thirty, which was the advertised starting time, he came in leisurely herding his family.

When Dora said she had been wondering if he had forgotten, he answered, "Oh, no. This is dairy country and everybody had to get their milking and chores done. Lots of time. They'll be coming along after a while."

Nine o'clock came and not one ticket sold. I asked the bishop if I might not just as well tell the people they could take their makeup off. "Oh, no," he said emphatically. "They'll start comin' pretty soon now. I think we'll have a real good crowd. You've got a pretty good reputation here. Some of our people saw you when you were in Pocatello a while back."

His optimism sounded great but a little hollow. It was nearly nine-thirty, and not a living soul besides the bishop's family.

Dora was standing disconsolately looking out the door when suddenly and with considerable excitement she called to me. "Glen, what is this?" I stopped pacing the floor and walked over to have a look. I had never in all my years in show business seen anything remotely resembling this. I have seen it many times since, but only in Freedom. Dear blessed Freedom.

The roads in Star Valley radiate out from Freedom like the spokes of a wagon wheel. On every one of the at least half a dozen such roads there was an uninterrupted line of headlights extending clear back to the foothills, and new lights were appearing at intervals from the mouth of canyons round the valley.

I couldn't believe my eyes. I called the bishop, who was stoking the big old wood heater against the chill that comes with night at these high altitudes. He came over unhurriedly and had a look. "That's them," he said matter of factly. "They're a-comin'."

By ten o'clock, to use a descriptive phrase coined by some showman of long ago, "the place was packed to the gills and they were hanging from the rafters."

In three nights we got two hundred and eighty dollars for our share. They loved us and, believe me, we loved them. For all the years we trouped up and down the Rockies, when other communities were crying the blues and we would be down to our last red cent, we would head for Freedom and everyone would get a window so we could watch the spokes of the wheel light up and then converge on that dear old Mormon hall. Boy, that sight gave every one of us a feeling of security. That would be the best way to describe Freedom and that old hall. It was our "security blanket."

Decimated as were our ranks and with the talkies maneuvering us into an ever more constricted category of smaller towns, I believe I came to appreciate how the Indians must have felt as the overwhelming power of the U.S. Cavalry squeezed them tighter and tighter. And we had a new enemy baying at our heels. The so-called Great Depression was beginning to make itself felt even in the places to which we had retreated to escape the talkies.

We headed up into Idaho, skipping the well-worn territory around Pocatello and heading for the smallest and most remote hamlets back in the hills as far as possible from population centers and talkies.

It became increasingly difficult to make ends meet. Dora and I bought a three-quarter-kapok camping mattress which was so thin it was little better than none at all, and took to sleeping in halls when it was at all possible. If circumstances prevented that, we would sleep on the floor of the truck. We also purchased a gasoline two-burner campstove and would cook our own meals and feed the others.

Dora became a cook and dishwasher for the whole gang. When Gladys, Dora's sister, was with us she would help, but at times we had a girl or two who would let Dora do it all alone.

Later, when people who had left started wanting to come back because there were no jobs to be had and they were hungry, we gave them to understand that they would be expected to help cook, wash dishes, lay out the wardrobe, and help pack up at moving time. By then things were so rough that they were glad to get a job on those terms. "The Great Depression" was on in earnest.

THE SEED Our first night's performance in Arco, Idaho, was greeted by a goodly crowd, and the show went over well. We were grateful for that because it generally meant that we would have a good crowd the next night. We were grateful that we had made a good impression for another reason also.

After the show a lovely lady, young of face but with snow-white hair, came backstage and introduced herself. I knew at first glance that she was some relation because of her startling resemblance to my sister Eleanor. She was Epha Taylor Sutcliffe, a cousin of mine and the daughter of my father's brother. We were invited to her home for dinner the next night.

Mr. Sutcliffe, my cousin-in-law, was a doggedly faithful Republican precinct committeeman. As a reward for his services in that capacity, he had been appointed postmaster.

While I was waiting for my cousin to prepare dinner, I relaxed in an easy chair near a homemade bookcase containing possibly fifty nondescript volumes.

I reached over and picked a book at random. That was the most fateful action of my life. The train of events triggered by this simple act was astonishing, to say the least.

The rest of my life and the lives of untold numbers of other people would be affected, altered, and made to flow in different channels because of that seemingly simple act.

Evidently human eyes had never scanned this spotless volume because, after no more than a dozen pages of reading, I came to one that had not been cut from its successor. I asked Sut if I might deflower this obviously virgin volume, because in reading those few pages I had become more interested in it than in anything I had ever seen in print.

So Sut took the book and thumbed through a few pages. Obviously he had scanned through this unorthodox treatise despite the fact of the uncut page.

His expression betrayed his feelings about it. He snorted his contempt and tossed the book back to me. "You can have the goddamned thing if you want it," he said, but admonished, "It's written by a bol-she-veeck."

Poor Sut. If he had had the faintest inkling of what was happening at that moment, he would have snatched the wicked essay from my hands and chucked it in the woodfire that was cooking our evening meal. "Hell on Wheels" was the way a writer would one day describe the force that Sut was innocently unleashing into the smug Republican controlled politics of Idaho.

The author of the book I had by chance selected hardly fit the role of "bol-she-veeck" in which he had been cast by my Republican cousin-in-law. In fact, the author of this book was a multimillionaire and founder and president of a giant corporation, which in turn was a shining example of capitalism in action. The man to whom Sut had applied one of the most stigmatic appellations known to defenders of the status quo was none other than King C. Gillette, the inventor of the safety razor. Surely Sut could not have taken the pains to see who the author was or he would not have denounced him in such a vehement manner, because this very likable shirttail relation of mine belonged to a tribe who respected wealth, power, big business, success, rugged individualism, private enterprise, capitalism, and the status quo. Gillette was presumably at the top of the heap in all these cherished categories.

The title of Gillette's book was *The People's Corporation.*

I approached his work with the respect for wealth that I had absorbed along with other standard mores.

The book make a more profound impression upon me because the author was a millionaire business tycoon. Surely, I reasoned, the ideas so clearly and persuasively presented in this book must be widely accepted by the writer's millionaire friends and associates.

If I could have known how wrong my assumption was, I might have decided that it was hopeless even to dream that his sensible and appealing plan could ever be put into action. I could not, however, believe that people would fail to respond to such lucid arguments and the hopefully better new day they promised.

Aside from some "how-to" books, I had never before read or owned a nonfiction book.

No scholar receiving a rare and priceless volume had ever been more appreciative than I.

Even the few pages I had read before coming to the providential roadblock, had implanted in my receptive mind the disturbing suspicion that I had been living in a fool's paradise, literally.

Up to this point I had, with only vague unformed doubts, accepted the status quo. I had accepted the economic system, starvation in the midst of plenty, and my own desperate struggle to live as practically preordained, inevitable, and unchangeable. A man doesn't think of change when he is ignorant of any alternative.

I was startled and angered to learn that depressions were not an inevitable part of an inevitable and unchangeable way of life. There were reasons for these things. There was a science of sorts that dealt with such matters.

The message of *The People's Corporation,* and the alternative offered, was "Production for Use." Gillette had nothing but scorn for "the profit system" and nothing but condescending pity for the millions of unthinking men who each day used his brainchild to keep themselves well groomed, while they starved in abject submission because, as Gillette wrote, "the system could not distribute the abundance it demonstrably could produce."

"The whole nation and its economy should be run much in the same manner as The Gillette Razor Co.," wrote the millionaire inventor of the safety razor.

"Each citizen, as his birthright, should receive one share of voting stock in 'The People's Corporation.' Everything possible or needed should be produced to satisfy the material wants and needs of all the people and sufficient purchasing power placed in the hands of the producers to enable them to buy all the goods produced.

"As long as the profit system continues," warned Gillette, "depressions, want and privation in the midst of plenty will continue.

"We should," Gillette continued, "plan for plenty instead of going off in all directions, every man for himself, like a flock of turkeys chasing grasshoppers."

As in any other treatise on technical subjects such as economics, there were references to source materials. I never wanted for a long list of books I planned to buy, as one book would refer to others.

I had read quite a lot in my life. Enough to pick up a fair command of the language, despite my woeful lack of higher education.

But when I cut this page it was the beginning of a period of study lasting seven long years that would see a flowering of my knowledge and an understanding of the economic forces that determine whether we partake of plenty or suffer privation.

Regardless of how desperate our circumstances may have been, I started buying books as fast as I could read them. I read with such intense concentration that many times I saw the sun rise before I could tear myself away from my exercise in futility, which I cannot truthfully say I enjoyed but pursued because of an inexplicable compulsion hidden away in my subconscious.

I am sure Dora must have wondered if the study of such dry subjects as history, political science, and economics had become an obsession with me, but she never mentioned that a book I bought could mean that we would have to eat less.

I spent seven years at the prosaic task of doggedly pursuing knowledge for the sake of knowledge, with not the faintest idea of why I was doing it except that I felt an urgent, irresistible compulsion. In my seventh year of reading I came upon this sage observation, "The object of all knowledge is action."

That was damn good advice, but what the hell was I to do? For one thing, I quit spending money for books. They had been getting more and more repetitious.

TICKETS FOR FOOD   The little Mormon community of La Sal in the red rock country of southeastern Utah was probably as far from a railroad as any inhabited spot in the country.

The people there were not affluent but they ate well. They raised everything imaginable, but they had little money. The Mormon bishop talked this matter over with us. If we would agree to take farm produce for show tickets, he told us, we would have a big crowd and the people would give us more than our money's worth in such an exchange.

If we agreed, he would spread the word. We agreed, and it worked out beautifully. We got enough cash for gasoline and enough foodstuffs to last us for days. Chickens, live and dressed, a turkey, a leg of lamb, a ham. Home canned string beans and fruits. All sorts of good things.

JUSTICE   There are those who recall the "Great Depression" with fond nostalgia because, in many instances, neighbors helped each other in their struggle for survival.

There was, however, a darker side to the picture. Take law enforcement. During those stark depression days many law officers, hard pressed like everyone else and scarcely able to feed their families, took advantage of their authority to become extortionists. Many small towns situated on main highways set ridiculously low speed limits and paid all the running expenses of their town with the fines collected from "speeders."

Another racket was to post a short stretch of highway with signs notifying truck drivers that for the next twenty miles the gross weight limit was some ridiculously low figure like ten thousand pounds. Naturally, if you came to such a sign and you were over the weight limit but there was no alternate route and no officer in sight you were going to go ahead.

A little farther along you would be stopped at a roadblock and asked to run one wheel of your truck onto a portable scale. You would have your choice of paying a fine right there on the spot, based on how much overweight you were, or you could go back thirty miles to the nearest town and see the judge. "However," we were told, "if you go back to see the judge you'll not only have to pay the fine but if you try to come this way again, you'll be stopped again. However, if you pay up now you can go ahead."

The excuse given for exacting this toll was that the roadbed had been softened by frost. If that was a fact, then why hadn't trucks been notified a hundred or two hundred miles back when they might have had an opportunity to take an alternate route?

The Glendoras were caught up in one of these traps. Our fine was fifty dollars. We did not have fifty dollars but we could scrape up twenty-five dollars if everyone emptied their pockets and purses. The two officers manning this highway robbery station held a council of war, made a loving exception for us, and took our twenty-five dollars.

Misfortune dogged our footsteps, and hard on the heels of the overweight incident we had another encounter with the law. It happened in the very town we were headed for. The lodge hall where we were playing had a huge woodpile behind the place. The man who owned the property next door also had a big woodpile. At the end of our three-day stay we were loading up preparatory to leaving when the town marshal came over and served papers on us for stealing wood from the man next door.

We were at a loss, at first, to believe such a stupid thing, so we started pointing out to the constable that we had a big woodpile. He shook his head and said, "You're wastin' your time talkin' to me. You'll have to come over and see the Judge."

The Judge was an oily bastard. He was very sorry but Mr. Jones had filed the complaint. It would be twenty-five dollars for the stolen wood and court costs.

"You can demand a jury trial if you want to," he informed us.

Of course! A jury trial. That's what we wanted. No jury would convict us of stealing wood when we had a big woodpile of our own. "Yes, we would like a jury trial."

"All right." He looked at a ledger that had nothing but empty pages and said as he wrote, "We will set that for two weeks from today."

"Two weeks from today?" I asked. "Why, we'll be three hundred miles from here by then. Why can't we have the trial today?"

"Well, Mr. Jones is out of town. He had to go to Spokane on business and he won't be back for two weeks," said the Judge. So we paid the twenty-five dollars, although the whole thing was a trumped-up deal to keep us from leaving town with that twenty-five dollars we had taken in during our three-day stay.

HEAP FINE TEPEE   Kamiah, Idaho, was a town of five or six hundred people, mostly Nez Percé Indians. Each Indian family had been granted two or three acres of land so the town was spread out all over the foothills overlooking the Clearwater

River. Kamiah is where the Nez Percé Indians started their famous march under Chief Joseph in an effort to escape to Canada.

It is also the town where I had walked with our eighth-grade ball team from Kooskia so many years ago to play the Kamiah eighth-grade team, which was one hundred percent Indian. That game ended in a free-for-all fistfight, Indians versus whites, and we palefaces had to beat a hasty retreat back up the railroad tracks the nine miles to Kooskia, forsaking a catcher's mask and a bat or two as the spoils of war.

Now I was back with The Glendora Players. The hall was on Main Street, and it was backed up against the hillside so that it had no back door. Ordinarily, we parked our house-car by the stage door but in this circumstance we had to find another place. The hall manager suggested the city park. Now the city park was not a trailer park or anything of that kind. It was indeed the "city park," located on rolling ground some two hundred yards from the hall. This was depression times, so the park wasn't kept up. The grass was dead as a mackerel.

There was a bandstand in the middle of the park some twenty feet in diameter, round, and it had a roof that came to a peak like an Indian tepee. The sides were open. The paint peeling or gone. There was a water faucet close by.

Our Ford truck had just played out on us back along the line and we were so crowded, with four of us living in that house-car truck, that we always took advantage of any opportunity to spread out. If there was room backstage, Paul and Gladys would move their bed into the hall.

The bandstand in the Kamiah city park afforded us an opportunity for spacious living the likes of which we seldom encountered. Its floor was just two or three inches lower than the door of our house-car, so we parked right against it and could step back and forth from one to the other.

In order to afford us a little privacy we enclosed its open sides with colorful diamond-dye backdrops. It took three of them to go all the way around.

One side was a northwoods scene with forested mountains cut through by a river. Another section was a western backdrop with a mesa in the distance and cacti in the foreground. The third segment was a farm scene with a barn, a haystack, and cultivated fields. It was really a gay, gaudy, and most interesting contraption. When we started decorating the bandstand curious Indians began to congregate, and by the time we had our brightly colored backdrops up there were at least a hundred Nez Percés, men, women, and children, standing about in open-mouthed wonder at the transformation we had wrought in less than an hour. One elderly redskinned gent who appeared to be the chief or headman voiced the general opinion by saying, "Damn fine tepee. Just like Indian but more pretty."

I imagine that some of my readers will ask, "What kind of people could these be to set up housekeeping right in the middle of town in such an outlandish and garish abode? Had they no sense of shame or pride?"

My answer to that would be: "Please remember that those were depression times. Emotions like pride and shame were a luxury and at a low ebb. Survival took precedence. Witness the park with no grass, and the unpainted bandstand. Once it had been a monument to civic pride, but now no one was willing to have their tax money spent on such nonessentials as grass and paint. The park was no longer serving any useful purpose, so if we could put it to some practical use, why not?

"Nearly every community had its Hooverville, a collection of shanties made from packing boxes, scraps of sheetmetal, and cardboard cartons. Compared to them, the miracle we had wrought was a mansion."

During the three nights we showed in Kamiah our audiences were preponderantly Indian; they could afford the price of a show ticket since practically all of them got a monthly check from the government.

From that time on we never missed a chance to play a community that had an appreciable percentage of Indians among its population or a reservation close by.

DIARY   The Depression was getting worse. Spreading like a flow of lava out over the rural areas, which had been relatively immune until recently. Business was bad. In one town we showed to one adult and twenty-nine kids.

To give you some idea of how rough things were, let's follow for a few days Dora's bookkeeping entries in a little ten-cent-store diary.

This entry is an all-time low record never equaled before or after. It reads, "Athena—Gross 90¢—Candy 40¢." We had no further towns booked so the next entry reads, "Went through Heppner. No hall. Ione—$3.00 license. Pretty broke."

Reading this entry really got to me. Dora never complained, but she couldn't resist crying a little on the shoulder of her tiny ledger with that forlorn notation "pretty broke." The three-dollar license ruled out playing Ione, of course. When you're grossing ninety cents, you can hardly afford three dollars for a license, and there had been no hall in Heppner. Broke or not, our forlorn wandering in search of a place to show was burning up precious gas.

The next entry reveals why we had to flee Oregon as though it was infested with the plague. It reads, "Jan. 6th—Arlington. Sheriff told us if we worked in Oregon we had to buy license for truck. Stayed all night, ate breakfast and started out of Oregon. Weather ten below."

We had no bookings, and we were nearly broke.

We decided that the situation was hopeless and that we should try to get jobs. In two days Paul, Gladys, Dora, and I canvassed the whole town of Walla Walla, which was a city of some fifteen thousand at the time. None of us could find a job of any kind or description. None at all. So there was nothing to do but hit the road.

It is interesting to contemplate what might have happened if I had found a job. It might have marked the end of our trouping, and changed not only my own life but the lives of a great many other people.

On January 12, 1932, Dora made this entry in her little book: "On this night we played Connell. Our gross was $8.10. It was booked for 70%–30% but the manager refused to take his percentage."

The next night, Friday, January 13, wasn't unlucky. In fact, it was wonderful. The manager, a Mr. Long, again refused his percentage of the five-dollar-and-twenty-cents gross, and in addition there is this item: "Mr. Long brought us an apple pie." If

Mr. Long should read this, I would like to say, "Thank you, sir, and may your God bless you."

Our third night in Connell we did better than we had on either of the first two nights, grossing eleven dollars and sixty cents.

Dora's diary bookkeeping, entry, and comment for this Saturday, January 14, says: "Gross $11.60—Mr. Long took his percentage, left us $6.90." It is apparent from Dora's comment that she was a little disappointed, obviously hoping that Mr. Long's generosity would last through our entire stay. Her further comments tell us, though, that Mr. Long was still a good guy.

Dora wrote, "The Longs gave us a graham cracker pie." Weren't they nice people? They were indeed. But wait a minute. Dora goes on to write, "After the show the Longs invited us to go with them to a dance at Kahlotus and they even bought tickets for us."

Let's include Mrs. Long in that "thank you" toast we proposed a moment ago. We had some bad times but we had lots of good times and met a lot of nice, compassionate people, too.

SNAKE IN EDEN   In the spring of 1935 we were in the area of Great Falls, Montana. Talking pictures were old hat by then but we kept plugging along. The Depression was letting up a little and we had bounced back from our three-people low to where we now had a seven-people show. We were grossing about fifty dollars a night, which just enabled us to get by with salaries pretty well pegged at two-fifty a day. That's without room and board. However, a room could be found in a private home or even in a cheap hotel for two dollars and fifty cents a week.

The truck went from town to town, driven by a kid who slept in it or in the hall. He also put up the scenery and tore it down, loaded and unloaded the truck.

The rest of us lived in Great Falls and drove back and forth. This arrangement made it cheaper for everyone to live. The fact that Dora would before long be having our first child, and would be unable to travel for a time, made this arrangement even more attractive.

For the first time in our seven years together, Dora and I were living in a house instead of in a house-truck. To be sure, it wasn't fancy. Five rooms on the ground floor of an old two-story wooden dwelling. Paul and Gladys lived with us; but it seemed like a spacious palace to us after all those years in the truck.

There were a lot of towns around Great Falls, and it looked like we could stay here for a long time. I had no sooner gotten used to this secure feeling than a snake showed up in our Garden of Eden. A fellow by the name of Bray came along with an outfit called "The Rainbow Players."

Their repertoire included some of the same plays we used. There were differences, though, and all of those differences seemed to be in our favor. All except one.

We had seven people. Bray had only five.

We had a truckload of scenery and lighting effects. They had neither.

The five of them traveled in a five-passenger car with a rack on top. If there was scenery in the hall, okay. If there wasn't, they performed on a bare stage. For two weeks we paid no particular attention to them. They weren't doing too well.

At the end of two weeks a friend met me on the street in Great Falls and told me that The Rainbow Players had been in his town the night before and that they had done two hundred and fifty dollars. We had done fifty there recently. How did that happen?

Well, you see, Bray had a gimmick. All of his five people played instruments and they had a hillbilly band.

Bray wasn't much of a drummer, but he banged the liver out of 'em and kept good rhythm. His wife chorded on the piano. Then there was a trumpet player whose wife played guitar.

He also had a young blond fellow who played the sax. Very fancy fingering, and everybody thought he was great. What if he did play sour? Who cared? The customers loved him. He had showmanship.

Every day they put on a thirty-minute radio broadcast from two to two-thirty. Several times during the program, Bray would announce their route. "Now tonight, folks, we'll be playing out in Cascade. We are putting on one of the funniest shows you ever saw, 'The Lure of the City.' That show is well worth the price of admission alone. *But!* After the show there will be a big free dance for everybody. The gang you've been listening to will be there to play while you dance as long as you feel like dancing."

After promising not only a show but also a free dance he got in a lick calculated to head us off at the pass. He said, "Now you folks just sit tight out there. We'll be coming to your community before long so just wait for us. Remember—only The Rainbow Players give you a show *and* a big free dance."

That spiel wasn't just a bid for customers, he was urging his listeners to stay away from The Glendora Players. It was a declaration of war. He intended to force us out of the country.

And do you know what happened? Our business did start falling off. Drastically. Things had been going so well, and now this.

We were expecting our firstborn any day now. If things had gone on like they were we would have had no trouble paying for the doctor and hospital, but now I had my back to the wall. I advertised "free candy" to try and perk things up a little and finally scraped enough together to finance the blessed event.

"AROD"   Our new arrival was a boy, born May 21, 1935. I was a father! I had a son!

Frankly, I was a little worried. I thought babies were supposed to be round and fat, but this—uh—baby wasn't round and fat. He was skinny and instead of looking like a baby he was as wrinkled as a sundried prune, and his face looked like he was about ninety years old. *My God,* I thought, *I've goofed.*

I mentioned our offspring's senility to Dora. She was incensed. "Why, the very idea! He does *not* look like he was ninety years old. He is a beautiful baby." Boy, was I glad to hear that. What a relief. Fathers can sure be stupid. Imagine not even knowing a beautiful baby when you see one. Honestly, though, as much as I wanted to believe it, I still thought he looked ninety years old. When I would see old men walking down the street with a cane, I caught myself scrutinizing their faces. This did not relieve my anxiety. My new son was more wrinkled than most of them.

Miracle of miracles! On the second day of his life my heir looked only fifty years old, and within a week his face had filled out, the wrinkles had disappeared, and he looked like a real baby.

Now we were faced with the momentous question and weighty problem of selecting a name for our handsome child. Partners in all things, Dora and I decided to each name him one name. Deferentially, I gave Dora the honor of naming her half of him first. She called him "Glen."

I was, of course, flattered to see my name perpetuated in the person of my firstborn son, but nevertheless it posed a very real problem. I have always despised the appellation "Junior." So we agreed that while his first name would be Glen, we would call him by whatever middle name I selected.

I wanted to be as generous as my wife, who had proven her love for me and all things associated therewith by calling her half of our common property Glen, but how could I do that? All I had to work with was Dora Marie and neither of those names could be considered fit for a two-fisted he-man.

I had read someplace in a book on "how to invent" that a cardinal rule which should always be the first step in inventing is: Before you start inventing anything, always ask yourself, "Can it be done better 'inside out,' 'upside down,' or 'backward'?" BACKWARD?!!

By God, I had it: "D-O-R-A" backward is "A-R-O-D." Eureka! We would call him "Arod." Not "arrid" like the underarm deodorant but Arod, with a long A and the accent on the first syllable. Arod was romantic sounding and it was certainly individualistic and easily remembered. You don't run into Arods every day.

When I broke the news of the bass-ackward recognition I had bestowed upon her, Dora was delighted. To have a son named after her made "her cup runneth over."

She agreed with me that Arod would be a wonderful name for a man to have if he were in show business or perhaps politics, where a distinctive and easily remembered name can mean the difference between failure and success.

I was right, too. Before he was three years old Arod became a local radio star, and thousands of people not only knew his name but would never fail to point out that Arod was his mother's name spelled backward.

The name became so well known in many areas of the West that you could walk up to any person on the street and ask them who Arod was, and nine out of ten could have told you with only the one word of identification as a clue.

THE TEN-DAY BAND I am not one to reject ideas that have been proven to be good, and I had not been letting grass grow under my feet with regard to Mr. Bray and his Rainbow Players.

Observing the proven success of his formula, despite the caliber of his band and his slapdash shows with no scenery, wardrobe, or lights, I said to myself, *If they can do that good with that corny outfit we will do better.*

I hied myself to the Muscians' Union and hired seven musicians. The boys were glad to work for our standard two-fifty a day. To hell with the union scale. This meant a morning rehearsal, two-thirty p.m. broadcast, and traveling an average of one hundred and fifty miles a day to and from our towns. They were also expected to play a part in the show, if needed, play in the orchestra during the show, then play for a dance lasting until at least twelve-thirty and possibly till three a.m. We would then start home, where we arrived sometimes as late as four or five a.m. All this for two-fifty a day, mind you, but they jumped at the opportunity. The Depression may have slacked off, but money and jobs were still hard to come by.

Swing was just becoming popular and these boys could really swing it. They could play "She'll Be Comin' Round the Mountain" with so many fancy frills and takeoffs you couldn't tell it from "Yes, We Have No Bananas." In fact, everything they played sounded like "Yes, We Have No Bananas." They were really good musicians.

So we went on the radio, broadcasting over the same station as Bray. The main reason we broadcast over that station was because it was the only one in Great Falls. We got the half-hour of air time free. They liked to have live entertainment.

We had better singers and musicians and with our far better show, with scenery and lights and everything, we couldn't help but be a much bigger success than Bray—but it didn't work out that way. No, it didn't work out that way at all.

Before Bray had appeared out of nowhere we had, as I have said, been averaging fifty dollars a night. After he got going our business had diminished to the point where we were losing money, and that we could not afford.

After we went on the radio and it began to take hold, our

business gradually picked up from our low ebb of twenty-five or thirty dollars a night to fifty, seventy-five, and as much as one hundred dollars a night. But there it hung up.

Compared to what we had been doing before we started broadcasting, one hundred dollars a night was wonderful, but in the meantime, Bray's business had increased until he was doing between two hundred and fifty and three hundred dollars a night.

With our new band we had fourteen people. Bray had five. Folks said we were good but Bray's outfit was better. Unbelievable! Incomprehensible!

I saw Bray on the street one day and we got to talking. He liked to talk, and I encouraged him. Obviously, he knew more than I did about this particular type of show business. His wagging tongue was his undoing, it turned out.

Now that the ice was broken and I had him going I jokingly asked, "How the hell is it, Bray, that you do the business you're doing with your corny outfit, and we don't do half as well with our seven-piece swing band?"

"Those boys are good," he said laconically. "That's your trouble. You're *too* good."

This frank conversation confirmed a suspicion that had been gnawing at me for some time.

I told the band boys, "Now listen, fellows, you are all good musicians but we're not going over. Quit swinging it and play 'Comin' Round the Mountain' so we can tell what the hell you're playing."

They looked at each other as much as to say, *What does this guy know about music?* and they were right. I couldn't read a note. The boys tried, though. They would manage to play one chorus straight, but then they would "take off" and "swing it."

I kept telling them to cut it out. "If corn is what they want, give it to 'em." It was no use. I was at my wits' end. Then one day Dora sat down at the piano and hit a few chords. This was an accomplishment she had kept from me. I asked her if she knew all the chords. "No, I just picked up a few when I was a girl, and I'm not sure what the ones are that I do know."

"How long," I asked, "would it take you to learn them all?"

"Well, if I had a book I could probably learn them in a few hours," she ventured.

We went to a music store and bought the most ramshackle old upright piano they had. We paid twenty-five dollars for it delivered. We also bought a book containing the chords and, sure enough, in a few hours you could say "A" and Dora could hit the A chord. Bass and all. We simply typed out our songs and wrote "A," "B-flat," "C," etc. over the syllable where a change of chord was indicated, and Dora had music. In an hour or so she was an accomplished "chorder," every bit as good as Bray's old lady.

In my chasing days I had played a ukulele to help lure the girls, so we headed back to the music store to get me a ukulele. I spied a beat-up old tenor banjo, and after a minute's experimenting transposing strings it could be tuned and played like a ukulele. To be sure, some of the strings were a little slack, and it didn't have the ring of a properly tuned banjo, but it put out a lot of good old twangy banjo noise. I bought it.

While we were in the store we bought my brother Paul a trombone, and a saxophone for his wife Gladys.

Paul had never played a trombone and Gladys probably wouldn't know a saxophone from a bazooka, but we would cross those bridges when we came to them. Namely, as soon as we got home.

A "how to" book came with the trombone, and one for the saxophone. Paul had a good ear. He could also read music a little. Just a little. He had taken music in the divinity school where Mama had insisted he go and learn the ins and outs of how to become a preacher. He attended briefly until he got kicked out for seducing his teacher. He always said it was vice versa.

At any rate, he experimented with the book and the trombone for a half hour or so by which time he had a rough acquaintance with both. Then he threw the book over in the corner and started playing the trombone. In fact, he played "She'll Be Comin' Around the Mountain" without a hitch. He had discovered that if he didn't hit exactly the right place on the slide, he could "lip it." If you are not an accomplished musician like Paul, to "lip it" means to tighten or loosen your lip to raise or lower the tone a fraction.

I don't know where we ever got it, but we had a kazoo among the crap we hauled around. So, in addition to playing my new tenor banjo, I blatted out the lead on the kazoo.

Paul, Dora, and I were in business.

The kazoo was, of course, just a temporary stopgap until Gladys could learn to play the melody on her sax.

We ran into a problem here. Besides not knowing which end of a saxophone you blew on, Gladys had a very poor ear and not much sense of timing.

Paul, Dora, and I were playing hillbilly or western tunes one after the other while poor Gladys stood around with a hangdog, left-out expression on her face, holding her shiny new sax and looking at it like a coon dog contemplating a bone too hot to handle.

It dawned on me that Gladys was a special case. I could chord on my banjo and Dora on the piano and Paul was just a natural with that trombone. Besides, he played baritone, and that doesn't change notes nearly as often as the lead instrument.

Gladys just wasn't a natural-born musician and, besides, she had to play every note of each tune, not just chord or fill in.

I called a halt to our corn-shelling session and we talked things over. We decided that learning to play a sax shouldn't be too difficult. There were only about a dozen pedals to push. The trouble was that we were just as ignorant about a saxophone as she was, and none of us knew how to go about teaching her. So we decided to send her to a music teacher. It shouldn't take long to learn which of those dozen pedals to push when.

I called a music teacher and reserved time for two hours instead of the regular thirty-minute lesson. I wanted her to learn how to play real good, but I told her to hurry it up. If she could get the hang of it in one hour, she should skip the second hour. Never mind the fine points; we had to get this show on the road.

Gladys was a smart girl, anxious to learn, so she took off down the street like she was going to a fire.

While she was going, Dora, Paul, and I impatiently whiled away the time with a jam session. We were getting real "hot" by the time Gladys got back from her lesson. She took the full two-hour treatment. We had hoped she could cut it short, but Gladys liked to do things right. She would probably be able to cut "Tiger Rag" when she got back. We could hardly wait for her to join us.

Pretty soon here she came, hustling along. She unpacked her shiny new secondhand instrument and affixed the mouthpiece. She had a little trouble but she got the job done.

Then she stood there, smiling brightly, and, I assumed, eager to show off. So I asked her, "Well, Gladys—what did you learn?"

"I learned," she said proudly, "how to hold the saxophone." And she proceeded to demonstrate the correct technique for holding a saxophone.

I do not remember for certain, but I do not recall any applause.

Of course, we "natural musicians" were a little taken aback, but after all, maybe it *was* very important to learn how to hold a saxophone correctly. In fact, any fool would know that you had to learn how to hold the damn thing before you could play it. Okay. She could learn how to play it the next day.

And the next day the three of us continued our extemporaneous self-improvement while Gladys took her sax and went tripping back to the teacher to get the lowdown on what was apparently a more complicated piece of machinery than we had at first surmised.

We had a chair drawn up waiting for her to join in when she returned.

When she did return, our hopes soared because of her professional behavior. Where she had been unsure as to just what went where yesterday, she was all business today. She went over and put her sax on the table, removed it from the case, put the mouthpiece in place, put the strap around her neck, and stood looking at us. I was evident that she wanted to display her newly acquired proficiency, but, womanlike, she wanted to be asked. So I asked her.

"What did you learn today, Gladys?" I asked.

"I learned," she said brightly, "to play A." She proceeded to place her fingers carefully on the right keys and tootled A. A little squawky, but Dora hit the A key on the piano and, sure enough, Gladys had hit A. A little off-center, but she did hit A. We waited expectantly for her to start playing, but that was all. That was "it." A whole two hours and two dollars and fifty cents, and A.

This was no business. At that rate, it would take a year and a thousand dollars for her to learn how to play "She'll Be Comin' Around the Mountain."

- "Now, that book you have there, it has diagrams showing the fingering for the complete scale, doesn't it?" I asked.

Upon inspection, we learned that the book did indeed contain this information—with diagrams yet. We sent Gladys to the back bedroom to learn the scale. Three hours later she emerged and passed our test with flying colors. We said "A," and Gladys hit A. We said "B," and Gladys hit B. The kid was ready to go. She even played a little off-key, like Bray's boy.

While Gladys was in the bedroom I had Dora type out, by syl-la-bles, the words to some of the numbers we expected to play, and by pecking around on the piano we had found the proper note for each syllable. Instead of music, we simply wrote "A," "B-flat," "C," etc., over the syllable, and Gladys had music that was foolproof.

If she had trouble with timing we simply jotted, next to the A,B,C, etc., a figure denoting how many counts she should hold that particular note. Like B-flat 4.

So Gladys picked up her sax, held it correctly, as she had learned for two dollars and fifty cents, tootled a practice A, which she had learned to tootle for another two dollars and fifty cents, and we proceeded to play "She'll Be Comin' Around the Mountain" with more verve and corn than Bray and his goddamned Rainbow Players ever dreamed possible.

Ten days after Dora exposed her hand by capriciously striking a few chords on the piano, we fired the seven swing musicians, hired an accordion player who, like us, couldn't read a note of music, and changed our name from "The Glendora Players" to "The Glendora Ranch Gang." With considerable trepidation, the five of us showed up at the radio station.

"What you gotta do to be a success in this business," Bray had told me, "is to give the neighbors what they want." And we gave it to 'em. There was corn enough for everybody, and to spare. We were better, or worse, than Bray. In this case the two antonyms were synonyms.

Paul got in plenty of arm's-length, circus-band slides on the trombone; he was sensational. He completely overshadowed Bray's fancy sax player.

Out in their old beat-up halls in those little farming communities and cowtowns, they loved us. We weren't "too good" anymore.

Nobody ever missed the seven swing musicians and Paul never missed a chance to get in an arm's-length slide on that shiny brass trombone. As they say in show biz, "We killed 'em dead."

"She'll be comin' around the mountain when she—WAAA-AA-AA," and every time Paul got in his "WAAA-AA-AA" and shoved that slide way out there with such elan and savoir faire, with his little finger sticking out like he was holding a fancy teacup, those cowhand Lotharios in thier high-heeled boots would let out a warwhoop you could have heard in the next county, jumping three feet in the air—"Yahoo!"

Three weeks later Bray gave up in despair and "snuck back to South Dakoty." A couple of days before he left, I saw Bray on the street, and he sure looked down in the mouth.

He said he's looked all over for a slide trombonist, but they were sort of out of style. Few musicians played a trombone at all anymore, and those that did played a valve trombone because they weren't so corny. Now to me a trombone without a slide would be sacrilegious. Like a bagpipe without a bag.

Poor Bray. He said he found one slide trombone player, but when he told him he wanted him to go "WAAA-AA-AA" like Paul Taylor, the guy turned purple in the face and yelled, "Paul Taylor? Why, that guy has only had that thing a week. How do you expect me to forget all I ever learned and play a trombone like him? WAAA-AA-AA, my ass."

A STAR IS BORN   Dora had worked until twenty-nine days before Arod was born, and five weeks after the blessed event both were on the job full time, going out with the show on our mad dashes of up to one hundred and fifty miles in all directions, over all kinds of roads in all kinds of weather. Arod traveled in a wicker laundry basket, with his considerable laundry.

The hubbub of dance music became to him what lullabies are to conventional infants. He would sleep like a dog as long as things were normal. Normal in this instance meant enough noise going on to wake the dead. He slept well during the show itself but when the dance started, with him in his basket right behind the piano on which his mother was beating out the chords as hard as she could hammer, that was when he really passed out.

On Sunday night, which was our day of rest, there was of course no music. This departure from the norm disturbed him, and he would fuss and fume while sleep evaded him.

Singing lullabies didn't help a bit. Such things might appeal to the tender eardrums of stay-at-home young fellows, but not to him. He was accustomed and attuned to Paul's brassy slides on that shiny new trombone, the twanging of my old secondhand banjo, and the thunderous chords emanating from the back of a piano.

It didn't take long for us to get the message. When bedtime came I would get out my banjo, Mama would open up the piano, and we would put Arod's laundry basket behind the piano and then go to work. Nothing soft or sweet. No, sir. He wanted noise. N-O-I-S-E—and plenty of it. We would really work up a sweat for five or ten minutes.

It wouldn't take long for our little trouper to feel secure and loved and relax in the arms of Morpheus.

When he was just three months old Arod made his first professional appearance. You have heard, no doubt, of a "walk on" role. Arod's first part was a "carry on" role.

We had a play called *Kentucky Sue* in which a mountain girl marries a handsome artist from New York. Unable to correct her mountain way of speaking and otherwise failing to adjust, she gives up and returns to the mountains; it looks like she and her old clansman sweetheart will surely "jine up" and everyone, including the audience, will be happy ever after. However, she finds she is pregnant and when the artist feller learns of this he comes into the mountains seeking a reconciliation, even though he knows that the mountain man has sworn to shoot him on sight. Sure enough, it happens, but just as the mountaineer is set to pull the trigger, "Sue" flings herself in front of the intended victim and tells the long-suffering, one-time sweetheart that she still loves her husband. Everyone is left to hope that things will work out better this time with a che-ild to hold things together.

I really think that our particular type of audience would have been happier if we had rewritten the show and let the heroic mountain man go ahead and plug that city son of a bitch, but I never got around to it.

At any rate, heretofore the expected blessed event had only

been talked about. We changed a few lines, and when Sue flung herself in front of her husband she had the baby in her arms.

We changed the name of the play from *Kentucky Sue* to *The Tie That Binds* and Arod made his theatrical debut as "The Tie."

He took to acting like a duck to water. He never cried or made a boo-boo of any kind, and he was a serious workman right from the word "go." In fact, after two or three performances, he would awaken from an apparently sound sleep just a few lines ahead of his entrance cue, and be smiling and eager to perform when Dora went to get him out of his laundry basket. To paraphrase an oldie, he must have slept "with one ear open."

I worked him into nearly every show after that and, if that wasn't possible, I would always take him out with me when I made my curtain talk before the last act so his fans could see how he was coming along.

He loved it and would laugh and gurgle, coo and kick, and always get a big hand. If there ever was such a thing as a natural-born actor, he was it.

FISHING   Things were going beautifully. Then one day a blizzard came howling in and we couldn't get out to put on the show. Every day for thirty days there was a blizzard. We couldn't pay salaries and our help all left us. In a letter to Papa, I had mentioned the terrible weather we were having.

We were actually going hungry when Papa called me on the phone. He told me that he had a wonderful business opportunity for me, fishing in the Gulf of Mexico.

I had always liked to fish, and Papa made this deal sound really good. It could hardly be worse than being cooped up in a tourist cabin in below-zero weather with the door so frosted we couldn't get it shut and with nothing to eat.

We went to Texas and I started fishing. The routine was to wade through the shallows after dark, dragging a net to catch shrimp for bait. If you were lucky, you might have enough bait by ten o'clock at night. At three a.m. it was time to fish. If you were good and lucky, you might make enough money to pay for your gasoline and have a dollar or two to show for the day and night of work.

This was more hopeless than trouping had ever been, and I was stuck here.

Papa was not about to offer me money so I could return to beating the dead horse of show business and I was not about to ask him to, but we couldn't stay there. I was having to dun Papa for grocery money every time I saw him. He had seen these poor people bringing in tubs of fish and thought they were getting rich. He just couldn't believe it when I explained how little they got for their catches.

One morning I abandoned my way of life as a fisherman. I dated some showbills for Dove Creek, Colorado, and mailed them. The chances that the hall was in use would be remote, and there was no money to waste on phone calls.

Before noon I had sold practically everything we owned that we could possibly do without.

Our two-burner Coleman gas stove went for nearly nothing, as did everything else. If we cooked now, it would have to be over a campfire. The portable typewriter that Dora used for typing scripts and parts went, as did any clothing we could spare.

Finally, we had about ninety dollars.

We put an ad in the San Benito paper and, miracle of miracles, found a young fellow who was a pretty good accordionist and singer. Even more miraculous, he turned out to be a pretty fair actor.

We started for Dove Creek. It had always been good and we were certainly counting on it now. We had a thousand miles to go.

Two hundred miles from Dove Creek the truck blew a tire. The spare was a sorry-looking thing with a boot in it. It didn't look like it would last a mile.

On the third day after leaving Port Isabel we pulled into Dove Creek. We had one dollar left, and practically no gas in either the car or the truck.

We picked our way gingerly over the rough, rocky terrain behind the hall, came to a stop, heaved a big sigh of relief that the old spare had gotten us there, and *bang!* The tire blew.

We were lucky beyond belief. Think of it. To have that old spare tire hold out for two hundred miles and then, at this exact moment—it was uncanny.

An event of far-reaching importance occurred in Dove Creek.

During our stay in Port Isabel I had had a lot of spare time. The fishing hours were ungodly but not protracted. I would get out my guitar and sing. Arod showed great interest. He had tried to sing when he was only eighteen months old and we were broadcasting in Montana.

During our stay in Port Isabel he would come a-runnin' whenever I started to play and sing. I taught him a dozen or so cowboy songs; some of them called for some yodeling. In May of 1937 he was two years old, and it was miraculous the way he could carry a tune. He could not yet talk plain. For example, in singing "Home on the Range," he would say, "and the kies are not keeoudy aw days."

We had been away from show business now for some five months. I called Arod onstage and asked him if he wanted to sing for the folks that first night in Dove Creek but he looked at the audience, got stage fright, and said, "No."

The next night he said he would like to sing. He was a sensation and from that moment on he was the unquestioned star of The Glendora Ranch Gang and would rather have taken a spanking than miss his turn in the spotlight.

We stayed our customary three nights in Dove Creek and did well. Since we had learned to play instruments, we made it a practice to play for a free dance after the show, our third night in town. It drew a big crowd and made the difference between a hand-to-mouth existence and actually making money. It is a question whether the free dance or Arod's singing was more responsible, but from there on we did well as we worked our way up through Colorado and Wyoming.

MAESTRO DORA   Dora learned to play a C melody saxophone by our quick method because occasionally we would play a hall where there was no piano. What she really loved, though, was that slide trombone. She confided her ambition to me, so I helped her write some of our trick music for the trombone we got her. She has a good memory and could shortly play all our numbers without—music?

Even as was the case when she was doing her first acting, she lacked self-confidence, so she kept her music book in front of her.

We were playing a school auditorium in a town of three or four thousand people, large enough to boast a school band and, of course, a music teacher who was also the major domo in charge of things for the evening.

He was what is called a "finished musician," meaning that he was finished trying to earn a living as a musician and had taken up teaching.

Assuming, I imagine, that we, being members of a practicing band, so to speak, were learned in the profession and would appreciate class when we saw it, the music teacher took us to his office and proudly displayed his credentials.

This fellow had proof of his competence. He had framed diplomas on his office walls from Paris, Hamburg, Heidelberg, and Budweiser.

We were playing for the dance when the maestro came up on the stage. He had his eye on Dora, who was sitting there with her beloved brass trombone in her hands as she relaxed between numbers.

When she saw him coming, she closed her looseleaf book of homemade music like it was the latest porno import from Denmark.

Sure enough, that's where he was headed.

Poor Dora, her eyes rolled around like marbles, she was so flustered.

The learned virtuoso drew up a chair beside her, but before seating himself gallantly asked, "Do you mind?"

Dora swallowed her Adam's apple and then told perhaps the biggest lie of her life. "Oh, no," she managed to croak. Actually, if she had had her choice of having this piccolo teacher sit there while she played or having him shot at sunrise, he would have been playing a golden harp these many years.

So he sat down, I gave the beat, and we shelled out "She'll Be Comin' Around the Mountain." Our friend sat there for several numbers registering no emotion at all. Approval? Scorn? Just nothing.

We played "They Cut Down the Old Pine Tree" and Dora, who had by now regained her usual reserved and ladylike demeanor, finished the old favorite with an arm's-length slide which called forth wild applause and whistles from the crowd.

The teacher arose and said, "Mrs. Taylor, it is a genuine pleasure and a privilege to listen to a really professional musician like you," bowed his best Heidelberg bow, and took his leave.

Dear, dear Dora. She is about as good at hiding her emotions as a hound pup that's just stuck his nose against a porcupine.

She blushed and flushed and said, "Uh—thank you," so gratefully you'd have thought the warden had just handed her a reprieve.

Dora was strictly a trombone woman after that. We could hardly get her to chord on the piano or play her C melody at all.

III

Introduction
to
Politics

GOVERNOR ROSS   In September 1937 I drove alone from Jackson, Wyoming, to Driggs, Idaho, to book the town. The hall manager was in Rexburg and would not be back until late afternoon. I did not know it at the time, of course, but this seemingly unimportant happenstance turned out to be another important turning point in my life. It would lead to undreamed-of things.

The hall was being used that afternoon for a political rally. Governor C. Ben Ross was campaigning for a fourth term. Here, I thought, must be a man with something on the ball, and for the want of something better to do I went in.

Ross was a rather successful farmer, and he looked it. In his sixties, big, rawboned, sandy hair, and ruddy complexion. If I ever saw anyone who inspired trust and confidence at first sight he was the man.

His English wasn't of the best, but he was full of understandable words and homey expressions. He was vigorous yet relaxed and informal. A few minutes after the meeting had started he came down off the stage, and while he talked he walked up and down the aisle.

Every few minutes he would spy someone he recognized, or pretended to recognize, and he would say, "Hello there, Bill," leaning over half a row of people to shake hands. "Say, I haven't seen you since the time I helped pull your old mare out of that mudhole over there by Victor—remember?" and he would laugh uproariously. "Yes, sir, folks, I came along and Bill's old black mare was stuck in the mud up to here," indicating his mid-belly. "Well, I had a big old rope in the back of my Ford and we tied it around her neck and to my old lizzie and I cranked her up and gave her the gas. Well, sir," and he wiped tears of laughter from his eyes, "that poor old mare's neck stretched out that long," and the governor spread his arms wide to illustrate, "but we got her out of there."

He laughed some more and the audience laughed, too. Ben Ross made it so vivid the voters had worked right along with him trying to get that poor old mare out of the mudhole and now that they and the governor had the job done, they relaxed visibly and enjoyed a good laugh at the picture conjured up of a poor old black mare with a neck long enough for a giraffe.

"Yes, sir," the famous man reminisced, "you folks used to have some pretty bad roads up here but we've finally got you out of the mud. That's sure a dandy road we built for you over to Rexburg. We came over it today and it's a humdinger. You know what? I saved you folks a lot of money when we built that road for you. I had the state highway boys go down in the river bottoms and get the gravel instead of buying it from that robbing outfit over there in Rigby. I saved you taxpayers a hundred and eighty-five thousand dollars on that deal. Ain't that right, Jerry?"

Jerry, the secretary of state, was a pretty good performer in his own right. He was campaigning with the governor but, instead of following the star into the audience, he had remained seated on the stage with a big ledger leaning against his chair. The plain fact of the matter was that the governor needed a straight man for his act and Jerry filled the bill quite adequately. Besides, his services were free. He was amply rewarded and assured of reelection by the simple fact of being associated with the popular governor.

At this moment Jerry was pretending that he had dozed and he failed to answer the governor's question. When the crowd's attention was turned to Jerry, they laughed at the picture he made with his chin on his chest and his lips vibrating with each breath he exhaled.

Old Ben got some sympathy for himself out of the situation by pleading with his listeners to excuse Jerry. "You know, I don't blame Jerry one bit for going to sleep. If I was a good talker he'd stay awake." This self-deprecation didn't hurt the veteran campaigner one bit and he knew it. He was probably the best homespun type of talker Idaho politics had ever known. He knew he was a good talker, and don't think he didn't. The act continued.

"Me and Jerry have been going day and night trying to get around and tell you folks the truth. These Republican papers sure won't tell you half of what we've done for you." And the governor stood pensively comtemplating his sidekick onstage.

Poor old Jerry, and the modest benefactor chuckled at poor old worn-out Jerry, who was at least ten years his junior, and the way he shook his head you knew he was deeply sympathetic and thinking, *Poor old Jerry, he's just all tuckered out.*

This byplay, besides serving the purpose of the moment, put the governor in the position of being something of a superman physically, arousing sympathy for this poor, overworked man who was making such heroic efforts to get the truth to the misinformed voters.

Then, with a complete change of pace, the governor thundered "Jerry!" so loud that the audience, which had been in a state closely akin to a moment of silent prayer for this dog-tired public servant, nearly jumped out of their skins.

Babies started to cry and the crowd roared with laughter as Jerry jumped with them. "Yes, Governor! What is it, Governor?"

"Didn't I save these people a hundred and eighty-five thousand dollars?"

"Sure you did, Governor, you-bet-your-sweet-life-you-did, Governor," and then, with timing that would have done credit to a Broadway performer, Jerry asked deadpan, "How'd you do it, Governor?"

This was good for a belly laugh, which was prolonged when the expectant electorate turned to catch the governor's reaction. Poor old Ben was shaking his head to indicate "you just can't win."

"Jerry," this good and patient man asked, "on that gravel deal, didn't I save these folks a hundred and eighty-five thousand dollars?"

"Oh," and Jerry raised his brows comprehendingly as he exerted obvious effort to horse the huge book onto his lap. The great ledger was four feet wide when it was opened, and Jerry fanned through the pages with a magnificent flourish. I could feel the breeze clear down in the audience.

Jerry presumably found the page and ran his left finger down the column. At precisely the right moment, and again with that timing so essential for setting up a laugh, which is so readily recognized and appreciated by a seasoned trouper (namely, me), the governor once again planted the question.

"Didn't I save these people a hundred and eighty-five thousand dollars on that gravel deal?"

"That's *right*, Governor," Jerry shouted excitedly, and on the word "right" his right index finger dramatically stabbed skyward at arm's length. When this picture had registered, Jerry again pointed to the irrefutable figures there on the page of the ponderous official ledger, proclaiming in stentorian tones, "You saved 'em a hundred and eighty-five thousand dollars—*and*—" he held up his left hand, palm toward the audience, to be sure they were silent and attentive so that they would be certain to hear the very important appendage he was about to proclaim. The audience held its breath, and at just the right instant Jerry excitedly shouted the gag line—"and—eighty-five cents," and on "cents" his index finger again shot skyward.

All these dramatics and then the unexpectedly ridiculous insignificance of the figure left the audience dumb for a split second, and then there was a big laugh.

The governor expertly milked the gag by happily repeating at just the right second " a hundred and eighty-five thousand—*and* eighty-five cents," as though that was just wonderful, and the eighty-five cents was more important than the dollars involved.

To say that I was extremely interested in this performance would be putting it mildly. It was a revelation.

This man Ross obviously must be a pretty good governor. He had been elected three times, but it was more obvious to me that he was a pretty good actor.

This whole thing had been more in the nature of a rehearsed vaudeville act. Be that as it may, this technique had worked, and it was obviously superior to the stuffy Shakespearean pronouncements of a Senator Borah.

As I sat there a light began to dawn. So this is politics? This man is a politician? And a very successful one. Regardless of what else he may be, or what other capabilities he may or may not possess, Ben Ross is an actor. And he's putting on a show for these people. Getting his points across, but putting on a show nevertheless.

The thought took shape. *If he can do this and get elected to office so can I, because I can do this sort of thing, too. But I can do it better than C. Ben Ross because he is an amateur and I am a professional.*

Before the rally was over my mind was made up.

This depression, this crime of people starving while food was deliberately destroyed, could be corrected only by electing men to office who were determined to make needed changes, who had studied the problem and knew what should be done.

My seven years of study had not been wasted. This afternoon was part of the scheme of things. If the object of all knowledge was action, then here was my opportunity to take action.

It was late at night when I returned to Jackson from my trip to Driggs, where I had been inoculated with the political virus.

Dora was asleep in our house-truck.

After I was in bed, I couldn't sleep for thinking of what I had seen and the new plan of action upon which I had decided.

Finally, I could contain myself no longer, so I nudged my Sleeping Beauty.

"Dora—Dora."

A sleepy "Huh?"

"Dora, I'm going to run for Congress."

"Uhuh," still not awake, and then as she reared up, *"huh?"*

"I'm going to run for Congress."

By now she was wide awake. I wasn't one to come home under the influence, as she well knew, but nevertheless this sounded a little funny. She had rolled over to face me, and I could tell from the sharp and prolonged inhalation that she was sampling my breath.

Evidently satisfied on that score, she probably thought she had heard incorrectly in the struggle to extricate herself from the arms of Morpheus.

"What did you say?" she asked, and I could tell from the tone that she was prepared to listen—very closely.

"I am going to run for Congress."

There was quite a pause, and then, "Huh." A hardly audible exclamation, but a sentence in itself that said, *Now, I wonder what's the matter with HIM?"*

I explained about the events that had led up to my decision.

"Well, what do you know about politics? You don't even know a precinct committeeman."

I had to admit she was right, but "The only way to learn is to get into it. I learned a *lot* this afternoon."

"But it takes money to run for office, doesn't it?"

"Well, we've got twelve hundred dollars we've saved up since Dove Creek," I reminded her.

I imagine Dora's heart sank at that. She had known some lean and sometimes hungry years as a girl and she had a real horror of being broke, and that fear had not been lessened by the years she had spent with me. We had thought we had the world by the tail with a downhill pull during the few brief weeks we spent in the Big Horn Basin, and more recently during our profitable sojourn in Great Falls, but the rest of the time we had nearly always been, as the old saying goes, "just one jump ahead of the sheriff."

Even that cliché is an exaggeration on the rosy side. At least twice during our struggle to *survive* we had been honored by visits from sheriffs, come to serve papers and take our car because of an overdue payment.

Years later Dora told me that the prospect of pouring our savings down the rathole of such a wild-eyed scheme as a political campaign made her sick to her stomach.

So she advanced another argument to dissuade me. "You can't run for office because we have no home," she pointed out. "You've got to be a resident of some place before you can run for office. We don't even have a permanent address."

"Well, we'll get one," I assured her. And so—we took up residence in Pocatello, Idaho. Paul rejoined us, and we hired an accordion player plus a man-and-wife team. They both sang. He played the guitar and she the sax. Once again we started the old grind of morning rehearsal, two p.m. broadcast, and a show and dance at night.

Arod took to radio like the pro he had become. From the start he got more fan mail than all seven of us adults combined. On Valentine's Day he got a bushel fruit basket full of cards besides many presents, cakes, cookies, and most everything imaginable.

The studio would be packed every day with children and their parents. Childless women would come to coo over him and, until we put a stop to it, to tug and haul at him in an effort to have him for their own for just one soul-satisfying moment.

People drove great distances to allay their suspicions that this prodigy we claimed was only two and a half years old wasn't really a ten-year-old midget.

In good weather Arod would do his number and then lead his young admirers outdoors and the sound of children's voices at play and the music of their laughter would penetrate the studio and mingle faintly with the beautiful tones of Paul's glorious voice singing "I Love You Truly." We made no attempt to shut out the age-old sounds of this enchanting background and many of our listeners wrote in to say it was the most unusual and wondrously fulfilling effect they had ever heard.

Arod loved all the attention, but he never became a spoiled brat because of it.

THE ORDEAL It was late February 1938. Soon it would be time to make known my political intentions. Doubts began to weaken my resolve. Should I embark on this wild-goose chase? We had a good thing going.

Then Arod came down with pneumonia. In those days pneumonia was a deadly killer.

Dora was staying home with our sick boy and the show was, of course, going on without them in the old tradition of show business. Each day over the radio I told the thousands of anxious listeners, children and adults, how their little cowboy was doing in his fight for life. Hundreds of get-well cards and handwritten, tear-stained letters were pouring in, and the religious wrote to tell us of their prayers for his recovery.

His struggle had gone on for several days now. Each day he looked more wan and worn, appeared weaker.

When I would get home in the wee small hours of the morning I would relieve Dora's vigil and sit with him until dawn. When she had gotten a little rest, I would catch a few hours' sleep before beginning another long day and night.

When I came home this particular night, so weary, so tired, I forgot my own spent condition as soon as I entered the door. We had Arod's little bed in the front room because the bedroom was so crowded. Besides, our only source of heat was the coal stove in the front room and the doctor had admonished us to keep an even, warm temperature.

Dora was sitting there by his crib, of course, never trusting herself to close her eyes or relax for a single minute.

All through this terrible ordeal she had been a pillar of strength, as she always was in a time of crisis. Dry eyed, businesslike, efficient.

Tonight she was crying. Not sobbing or hysterical. Just sitting there with her beautiful hand on his fevered brow, as silent tears of anguish trickled down her lovely unblemished cheeks.

The doctor had made his daily visit and had frankly told her that the time of crisis was not far away. This is the time when those with this sickness either got better and then got well, or they would take a turn for the worse and probably die.

"Hope for sunshine and warmer weather," the doctor had said.

I could see that Dora was in bad shape, not far from collapse. She did not want to leave her baby's bedside for one minute, but I finally convinced her that it would be infinitely better for her to get some rest and be available for an emergency during these dark hours than for her to force herself to the breaking point.

I helped her to the bedroom, kissed her goodnight, and reluctantly left her gently crying on her tear-stained pillow.

I took up my vigil, fighting back my own tears, and started walking back and forth in order to stay awake. Occasionally, I ceased my pacing to feel his forehead. He was so tiny, and so frail.

This was the day. He would either get better or we could prepare ourselves for the worst.

Dora placed her hand on his brow and then the other hand, as if disbelieving the first. She breathed a sobbing cry of joy. "He has no fever! He is better!" she quavered. He opened his eyes and for the first time in days they were clear, free of the glitter that warns of impending doom. There were no fevered mutterings, and he smiled. A weak little smile, to be sure, but he smiled. Dora could not speak. She was biting her lip to keep from breaking down in sobs. I said, "How do you feel, son?" and he whispered, "Fine." Dora could no longer restrain herself. I took her in my arms and we both sobbed unrestrainedly.

After this release of tension we felt our world, which had been so close to crumbling, re-forming about us. For the first time in days the sun came shining through the window, and we sat beside his bed holding hands and marveling at the unmistakable signs of his recovery.

THE POLL   I started racking my brain trying to figure some way to ascertain what appeal my "Production for Use" program would have for the voters.

I came up with an idea whereby I could not only test public opinion, but induce those tested to pay for the privilege.

For the purpose of my "poll," I wanted an out-of-the-way place where I hoped I would not attract attention.

I announced over the air that, because the wonderful people in this particular community had been such faithful customers and treated us so generously, we were going to show our appreciation by putting on a "free show" there on such-and-such a night. However, I made no mention of a free dance, as we always had.

The age-old lure of "something for nothing" drew a much larger crowd than we had ever before played to in that community.

When I made my customary curtain talk after the third act, I told them that I was thinking of running for Congress and that after the next act I wanted to talk to them for twenty minutes and then take a poll to see what they thought of my ideas.

I told them that if they would help me out in this manner, it might save me from wasting my time and cluttering up the election. "If you folks will do this favor for me, then we will give you a twenty-minute musical concert free," I promised. Practically everyone stayed.

I talked straight King C. Gillette: "Production for Use."

My talk was well received.

There was no handclapping, but then I had not yet learned that by playing on words and phrases a clever speaker who has some understanding of semantics can get applause at almost any point that he chooses. I had just bought a book on semantics and it was amazing me. You can make a statement that won't cause a ripple, change the wording around a little, and that same statement will get a big hand.

So while there was no applause on this night, there was considerable nodding of heads in agreement with what I said.

When I had finished my talk, I explained that now we would pass out blank pieces of paper and pencils. They were not to sign their name but should simply write "yes" or "no." "Yes," if they liked my plan and would vote for me on such a platform, and "No," if they disagreed. I urged them please not to write "yes" unless they really meant it because otherwise they would mislead me.

I asked a well known local person to help count the ballots and then I announced the results. The poll was 90 percent "Yes." What a surprise! What a boost to my morale!

There was a nice round of applause. I was on my way. I had it made. All I had to do was get my message to the people.

We then played and sang for *thirty* minutes instead of the twenty I had promised. I feigned surprise that we had been so carried away and apologized for keeping them "ten minutes longer than promised."

I announced that the free entertainment was over, and pointed out that since the show was free we had not advertised or planned on a dance because we had to pay our people extra for playing for a dance.

"However," I said, "a number of young people want to dance and we do not want to disappoint them so we will play for it. No one is obligated in any way to stay." Admission for the dance would be the same as always. "Always" was fifty cents. We always charged fifty cents whether a customer came for the show and dance or just the dance.

I thanked the crowd again for their cooperation. "I really appreciate it," I said, and to prove it we would give those who stayed for the dance another twenty minutes of songs after the midnight lunch.

At this point I was keeping my fingers crossed because the local ladies who were sponsoring us always served the lunch, and if few or none stayed they would be stuck with a lot of unsold lunches. We were prepared to make up the difference to them if that should happen.

Practically everybody stayed, and everybody was happy and paid the fifty cents. We actually took in more money than if we had come in our customary manner.

During the dance I circulated around and got many favorable comments on my talk. I was elated but somewhat suspicious that something was amiss. Ninety percent! It seemed too good to be true.

Results in the other two communities I had selected for trial balloon runs and soundings confirmed what had happened in the first one. It was unbelievable.

After the success of the "free show," we went right on using it—speech, poll, and so on. For all practical purposes the campaign was under way. The amazing results of the polls convinced me that I had read the signs correctly. I had no doubts. I was resolute. And supremely confident.

I ANNOUNCE   I wrote the secretary of state for nominating petitions and cooked up a deal with a reporter I knew to break the news using the exact heading and wording I had given him.

The little story rated the front page, top and center, right under the headline of the day.

The heading I had written got by unchanged. It was in the form of a question. This was something else that I had long since learned. People will read an article with a question for a headline to find out what the answer is, when, if the heading is a flat statement, they will read the heading and pass up the details.

In this instance, my "comeon" asked: TAYLOR CANDIDATE?

That was good. People like a mystery; it causes talk. The article itself said:

> Glen H. Taylor, radio entertainer and team member or The Glendora Players, said today that primary nominating petitions he secured from the Secretary of State's office were for his own use. Taylor refused to designate the office sought saying, "Maybe I'll have some announcement to make in a few days, but right now I am undecided as to whether or not I will use the petitions."

Things worked out the way I had planned. I got two exposures in the press instead of one. When I did announce, it was of more interest than if I had spilled the beans at first because it was not only my announcement, it was also the answer to a mystery that had caused considerable speculation.

The statement I presented to the press was brief. The whole thing, including a one-column-by-three-inch picture of Dora, Arod, and me, was eight column inches. I was wearing my cowboy hat. Dora and Arod were included for several reasons. For one thing, a picture including a pretty woman and a child will attract much more attention than one of a man alone. Second, because I was an actor (and people generally think of actors as high livers), I wanted to build an image as a respectable family man. Third, a picture of the three of us would also be different from those ordinarily furnished by candidates. The most important reason, however, was the fact that both our radio and stage fans had become used to seeing us together in all our publicity. If all of a sudden I were to divorce myself from them to the extent of excluding them from their usual place beside me, people, particularly women, might be resentful and feel that I had an inflated idea of my own importance. I had my announcement made up in the form of a mat which most small papers used. Most people aren't anxious to do things the hard way, especially if there is an easier way at hand. The mat saved the editor the trouble of setting type (unless he wanted to change the wording). Nearly all papers ran the mat as is. No other candidate thought of using my "gimmick."

My announcement read: "I wish to announce my candidacy for the U.S. Congressional nomination on the Democratic ticket. I was raised in Kooskia, Idaho. I am not a politician. If elected I will do the very best I can. My father is P. J. Taylor, for many years prominent in Idaho County and a delegate to the 1920 Democratic Convention in San Francisco."

This, of course, removed any possible taint of carpetbagging by making me at least a second-generation Idaho Democrat. Nineteen hundred and twenty? Hell, I was practically the dean of the party.

By some incomprehensible oversight, I had stated in my announcement that "I was raised in Kooskia, Idaho," and forgot to mention that I was born in Portland, Oregon. I had also failed to mention that my father had not lived in Idaho for some twenty-eight years.

Such little slips will occur, and I am sure you will forgive me for failing to mention these really unimportant and trivial details.

In addition to printing my announcement, the *Pocatello Trib*, in its daily gossip column, gave me this mention.

> Glen H. Taylor, handsome stage and radio entertainer, who with his wife is co-owner of The Glendora Players, just rolled into the office togged out like Tom Mix and announced he is also to be a candidate for Congress. There is a "colored gent in a woodpile some place."

I did not actually "roll" into his office. He was referring to my rolling gait in high-heeled cowboy boots. I was, as he says, though, "togged out like Tom Mix." That was my usual form of dress, and I continued it into the campaign to distinguish me from the more prosaic members of the pack.

The reference to a "colored gent in a woodpile" was the writer's way of saying that he thought my candidacy was not on the level. He was implying that maybe somebody was paying me to get in the race to drain votes away from somebody else. This is an old political stratagem.

The campaign was under way. What a field! Nine. Eight caballeros and one ancient señora. The attorney general, the secretary of state, the head of the relief agency (the WPA), and five lesser lights.

If there was one other person on earth besides me who thought I had the faintest chance of succeeding with my wild scheme, I do not know who it might have been.

BATTLE WAGON When you lack the resources to do a given job right, you have to use your imagination and make the most of what you have. I built a platform five feet wide and ten feet long on top of the car. That was the stage on which the band would play and entertain, and from it I would speak.

I had two thirty-by-forty-eight color enlargements made of the family picture we were using, in which I was wearing my mammoth white Tom Mix–style cowboy hat. The handsome enlargements were attached to the sides of the platform on each side and just behind the rear doors of the car, so they would not interfere with their opening and closing.

I nailed a one-by-six-inch board to each side of the platform, extending the eight feet from the pictures to the front corner of the platform. I painted them white and lettered each one to read TAYLOR FOR CONGRESS.

I painted the signs myself. Red letters outlined in black. While the finished product wasn't exactly a triumph of the art of sign painting, it was exactly what I had in mind, discernibly "homemade"—in keeping with my "poor man's" campaign. My very best effort filled the bill to a tee. Not messy, but something less than perfect.

Our old P.A. system had become obsolete. We couldn't buy parts for it anymore. We had to dip into our jealously hoarded twelve hundred dollars to the tune of one hundred and eighty dollars to purchase a new one. It was a beaut. Three (count 'em)—three big black loudspeakers that looked like big fat megaphones with sixteen-inch bells. One mounted on each front corner of the platform, and one on the back.

REPUBLICAN MONEY   I am sure that Dora felt that I was a good actor and the fact that I had designed and built our house-cars and kept them running for years over every kind of road imaginable had probably convinced her that I was an all-around handyman, carpenter, and mechanic.

Certainly, though, up to this moment I had done nothing to indicate that I was a genius or a superman who could fly in the face of providence and produce miracles. That's what it would take to ever make a reality of the conviction that I would climb to heights so recently undreamed of.

Call me a nut if you will, and I do not blame you. Imagine anyone so far gone as to believe he had a hot line from the power which created the Universe, including the earth and all the crazy people who are ruining it.

Imagine "The Power," or whatever you wish to call it, working through a stupid jerk who for years, and without protest, starved in the midst of plenty. Didn't even have sense enough, in fact, to settle down and get a permanent address so he could get on relief, like everybody else. Oh well, it takes all kinds.

Now that the filing period was officially open, there remained the little matter of getting my petitions signed and delivered to the secretary of state's office in Boise. Getting two hundred signatures, no more than twenty-five from one county, could be a time-consuming, slogging chore.

I imagine that the other candidates would have turned green with envy if they could have seen how ridiculously easy it was for me to get those necessary signatures. As was the case with the poll I took, the voters again came to me to sign up.

We took the petitions with us when we started the overt phase of our campaign and collected signatures at our "free show" night meetings.

The time came for our first cartop street meeting. We pulled into American Falls, a town just twenty-five miles from Pocatello. While I shook hands up and down Main Street, Paul drove around the residential district playing brassy marches and announcing over the loudspeaker that starting right away there would be free entertainment by The Glendora Ranch Gang on Main Street and Glen Taylor, candidate for Congress, would speak.

Paul and I finished our chores in about thirty minutes, then parked our bandwagon on Main Street, where a crowd was gathering in response to his tour of the residential district.

He played another Sousa march while waiting for the crowd to assemble, and then the seven of us climbed up on the platform and entertained for fiteen minutes. There was a crowd of several hundred people around the car.

Arod was not yet three, but he would sit with his feet hanging over the edge of the platform and play up a storm on his ukulele. The strings were so loose they made little or no noise, so he could bang away to his heart's delight. He had a fantastic sense of rhythm and was so clever at moving his fingers that only an accomplished ukulele player could possibly have been able to detect that he wasn't playing the hell out of it.

We tore into our theme song "Tavern in the Town," and wound up with Dora and Paul both doing a big slide on those shiny brass trombones.

If there is any one thing in music that can make the hair stand up on the back of my neck it is a good, uninhibited, corny, circus slide on a brass slide trombone. A lot of people must agree with me, because we found that we could always get a big hand on any old number if we ended with the trombone doing an arm's-length slide.

If you've got two trombones, then it's just twice as good. It laid 'em low.

Frantic applause, warwhoops, and whistles. Even that storekeeper standing there with a big chaw of tobacco in his mouth, who had been sneering at the shameless spectacle when this nutty candidate climbed up with all that gang to make a fool of himself, lost some of his supercilious demeanor and applauded in spite of himself.

We played for fifteen minutes, and then all the gang got down and stood back against the building so as not to distract attention from me while I spoke.

I talked for ten minutes and then I noticed attention beginning to waver so I called Johnny up to sing them a song. Using this technique, we held forth for an hour and a half without losing a listener. This was due in no small part to the fact that I kept promising that Arod would sing again pretty soon.

I was so full of things to say that I talked too much. I had not written anything out. It was completely extemporaneous and I kept thinking of important things I had not mentioned. Fortunately, I had sense enough to do something that very few politicians seem to have sense enough to do. I cut it short at the next meeting and trimmed the hour and a half program down to forty-five minutes, largely at the expense of my own verbosity.

This first meeting was of particular significance because we were seeking to establish a technique and to gauge the effectiveness of my presentation.

I kept watching that "doubting Thomas" storekeeper. He fascinated me for two reasons: that prodigous hunk of cut plug in his cheek and the fact that he was, at least to begin with, very skeptical.

Occasionally, he would make some remark to his friend. He started out sneering and after the first number I was quite certain he said "Well by God he may be a nut but they sure make good music," and he quit sneering.

After I had talked for eight or ten minutes and just before the first break for a song he turned toward his friend and, without taking his eyes off me and speaking out of the corner of his mouth, he said, "This guy is no fool."

Two songs later I was into my third ten-minute segment of speechifying. I made some quip and my grocer friend laughed. He immediately caught himself. I looked straight at him and held his eyes for a second and then asked him, "Well, that's a fact, isn't it?" He nodded his head in agreement and then burst out guffawing. His friend had to jump, and quickly, to escape the spray of tobacco juice.

I got the impression he was laughing at himself, recalling how he had started out completely disdainful and had been taken into camp in spite of himself. At the end of my speech I made a pitch for contributions. Several people came up and dropped a coin or two in the hat we had on the hood of the car. I was anxious to see if the storekeeper would contribute. He looked uncomfortable but kept his hands in his pockets. I was disappointed.

When I became aware that someone was standing at my elbow, I looked up. It was the storekeeper. He glanced around apprehensively and spoke in a low voice. "I am the Republican precinct committeeman," he said. "I couldn't let anyone see me give you anything. That's why I didn't put anything in the hat. You're all right, young feller, here," and he surreptitiously pressed a well folded bill into my hand. "Good luck," he said secretively, out of the corner of his mouth, and sauntered back to his store in an overly casual manner.

I slipped the money into my pocket without looking at it. As soon as we were on the road, I handed the storekeeper's under-the-counter offering to Dora. "Here is something from the storekeeper who happens to be the Republican precinct committeeman," I said. She unfolded the contribution. It was a twenty-dollar bill.

I was elated and said to Dora, "If we can do that to a Republican precinct committeeman, we must be doing pretty good with the rest of the folks, huh Mom?"

In the next town we learned that one of our opponents, Ira Masters, the secretary of state, was holding a rally in the town hall. A man who had been in attendance and was lured away by Paul's ballyhoo told us that Ira had twenty people at his meeting and all of them were his known supporters, so there was no remote possibility of his making any converts, and therefore his ritualistic appearance would get him few if any votes.

In contrast, we had at least three hundred people out here on Main Street, practically all of whom would be open to persuasion and conversion.

We had a good thing going. No doubt about it.

COCKLEBURS At our very first street rally we ran into an unforeseen problem. Campaign buttons. The excited voters wanted "campaign buttons." Now that would take money and, besides, they were so unimaginative. Every candidate passed out campaign buttons to all and sundry, but few were ever worn.

Surely I could dream up something with a little more schmaltz and pizazz than plain old campaign buttons, but what? Inasmuch as I was working at being the poor man's candidate, I needed a lapel button in keeping with that theme. My problem was solved that very afternoon. Uncanny how these things happen at just the right moment. Isn't it?

We were playing Aberdeen, a little town twenty-five miles from Pocatello on the shores of the American Falls Reservoir, and while the rest of us were busily engaged getting ready for our evening's "free show" Arod went out to play. The door had scarcely closed behind him when he came back in again, and he was a mess.

The area behind the hall was just a solid patch of cockleburs. Cockleburs are about the size of small olives, and each one has about a million stickers on it.

Arod had fallen down in the cocklebur patch and he had cockleburs all over him, sticking to his playsuit. He looked like a weirdo from outer space. It took Dora an hour to deburr him. They stuck like crazy.

I had an idea. I picked up an empty cardboard box and said, "Come with me."

"Where to?" Dora asked.

"To pick cockleburs," I answered.

"Why, Glen, you can't clean up all the cockleburs out there. There are millions of them," she protested.

"Never mind, just come on. I've got an idea. I'll explain while we pick."

This was without doubt the first time in all history that anyone ever "picked" cockleburs. As soon as the scenery was up and we were ready for the show, I had the rest of the gang go to the store, get more boxes, and help us in our unprecedented task.

These were prime cockleburs. Last year's crop. Well dried so the stickers were very strong and stickery. If you took hold of them firmly (but not too firmly) you could handle them.

We picked several boxes full of cockleburs. Thousands of them. After carefully spacing the cockleburs so they would not make contact horizontally, we laid a piece of newspaper over each layer so they would not make said contact vertically. If we hadn't done that, we would have wound up with just one big cocklebur. The next morning we went downtown and bought a hundred yards of ribbon three-fourths of an inch wide, and any color we could get. We practically deribboned Pocatello.

We had a rubber stamp outfit with interchangeable letters which we set up to read TAYLOR FOR CONGRESS. We stamped the ribbon with this message every three inches so that there was a one-inch blank space before each stamping. We cut the ribbon in three-inch pieces, then stuck a cocklebur to each piece of ribbon. These ugly ducklings would be our campaign buttons.

No messing around trying to fasten a pin to hold them on. Just pick it up firmly (but gently!), just as I have said—push it against the man with the ribbon next to the lapel (the stickers went right through the ribbon), and presto! There it sticks. And God help the smart alec who tries to remove it.

Of course, this baby porcupine would also stick to everything else with which it came in contact, including any amorously inclined person so foolish as to attempt to embrace the wearer.

But this was no time to worry about such minor details. People like to suffer and shed a little blood for a cause they believe in. Witness the blood-letting initiation ceremonies of secret and fanatical groups down through the ages.

Three or four students volunteered as campaign workers. I put them to work making cocklebur campaign badges. When the supply of the principal component ran out, they drove the twenty-five miles to Aberdeen and shed their blood picking more cockleburs.

But that was not the end of it. They gave the campaign another transfusion when they set about fabricating the vampirish little gadgets. And when at last the gaily colored little pieces of ribbon were attached to the lapel of the recipient, almost invariably they would be valorously stained with the pinkish fingerprints, if not from the blood of the martyr who made it, then almost certainly with gore from the unsuspecting recruit who was unaware of the lethal nature of cockleburs. I took considerable good-natured ribbing from thumb-sucking supporters, but there were no lawsuits and the word spread until even the press carried a little story about this oddball banjo-playing candidate who had these home-grown campaign buttons because he did not have any money to buy buttons like all the other candidates.

Meanwhile, the demand for cockelburs was overwhelming. They were going like hotcakes. I had to either curb the demand by setting up restrictive rules and priorities or set up a factory.

I had some postcard-size cards printed up with a picture of Dora, Arod, and me on one side and on the other side a message and a place for people to sign up to receive their cocklebur badge.

The printed side read: "Membership Card—Cocklebur Club of Southern Idaho." Under that, in print not much larger than newsprint, was the pledge:

"In accepting this membership in the Cockelbur Club, I solemnly pledge myself to support Glen H. Taylor for the Democratic nomination for Congress, and stick in the fight like a cocklebur in a sheep's wool. I will wear my valuable Cockelbur badge at all times and defend it to the last sticker."

And there was a line for a signature under which was "Cockle-bur Member and Sticker."

Below that was my pledge to the member, "I hereby pledge myself to stick to the above signed Cocklebur and the people of Southern Idaho, and if elected I will do my best, stick on the job and not sit on my Cocklebur."

Under the pledge was my title, "Grand Cocklebur." Above that high-flown oriflamme, a place for my signature was indicated by a line—and the voters lined up to get 'em.

Having to sign up for a cocklebur brought the situation under control: asking for one out of curiosity was one thing, having to sign a pledge of support was something else. So we accumulated a list of true believers.

And now a very strange thing happened.

Service clubs like the Lions, Kiwanis, and Rotary became infected with cocklebur fever. It spread to the Chamber of Commerce. Few of these people were Glen Taylor supporters, you understand. I was, to most of them, a clown, and the best joke to come along since Herbert Hoover.

The reason some of these upper-crusters shamefacedly stood in line, and committed perjury by signing a pledge to support me, was because cocklebur badges were a "horseplay" addict's dream come true. They were the ultimate weapon for practical jokers.

How simple it was to stick one on the lapel of the chairman's coat without his knowing it, and then when he got up to open the meeting ask him, "What's that you got on your lapel there, Bill?"

Imagine Bill's shock and redfaced confusion upon finding that he was wearing a badge branding him as a supporter of that nut, Glen Taylor. And imagine the belly laughs and tear-inducing glee at his expense.

The gag even became a favorite bit of hokum to liven things up at Republican committee meetings.

THE HANDSHAKE   During that first day of campaigning I encountered another problem. I would approach a man, offer my hand, and say, "I am Glen Taylor, I'm running for Congress." Then the man would say, "I'm Bill Jones," and I would follow up that formal exchange by saying, "I'd appreciate it, Mr. Jones, if you would vote for me." He would probably answer, "Well I don't know. Are you a Republican or a Democrat?" The minute you answered that question, you lost about 50 percent of your prospects.

"Well, I'm sorry but I can't vote for you. I'm a Republican."

If I had not opened that door he couldn't very well have closed it, and he might have decided that he liked my looks or just appreciated the fact that I was the only candidate who had shaken his hand and asked for his vote. In the privacy of the voting booth, he might have put a little X after my name.

If he turned out to be a Democrat and you got by that first hurdle, then he would probably start asking you how you stood on various issues. You might hit it off fine for several minutes and agree on most issues. Then he might ask, "Well, how do you stand on vivisection?" If you gave the wrong answer to that one stupid question you were finished.

I was not only losing votes, I was wasting too much time. You get no place shooting the breeze for thirty minutes with one guy. He has only one vote.

That night I lay awake until I came up with the answer. Semantics again.

The first voter I approached the next day I stuck my hand out and said, "I'm Glen Taylor. I'm running for Congress and if you don't know anyone you'd rather vote for I'd appreciate your vote." And the voter thought, *Now that's pretty darned nice of him. Just around trying to pick up a few stray uncommitted votes.* You have asked him nothing and said nothing that requires an answer and while he's standing there slack-jawed, trying to figure out what it was you said and frame a reply, you have shaken his hand and gone on to the next one. With this technique, I found I could shake hands with hundreds of people a day instead of a dozen or two.

My approach to politics differed from the norm in other respects. My opponents would spend a great deal of time hunting down precinct committeemen with whom they would then be obligated to visit at some length. I never went ten feet out of my way to contact a committeeman, for two reasons: I had nothing of a material nature to offer him, and if I won him over by spending a half hour outlining my program, he still had only one vote, and while I had been wooing him I could have been shaking hands with a hundred ordinary voters.

The same goes for county chairmen. If you are clearly the front-runner, they will probably support you anyway. Most committeemen or chairmen like to support winners. Jobs, patronage, and favors come from hard-headed winners, not from idealistic do-gooder jerks with no chance of winning.

Most candidates, practically all, are or fancy themselves to be important people, and inasmuch as like attracts like they have a hangup about calling on important people. They would, for example, cover Main Street by looking up the manager of a department store or whatever, sitting down for a chat, with all its pitfalls and perils, while I was downstairs shaking hands with fifty employees, each of whom had one vote, just like the manager.

PASS THE HAT   Bearing in mind the old adage that people place a greater value on something they have to pay for than they do if the same something is given to them free, plus the fact that voters who contribute to a candidate tend to have a proprietary interest, plus the additional fact that we just plain needed money to keep going, I told my listeners at each stop that: (1) I was not a rich man; (2) I would not accept large contributions with strings attached; (3) ditto any contributions, large or small; (4) I would appreciate, subject to the foregoing conditions, any contributions they might wish to make; and (5) Dora would stand by the front of the car with my petition while we packed up, and she would be happy to receive said contributions.

I made this pitch at the end of my speech, which was also the "livin' end" of the meeting. The results left something to be desired. As soon as it was apparent that the show was over the crowd started breaking up. I noticed that some voters stood around until the crowd had dispersed, and then came up and surreptitiously handed Dora a coin or two. There was something wrong here. We had to make it easier and less conspicuous for the folks to contribute, and we had to hold the crowd until they had had an opportunity to contribute. At the next stop I made my pitch while we still had a couple of numbers left to play, which I promised would be forthcoming, and I told the crowd that during our final two numbers Slim and Johnny would pass the hat. That worked better. We substantially increased our meager take. Two or three days later, just as it was time to pass the hat, Johnny was caught short and had to run. Dora took over in his place. She collected twice as much as Slim.

At the next stop I had Audrey and Dora do the hat passing. They did twice as well as the boys.

I noticed that often, as the girls passed through the audience, men who had their attention on the entertainment would not realize the hat was passing them until it was too late. They would hurriedly reach in their pocket and then, seeing the hat had moved on, would hesitate a moment and then put the money back in their pocket. That wasn't good. I told the girls to stop in front of each man and, not too obviously, act as though they expected him to drop something in the hat.

Now I ask you—what's a guy to do but divvy up when a good-looking girl is standing there holding a hat, patiently and expectantly *and* smilingly waiting for him to join all these other sporty guys and fork over?

That technique doubled the kitty again.

Arod unintentionally got into the act. At the next meeting he climbed up on the hood of the car and sat there during the hat passing. He got more money than anybody, and with no hat at all. He had three nickels, five dimes, and a quarter, plus three silver dollars and a one-dollar bill.

He was all steamed up over his spectacular success, and at the next stop he could hardly wait to get up on his perch atop the hood of the car to make sure he'd be ready for business. He didn't get a single contribution. Not a red cent. We'd have to have a shill give him a dollar to get the ball rolling or something. It would probably work, but the word "shill" had a sound I didn't like. I thought up a better idea.

At the following rally I gave him a plug. After I had told the crowd that Dora and Audrey would now pass the hat I said, "Now if any of you boys are bashful or don't want your wife seeing you giving money to a strange woman, Arod will be right there on the hood of the car and you can give your contribution to him, if you'd rather."

Several did. Again, he got more than either of the girls.

I would rather have ended things after my speech while it was fresh in their minds but I realized the fact that people are much more apt to give when music is blaring and no one is paying them any attention. So it had to be that way.

We needed the money. We had to have it! If we were to keep going and have anything for a few ads and maybe a little radio time down in the home stretch, we just *had* to have every nickle we could beg, borrow, or—scrounge.

After all this fuss over "collection techniques," perhaps you are wondering just how much we were raking in. Holding five to six meetings a day, we averaged between twenty and thirty dollars. That's for the whole day, folks! Not twenty or thirty dollars a meeting.

The Depression. Remember? It was still with us.

MY WAY   There had never been a campaign like this before, noisy street rallies with a cowboy band entertaining from atop an old Ford car, and a candidate for Congress dressed like Tom Mix, not mention blood-letting cocklebur campaign badges.

Heretofore, campaigns had been a terrific bore, dull, uninteresting and stereotyped.

For the first time a lot of people were *enjoying* a political campaign.

I thought things were going just great. Better than I had planned and hoped they would.

Not everyone was pleased, of course. The conservative "haves" were shaking their heads and clucking their tongues. Others just didn't know *what* to make of it. One of these undecided voters voiced their dilemma. This man approached me after a street rally and said, "Taylor, I like you, you've got a fine family, and I like what you have to say but dammit, man, you're so undignified. I know you're just putting on an act and you're sure getting known in a hurry, but are you getting known in the right way? Don't you feel like a fool when you get up there on top of that car like that?"

I explained how I felt. I said, "Friend, when I started this campaign comparatively few voters had ever heard of me. Fewer had ever seen me, and not one had ever heard me make a speech setting forth my ideas. If I had conducted a campaign like the others, practically no one would ever have seen or heard of me, much less heard me talk, because I have no money for radio or newspaper space, and since neither the radio nor the press is going to devote much time or space to an unknown run-of-the-mill candidate, I would have been doomed before I started. I believe," I said to him, "that it is infinitely better to have the newspapers rave at my unorthodox behavior and in doing so unwittingly help me to become known, even unfavorably, than it would be for me to never become known at all. If by using these unconventional and, as you put it, undignified tactics, I can become known, even unfavorbly, people will come to my rallies just to see what kind of nut I really am."

He nodded to indicate he understood what I was saying and I went on. "Now—if they come out of curiosity and I have something to say that makes sense, they will be convinced that I was not the nut the press and stuffed shirts had represented me as being and their unfavorable opinion may become favorable. I'll have another convert. An angry convert, for he will be outraged at the press maligning me and deceiving him. But," I pointed out, "if I had not done these things to make that man curious he never would have come to hear me and I would have wound up just like I started—an unknown 'lost ball in the tall grass.' " I paused and added, "But to answer your last question, No, I didn't like getting up on top of my car the first time, but I knew I had to do it or just forget the whole thing. Look, my plan is working. You can see for yourself. Look at this crowd here today." I finished what I had to say by adding, "So you'll see me around—on top of my car."

My friend stood for a few seconds, head bowed, thoughtfully scratching his chin. Then he looked up, nodded his head very positively in agreement, and stuck out his hand. As he turned to go he said, "Give 'em hell."

After I had written the foregoing, I read the following, which appeared in a newspaper column of quotations from current statements by prominent figures:

"You have to shoot somebody, burn yourself alive, do something violent, in order to get any attention at all, however good your cause or causes.

"There is an absolute stone wall of indifference all over the world."

From the foregoing, one might assume that this guy was some kind of a nut. "Shoot somebody?" You'd probably get hung. "Barbecue yourself?" Remember, pal, you're a long time dead. Actually, the quoted statement is a cry of utter frustration from a very famous and distinguished man. I agree with him in principle or vice versa, but his suggested methods of breaking into print strike me as being a little drastic. However, the abhorrent idea of doing some outlandish thing to accomplish an objective is so unthinkable to such a man, a highly educated, cultured, serious-minded, and dignified man that the thought of compromising his dignity does not even enter into his reasoning.

The source of the anguished statement I have just quoted is none other than the eminent English historian Arnold Toynbee.

He would literally, in all probability, rather shoot someone or immolate himself than climb up on my sound car with a group of western entertainers, or dash about grabbing voters' hands and shaking them, or lower himself by sticking cocklebur badges on people.

You do it your way, Mr. Toynbee, I'll "do it my way," to paraphrase Mr. Sinatra. It's not too bad, not really—not after the first shock to your sensibilities has worn off.

I thank Mr. Toynbee, however, for verifying conclusions that I arrived at way back in 1938.

VOTE RIGHT   The day after my announcement, Henry Fletcher, the manager of the radio station, buttonholed me to caution that I would have to be careful and not let politics enter into our broadcast or some of my opponents might object and we would have the Federal Communications Commission after us.

We adhered to this rule strictly. However, we all know that educational campaigns urging people to vote are perfectly legitimate. In fact, they are patriotic and in the interest of good citizenship, so I spoke to Henry about the matter. I convinced him that the idea I had in mind would not violate the FCC rules. He shook his head rather dubiously, but he had to smile at my ingenious *and* ingenuous guile. He was a pretty good egg.

From then on, at the end of each day's broadcast, while all the gang were playing and singing our theme song, Cal the announcer would lower the volume on the music and Arod, who was not yet three, would chime in with a public service exhortation, "Be sure to vote right."

LAUGH-IN   I had been doing comedy since 1921 and, believe me, there is no sound more welcome to the ears of a comedian than a good belly laugh. It's good to be able to keep an audience laughing while you are trying to get across a serious message, like Governor Ross did that afternoon in Driggs when he so impressed me and started me off on this "save the world" kick.

There is, however, a happy medium to all things, and a limit beyond which the law of diminishing returns starts to work. This happened to me. My evening meetings, and to a lesser degree my street meetings, were becoming hilarious "laugh-ins." Entertaining, perhaps, but hardly calculated to impress the voters with one's qualifications to represent them in the Congress of the United States.

At Blackfoot, we held our biggest meeting to date. My fame as an entertaining speaker had spread. It was a good-sized hall, and the place was packed. Rising to the occasion, I really outdid myself. By now I had padded my presentation with well tried and polished humorous sequences and I really slayed 'em. I had the audience rolling in the aisles, almost literally.

After the rally I stepped out the stage door, hurried around front, and stood in the shadows to hear what the voters had to say as they filed out.

They were still laughing. One man said to another, "Well, what did you think of him?" The answer was, "W-e-l-l, I don't know. I don't know what kind of congressman he'd make, but if you want to laugh yourself to death, he's the best I ever saw."

That's exactly what I had begun to worry about. I had had a suspicion I was overdoing it, but trying to get a comedian to pass up surefire belly laughs is like trying to drag a dried-out mule away from a water trough.

Reluctantly, I realized I had to get things more in balance.

MONKEY BUSINESS   Perhaps you have a mental picture of me telling one joke after another and then laughing at my own gags, like most comedians do.

Not so. I never, never, told jokes and I never, never, laughed at my own humor.

"Then what type of humor enabled you to convulse an audience?" you may ask.

My style and technique were my own. I cannot point to any comedian and say, "My style was like his." I had a "gimmick," and I have never seen another comedian use it.

I stumbled on this "secret weapon" quite by chance.

I was visiting the zoo in Salt Lake City and stopped at the monkey cage. Eight or ten of them were cat-napping up in a big old dead tree, but one was down front entertaining the spectators.

He would do something outrageously funny that would convulse his audience, but instead of acting like he thought he had done something funny the chimp would look at the spectators with a deadpan, ever so serious face as though he was trying to fathom, "what in the hell are these stupid people laughing at?"

Fed by the monkey's childlike puzzlement, the laugh would double and when this second wave of laughter still failed to faze him, and he just kept looking as though he was deeply puzzled by all the hilarity, the laugh would last an unbelievably long time and grow to uproarious proportions.

I had been doing comedy for several years, and it occurred to me that perhaps I could add this technique to my repertoire of laugh-getting gimmicks.

I was on the verge of turning away when suddenly it dawned on me. The eyes. This master comic had a gimmick. Monkeys do not blink their eyes like homo sapiens. It isn't really a blink at all but more of a mechanical, slow, lazy one-two, closing and opening of the eyes. They may be kept open for varying lengths of time, but they are kept closed a good long second.

I had it. I tried it on an audience. It worked! And the best part of it all was that the viewers never caught on.

This subliminal technique, which we will call "the one-two," enabled me to get protracted belly laughs without it ever appearing that I was trying to be funny.

The following is an example of the type of humorous sequence suitable.

In 1938 the Honorable William E. Borah was Idaho's senior senator, and had been for too many years to count. He was known as a great orator. Because of his oversized head and his great mane of hair, the press had for years called him "The Lion of Idaho." Borah was without doubt the most famous Idahoan of all time.

If it is at all possible, it is always good politics for a candidate to associate himself with such a famous personage. I did that, and here is how.

During my speech I would say, "A lot of people have asked me, 'Glen—when did you first think about running for office?'

"Well," I would say, "I have wanted to be a congressman ever since I was a small boy up there in Kooskia. In case you never heard of Kooskia, it's a little town about seventy-five miles above Lewiston on the Clearwater River.

"Well sir, Senator Borah used to come to Kooskia campaigning, and I did love to hear him speak. He became something of a hero to me, and right there I decided that I'd like to someday follow in his footsteps."

(Now that statement wasn't exactly 100 percent correct, *but* it was essential to my presentation. Senator Borah was a great orator, all right, but his stuffy, pontifical style and resonant, droning voice would put me to sleep before I was comfortably settled in my seat.) Now that I have confessed to that little fib, let's get on with my story, as I told it to the voters—and no more fibs.

"When Borah came to Kooskia," I related, "he would always stay at our house, although he was a Republican and my father was a red-hot Democrat.

"I know that sounds strange," I would admit, "but I'll tell you why that happened. You see, Senator Borah is a relation of mine. Now, I don't want you to think I am trying to get into office by claiming a relationship with Senator Borah." (Author's Note: Obviously that disclaimer was something less than 100 percent honest.) "He's no blood relation, but he is some kind of shirttail relation of my father" (fact).

"I don't know exactly how it is, but it is something like this. Senator Borah's great aunt's nephew married my father's cousin's stepsister's half aunt" (wait here for a little laughter and then add) "or something like that" (good for another little laugh).

All this done straight-faced, with never any indication that I meant it to be funny or even humorous. Each time the audience would laugh I would wait them out, using the one-two.

The statement that starts the laugh, of course, has to be of such a ridiculous nature that no one would take it seriously, but it must be said with the utmost seriousness, and then the speaker must *remain* sober-faced. When he fails to give the slightest recognition of the obvious fact that what he said was ridiculous, a little laugh can often build into an almost hysterical situation.

But, to pursue this bit of campaign tomfoolery, I said, "Anyhow, the relationship was close enough that Borah would stay at our house and he would call my father 'Cousin Pleas.' His name was Pleasant John. Senator Borah would kiss me when he came and he would kiss me when he left." (This was good for a measurable laugh which I waited out using the one-two.)

When the laugh tapered off, I would add, "Oh, I've kissed Senator Borah several times." (This would get a good laugh.) I just stood straight-faced using the one-two.

"The Lion of Idaho" was probably the most dignified of all the dignified senators. My original statement that Senator Borah kissed me when he came and kissed me when he left conjured up an innocent picture of the senator kissing a small boy. It got an innocent little laugh because it was difficult to imagine the stony-faced senator kissing anyone—even his wife—but my follow-up statement, "I've kissed Senator Borah several times," made it a matter, by inference, of Glen Taylor, the speaker, and Borah, the sedate senator, kissing each other.

If I had, by the faintest trace of a smile, or any other sign, given the slightest hint that I was making jokes at the expense of the revered senator, it would have been resented. But when I did not, my convulsed listeners could not blame me for all the hilarity. All I had done was tell a harmless little story about a little boy who cherished the memory of being kissed by a famous senator.

During all this I remained absolutely solemn and relaxed, as though nothing at all funny had been said and I was about to offer a benediction, meanwhile blinking my eyes one-two.

Then, as quickly as I could be heard, I would add rather pensively, "Of course—he was a lot younger and better looking than he is now," and that would really slay 'em. But don't change expression, just stand there and soberly blink one-two.

It would take some time for that laugh to die. Then, almost invariably, just about the time things had quieted down but everyone was suppressing chuckles, somebody, generally a woman with a good imagination, would take another look at my completely innocent face and their mental picture of me and Senator Borah osculating. That would do it. If it happened to be a man who could no longer contain himself, his suppressed mirth would explode with a snort and a guffaw. If it was a woman, she would give forth with a piercing "tee-hee-ee-ee," and the whole thing would erupt again, probably resulting in a bigger laugh than the gag had gotten in the first place.

All the laughs I built into my talks to relieve the tedium of a serious discussion of my program and the issues were directly related to the subject at hand. I never used extraneous, obvious jokes or stories.

COUNTDOWN   Anyone who has not experienced it cannot possibly imagine my feelings of frustration during the last ten days of my campaign.

Radio spot announcements poured forth in a constant stream extolling the virtues and accomplishments of the other candidates and urging the populace to vote for one or another. Speeches by the candidates, and speeches by prominent citizens in behalf of candidates, monopolized the air. Quarter-page, half-page, full-page ads for my opponents filled the newspapers. How can a candidate with none of these things hope?

You've got to hope. Without hope to sustain you, you would collapse from utter weariness. Keep a stiff upper lip. It's almost over. Just a few more hours. When you are a candidate, or a candidate's mate, listening to election returns can be more exciting than any gambling game.

If you have worked until you felt you must surely drop in your tracks, gambled all your financial resources and do not know how you will feed your family next week, the terrible strain is infinitely compounded.

Trying to make a living was becoming more and more difficult. It was a blind alley. Jobs were practically nonexistent. I had no training for any job and even jobs for skilled workers were so scarce the WPA roll of educated unemployed was fantastic.

This was election night.

As I sat there at this last supper, fiddling with my fork, I thought how wonderful it would be to have an income so that you could run for office without the awful emptiness of reckoning with the days beyond election night.

The four of us—Gladys, Dora, Paul, and I—had pencils and paper. There were nine candidates. We discounted Larsen. No one had seen him around or talked about him. Each of us took two candidates to keep track of as the returns came in.

The voice of the announcer who handled the Glendora broadcasts, Calvin Hale, interrupted a recorded musical selection.

"Ladies and gentlemen, here are the first election returns.

"The first precinct to report is Pocatello precinct number 5." Unless you have run for office you cannot begin to imagine the strain, the excitement. I know of nothing to compare. Aside from all other considerations, you are going to learn what people think of you. The people of your congressional district, your home county, your home town, your own little precinct. That's where your home is, where you live. Your close neighbors will be passing judgment on you. You are supposed to have a big advantage here. No other candidate lives in that precinct.

The announcer said, "That's Pocatello precinct number 5, and here are the figures." But instead of giving us the figures, he proceeded to dangle us on the hook with a little jocular suspense building. "All ready? Got a pencil and paper? Okay." Damn Cal, anyhow. It was all right for us to kid back and forth and rib each other during our broadcast but not now, Cal, for God's sake, not now!

"Pocatello precinct number 5—Leo Hood, 92; Jonesse, 5; Larsen, 4; Masters, 46; Miller, 25; Taylor—" The blood pounded in my temples as though I were surrounded by wild Indians, with only one bullet left. "Taylor, 22—" The bottom fell out. Jesus, that was terrible. I felt like someone had hit me in the stomach with a ball bat. I wanted to vomit.

Cal went right ahead, unaware of the blow he had dealt to my hopes, my pride, my ego. "Thornton, 1; Whittle, 1; Ray, 23."

A little figuring showed that Hood had received more than four times as many votes as I had: four to one. I remember expelling my breath between loose lips with a "phew" sound as the terrible truth soaked in. What I had feared most had happened. I was a joke. I had not been taken seriously. And, after all that work, the friendly audiences, the promises of support, the hundreds of cocklebur badges so eagerly sought and worn. The fabulous street meetings and the fantastic crowds. Gags and gimmicks might draw crowds and get attention but they sure as hell didn't get votes.

Ira Masters, who hadn't lived here for ten years, had gotten twice as many votes as I had. "Even old Doc Ray beat me."

"Well he only beat you by one vote, and he has lived here for sixty years. He is state senator. I think you did pretty well to tie him." Dora was in there trying to cheer me up, encourage me, as she always did when the heaviest blows were falling. "Bert Miller is attorney general. He's been in politics for years and he only got 25 votes. He only beat you by 3 votes," she pointed out.

I grasped this straw in my sea of despondency. "That's right. I guess it's not really a disgrace, but I had so hoped I might win."

"Well look at Jonesse and Larsen and Thornton and Whittle," she said "They got hardly any votes at all. You got six times as many votes as Jonesse or Larsen and twenty-two times as many as poor old Thornton. He only got one vote. And so did Whittle. I think you did real well. Look." She showed me the figures. "Four of them got more votes than you did and four got fewer. You are right in the middle."

Paul had been sitting there completely in the dumps. For the want of something better to do he was looking at a precinct map. All of a sudden he hit the table. "Say, do you know what? That's Leo Hood's snooty home precinct." Sure enough! Sure enough! Maybe I'd do that good in my home precinct.

The next precinct to report was Pocatello number 9—Hood, 87; Masters, 97; Miller, 27 (only 27?); Taylor, 86. Hooray, yippee, only one vote less than Hood. Doc Ray, only 46. I was third high man in the ninth instead of fifth, as in the fifth precinct.

That made it Hood, 179; Masters, 143; Miller, 52; Doc Ray, 81; Taylor, 108. "And now here's precinct number 15," Cal was saying. Number 15? That's our home precinct. My heart nearly stopped beating. "Precinct 15," Cal was repeating. All right, Cal, let's have it! Let's have it, man!

"Hood, 97." Hell, that's a lot of votes! "Jonesse, 8; Larsen, 9; Masters, 86; Miller, 16 (only 16?); Taylor, 106."

Yippee! I carried my home precinct. Not by much, but by God I carried it.

Dora had the totals again. "We can just forget everybody but Hood, Masters, and Taylor," Dora suggested. "Hood, 276; Masters, 229; Miller, 68; Taylor, 214. We're 15 votes behind Masters and only 62 behind Hood." I was in third place!

Cal again. "Here's Alameda number 1." Alameda was a suburb where mostly working people lived. "Hood, 72; Masters, 68; Miller, 20; Taylor, 90." We raised the roof. "We beat everybody," Paul yelled. Dora was busy figuring. "Let's see, that's

Hood, 348; Masters, 297; Miller, 88," Dora said. "Forget him. Taylor, 304. Only 44 votes behind Hood and 7 ahead of Masters."

Cal with more—Alameda number 2. Hooray for Alameda! Hood, 64 "Only 64," Dora shouted. Masters, 36. "Only 36!" Paul this time. Taylor, 109. We did a war dance, yelling to match.

Dora busy figuring again. "Hood, 412; Masters, 333; Taylor, 413." I had to yell. "Boy oh boy, we're ahead of Hood! We're ahead, by 1 vote."

"Here is McCammon" (McCammon is a small town about twenty miles south of Pocatello. It was one of the communities where we played regularly once a month with The Glendora Ranch Gang.)

"Hood, 19." Swell! Obviously, Hood didn't have it outside Pocatello. "Taylor, 70." "We're going! We're going!" Dora again "Totals—Hood, 431; Taylor, 483!" "We're pulling away," I whooped. Even Dora joined in the pandemonium and Arod, who was accustomed to sleeping through almost any noise, had been roused by the din and appeared at the bedroom door. When he heard the news he went into ecstasies with the rest of us.

Then returns started coming in from Boise and Twin Falls, where I was not so well known, and with one report on several precincts we lost our lead. We never got it back. That was our high point.

It was better to have had our brief moment to let off steam than it would have been if we had never gotten our head above water. Everything considered, we did well. Miller finally won with 9,996. Masters was second with 9,803. Hood was third with 8,530, and I was fourth with 6,742. The other four candidates were also-rans with only 2,000 some odd votes each.

My showing proved that it could be done. I was no joke. We would try again next election.

In the meantime, there was the urgent matter of making a living. There was no doubt that I had added to my fame by becoming a serious political contender but the important question right now was: Would my achievement help or hurt our business? We did have to eat.

MORNING AFTER   The morning after election I awoke with more of that gnawing tension gut ache than I had ever known before. I was thirty-four years old and my prospects for the future were practically nil.

We were down to our last few dollars.

All I had to look forward to was the depressing prospect that my family and I, by working sixteen to twenty hours a day, could perhaps eke out a bare existence.

I had to be right here in early 1940, prepared to campaign again. It was evident that I had been taken seriously, and that my theatrical background was not the political cyanide I had feared. Several editors and political writers tried to explain what had happened. They all agreed that my street rallies, instead of making me a laughing stock as they had expected, had been very effective. They attributed this to the stupidity and lack of discrimination on the part of the voters, and hinted that some way should be found to keep such ignorant oafs from voting. Not one of the experts ever mentioned the most remarkable aspect of the matter, which was my almost total lack of campaign funds. You just don't run a political campaign without money, you know.

I was what they liked to refer to as a "political phenomenon." Those few county chairmen, county officeholders, and committeemen who had supported me were sure I had what it takes to go far in the rough-and-tumble game of politics, if I would stick with it. That was the sticker—how to stick with it.

My mode of life was not conducive to staying in one place long enough to wait for the brass ring to come round again. That was my problem and, hopeless as it might seem, I felt I had no choice but to pursue the matter until I had exhausted every resource.

My fame as a campaigner and a political figure had not helped business, which was off nearly 50 percent.

When familiar faces would be missing from our audience the absence would be accounted for with the matter-of-fact explanation, "Oh, he's a Republican."

How much of our poor business could be blamed on this attitude there was no way of telling. To Republicans, I was no longer "good old Glen" or "Toby," but Glen Taylor, the Democratic politician.

In fact, we now had a Democratic show and it would be very, very difficult to make it on that basis.

We should have gone where this political factor would not hamper our efforts to make a living, but somehow we had to stay in Idaho until 1940 or just forget politics.

We literally starved it out.

MIRACLE TIME   The 1940 election had particular significance. The most distinguished Idahoan of all time, Senator William E. Borah, had died, and the question of who was to succeed him was to be decided.

I had decided to run for the seat as soon as I heard of Borah's death. The reasoning which prompted this presumptuous move was not based on an appraisal of my strength. No one asked me to run. No one even suggested that I run. I am quite certain I would be perfectly safe in saying that no one had even considered the possibility of my running to succeed the renowned Senator William E. Borah.

The reasoning behind my decision was simple. If I ran, even for the congressional seat, and won, it would be a miracle. All right. As long as we were dealing in miracles, why settle for a little old second-rate miracle? Why not go first class?

I wanted to get where I could be of maximum service in helping to end the vicious nonsense of "scarcity and starvation in the midst of plenty." So be it. Everyone knew a senator was infinitely more important and influential than a congressman so there was no use being satisfied with half a loaf, no use being chicken about the matter. A really heroic, bona fide crusader should think big.

The Senate it would be.

If I had been looking for some measure of the security I had never known, then I might have run for Congress because there would be only half instead of all the state to cover.

I decided to ask some of the people who had supported me in 1938 what they thought about me running for the Senate. The first two I asked were openly astonished that I would even think of such a thing.

"Oh no Glen," they said, "you should try for Congress again. If you make that and serve a term or two, *then* try for the Senate."

They just could not conceive of such derring-do. That was enough of that. If you think big, do not seek advice from timid people who think in conventional terms.

I realized that these two people would feel resentful when I disregarded their sincere advice. Asking advice was a good way to lose friends and alienate people. I let the matter drop after approaching those two.

The first political stirrings of the 1940 campaign year came January 28, when the *Idaho Daily Statesman* ran a two-column article under the heading HOT SENATE RACE PREDICTED BETWEEN THOMAS, DONART; OTHERS MAY ENTER CONTEST.

The implication was clear. Donart already had it in the bag; if there were any jerks around foolish enough to contest Mr. Donart in the primary they were free to do so.

John Thomas was a man in his seventies, a banker and big sheep rancher, whom the Republican governor had appointed to fill the vacancy created by Senator Borah's death. He had to return from retirement in California to accept the honor. Years before he had been appointed to fill a similar vacancy and lost his seat when the voters got a crack at him.

It was conceded that he would be the Republican candidate in the general election. He had money and nothing is so dear to the hearts of politicians as a "fat cat." The fact that he had been defeated under similar circumstances before gave hope, however, to the Democrats that history might repeat itself and that he could be beaten again.

For that reason the Democratic nomination was an eagerly sought opportunity.

George Donart, a prominent attorney and long-time state legislator, was conceded to be a formidable man, and he was obviously the Democrat most acceptable to the *Statesman* or it would not have arbitrarily paired him as Thomas' opponent.

My name was never mentioned in the prefiling period as a possible senatorial aspirant. The idea was unthinkable.

Since the 1938 election I had made it a practice to furnish free entertainment for picnics and celebrations of one kind or another if I could be assured of a good crowd. This type of activity was doing me more good than any amount of political campaigning.

The following is a letter thanking us for one effort along this line.

> This letter is to express the appreciation of the Ladies Aid Society of The First Presbyterian Church of Pocatello for the fine performance of *The Ghost Fighter* which you presented at the church two weeks ago. We are glad to report that we cleared $62.00 which was turned over to the American Legion toward the purchase of an Iron lung. Everyone who attended the performance was well pleased and we are anxiously awaiting several return engagements in the future.
>
> Very Truly Yours,
> Ladies' Aid Society of
> The First Presbyterian Church

There was a postscript. It read:

> Mr. Taylor:
> You may read this letter over the radio if you care to, and thank all those who attended.

Of course, I was glad to do these very nice ladies this favor and read their letter. I thanked those who, by their attendance, had made possible this contribution.

I also bragged about what good cooks this group of lovely ladies were and what a fine midnight lunch they had served.

Naturally, I did not forget to laud the American Legion for their magnificent humanitarian project, and explained how an iron lung would save the lives of little children.

It was a poor week indeed that I didn't have at least one or two such letters to read.

Incidentally, I'll bet that was the first dance ever held in a Presbyterian church. After all, though, those danged Mormons were doing it, and then having me brag on the air about all the money they were making. And doesn't the Good Book say something about "where your purse is, there also is your heart"?

On March 7 George Donart of Weiser became the first Democrat to announce for the United States Senate. He caught me flatfooted. I had hoped to be the first.

Political writers attributed his early entry to the fact that he felt he was in such a strong position that by making his intentions known he would scare away other hopefuls. His announcement rated twenty column inches. It was printed in its entirety by the *Boise Statesman*, and I imagine by most other papers, because Mr. Donart was a big man.

His statement was a typical fence straddler. He was for Roosevelt, but "I do not mean to convey the impression that in my opinion all of the new deal measures have been entirely satisfactory." From there Mr. Donart went on to discuss tariffs, foreign relations, parity, and trade agreements, winding up with, "The most favored-nation clause in each treaty should be limited in its appliction to the articles specified therein." Hooray for George Donart! Can't you just see the truck drivers, sawmill workers, and practically every ordinary voter throwing their hats in the air and cheering that last erudite pronouncement?

Mr. Donart probably knew the law, but he sure as hell didn't know people. Who would ever read that crap, much less understand it?

The fact that he was a profound thinker was one of the reasons this great man felt that no one would dare oppose him. Listen to this: "Senator Donart received his grade school and high school education in Weiser and attended the University of Idaho. He owns a large irrigated farm; is a director of the Wulf Hardware and Farm Implement Company, president of the Hotel Washington Company, and practices law. He is a former Washington County prosecuting attorney and has served four terms in the state senate." How do you like them apples?

Obviously (to Mr. Donart), anyone who would think of going up against such a formidable man would have to be nuts. The press was very respectful.

When I announced, there wasn't a single editor in the state who considered my candidacy seriously, but my picture with the cowboy hat was too much to resist, and most editors succumbed to the obvious and used the "Hat in Ring" caption. The *Coeur d'Alene Press* headline was HILLBILLY SEEKS SENATE NOMINATION.

On March 29, the *McCammon News* became the first paper to concede that I had any chance of beating Mr. Donart. The editor had this to say: "Glen H. Taylor, radio and stage entertainer, has announced his candidacy for the United States Senate on the Democratic ticket this year. Taylor came in fourth in a field of nine aspirants for representative in the last primary election and he would not be a safe bet either way this trip."

I have often been asked how I was treated by the Idaho press. My answer was, "There are eleven daily papers and they were all against me but one and it was neutral." That one paper was the *Lewiston Tribune*. Lewiston is the largest town in northern Idaho.

In 1938, we had twelve hundred dollars when the campaign started. In this year of 1940 we had only one thousand.

THREE-HEADED CANDIDATE   Soda Springs and Rupert were the only towns within reach of the Pocatello radio station where we had not used the "free show" gimmick in the 1938 campaign so we decided to start our '40 campaign with those towns. On May 2, we started the ball rolling in Soda. It's a community of some five hundred souls, about seventy miles from Pocatello.

The editor of the local paper had some observations that were interesting. He wrote: "Mr. and Mrs. Glen Taylor, their young son Arod and a couple of handy cowhands started the year's politcal campaign in Soda Springs, Tuesday night. They gave a variety program in Sodora Hall before a SUPRISINGLY LARGE CROWD. Mr. Taylor expounded his own unique plan for bringing about 'plenty for all.' His discussion indicated that this musician has done a lot of thinking. He is a fluent speaker and held the interest of his listeners very well."

The editor wound up his coverage of the event with a statement that gave me a chuckle and proved he was a man who recognized the obvious. "Mr. and Mrs. Taylor and their son Arod are a candidate for the United States Senate."

At Rupert, which was the second day of our campaign, we had a big crowd. The local paper reported: "Mr. Taylor, after presenting his views and plans to carry out his convictions, gave out approximately two hundred straw votes. The poll taken showed all but eleven of the two hundred favoring the Taylor Plan." The size of the crowd and the results of the poll had us walking on clouds. It looked like we were on our way.

From Rupert we made a three-hundred-mile jump to my old home town of Kooskia, where we had a big crowd, and the results of the poll were 126 "Yes" and 14 "No."

After Kooskia we had ten towns booked and billed for evening meetings.

We planned to try a somewhat modified approach in these towns where we weren't so well known, since we had not played them for several years and they had not been exposed to our radio program.

Although our "free show" bit had proven successful, drawn big crowds and no complaints about having to pay for the dance, my thin-skinned conscience had bothered me.

On the thousands of new handbills I had had printed I used the "Big Free Show," but at the bottom of the bill was this clarification: "The entertainment and speaking from 8 till 9 is free. No strings attached. Admission for the play and dance starting at 9 o'clock is—Children 25¢ Adults 50¢."

That did it. My attempt to be absolutely honest and forthright backfired. That "Children 25¢ Adults 50¢" made the folks stay away in droves and, before we could throw the misbegotten bills in the garbage, have more printed with the old "free show" gimmick and no mention of any charge, we had goofed off ten or a dozen towns.

We managed to get back to Pocatello, but we were down to our last dollar. The campaign was perilously close to collapse. It had to be self-supporting or we were finished, so I took measures to cut expenses to the bone.

I let the three salaried people go. The car which had carried them and our baggage was permanently parked in the backyard. This meant that from here on Dora would have to drive around town announcing our street meetings while I shook hands up and down main street. It also meant that Dora, Arod, and I would be the only entertainment.

An item on the plus side was the fact that, instead of one evening meeting in a hall where we had to pay rent and depend on the voters coming to us, we could now hold two or three street meetings which drew better crowds than daytime rallies and, seeing more people, we collected more money by way of passing the hat.

I put the twelve-foot canvas boat back on the platform atop the Ford car to carry our clothes, advertising, and instruments. It would not be as convenient as having the clear platform to work on, but it had to be.

PEACHES AND COOKIES   I worked the Ford car over so the back of the front seat could be lowered to form a bed of sorts. "Of sorts" is a generous description. It was a damned poor excuse for a bed.

I cut a piece of plywood about twenty inches wide to rest on the two front windowsills, with a hole to fit around the steering wheel. This would be Arod's bed.

While I worked at these chores, Dora was busy baking oatmeal cookies. Not just a dozen or two or a few dozen, but hundreds. A five-gallon can full. We decided on oatmeal cookies because sealed up in that airtight can they would remain moist and soft for days or even weeks.

The previous summer a friend who had a peach crop he could not sell had given us permission to pick all the peaches we wanted. We had really loaded up and Dora had canned them, standing over a hot stove day in and day out while the temperature hovered around one hundred degrees.

Two days at home, and we were ready to hit the campaign trail again.

Into the trunk of the car we loaded tack cards, bumper strips, and campaign buttons, plus the five-gallon can of oatmeal cookies and three dozen jars of peaches. On top in the boat we packed our bedding, clothes, and instruments. We kept the back seat free of clutter so Arod could nap there as we traveled.

For the balance of the campaign—from May 25 on through June, July, and until August 13, primary election day—the three of us lived in that Ford car.

We would find a secluded spot, shady if possible, where we could park overnight to sleep. Two or three times a night Arod would roll off in his narrow perch. We would boost him back up and try to resume our fitful slumbers.

We made sure that our gas tank was nearly empty at the end of each day so the next morning we could drive into a gas station and say, "Fill her up." While the car was being serviced we would go to the restrooms to wash and shave. Then we would have breakfast in the car. Peaches, oatmeal cookies, and milk, which was the only item we had to buy. We would hold a street meeting at ten a.m. and another at ll:30 a.m., and five to six more during the afternoon and evening.

We no longer had the band to attract a crowd, but when Dora returned from ballyhooing the residential district, parked on main street, and those horns started blaring a rousing Sousa march, the crowd would gather and the band was hardly missed.

While I was speaking at the eleven-thirty meeting, Dora would take Arod to a restaurant and get him a bowl of hot soup. That was the only deviation from peaches and cookies.

Peaches and oatmeal cookies are good, but after a while it gets a little monotonous, and a steady consumption of such delectable goodies can have distressing side effects. After two or three days this uncustomary diet gave us the trots, or to put it less euphemistically, the runs.

When we left Pocatello on this trip, we were so strapped we could not afford the little ads announcing our appearances and found that our street rallies were not nearly as well attended without them. You can't imagine how frustrating that was.

With our three people setup and no salaries to pay, we were beginning to accumulate money for campaign expenditures at a surprising rate. We started placing the ads again and our crowds picked up. Now we could either start staying in motels and eating in restaurants or we could stick by our guns and plow that money back into ads and hopefully a radio talk or two, as well as a few spot announcements just before election.

We chose the latter and stuck to the peaches and cookies. It wasn't so bad, really. We had sort of forgotten that there was anything in the world to eat besides peaches and oatmeal cookies.

The rest of the campaign was in ten-day segments. At the end of each ten-day jaunt we would return to Pocatello, all take badly needed baths, Dora would wash our clothes, we would load up with more peaches, cookies, and advertising, get a few blessed hours of sleep in a real bed, and set out, probably at midnight, for the distant spot where the activities of our next ten grueling days were to begin. In the early mornings before our ten o'clock rally we would tack up cards, get our little newspaper ads in the mail, and date handbills which we mailed to friends to distribute in out-of-the-way communities. Not having previously campaigned in the northern part of the state, we had no political friends there and any handbills that went out had to be mailed.

After the last rally of the day, at ten or eleven p.m., we would sally forth again to drive the highways and byways until two a.m., tacking up cards and bumper strips by the light of our car's headlights. We tacked the cards on roadside posts and telegraph poles and the bumper strips on horizontal surfaces, like board fences and abandoned buildings. Unless there was a card or cards already there, much as we hated to pass up a good place close to the road, we never risked the possibility of offending and thereby losing votes by defacing a virgin surface.

We never wasted a minute. Arod slept whenever he felt like it in his comfy back-seat bed, but Dora and I drove ourselves relentlessly.

HOME STRETCH   I have an observation that I must get off my chest here.

I cannot for the life of me understand how anyone could rate George Donart as a good campaigner or speaker. He was possibly five feet seven or eight inches tall and had a noticeable paunch. He walked so stiffly he gave the impression that he was afraid he might tear his dignity.

You can't be a good campaigner and see very many people if you move around like a constipated turtle.

I had sneaked into one of his meetings and listened to him, and he talked even slower than he walked. I spent fifteen minutes listening to him, and he almost drove me crazy thinking of all I could have said in that time.

As luck would have it, he told a story about me. I was beginning to worry him, or he would have ignored me. No doubt he meant the humorous incident he recalled to present me as a harum-scarum scatterbrain but it backfired. It not only got a good laugh but it wound up turning into a big round of applause, which I felt sure was more for me than it was for him. Here is the story. I could have told it in one minute. It took George fifteen. Remember now, he talked like a 78-rpm record being played on a 45-rpm turntable.

To start with, he made some belittling remark about me calculated to furnish comedy relief for the campaign, and then he launched into this story. By "launched" I mean he was as ponderous, slow, and deliberate as would be the launching of the *Queen Mary* on a well sanded track. He said, "Theee firrrst ti-i-m-e I sa-a-aw Gle-e-n Tay—lor."

Now that you've got the idea of his long-drawn-out delivery, we'll proceed without the boring spelling and let you imagine it. V-veery s-l-o-o-w-ly n-o-o-w.

"The first time I ever saw Glen Taylor I was standing on the street corner in Burley. I was campaigning and I had been to see all the committeemen and the county chairman and I was just standing there trying to figure out who I'd see next.

"Well sir, I looked up the street and here came a fellow wearing a white cowboy hat, and he was shaking hands with everybody faster than I had ever seen anybody shake hands before.

"He rushed up to me and he grabbed my hand and he said, 'I'm Glen Taylor and I'm running for the United States Senate. If you don't know anybody you'd rather vote for I'd appreciate your vote.' I opened my mouth to tell him that I was George Donart and I was running for the Senate too, but before I could say anything he was shaking hands with the fourth fellow down the street."

That's where he got the big laugh that turned into a big hand, and I still think the laugh was for the good story George had told and the hand was for that crazy handshaker, Glen Taylor.

By living in our car we had saved up enough money to put a one-column, five-inch ad in every paper published in the state to appear during the last week of the campaign. It read: "Glen H. Taylor Democrat—U.S. Senate." Then there was the picture of the three of us.

Under the picture was this copy: "The people must cooperatively own and operate the business of the nation so we can plan to put everyone to work to produce plenty for all and not profits for the few."

There were three more sentences: "I'll make you a good progressive Senator. There are just two things the matter with me. I am not rich and I am not a lawyer."

In the closing hours of the campaign, the political "analyst" for the *Idaho Daily Statesman* put down his glass long enough to concoct a barefaced lie about me. He wrote: "In the Democratic senatorial primary there are three candidates. One is Glen Taylor, the cowboy, vaudeville, sound truck artist. He doesn't expect to be nominated he has told friends."

That outright falsehood made me see red. If he had said he thought I was an idiot that would have been his privilege, but to attribute such an idiotic statement to me was just too damn crummy. It was typical, though, of the *Idaho Daily Statesman*.

After trying, in such an underhanded way, to plant the idea in the minds of my supporters that they were simple-minded parties to a cheap publicity stunt, he admitted that I wouldn't be a complete washout, as follows: "He will nonetheless poll a surprising number of votes. The real contest however is between Donart and Bothwell." (Judge James Bothwell, a late starter, was elderly and stodgy. He could take votes away from only Donart.)

The election was at hand. It was customary for the state house employees to take an election eve poll of their members, the results of which had been amazingly accurate in the past.

On the Senate race, these bureaucratic prophets of old came up with these figures: Bothwell, 20—Donart, 19—Taylor, 2.

All right, let's vote.

D-DAY   On election day the pundits relax and enjoy a brief respite from the strenuous exercise of getting their feet in their mouths. So we move on now to August 14, the day after election.

Here is the front page of the *Idaho Daily Statesman*, with a banner headline clear across the top:

THOMAS, CLARK, DONART LEAD

Under the big black headline was a subhead that also extended clear across the page, and it was all devoted to one candidate. Guess who? It read, COWBOY CANDIDATE SPRINGS SURPRISE IN DEMOCRATIC SENATORIAL RACE. Below that teaser, occupying four columns on the right, was a headline in even heavier type shouting, GLEN TAYLOR GIVES ATTORNEY PRIMARYS ONLY HOT CONTEST. The details must have been a bitter pill for the *Statesman* to print, if you will excuse the mixed metaphor. Here they are: "Favorites were emerging in all but one of the contested positions in Idaho's 1940 primary election Tuesday night with only the contest for the Democratic senate nomination developing into a struggle—between a youthful sound-truck campaigner and a party stalwart." At this point there was a subheading: TAYLOR CROWDS DONART. After that, the account continues:

> Glen Taylor who traveled the state with his wife and ballad singing small son lacked only 261 votes of matching State Senator George Donart of Weiser known throughout Idaho as a Democratic wheel horse.
>
> Taylor counted 2,472 votes against Donart's 2,733, with 89 precincts reported of the state's 702. Third man in the contest, former Judge James R. Bothwell of Twin Falls had 1,921 votes.

Donart's picture was on the front page.

Whew! That's a cliffhanger. The *Statesman* was a morning paper. Let's see what the *Pocatello Tribune* had to say. It's an afternoon paper and will have later, more complete, returns. Here it is, a headline clear across the top of the front page:

POCATELLAN LEADING U.S. SENATE RACE

> The vote is Taylor 17,740 Bothwell 17,083 and Donart 15,604 with only small isolated precincts unreported.

I almost heaved a sigh of relief. They'd never catch me now. Remember that the remaining precincts are "small and isolated." While Donart and Bothwell were stalking around the county seat, honoring the officeholders, party Pooh-Bahs, and establishmentarians with their august presence, we were out yonder racing from one to another of those "small isolated precincts."

That's all there was left. No—they'd never catch me now.

On August 15 I received the following letter from George Donart:

> Please accept my sincere congratulations. You started this campaign without the support of a single county organization, and probably not even the support of a half dozen precinct committeemen, and came through high man in three quarters of the counties.
>
> It was your own power that put you over. Keep up the

good work. More power to you in the future. Yours very truly, George Donart.

Wait a while before you throw your hat in the air for "good sport" George Donart.

IF Shortly after the primaries, it was suggested to me that I have a conference with the gubernatorial nominee, Chase Clark, to plan campaign strategy.

I didn't know it at the time, but the meeting was *not* for the purpose of planning our campaign. It was simply a probing session to find out if I could be turned into a "safe" candidate. The machine would have liked it if I could be. They just loved a good vote-getter—*if* he could be persuaded to be "safe."

Chase tried to get me to dump Gillette and listen to reason. There was money to be had for a "respectable" campaign if I would just get rid of some of my "wild ideas" and talk things over with "the boys." I wasn't told just who "the boys" were. Later, I would have a pretty good idea.

Chase pointed out that "the boys" would be glad to get behind me. "Even a good many Republicans are not anxious to elect John Thomas. He's too old," I was told.

I said "I couldn't change my beliefs," and I scarcely saw the candidate for governor from there on out.

The day after my talk with Chase Clark, I received a handwritten note from a Robert Coulter. It read:

> Dear Mr. Taylor: Accept my congratulations on your nomination for the U.S. Senate. I wish you a successful campaign in the coming election.
>
> Sincerely yours,
> Robert Coulter

Now, I did not know who Robert Coulter was. Later, I was to learn that he was a former state chairman and known as a ruthless, no-holds-barred operator.

Immediately after my talk with Chase Clark the machine had called Coulter back from retirement to mastermind the job of getting rid of me. The first thing he did was to write me that note to anesthetize me for the kill. I didn't forget it either, because his letter of congratulations was the first one I received addressed to the "Honorable" Glen H. Taylor. I had to hand it to Coulter. He knew how to win friends and influence people. He knew that one of the shortest routes to a jerk's heart is via his vanity. Boy, look at that! Now I was "Honorable." Of course, the implication there was that heretofore I was *not* honorable. At the state convention in Idaho Falls I met Bob Coulter in person. He was sixty, at least. No more than five feet six inches tall, frail looking. He reminded me of an underfed prairie dog, but a soft-voiced and smooth little underfed prairie dog. He put his arm about my waist (he couldn't reach my shoulders) and calld me Glen and congratulated me on my great victory and promised that he would do great and wonderful things for me.

At the time, of course, I did not know of Coulter's perfidy, but years later I learned that Robert Hannegan, the Democratic National Chairman, had called him a few days after the election and said, "Say it looks like we've got a winner out there in this Singing Cowboy Taylor. Hell, he's been hogging the show back here in the newspapers. What can we do to help you elect him ?"

To that open invitation to ask for money and nationally known speakers, Coulter had answered, "Aw, forget it. The guy's a screwball. Just skip it, and we'll try to do better next time."

On August 24, two days after my conference with Clark, the *Nampa Free Press* carried a heading:

DONART TO SUPPORT GLEN TAYLOR—MAYBE

The article with that snide heading reads:

> George Donart, unsuccessful opponent of Glen Taylor for the Democratic nomination to the U.S. Senate, today promised full support of Taylor—on the condition the Pocatello cowboy entertainer adhere to the regular party platform and drop his own semi-socialistic campaign stand.
>
> "I'll vote for Taylor myself regardless," Donart said, "but I'll campaign for him only if he follows the regular party platform."

Well, *thank*—you—George. It's been real nice knowin' you. On August 26, two days after Mr. Donart had issued his statement to the press qualifying his early-on congratulatory telegram, and fifteen days after the primary, I received a belated letter of congratulations from the Honorable Judge Bothwell, the other poor loser I had defeated.

Some of the words were different than those used by Mr. Donart, but the message was the same: "I'll support you—if."

While I did not grasp the significance of the double-barreled, delayed-action shot in the back at the time, what had happened was very plain to those familiar with the workings of the machine. That nefarious and despicable organization which had controlled Idaho politics for decades, before I stuck my nose into their stinking tent, had gone into action.

The "powers that be" had laid down the law. "None of this 'good sport' stuff, fellas. The word from on high is 'close ranks and teach this lad Taylor a lesson.'"

THE MACHINE   Poor, naïve, ignorant me. The "machine" was out to get me, and I didn't even know there was a machine. Believe me, there was. I would learn about it the hard way, and my education was about to start. While I had not yet learned about the machine, and describing its workings at this point is not in chronological order, it will help us understand what's happening if we learn about its devious doings here and now.

It wasn't a case of two machines, one Republican and one Democratic, plotting against each other and fighting over the spoils. Not a bit of it. There were two organizations on the surface, for appearance's sake and to kid the public into believing that they had a choice, but when general election time rolled round it was really one big machine.

Its membership was composed of the rich and conservative business people, and lawyers scattered throughout the state and directed from Boise, the state capitol.

The object of the machine was to keep a tight rein on Idaho politics so the big corporations could have access on favorable terms to the state's resources of timber, metals, hydroelectric dam sites, enjoy ridiculously low taxes, etc., etc.

The active machine workers all seemed to do better than average, whatever business they might be in. At heart, the members of the machine were reactionary Republicans and/or out-and-out mercenaries who couldn't care less about party labels as long as they got paid for their services. Obviously, though, somebody had to pose as Democrats. They sort of chose up sides. They drew straws, perhaps, or they may just have talked things over and dished out assignments.

For example, two of the best known lawyers in Boise were brothers. One was a Democrat and the other a Republican, but you couldn't tell which was which by what they said.

The machine was financed with corporation money so its members could devote time to politics the year round. The corporations had learned that it was much cheaper to elect senators, congressmen, and governors in small states than in larger ones.

A certain eastern Idaho lawyer was famous for being the corporation bagman. Each election he would set out loaded with greenbacks and go about the state handing out sizeable chunks of cash to favored candidates and machine operators. The press was more or less subservient to the machine. How come? Well, for example, the Idaho Power Company placed ads in practically every paper in the area it served on a regular basis. No real reason to, they had a monopoly, but they did it. Not earth-shaking, perhaps, but it was a steady source of income not to be sneezed at by struggling country editors.

What else? Well, at least 75 percent of all businessmen were conservative. They knew that machine candidates were screened, safe, and reliable. Businessmen and firms all place ads in newspapers. Ads are the lifeblood of newspapers. Support the wrong candidate, and terrific pressure can be brought to bear.

Owners and stockholders in the larger newspapers were businessmen who either had their own racket going which benefited by the election of "safe" candidates, or they owned stock in the larger predatory corporations.

The machine's job was to nominate safe candidates on *both* tickets in the primaries. Generally they did. Then they could sit back and relax. They had it in the bag. The voters had a choice, but no matter who was elected the machine boys had it made.

Then they would make bets among themselves as to whose "boy" would win. They'd put on a big show and get out there and really try. An election turned into a sporting proposition. *But* if by some fluke a maverick won the nomination on *either* ticket the machine closed ranks, party labels were forgotten, and both machines threw their combined weight behind the safe candidate—and God help the maverick. Any amount of money necessary would be spent to beat him. The press would belabor him unmercifully.

Now the machine was out to show me what politics was all about. The first item on their agenda was to destroy the image I had built up as the champion of the people. They went about it in a workmanlike manner.

I was called to Democratic headquarters in the Hotel Boise, ostensibly to see what I thought of a piece of campaign literature.

PENTHOUSE   There were a dozen nice-looking young men and women manning the headquarters.

One of them innocently asked where I was staying. When I told them that Dora, Arod, and I were still living in our old Ford and eating canned peaches and oatmeal cookies they were, or pretended to be, horrified.

The Democratic Party couldn't have its senatorial candidate doing a thing like that. "We'll get you a room here in the hotel," their spokesman said. I couldn't see anything wrong with that so I agreed.

The "room" turned out to be a penthouse suite. *Man, Idaho Democrats must have money, to put out for a joint like this,* I thought.

Dora was very happy, and who can blame her after those weeks and months of living in our car?

I was too proud to mention that we were stone broke and could use a meal ticket so we smuggled some peaches and cookies up to our penthouse and for our evening meal it was the same old fare.

On the second page of the *Statesman* there appeared a daily column "Boise Visitors." I would have skipped over it, but the word "Taylor" caught my eye. The subheading read: "Glen Taylor of Pocatello, Democratic candidate for the U.S. Senate, has reserved one of Hotel Boise's eleventh floor penthouses for four or five days. The penthouse was formerly occupied by E.T. Fisher, Idaho Mining magnate." It was just an innocent coincidence, of course, that Mr. Fisher moved out so the trap would be vacant.

I wasn't too happy to see the item in print. It certainly wasn't in keeping with my image of the poor man's candidate, but I didn't take it too seriously. Just a routine job of reporting, I thought.

How mistaken I was. This seemingly unimportant squib turned out to be the fuse that lit a chain reaction. Practically every daily in Idaho editorialized about it. Here is a typical example from the *Idaho Pioneer*:

> A lot of things happen in politics. For instance, there is the candidate Mr. Taylor who makes me wonder if this running for office pays more than I am sure it doesn't.
>
> The gentleman now lives in a penthouse atop the Boise Hotel, and we wonder if he pays for it with the money collected for the songs and dances he attracted attention with during the campaign.
>
> Do you suppose the folks up Willow Creek that gave him these nickles and dimes expected him to rent many penthouses? It may be that someone else is furnishing the money,—and if so why? And what do they expect?
>
> Perhaps Mr. Taylor figures that if elected, he can represent Willow Creek money and Penthouse money at the same time. He has always said he is a common man but between you and me, very few common men live in penthouses.

This would never have occurred if I had been a machine "boy" of either party. My sponsors could have rented the whole top floor of the Hotel Boise for me and no one would have raised an eyebrow.

If I had the faintest inkling of how closely knit, powerful, and merciless the political organization that controlled both parties was, I might have smelled a rat and stayed in my goddamned car until I rotted. But I didn't. So I had authorized that damned reservation.

APPLAUSE My first opportunity to show my stuff and get acquainted with my new political bedfellows came when the Young Democrats invited me to address their convention in Grangeville, the county seat of Idaho County, where I was raised.

The *Idaho Daily Statesman* carried a fairly comprehensive account of my talk and, surprisingly, without any snide asides.

> The Young Democrats of Idaho in their fourth bi-ennial convention heard Glen Taylor of Pocatello accept his nomination as the Democratic candidate for United States Senator.
>
> "The New Deal has not cured the fundamental ills affecting our economy but it has saved us from revolution and Communism or Fascism," Mr. Taylor told the young people. The actor went on to say, "The promise of plenty for all in America is an ideal that can be fulfilled through courage and cooperation. If I can hold to the course I have charted and come out victorious it will be a great victory for the people over the forces of greed and private profit that are starving the American people in the midst of plenty.
>
> "Only one vital element is lacked by the nation," Taylor said, "and that is a plan to produce and distribute all the good things it is possible to produce.
>
> "I don't like the profit system because it is failing to provide the plenty that could and should be produced and distributed.
>
> "But instead of changing our system to fit our new conditions of plenty we are trying to change our conditions of plenty back to scarcity to fit our old profit system.
>
> "We can't balance the budget and we can't go on spending so I think it is time we thought about some new ways of doing things. President Roosevelt has held the bridgehead for eight years. He can possibly hold it for another four. If by that time we haven't found the answer to our troubles we will go the way of France." (Which had a Fascist dictatorship under Marshal Petain.)

There was no mention of how the talk was received so let us pursue an item from the *Nez Perce Herald*, a small weekly published in the town of Nez Perce, which is not far from Grangeville. It says in part:

> Following recent charges that Glen Taylor's program was a share-the-wealth scheme that bordered on Communism, the delegates were somewhat dubious about Mr. Tay-

lor, and insisted that he clarify his position.

When Taylor got underway he took the crowd by storm
and his disavowal of Communism was convincing. He con-
cluded in a burst of applause and left the impression that he
will make a vigôrous campaign.

The press continued editorializing about my lack of education
or any other serious qualifications but their main attack was on
the primary law which allowed such people as me even to get on
the ballot. It should be changed back to the convention where
"responsible people" (the machine?) could have the say as to
who should and who should not run for high office.

On August 29, the *Pocatello Tribune* took another backhanded
slap at me for insisting that Dora and Arod share the platform
with me at party-sponsored rallies. The caption is typical
Tribune—OH WELL! IT'S SOMETHING TO READ ANYWAY—and goes
on in similar manner:

> Glen Taylor, Democratic nominee for United States
> Senator, his wife and son with their traveling campaign
> outfit, which consists of a sedan with a stage mounted on
> the top and loudspeaker system attended a big Democratic
> rally at Caldwell. Taylor insisted his wife and son be intro-
> duced with himself, because "they are my campaign man-
> agers." They seem to have been quite efficient.

The reference to the "big" campaign rally is indicative of what
was going on. The pros were amazed at the size of the crowds I
was drawing at these precampaign parties. They were intended to
be pep sessions for party workers, but the general public was
crashing the gates in great numbers.

The machine employed a hack political writer who wrote supposedly objective articles that were distributed statewide. On
August 31, he wrote:

> Many Republicans feel that the victory of Glen Taylor,
> cowboy songster, and former actor, in the primaries made
> the world safe for Republicanism and Senator John
> Thomas. Such a viewpoint is highly dangerous and should
> be discouraged by the Republican high command.
>
> This warning is based upon the enthusiastic reaction of

the Young Democrats who have returned from the Grangeville convention of their club, praising the personality, platform manner and intelligent outlook of their candidate.

Many of them went there to scoff and remained to pray.

WOLVES   On the second day of September the Democratic state platform convention was held in Idaho Falls.

I had met the young leaders at the Grangeville convention. At Idaho Falls I met the movers and shakers, the bigwigs, the dispensers of corporation money, the schemers and plotters, the decent, dedicated Democrats, and the slimy sons of bitches. What an innocent young lamb I was among a pack of wolves!

Never dreaming that my downfall was being plotted, I smiled and chatted, shook hands, and did not spare myself in the arduous task of showering each and all with that mysterious, unfathomable thing called personality (more recently, charisma). I knew I had that inexplicable and all-important gift. Donart didn't have it. Bothwell didn't have it. That was the reason I was here now instead of one of them.

For this important occasion I wore a suit and a small red silk handkerchief tied like a necktie around my neck. The suit, five years old and the only one I had, wasn't exactly senatorialish. It was blue with a red thread woven in. The overall effect was sort of a dismal purple. I had on my high-heeled boots which I had purchased years ago in Texas. They were of Spanish design with exceedingly high heels that tapered down to a spiked point no larger than a silver dollar. They served two purposes: they were an important part of my "cowboy" trademark and they made me stand two and a half inches taller than my five feet ten, which kept my broad shoulders from making me look stocky. They gave me that "range" look.

The self-appointed managers had wanted me to enter with all the other candidates and sit there throughout the protracted business of electing a chairman and knocking out a platform.

When I objected to sitting on the platform until my butt was paralyzed, and assured the other candidates that this was not good show biz psychology, they were delighted and decided that none of them would sit on the stage. So each one of them enjoyed his own grand entrance. And they thought I was the Wizard of Oz. By God, we'd put a little show biz into these corny old political routines.

When I was given a flowery introduction and made my entrance from the wings, I wore my white Stetson. As I reached center stage, I removed it and bowed repeatedly to a standing ovation. I was a celebrity and, whether or not they like you and what you stand for, people just love celebrities.

Let's see what the newspapers had to say about our convention. D. L. Carter was chairman of Donart's home county delegation. It could be expected that these people who had solidly supported Mr. Donart might be something less than enthusiastic about this singing cowboy who had humbled their champion and, in turn, been publicly demeaned by him. Not so. In reporting to the Weiser paper, Mr. Carter says:

> The highlight of the convention was the address by Glen Taylor, the successful candidate for United States Senator. Taylor took the convention by storm. He had the audience in an uproar much of the time but he also got down to fine points on the campaign issues.
>
> A natural born, as well as a trained actor, he amused and held the audience spellbound throughout his address. The delegation predicts that he will receive a tremendous vote in the November election. Contrary to the usual opinion that he is a mere cowboy entertainer, they state that he is scholarly and able and instead of being a wild-eyed Socialist, he is a progressive, forward thinker, with both feet on the ground.

The way I am winning friends you might think I was backing away from my "Production for Use" platform. Not so. I did perceive this apprehension, however, so I began to assure my listeners that all I was advocating was an extension of the idea of cooperation similar to the cooperatives set up by the Farmers Union and the Grange.

This approach did not make retail merchants happy, for co-ops were a thorn in their sides. It did make it more difficult for my enemies to attack me and call me a socialist or communist without, indirectly at least, seeming to attack the co-ops, and co-ops were a power to be reckoned with. My new semantics did help to allay the apprehensions of most.

John Corlett, whom I always felt would have been a pretty decent guy if he had not received his paycheck from the *Statesman* for being their political hatchet man, had this to say about the convention:

> Senatorial Candidate Glen Taylor was at the convention. Frankly, he assumed a dignity over some of the leaders. He entered into no controversy and the leaders came to him. Though some of the leaders tried to soften him down, he still insists that he will go into the campaign this fall on his platform of a "cooperative society."

That is the first time my name and dignity have been associated. Pardon me while I take a bow.

In reporting on the convention to its readers, the *St. Anthony Chronicle* quoted me as saying: "There has been some doubt about whether or not I would line up with the party inasmuch as I failed to contact central committeemen and other 'big wigs' before the primary. Now let's be reasonable and practical. None of the county chairmen or committeemen had ever even heard of me. Calling on them would have been a complete waste of time. If I had spent my time trying to win them over I'd be there yet." (That got a laugh that turned into a hand, indicating that they recognized and admitted the truth of that statement.) The reporter goes on to quote me as saying, "I knew the votes were with the people so I went there and got them." (Another hand.)

> In closing he said, "I will support the National platform and what's more I have read it. How many of you can say the same?" That got a big laugh and Taylor left the platform to a standing ovation.

The keynote address at Idaho Falls was delivered by an attorney from Coeur d'Alene. Later, I learned that he was an up-and-coming underling of the machine.

In the *Idaho Falls Post-Register*, we find this significant paragraph:

The keynoter failed to mention Glen Taylor, of Pocatello, or any other candidate for State or National office other
than Mayor Chase Clark, the nominee for Governor, and
President Roosevelt.

I did not know it, but this slight had been planned. It was the
signal. The machinery had been put in motion. The hierarchy of
both parties had sent out the word that the bipartisan machine
would support Clark for governor and Thomas for senator. The
lesser offices were unimportant.

THE CLARK DYNASTY   This was my first encounter
with the Clark dynasty. D. Worth Clark, a nephew of Chase, had
started it by getting elected to Congress in 1934, posing as a
liberal young New Dealer.

In 1936 two Clarks were on the ballot. D. Worth was reelected
to Congress and his uncle Barzilla Clark, who was mayor of
Idaho Falls, was elected governor.

In 1938, D. Worth ran for the Senate against James Pope the
incumbent, who was too liberal and too incorruptible to suit the
machine.

This coldly efficient combination of corporate money and
brains plus professional politicians was now called "the Clark
machine."

In that 1938 campaign word went out that those minions of the
machine who generally worked within the Republican Party were
to cross over into the Democratic primary and vote for D. Worth
Clark against Pope. Pope had been considered practically certain
of reelection, but the devious tactics defeated him in the primary
and D. Worth Clark was elected senator.

However, C. Ben Ross, the old warhorse whose speaking
ability caused me to enter politics, defeated Barzilla in those
same 1938 primaries. The machine evened the score by defeating
Ross in the general election.

Now in 1940 Chase Clark, who was Barzilla's brother and D.
Worth's uncle, had succeeded Barzilla as mayor of Idaho Falls
and from this family springboard had become the Democratic
nominee for governor. If I had been familiar with all this, the
failure of the keynote speaker to mention my name would have
alerted me to the fact that I was being set up. If I had known that,

I would have done something unheard of, attacking Chase Clark and the machine in my speech to the convention.

I might—or might not—have pulled down the whole house. But at least I am confident I could have nailed Chase.

But I *didn't* know, and I proceeded trustingly on my way. The Clarks and their heirs played for keeps. You were either with them, on your knees, or you were out.

MONEY—PLEASE   According to long established custom the campaign would not start until the first of October. This fiddling while Rome burned was just downright hell. If I had been susceptible to ulcers, I'd have had a belly full of them. I wanted to get back on the road the day after the primary. But even I, with my penchant for disregarding custom and precedent, could not throw a custard pie in the face of the party. The only thing that kept me from going completely nuts was the fact that some county organizations just could not wait to show off their "Singing Cowboy" who had made such a hit at the convention. We were invited to be the featured attraction at a dozen or more "preview" rallies. There were many good honest people associated with the Democratic Party. The machine made no effort to control them. All the machine wanted was a majority.

It was now September 25. Some forty odd days since the primary. Not a penny coming in. On the strength of my newly-come-by fame, we had run up sizeable bills at the grocer's and the gas station. Although the campaign had not officially opened, we had also traveled five hundred miles to north Idaho and five hundred back to attend and help spark county organizational meetings, where we met local party officials, county chairmen, and precinct committeemen.

God knows this was my weak point. I had not met a handful of these people in the primaries and only a relative few at the Young Democratic Convention in Grangeville and the state convention in Idaho Falls.

I did as well as the next fellow might have in meeting these party workers in small groups but I did not like it.

My long suit was addressing the multitude. Dora did great at pink teas and of course Arod would sing the ladies a song and always stole the show.

We had made three or four trips to Boise to help plan routes and itineraries for the campaign and approve my page in a campaign brochure that state headquarters was getting out.

Even with running up bills, we had now come to the end of our rope. Our creditors were getting fidgety and pressing us.

We were desperate. In a drowning effort to stay afloat I placed an ad in the Pocatello paper. It was a small ad but it almost cleaned us out.

It was simply the one-column picture of the three of us with this copy.

> We need some campaign funds. Must be no strings attached. Anything over one dollar I'll repay double if I win. If I lose—nothing.
> Will be home Wednesday September 25th only.
>
> Your friend, Glen
> 129 So. 10 St. or phone 1248-J

Believe it or not, all we got out of that forlorn appeal was about a hundred dollars, all in one-dollar and five-dollar contributions, except for one twenty-dollar bill. All of the givers said "forget it" about the double-or-nothing deal: "This is a contribution." All of them said that, except the twenty-dollar friend. Years later he wrote me, reminding me of the "twenty," explaining that he had considered it a straight loan without the double-or-nothing gimmick, and he could use the twenty. I sent it to him.

I imagined at the time, and still do, that the "penthouse" flap accounted for the lack of response. When the press is solidly against you, they can make a *cause célèbre* out of most anything.

We took nearly all of the hundred and split it between the grocer and the gas station and temporarily stalled them off.

It was getting close to October 1 so we loaded up with peaches and cookies and headed for Boise and the start of the campaign. Before we left Pocatello and drove off to war in our battered old car, the Bannock County Central Committee raised one hundred dollars and presented it to us. At least we would have enough for gas to Boise.

When I arrived there I looked up Bob Coulter, the state chairman, and asked him about some money for campaigning. He said, "Oh no Glen, the state headquarters is only supposed to help state candidates. The senatorial campaign committee in Washington is supposed to help you." I asked him for the address, and he wrote it on a piece of paper. (I never received any answer to the letter I wrote because of what Coulter had said to Hannegan.) When I pointed out to Coulter that I was broke and couldn't even start out with my group, he grudgingly gave me two hundred dollars. That was it, aside from a few modest contributions we picked up along the campaign trail.

The itinerary worked out called for the big opening rally to be held in Nampa. Chase Clark and I would both be there, as well as all the other candidates.

As was customary, Chase and I were scheduled to hold six joint meetings in major cities during the campaign. Again, according to custom the candidates would be divided into two groups. One led by Chase Clark, the other by me. I was unfamiliar with the candidates, and did not realize that they gave me those for whom the machine had no great love, and Chase Clark got the old reliables.

Meanwhile, the press was making a big deal out of my ad asking for campaign contributions. A dispatch out of Boise commented under the heading, TAYLOR VIOLATES LAW IN APPEALS FOR $1 DONATIONS.

The article read:

> One of the weird things about the Idaho election laws, especially the Corrupt Practices Act, so called, is illustrated by the dilemma of Glen Taylor, Democratic candidate for United States Senator, who advertised for $1 contributions to his campaign fund with the promise that if elected he would return them with 100% interest but if he lost the donor got nothing.
>
> Now the advertisement was inserted in all good faith, and undoubtedly Taylor would have made good on his promises, especially the second. But unwittingly he violated the Corrupt Practices Act which forbids a candidate to offer any consideration of value for support of his election.
>
> The Taylor offer was small potatoes beside some of the offers of his colleagues on the ticket but because of its unusual form it has drawn wide publicity.
>
> The Republican high command probably will take but little notice of his unique campaign stunt—the latest infor-

mation was that the chieftains don't take the Taylor candidacy seriously enough to bother with this particular angle.

This ad was reprinted widely. Perhaps it stimulated the flow,
or trickle, of campaign contributions. If it did, I can only wonder
how minuscule that trickle would have been without it.

NOT MARRIED?   The day before we were to open the
campaign, Bob Coulter sent word for me to come to headquarters.

After we had exchanged pleasantries, he came around the desk
and put his arm around my shoulders. He could do that because I
was sitting down, whereas I had been standing when he was
buttering me up at the convention.

"Glen," he said in his gentle voice, "I've got some bad news
for you."

"What?" I asked bluntly. If there was any news worse than the
penthouse flap or the stupid ad for money it must really be rotten.
"Glen, " Coulter repeated, "you've got to resign from the senatorial race."

My reaction to his statement was a hodge-podge. Had I heard
right? My hackles rose. "What do you mean, resign from the
race?" I demanded.

"Glen," our state chairman repeated (boy, he sure liked to call
me Glen). "You have been married before, haven't you Glen?"
What the hell was he getting at?

"Yes," I admitted angrily. "What of it?"

"Glen," he said again, "I'm sure you did not know it and that
you were innocent of any intentional wrong, but when you married Dora your divorce decree was not yet final. In the eyes of the
law you are a bigamist."

I had read in the theatrical trade paper the *Billboard* that my
first wife had been granted a divorce. It didn't say anything about
final decrees or anything else. I had assumed I was a free man
and married Dora. As recounted earlier, I had been married for a
brief period, but we were not suited to each other and I could see
no use in even mentioning the matter. Now I was momentarily
struck dumb. Coulter took advantage of the brief silence to say,
and this time he didn't call me Glen, "You realize, of course,

what this means. You will have to resign from the ticket."

"The hell I will." I had my voice back now, and I fairly bellowed my profane refusal.

Coulter backed away as though he was afraid I might hit him, and if that was what he was thinking he was not too goddamn far wrong. I was on my feet. I had had enough *banderillas* stuck in my withers the last few days, and I was beginning to see red. "I haven't done anything wrong intentionally or knowingly," I gritted out, "and if anyone wants to arrest me for an unintentional mistake I made ten years ago I'll be glad to face any jury anywhere in this goddamn state and I don't think you'd find a jury in the state that would convict me. It's as plain as the nose on your face that you guys have been looking for something, for some way, to get rid of me. This is a cheap john shitty trick if I ever heard of one. Hell no, I won't quit." During my outburst I had backed Coulter clear around the office, and now we were back where we started from. All the while he had been motioning with his hands outspread trying to soothe and quiet me.

I am sure he had expected me to tuck my tail and run. My vehement explosion had come as a surprise to him, but he was not known as "Foxy Bob" for nothing. He was not about to give up. His next words were a calculated blow below the belt. Still using his unctuous, oily voice, he said, "But Glen, think of your wife and son. Think of the scandal. You're not legally married."

"Then, by God, we'll get married again!" I shouted, with my face close to his.

"But Glen," he argued, "don't you think you had better talk to Dora? See what she says?"

"I know what she'll say. She'll say the same as I. To hell with 'em!" And with that I stormed out and slammed the door so hard the girls in the outer office got the lead in their fannies a foot off their chairs.

I went over to the capitol building across the street to see Bert Miller, the attorney general. He is the one who had been nominated to Congress in that nine-man race in '38. He had not made it in the general election, but he had retained his job as attorney general. Now he was the Democratic candidate for reelection to that post.

I had met him several times, and he appeared to be a nice

fellow. Always friendly, polite, and courteous. Later, I was to learn that he was "in" with the machine but only in a nominal sort of way. I was immediately ushered into his office.

He heard me out and said with no hesitation, "Well Glen you can't stop the word getting around, but as far as any legal action against you the statute of limitations has run out so you need not worry on that score."

"Well what about this business of Dora and me not being legally married?" I asked.

"Your marriage may not have been legal at the time, but after all these years of living together you'll be considered legally married all right. If you don't think so just try any fancy stuff like moving out on Dora, for example, and you'll damn soon find out whether you are legally married or not."

I thanked him and, believe me, it was from the bottom of my heart.

Bert was a professional politician, to be sure. He had made a career of it. It was his livelihood, and in his defense there is that old saw, "Well if I don't work for these boys, someone else who might be considerably worse would."

I told him I was going back to have it out with Coulter, but I guess my general attitude warned him that this might not be a wise thing to let happen so he said that perhaps it would be better for him to talk to Coulter—as my lawyer, so to speak. I agreed, and that is the last I heard of the whole shiteree.

Those louses (I didn't know who they were exactly, although I had pegged Coulter) had gone over my life with a fine tooth comb to find that out, goddamn them, and what kind of yellow-livered bastard had Coulter thought I was to imagine I would just bow out?

The machine tentatively tried spreading the story but Dora, Arod, and I had built up such an image as a talented and devoted family that they found out the very idea of such a crummy story being bruited about got people's dander up, so they abandoned the slimy tactic as a bad deal.

However, this was not the end of it. When I returned to Pocatello, a Republican lawyer who considered himself to be a big wheel in the machine phoned me and unctuously said he had a matter of importance to discuss with me. My recent encounter with Coulter gave me a pretty good clue about this "matter of importance." I took Dora with me to the lawyer's office. When I was seated opposite him the old slicker got right down to business.

He said he was representing my former wife, and that she wanted $9,997.

I told him that I felt I owed her nothing, and that he knew I had no such sum of money. In his oiliest style, with his hands clasped over his paunch, he said, "Well, Mr. Taylor, a man in *your* position can always *raise* money."

I told him that I understood his insinuation. I could go out and sell a controlling interest in myself to his well-heeled political pals. "But you might as well forget that," I told him, "because I have no intention of doing it."

His eyes narrowed and his voice became somewhat acid. "If you don't, we'll spread this all over the papers, and you know what that will do to your chances of being elected."

If we had been someplace other than in his office, I would have flattened him. Regardless, I was hard put to hold myself in check. Without answering I got up, took Dora's arm, and steered her to the door. As I reached for the knob and we started out he shot after me, "Better think it over."

I turned and shot back, "Go to hell!"

For several days Dora and I lived in an agony of uncertainty. Every time we looked at a newspaper or turned on the radio or even when the phone rang, we would die a little. But it never happened.

They had tried to blackmail me out of the race, and when that did not work they had tried to buy me out, but they had picked the wrong boy. I did not scare worth a hoot. What would the bastards try next?

NO THOUSAND DOLLARS   The largest crowd ever to attend a political rally in the history of the state jammed the auditorium in Nampa. It was the first official rally of the campaign. Here is an account of it, as reported in the *Nampa Free Press:* 1200 ATTEND RALLY THAT OPENS STATE CAMPAIGN was the thrilling heading. The subheading in the same type was TAYLOR'S SALLIES DRAW LAUGHS.

The entire sixteen-inch, one-column story was about Glen Taylor and poor Chase Clark wasn't even mentioned. Here is the story:

>   Glen Taylor was the hit of the evening, bringing Mrs. Taylor and their handsome little son on the platform with him, the latter to sing.
>
>   Speaking with Will Rogerish humor Taylor brought repeated laughs and chuckles and at times brought down the house. The candidate took a few witty cracks at a front page story in last night's *Boise Capitol News* which said, he might be prosecuted for placing an advertisement in a Pocatello paper asking for campaign contributions which were to be refunded double if he won, nothing if he lost.
>
>   In answer to that threat Taylor quipped, "They say, I may be fined $1,000 and sent to jail for five years," he drawled, eyes twinkling. "Well, those rich Republicans may send me to jail but that won't do them any good because Dora and Arod would carry on my campaign just as good, or maybe better without me.
>
>   "But, I'll guarantee you one thing, they'll never get a thousand dollars out of me." This reference to his strapped financial condition got a big laugh and applause. Taylor continued, "I could get plenty of campaign money if I'd just forget some of the things I said in the primary and here tonight, but I'm not going to do it even if I have to hitch hike around the state."
>
>   Mr. Taylor said, he'd been warned he would be unhappy among the stuffed shirts in the Senate. "I don't think so," said Taylor, "I'll be too busy. They've got a lot of smart men back there but they've just gotten in the habit of doing nothing. I'd just love to take a stick and stir 'em up. I may not be smart, as the Republicans say, but I can always let you folks do my thinking for me. Just let me know what you want done and I'll do it," the Candidate promised.
>
>   Taylor then held up a full-page advertisement for Wendell Willkie on the back page of the same paper he had read from earlier, and jibed, "Look at this. Just look at that, a full page ad for Wendell Willkie. Those Republicans have sure got plenty of money, haven't they? A full page ad and all there is on it is just this little bit right here in the middle. Just five words. Yes sir, that's all, just five words. It says

'WENDELL WILLKIE' and under that it says 'BORN TO WORK.'

"And Mr. Willkie is a hard worker all right. He works for big corporations and he works long hours, trying to find new loopholes in the tax laws so his bosses can pay less taxes and we can pay more.

"You know, this ad isn't quite honest. There should be two more words here. Instead of reading 'Wendell Willkie Born to Work' it should read, 'Wendell Willkie, Born to Work—the people.' " This got a big laugh, but Taylor wasn't finished with the Willkie ad. He went on to say, "Look at this. Just look at it. A whole page and just five words. Look at all that blank space. Just think how much all that cost," Taylor said and shook his head sadly. "Those poor rich Republicans. I guess they bought this full page and then couldn't think of anything good to say about what they had done, or about Mr. Willkie, so they just had to leave the whole thing blank."

An encouraging report from the *Statesman,* on this Nampa meeting, says:

> Senatorial candidate Glen Taylor redeemed himself last night in the eyes of Democratic leaders in his Nampa speech. He had slipped considerably between the Grangeville speech in August and the Nampa talk.
>
> He was applauded, not for his handling of national issues and any explanation of his own platform, but for his deft handling of an embarrassing situation arising from his advertisement for campaign funds in a Pocatello paper.
>
> Several Democratic leaders, who had decided that Taylor was hardly the man to bear the Democratic senatorial banner, were converted or "reconverted" to his cause.
>
> Taylor probably is the most effective speaker of all the Democratic candidates, primarily because of his knack of showmanship and his apparently "unconscious" use of humor. Issues are not his forte. In fact, one would say, he is not in the least concerned with them.
>
> As far as is known to this writer, he has never spoken on the important national issues of the day—national defense, conscription, tariffs, reclamation, etc.
>
> But he has a flow of "Down on the Range" speech that is

remarkable. He never falters.

He has the voice and inflections and mannerisms of the actor that he is.

His wife, Dora and his son Arod, travel with him wherever he goes. Each of his talks is preceded by a song or two by five-year old Arod.

The song that bowls the audience over is Arod's rendition of a song in Chinese, sung to the tune of "It Ain't Gonna Rain No More."

This chap, while fairer than most, is as muddled as the others when he says I do not "discuss the issues." To me there was only one tissue, and that was how to end the absurd situation of artificial scarcity in the midst of plenty. Solve that problem, and all the other issues would cease to have any meaning.

BRONC BUSTER   The campaign was now under way, and the two groups of supplicants took off and went their separate ways to beat the brush.

A few days later we received word that there would be no more joint meetings like Nampa, where Chase and I and all the other candidates had shared the same platform. The explanation was that, inasmuch as I had been an unknown quantity, it had been thought that the joint meetings would be advisable so Chase could help carry me along if necessary. Now, however, I had proven that I was able to carry my share of the load without the help of Mr. Clark. Under these changed circumstances, State Headquarters felt it would be a wasteful duplication of effort and a waste of talent to hold joint meetings. We could cover more ground, hold more meetings, and get to more voters if we held no more joint meetings. This sounded reasonable so I made no objection.

Later (after the election), I heard that Chase had a fit in Nampa, because I stole the show, and refused to participate in joint meetings. Now, while Chase doubtless did throw a wing-ding, in retrospect, I am sure the machine wanted us kept apart so they could build up Clark's meetings and let me wither.

I had planned to go my own way during daylight hours, holding street meetings and passing the hat, but my group insisted that they wouldn't think of letting me go off all alone that way. It would look like there was dissension in our ranks.

What could I do? There was no way I could gracefully say "No," so I was forced to share my meetings, which I advertised out of pocket. It is a well known fact that there is nothing on earth more difficult than trying to get a politician to stop talking when he has a good crowd and that old postulate held true here.

My remarks were reduced from twenty minutes to five and sometimes less.

We had a schedule, and we couldn't overrun or the whole thing would come unglued. No matter how firmly I admonished my sidekicks to make it short, they couldn't resist the temptation to get in just one more point. They would always apologize for running over, but that didn't help me a bit. I had to take my time to be effective, and now I couldn't. The worst of it was that with these others sharing the platform, I could not pass the hat. The only financial help I got from my little helpers was an occasional tank of gas.

I had to use practically all the two hundred dollars I got from Coulter to appease creditors who were hounding me. To make matters worse, we were bound to a schedule that did not take us home every ten days so we could load up with peaches and cookies.

It had been tough in the primary. Now the situation was desperate. It was also embarrassing because my more affluent team members would, at day's end, put up at the best hotel, while I lied and said that we were staying with friends, and we would sneak out of town to find a billboard or some other concealment where we could park our car to spend the night without advertising our paupery. Cornflakes, cheese, and crackers replaced cookies and peaches.

On the subject of my finances, an article in the *Twin Falls Times* had this to say: "Taylor is absolutely candid in asserting he needs campaign funds. 'We'll get our funds from passing the hat, unless we find some rich angel' he stated."

About that "rich angel" quote. Shortly after I started campaigning in 1938 and began to realize how important money was in politics, I kept thinking, surely, one of these days someone with money who agreed with my philosophy would hear me talk and he would come up to me and say, "Taylor, I agree with what you say 100 percent. If I could talk like you can, I'd have been out here long ago saying just what you are saying. I can't talk, though, so I'm going to finance you; not just for this campaign, I'll finance a political career for you, and maybe one of these days you'll be President and you can make this dream of 'plenty for everybody' come true!" That pipe dream helped me to keep my courage up and go on fighting against odds that might have overwhelmed me without the well known "hope that springs eternal." That mirage never materialized.

The reporter continues his coverage by saying, "Taylor has worked as actor, singer, orchestra leader and rodeo performer."

Where he got that "rodeo performer" thing, I do not know. I was never a rodeo performer. I never rode a bucking horse in my life.

But from the beginning, when I first started getting into print as the "Singing Cowboy," I received letters from hither and yon, from people I never heard of, recalling the good old days when we followed the rodeo circuit together. Thrilling descriptions of how I rold old "Midnight" at the Calgary Stampede, etc., etc.

I have won, according to my new old friends, practically every imaginable type of rodeo event from Pendleton, to Calgary, to Cheyenne, to Madison Square Garden, and I've got witnesses to prove it.

I never objected, though. Those old rodeo riders vote, you know, and nobody is going to vote against you because you were a champion bronc rider.

On October 6, the *Twin Falls News* boldly proclaimed the strategy of the bipartisan machine that ran the state's politics with this headline: TWO CANDIDATES CENTER DRIVES. A subheading named the two lucky people: REPUBLICANS FOCUS ON SENATOR THOMAS, DEMOCRATS ON CHASE CLARK. The machine was throwing Republican gubernatorial nominee Bottolfsen to the wolves, supporting Chase Clark, giving me the old "heave-ho," and closing ranks behind John Thomas.

"COME ON, FRANKLIN!"   On October 12, at a big rally in Pocatello, I used a new finish to my talk that began to call for encores, something new in politics. No one had ever heard of anything like this happening before. My carefully thought out new climax went like this:

"Some people have been asking whether or not I was a supporter of Franklin Roosevelt. I haven't made a big deal out of proclaiming my loyalty to our great President because I knew I was for him and I just assumed that everybody would take it for granted that a man running for the U.S. Senate on the Democratic ticket would naturally be for the standard bearer of his party and I didn't want you folks to think I was a coattail grabber. I am sort of an independent cuss and I like to stand on my own two feet. Of course, I am for Roosevelt. Yes *sir*—I'm for Roosevelt. My father was the first Idahoan ever to vote for Roosevelt. That's right. He was a delegate from Idaho to the 1920 Democratic Convention in San Francisco. I doubt if many of you remember, but at that convention, Franklin D. Roosevelt was nominated for vice president. That's right. And when it came time for Idaho to cast its vote, it was my father, P. J. Taylor, who stood up and shouted, 'Idaho casts four votes for Franklin D. Roosevelt.' "

And maybe you think I didn't give that all the lungpower I had. I used that old favorite gesture too, and wound up with my forefinger pointed skyward as far as I could put 'er. It was always good for a big hand.

And then, after things had quieted down, I'd say very quietly but with as much scorn as I could put in my voice and fighting to keep back the tears, "And then they have the nerve to ask, if I'm for Roosevelt?—Why—Taylors were voting for Roosevelt when most of these ya-hoos were still wearing three-cornered pants.

"I'll guarantee you one thing, though. If you send me to the United States Senate, you won't find me throwing stumbling blocks in the President's way and pulling back on his coattails, like some of those corporation boys who are questioning my party credentials and loyalty to Roosevelt.

"No sir—you won't find me hanging back. I'll be out ahead breaking new sod for new ideas.

"I'll be out there with the front skirmish line and I'll be yelling, 'Come o—n Fer—anklin.' " I'd draw out the "Come o—n Fer" and then bite off the "anklin." As I was saying it, I'd crouch down like I was jugging a Fourth of July footrace with my arm extended thumb up toward the oncoming runners. I'd wave the winner through with an elaborate flourish and follow my thumb right on around until my back was toward the audience and I'd never stop. I'd just keep right on going upstage and make my exit without ever looking back.

Hell. They didn't applaud. They tore the joint down. They came to their feet, not a few at a time as sometimes happens—they all came up at once and with a roar, as though the seats were wired and the juice had just been turned on. Hyperbole? Here is a paragraph from a story appearing in the *Statesman:*

> Glen Taylor is probably the only candidate in the history of Idaho who has to take curtain calls when he has finished an address. Out at Franklin School, the other night, Glen finished his address and left the stage, but his listeners were so enthusiastic that he had to come back to the speaker's platform and continue.

Can you imagine a greater tribute than that? But it was happening. Being able to sway an audience and arouse such empathy is a soul-satisfying and infinitely gratifying experience. The account of our Lewiston meeting on October 30 carried this heading: TAYLOR THRILLS RALLY AUDIENCE. CROWD DECLINES TO LET SENATE CANDIDATE QUIT AND YELLS FOR MORE.

The account of my meeting reads:

> When he had talked for an hour and thirty-five minutes, the crowd declined to permit him to stop. Applause, cheers, whoops, and hurrahs greeted his attempted conclusion. Yells came for more and Taylor complied. He donned his cowboy hat and went back for another half-hour of his suave humanitarian chat, concluded with a vocal trio, including his wife Dora, son, Arod, and himself. The audience was still reluctant to let him quit.

Lest you get the false impression that, to be able to arouse an audience so, I must be a "hellfire and brimstone" orator or a screaming, gesticulating rabble-rouser like Hitler or Mussolini, let's read another sentence or two from the Lewiston coverage.

> Throughout his entire address, Taylor couched his terms in words that appealed to the common people. He seldom

raised his voice to oratorial heights, made few gestures and spoke throughout in a mellowed conversational tone.

SANTA   Here is the type of press release that can really get printed, get talked about, and, I believe, get votes, particularly among the women. The following episode actually happened. I recognized it as a good story and had Dora type it up and mail it statewide as a press release.

An interesting phenomenon is the fact that a newspaper that will lie about you and say practically anything they can think of that is bad about you will turn right around and print a human interest story like the following, which will undo much of the damage their editorial policy may have done you. In the *Pocatello Tribune,* the heading on the one-column, five-inch article reads: TAYLOR'S SON WANTS SANTA CLAUS' AID IN ELECTING FATHER. (The *Nampa Free Press* carried this heading on the same article.) LITTLE AROD. GOES AFTER SANTA CLAUS VOTE FOR HIS DAD. All right, let's read the story.

> "Cowboy" Glen Taylor, the booted, big hatted, Democratic candidate for United States Senator may have talked himself into a trip to the North Pole.
>
> Taylor told today, how his five year old son, Arod, termed by his father "America's youngest campaign manager," had inquired whether or not Santa Claus would be able to find him in Washington, should the campaign be successful.
>
> Assured Santa would have no difficulty, young Arod then asked whether Santa and his helpers could vote. His father unwittingly answered "Yes." Now, Arod has decided that the Taylor family had better take off immediately for the North Pole in their sound equipped campaign car so he can sing a few songs for Santa and sew up the old gent's vote before someone else beats them to it.

SKELETON OF A LADY   Things were going well. Everything looked rosy. Then on October 24 a letter was mailed out to merchants statewide. It was signed by twenty of the Boise Valley's most prominent businessmen. They were largely Republican movers and shakers in the machine, but the merchants and business people of the state would not know that. The letter's heading identifies the correspondent as the "Idaho Businessmen's Committee," and it says:

> Glen Taylor has a scheme to wipe out all private business. He does not believe in the profit system. His philosophy of government is based on a book by King C. Gillette, entitled "The People's Corporation."
>
> In order that you may be informed, more in detail, as to King C. Gillette's "solution," we enclose excerpts from his book.

Oh, ho! So *that's* where my book went. Until now, I thought I had laid it on the fender of the car when I had finished my talk at Nampa and just left it there and lost it. But that wasn't the fact. These fine-feathered prime examples of profit system morality had deliberately sent someone out to steal the book. That had to be it because I tried for years to get another copy and offered any price, but to no avail, so where could *they* have gotten one?

So let's see what further my thieving friends have to say. The letter had this enclosure:

EXCERPTS FROM KING C. GILLETTE'S BOOK
The People's Corporation
Glen Taylor says this is the book upon which he bases his program.

P. 219, *Constitution, the People's Corporation*

> The People's Corporation shall have plenary power . . .
>
> All property and wealth of the world . . . shall belong collectively to the people thereof; and no individual or association of individuals, as such, shall own or possess in his, her or their individual right, exclusive title to anything of value, other than moveable personal effects and credits of labor units with the corporation.
>
> The control of all property, industry and production, shall be vested in the People's Corporation.

Pp. 188–189

> Under a corporate system there will be very few cities and no towns other than pleasure resorts; no shops or stores where food products are sold to individuals. . . . The whole system of retail and wholesale stores, brokers, agents and traveling men will pass away.

Pp. 189–190

> There will be no country towns, no individual farms, no fenced-in fields; there will be one vast sweep of land, divided into large tracts for production, and labor will be moved in organized bodies from one field of production to another.
>
> The people's corporation will of course take possession of land, which is the source of all raw material. Farms, forests, mines and oil wells will belong to the people and be exploited for their benefit. Under such conditions, "This is mine" will pass from man's vocabulary, and personal ownership will be so limited that everyone can almost carry his possessions in his automobile.

The legal-sized mimeographed page of quotes was dynamite. Whatever one may say of King C. Gillette, one thing is certain. He was not devious. He obviously knew nothing of semantics and presented his ideas in, shall we say, an indelicate manner. Whereas Gillette had envisaged a planned economy where want, hunger, and worry over economic matters would be banished from the human experience, these stark, unlimned passages presented one after the other in cold print made Gillette's dream of Utopia appear a harsh blueprint for totalitarian regimentation.

It was like looking at a skeleton that had been a beautiful woman when clothed in flesh. It was devastating.

This piece of literature, the preparation and mailing of which had cost many times the total I had spent on my entire campaign, dealt me a blow in the solar plexus. The optimism I had felt the day before left me—but I didn't give up. I worked harder.

SINKING SHIP   Since the "businessmen's letter," three of the candidates who had been traveling with me had left. They had all offered plausible excuses for leaving: "somebody at home was sick," "pressing personal business," etc., etc. But a news article said they were campaigning in Shoshone County. It struck me in the face. My former group members had lied. There was no sickness in the family—no business that needed attending to. They had simply been deserting a sinking ship!

As election time drew close, it became more and more obvious that my situation was desperate to the point of being hopeless.

I would have given anything if I could have placed a copy of Gillette's book in the hands of every Idaho voter, but taken in bits and pieces this way and connected with the charge of communism, it was deadly.

Election night, there were celebrations up and down the width and breadth of Idaho. Celebrations because Roosevelt had carried the state by 21,000 votes. Uneasy celebrations because Chase Clark had squeezed through by something more than 2,000 votes. Lesser celebrations because every Democratic candidate for state office had been elected. The biggest celebrations in the swankest surroundings by the state's most important people were not because anyone had posted a great victory, but because a hated and feared enemy of the status quo had gone down to an ignominious defeat.

THE CLARK MACHINE   The machine, now openly called "the Clark machine," had defeated the "Singing Cowboy." While Roosevelt was winning by 21,000 votes and all the Democrats on the state ticket were being elected, I had lost by 13,000 votes. That would take care of Glen Taylor for all time. In politics, you just don't come back from such a shameful public whipping as that.

After the election, I heard numerous stories of vote stealing. Some were firsthand accounts. It was simple to do. Idaho used paper ballots. There was no recount provision in the election laws at all. Where the machine controlled the appointing of election judges, it was just too bad. They would appoint wives of machine underlings. One old pro to run the show and three figureheads who were told to "just let Mrs. Jones take care of things." Mrs.

Jones might send the others out for coffee, write down some fictitious totals, lock the box, and that was it.

I was told how I would get 200 votes and Thomas 75 and the judge who was writing the totals would reverse them. No danger of repercussions there. Everyone makes mistakes.

Through the years I have had people who were known as honest, upright citizens brag to me about how they stole votes one way or another. They seemed to look upon it as a game, the object of which is to see who is the slickest cheater. Whoever said "All is fair in love and war" should certainly have included politics.

Stolen votes or not, practically everyone agreed that if I had been willing to forsake or even soft-pedal my advocacy of Gillette's theories, I would have beaten John Thomas easily, and would have become a United States senator, enjoying the emoluments, privileges, and honors that went with the high office. I knew they were right and it caused me to wonder about the validity of my blind faith that if I but followed my conscience, or whatever it was, I could not fail. That faith had caused me to follow my suicidal course and I *had* failed. But had I? Did one failure (two, counting my primary defeat in 1938) mean that I was washed up—completely and forever? I refused to accept that weak-kneed premise. I still had faith. There would be other elections.

I could only surmise what thoughts were in Dora's mind. What *must* she think of a husband who had had a golden opportunity to achieve fame and fortune, provide security for his family, and end her life of drudgery, only to spurn it all in dogged pursuit of an ideal for which the people were not prepared?

We rounded up our gang and resumed the old show and free dance routine.

On October 9, 1941, my concern over the menace of Hitler prompted me to send the following wire to President Roosevelt.

> Dear Mr. President: In my campaign for the United States Senate at the last election I told the voters of Idaho that if elected I would never consent to our participation in a foreign war.
>
> I have become convinced that we must destroy Hitler, or he will destroy us.

If we must fight, better to fight abroad than to subject our women and children to the horrors of a war at home. As a private citizen with no campaign pledges to keep, I want to add my name to the list of loyal and patriotic Americans who believe we should fight now while we have help, to preserve our country, our democracy and our freedom.

Later, this unequivocal statement, some eight weeks before Pearl Harbor, put me on record when the question was being argued as to who foresaw the inevitability of war with Hitler as opposed to those who clung to the forlorn hope that Hitler could be appeased and another, fascist-minded group who contended to the last that Nazism was "the wave of the future."

On December 7, 1941, we were right in the middle of the show when the hall manager came backstage and told me that the Japanese had attacked Pearl Harbor. I stopped the show and told the audience the news and we refunded their money.

Shortly, two of our band members received their draft notices, so we closed the show.

Older men who had families were urged to seek employment in defense plants, so that's what I did. There were no defense plants in Idaho so we went to San Francisco, where I got a job as a sheet-metal worker in a plant fabricating components for liberty ships.

AGAIN?   The senatorial election of 1940 had been for the rest of the term of which John Thomas had been appointed. In 1942 he was up for reelection to a full term. I planned to run against him, so we returned to Idaho.

Before leaving California, we had addressed some two thousand postcards to people we had met during previous campaigns. As soon as we got to Pocatello and our old mimeo machine, Dora cut a stencil and I ran off this message on the cards:

Dear Friend,—My only stenographer is busy tending our new son, born January 26th (MacArthur's birthday) so I started to write all my friends in long hand. After one county, I decided that Hitler and Hirohito would be gone and forgotten before I finished. Besides, this postcard saves money which appeals to the Scotch in me. During the last campaign, a clique of our richest, home grown, economic royalists spent more money shipping out bales of propaganda calling me communistic than I could afford for my entire campaign, because I said we should plan our production and that $100,000 a year was enough for any man. Now the President wants a $25,000 limit on incomes and they have more plans back there, than I ever dreamed of. So if you don't think I am too conservative I'd appreciate your support and a word of encouragement.

Your friend,
Glen H. Taylor For U.S. Senate

That's quite a lot to get on a postcard and still keep it chatty, informal, and not like a telegram. I am also proud of the semantics I used to try and overcome the communistic label they hung on me in '40.

I wrote copy for a one-page letter to be mimeographed and mailed to every labor union in the state, and left it for Dora to take care of after I had begun my campaign.

HAYBURNER   It was June 20, 1942. The primary was August 11. This would be my shortest campaign ever. We had decided that it would just be too much to subject our second-born son to the rigors of a campaign, so Dora was going to stay in Pocatello. As long as she was not going along, I couldn't very well take Arod, so I was alone. One thing for sure, this time they couldn't accuse me of exploiting my family.

I had to figure some angle that was effective and cheap. I did. I left Dora three hundred of our five-hundred-dollar bankroll, and I took two hundred. I bought a bus ticket to Coeur d'Alene, which is in the northern panhandle of the state. To get there, I traveled through Pendleton, Oregon, to Spokane, Washington, and then back into Idaho. All I had with me was my toothbrush and razor, a change of socks and shorts, plus the same cowboy clothes I had worn in previous campaigns. But something new had been added.

I arrived in Coeur d'Alene on July 2. I had a good core of supporters among the workers in this sawmill town, and they pitched in to help me put my bizarre plan into action.

The first order of business was to find a horse. That's right, a saddle horse. Very shortly, one had been located. He belonged to a well-to-do businessman who had gotten so busy making money out of the war preparations that he no longer had time to ride, so his saddle horse was for sale. He was asking one hundred fifty dollars. That was a real bargain, the reason being that although the owner no longer had time to ride, the feed bill was continuing unabated. The one-hundred-fifty-dollar price was without saddle or bridle, which I needed. I haggled until I got the horse, saddle, bridle, and saddlebags for one hundred sixty dollars, which was every cent I had.

Even though this purchase left me dead broke, I sure loved that horse. Everybody remarked on what a handsome animal I had, and handsome he was, indeed. I have never seen a more beautiful horse. And he had a glamorous name to match: Ranger!

He was a blue-rinse dapple-gray Arabian, with a long, flowing, nearly white mane, and a tail the same color which came within inches of touching the ground. God, what a beautiful animal! He was the proudest piece of horseflesh that ever carried a proud man. He held his head so high that I was perpetually looking right between his ears, which were always erect and pointed forward.

This sounds too good to be true, but it *was* true. Considering all this, I dislike having to tell you that, despite all I have said, this beautiful creature was not perfect. He had one fault. A very serious fault. Hell, what a fault! He was the hardest riding mount I had ever had the misfortune to straddle. He raised his front feet so high and set them down so firmly that my teeth rattled wtih each step.

This parade ground deportment was very impressive and thrilling to watch, but jee-sus! Forget the rattling teeth, if you will, but just imagine what would happen to my *derrière* in the long run. And this was to be a long run. That's what I had in mind. I would ride Ranger as far and as long as the thirty-five days until primary election day permitted.

Before leaving Pocatello, I had mailed a statement to the press announcing my candidacy and gotten my mileage out of it. Then I had called the AP and UP in Spokane and announced that because tires and gasoline were rationed I thought it would be something less than patriotic to ask for special rations of gas for campaign purposes. So, in order to conserve the scarce rubber and gasoline needed in the war effort, I had put on my thinking cap and come up with a happy solution to the problem that would enable me to travel the highways and byways and personally contact the voters, as had been my custom in the past, but without impinging on the war effort. "I am going to use a time-honored means of locomotion which will require neither gasoline or tires," I said. "I shall use fuel supplies which will be readily and abundantly available wherever I go, namely grass, hay, and an occasional bucket of oats. I am going to ride a horse. Idaho is the ideal state for this type of campaining," I pointed out, "because there is just one road traversing the entire state from Coeur d'Alene to Boise to Pocatello to Idaho Falls. There is a parade in Coeur d'Alene on the morning of the Fourth of July and to start my campaign, I shall join in that patriotic event, ride in the parade, and keep right on going, headed south. I expect to ride five hundred miles by primary election day."

As you may imagine, that tongue-in-cheek story of a cowboy candidate so patriotic as to undertake a gruelling five-hundred-mile ride to save gasoline was printed even to the far corners of the land.

Publicity was what I needed. I had to have it, and I had to get it free. And I did.

PARADE   Bright and early on the morning of the fourth, I was at the park where the parade was to start. A group of some fifty supporters were on hand at the park. Some carried home-made signs with such slogans as WASHINGTON OR BUST, HAY—HAY—ALL THE WAY, etc.

At this point, politics reared its ugly head. While 90 percent of the precinct committeemen in the county were sawmill workers, the Democratic state committeeman was a corporation lawyer who was head man of the machine in north Idaho. He had been committeeman since God knows when. Not because he was popular with the laboring people, but because he ran the show with an iron hand and no one had ever even thought of challenging him. The working people of Coeur d'Alene and Kootenai County were solidly for Glen Taylor. Bob Older was for "anybody else but." When he read that I planned to use the parade as a launching pad for my campaign he flew into a rage. When he calmed down, he figured out how to block me.

I had hardly showed up, nearly an hour early, when the guy who seemed to be ordering everybody around spotted me and purposefully headed in my direction. "Mr. Taylor, I'm sorry, but there is a rule against any thing of a political nature in the parade."

"Does that mean I cannot ride in the parade?" I asked.

"That's right," he said, and turned on his heel and walked away.

My supporters' first reaction was, what a shame that this should happen in their town, to their champion. Then they became furious. Some of the hulking lumberjacks were all in favor of stringing up the smart-alec parade boss.

I calmed them down and told them I had an idea, which I explained. Inasmuch as I could not ride *in* the parade, I would follow immediately *behind* the parade. Nobody could stop me from *following* the parade. To make some hay out of the situation, I told my gang, which had now swelled to nearly a hundred excited partisans, to go downtown and noise it around up and down the streets that I had been barred from the parade, but would tag along at the tail end, and for everyone to pass word so that no one would leave before I showed up.

This bit of strategy impressed them as being most clever, and they hastened away with a promise to be back before the parade started so they could fall in behind me and not let me suffer the ignominy of being "the old cow's tail."

When they returned, they were all full of chuckles at the outraged response of the citizenry over the dirty trick that Bob Older had played on me. "How do you know it was Bob Older?" I asked. "Well, it must have been him, he gives all the orders around here" was their logical explanation.

By this time the word had spread throughout the assembling parade about what "that dirty Bob Older" had done, and some of the sponsors of floats and most of their operating personnel were in open revolt and threatening to desert their posts and walk behind me. The parade managers were frantically trying to soothe ruffled feathers and get their shows on the road. I had in fact become the arbiter of whether or not there would even *be* a parade.

I decided to play it cool and be noble and self-sacrificing for "the greatest good of the greatest number." Standing tall in my stirrups, I made my first and only speech of the campaign. I pointed out that "there are hundreds of people lining the streets expecting to see this handsome parade with all these beautiful floats which you people have worked so hard to prepare. It isn't going to hurt me to ride last. In fact, it will probably help because the good people of Kootenai County and this fairest city of Idaho believe in fair play and when the word gets around they will in all probability express their disapproval of all this by voting for us. On the other hand, if we sabotage the parade and they are disappointed, they will be resentful toward us. Let's everybody return to our posts and let the people see your handiwork."

There was some grumbling but the parade finally got organized, albeit some thirty minutes late. When it became apparent that it was about to get under way, a committee of three, chosen to represent all my friends present, stepped forward and one of their number, a big burly Swede, made a little speech in a delightful Swedish accent. "Glen, ve vant that you should take this gift to feed you-er se-elf and you-er ho-urse and keep vorum." And having delivered himself of this heartwarming oration, he handed me a nearly new army blanket with the corners held together. Obviously, it contained something. Whatever was in the blanket, it wasn't very large. I opened the corners enough to peek in.

"Money," I exclaimed. "Well, thank you. Thank you ever so much. Come to think of it, I was about to start a five-hundred-mile ride without five cents. This campaign is not going to be so bad after all. Now I can eat once in a while." That got a little laugh.

I called to an old retired worker who would, I believe, have gladly stepped in front of me if someone had taken a shot at me. "John," I asked, "will you ask someone to count my loot and wrap it in a bandana so I can put it in my saddlebags? And have someone roll up the blanket so I can tie it behind my saddle." The old fellow was tickled pink to be singled out this way and started giving orders like he had just been made Treasurer of the United States.

While he was attending to the chore with which I had honored him, I asked the Swedish union official why in a town like Coeur d'Alene, which was overwhelmingly sawmill workers, they let a man like Bob Older run the Democratic Party. His face fell, and his expression was a complete blank. "Vat do you mean?" he said. "How many of your precinct committeemen vote for Bob Older for state committeeman?" "Vy, ve all do. Vy?"

"Why do you vote for him?" I persisted.

He looked puzzled and scratched his head. "Because," he answered, "he is de only vun."

"You mean that no one else is ever nominated?" I asked.

"Ya," he said.

"How many committeemen are there, Pete?"

"Oh—feefteen or t-venty."

"If there was someone else to vote for, how many would vote for Bob Older?"

"Vy, nobody would vote for that—Oh, maybe four—maybe five," he guessed.

"Then if you wanted to," I said, "you could vote him out. Why don't you?"

I could see that the thought had just never entered his mind. Bob Older *was* the Democratic Party in Kootenai County. Poor Pete was just standing there with the light slowly dawning in his pale blue eyes. "All you have to do," I explained, "is the next time you have an election of a state committeeman, you fellows just decide who you want, one of you place his name in nomination, and simply vote Bob Older out."

The light finally dawned. Pete struck the palm of his hand with his fist. "Py golly, ve do it," he exclaimed, and they did. That was the end of Bob Older showing up at state conventions, throwing his weight around as chairman of the Kootenai County delegation.

The band struck up and the parade was under way. I stashed my money, sixty dollars in dollar bills and small change, in my saddlebag, checked to see if my blanket was securely tied behind my saddle, and we moved out.

Oh, yes. The modification of my cowboy togs, which I mentioned earlier, was calculated to make it easier for me to be recognized by friend or foe, no matter in which direction they were headed. Across the front and back of my maroon shirt, Dora had sewn white letters, three inches high, which spelled

TAYLOR, and under that, in two-inch letters, the word SENATE.

There were many fine-looking horses in that parade but, compared to Ranger, they all looked like nags.

We waited until the last float was perhaps one hundred feet down the street before we swung into line with the hundred or more sawmill workers and miners, their wives and kids marching four abreast behind me. Half a dozen oldsters hobbled along each curb haranguing the onlookers with authoritative exhortations such as "That's our boy" and "Taylor's the man us common folks want to vote for." A covey of twenty or so children danced and frolicked dangerously close to Ranger's trim hooves, which were striking the pavement with such vigor that sparks were flying. I heard one man say, "Goddamn, look at that horse! He's marchin' to that music better'n the people," to which his friend replied, "He shore is. By hell, look at him bring his feet down. He looks like he's killin' snakes." And that was about the best description of how Ranger strutted along that I ever heard. And he went right on killing snakes all day. Not with as much determination as he did here with the band blaring and the crowd watching (he was a born show horse), but he did keep rapping the earth with unbelievable vigor hour after hour and mile after mile.

SADDLEBAG CARDS   As we pranced down the street, I had two boys running along either curb passing out campaign cards. People were not throwing them away, either. They were looking them over carefully, and then they would smile and turn and show them to those behind them who hadn't been so fortunate as to get one, and a knot of curious bystanders would form around the lucky one to see and admire and envy. Then someone started running trying to catch up with the boys who were passing out the cards, and then another deprived citizen started running, and in a few seconds everybody was running and shouting at the dispensers of my campaign cards. "Stop—Hey—I want a card!"

These were not ordinary campaign cards. They were smaller, much smaller. They were the size of a postage stamp. On one side was my picture wearing my cowboy hat and holding my banjo. On the other side was printed "Glen Taylor for U.S. Senate" and below that "Saddle Bag Campaign Card," and that's what they were. My saddlebags were full of them, and down the country at intervals were fresh supplies waiting in road-side farmhouses. I had sent them to political supporters with instructions to hold them till that day uncertain when I would ride into sight and claim them to refill my saddlebags.

And so I rode down the main street of Coeur d'Alene with the populace applauding and children running alongside, breathlessly asking if I was Gene Autry or Roy Rogers, while my unbeliev-able mount struck fire from the concrete paving.

In 1940 the threesome of Glen, Dora, and Arod and our sound-equipped automobile with the platform on top had been described as a "compact little campaign machine." Compared to my present "machine" that was an extravaganza. Now, there was literally no "machinery" involved. No car, no electronic amplifiers. No bed. Just a single blanket. No peaches and cookies—and, worst of all, no Dora and Arod.

When the parade turned off at the end of main street, I contin-ued on, grateful that I could now get off on the shoulder of the highway and save Ranger from going lame. We have all heard the phrase "pounding the pavement." Well, Ranger did that liter-ally, and he couldn't possibly have lasted long on a hard-surfaced road.

I hadn't ridden a horse in twenty years. By the time Coeur d'Alene had disappeared from view, I was beginning to be re-minded of this fact through the seat of my pants.

KING OF THE ROAD   The advance publicity that my ride had received alerted the populace along my route and the lettering on my shirt heralded my passing. Quite a number of motorized voters stopped me that day—some to wish me well, and some just out of curiosity. They simply wanted to be able to say they had personally shaken hands with that guy they had been reading about and hearing about on the radio. I discovered that the radio was giving me more publicity than the papers. Radio announcers like a light human interest type of story to wind up their news-cast, and this ride was right up their alley.

Some of those who stopped did so at the risk of life and limb. They would come roaring along at sixty-five mph and not realize who I was until they saw the name on my shirt as they zipped past. Then you would have to allow a few seconds for them to do a double-take and digest what they had seen. Now, add to that a few seconds for formulation of a decision to stop. Then I'd hear it. The awfulest squealing of brakes you ever heard, while they burned up ten dollars' worth of rationed rubber—fishtailing a hundred yards or so to a stop. Occasionally they'd wind up in the barrow pit, but nothing very serious ever happened.

When one traveling voter stopped on that narrow road, others would slow down, and then most likely they'd stop too. Sometimes there would be three or four cars stopped, headed in both directions. The road would be completely blocked, and I'd be busy as the proverbial cat on a tin roof passing out my valuable little pieces of cardboard. One man said that when he first saw the jamup, he thought I was running a roadside fruit stand.

Everybody was friendly, though. They wished me luck, and a good many said they would vote for me. Several of those who got involved in my miniroadside rallies said they were Republicans but would vote for me in the general election.

I gave everybody a saddlebag campaign card, and everyone was tickled as could be. But a problem arose. Those saddlebag campaign cards were so doggoned cute that everybody wanted a handful to give to their friends as proof that they had seen me riding Ranger and had shaken hands with the man who was being mentioned on every newscast and in every edition of every newspaper.

They didn't want to settle for just two or three, or even two or three dozen. They wanted a handful. I had to become stern and ration them out like they were gold nuggets.

Ranger was still killing snakes, and I was getting stiffer and stiffer, so I got off every twenty minutes or so, house or no house, and led Ranger while I walked for a ways. That didn't help either. I kept getting more and more sore.

To add to my discomfort, I snagged the palm of my right hand while opening a farmer's barbed-wire gate. Not too bad, but it bled some, and to keep from getting my customers bloody, I had to shake hands with my left hand and explain what had happened. It was an inconvenience and hurt some, but it wasn't much of a wound.

No, it wasn't a bad hurt. The fact is that it turned out to be a blessing in disguise, and, believe it or not, the next day the whole

United States and some foreigners knew about it.

It was late afternoon. It was such torture to get off and on my horse that I had ceased to do so. I planned to ride as far as Worley, some thirty miles, this first day. I still had five miles to go. In that five miles there wasn't a farmhouse close to the road, so I was not called upon to dismount, and I didn't, but I paid the price.

As I neared Worley I kept a lookout for a likely place to spend the night. It was growing dusk. "Here we are, here is a place," I said to Ranger. It was a schoolhouse.

The school grounds were fenced so stray stock had not been able to get at the grass, which had been left to grow since school was out in late May.

It took an agonizing effort for me to get my leg up and across the back of the saddle. It seemed like I had been molded in this shape and meant to stay that way forever.

I unsaddled Ranger, and turned him loose to graze. There was a trough with a faucet at one end of the shed where he could drink. In the last light of a dying summer day, I took two post-cards from my saddlebags. They were preaddressed to UP and to AP, the two news services in Spokane, Washington, which was the nearest city with such facilities.

I wrote the same report on both cards, which would, of course, be postmarked "Worley." No use wasting space repeating it. There was all too little room. The dispatch read: "Arrived on schedule. Except for saddle soreness feeling fine, but had terrible accident. Lacerated right palm opening barbed-wire gate to farmer's lane. Unable shake hands. Can think of no worse calamity to befall a candidate. Best regards. Glen Taylor."

Can you imagine a better tongue-in-cheek horror story? Here's a poor goddamned patriotic candidate starting out to ride a hay-burner for five hundred miles to save gasoline, and on the very first day he falls victim to an accident that robs him of a politician's most cherished asset, the ability to shake hands.

Isn't that awful?

The story appeared in practically every paper and was told on every radio station—not only in Idaho, but in the whole cockeyed country, as well as foreign countries.

Who can't laugh at a joke like this, particularly if the seriocomic misfortune features a politician as the butt of the joke? I walked the quarter mile to the store and post office and mailed my first press release.

I had met this storekeeper-postmaster in previous campaigns when I held street meetings in front of his store, and he was quite friendly. Upon learning that I had not eaten for more than twelve hours, he invited me to eat with his family. (He did not close the store until eight p.m., and then ate dinner.) It was a delicious country meal: corn on the cob, lettuce salad, string beans and radishes, all from his wife's garden, plus fried chicken from her flock. I bedded down for the night in a manger in the school stable, which still had some six inches of dried-out hay left in it.

MOONLIGHTER   I was up before dawn and on my way. It was still not daylight when I came to the first farmhouse, but the people were up and had the lights on. It was a rather pretentious home, not the type in which my supporters generally lived.

I rode up the oiled driveway to the house, dismounted, and knocked on the door. A tall, lean man opened up, and I recognized him as the Democratic county chairman. He had worked for Donart in the 1940 primary. He looked at me and then at Ranger in disbelief. I said, "Good morning, Mr. Acuff."

That seemed to convince him that he wasn't seeing things, and he managed to say, "Glen Taylor, well I'll be goddamned. What the hell are you doing out here before daylight?"

"I'm campaigning. They say the early bird catches the worm. I am out trying to drum up a little support, and I know of no one in Kootenai County whose support I'd rather have than yours."

"Well, I'll be damned," he repeated, and then he seemed to come to and stammered, "Well I-uh-that-is-have you had your breakfast?"

I admitted I hadn't. "Git down! Git down!" he commanded. I did, and he opened the door wide and invited me in. "Martha, this is Glen Taylor, the man they were just talking about on the radio."

"Yes, I know, I met Mr. Taylor in 1940," she said pleasantly from where she stood in the kitchen door.

I walked over and shook hands with her, and about that time two teenagers came bursting in, freshly washed and combed—a boy about sixteen and a girl about fourteen.

"Jack," Acuff said, "this is Mr. Taylor, the candidate for Senate that's riding the horse."

"Gee, yes," Jack beamed, "you've been on the radio all morning. Everybody's talking about you riding the horse to campaign. I thought maybe you'd already gone by."

"No, I'm not traveling very fast. Stopping to shake hands and talk to people," I explained.

"And this is our daughter, Kathy," Mrs. Acuff introduced the girl, and then spoke to the boy. "Jack, run out to the barn and get some eggs," she said in an offhand manner, as though he had to go get eggs every morning before breakfast, but Jack told me that they didn't have eggs every morning for breakfast and my being there called for something a little special. Jack didn't say that in so many words, but he might as well have. What he said was, "Eggs, boy oh boy! Eggs for breakfast! Gee!" and he almost ran me down in his eagerness to get to the henhouse so he could have eggs for breakfast.

Kathy had gotten a glimpse of Ranger, and she went to the door and clasped her hands in ecstasy. "Oh, look, daddy," she enthused. "Isn't he a beauty?"

And the chairman agreed. "He certainly is. That's the finest looking animal I've ever seen." And he sure might well have been. Instead of standing there hipshot, and with his head hanging as most horses will the moment the rider dismounts, Ranger was as erect and alert as a sentinel on night watch in "Injun country." Head high, eyes wide open, nostrils flared and ears pricked up, looking about with quick jerks of his handsome head as though I had, indeed, left him on guard. Hell, he was pretty!

At this point the chairman's farmer instinct to think of animals first and people second came to the fore, and Mr. Acuff directed Kathy to "take Mr. Taylor's horse to the barn and give him a good feeding of oats." The girl was obviously thrilled to death at this opportunity to care for such a handsome animal who belonged to such a distinguished guest, and she ran toward Ranger so eagerly I was afraid she might spook him. She was a real farm girl though, and as she stepped off the porch she caught herself and approached Ranger slowly, cooing soothing words.

Acuff motioned me to a chair, but it dawned on him that he had forgotten something. "Want to wash up?" he asked. I said I would, and he pointed down the hall. "Second door on the right," and then with obvious pride, "Running water, hot and cold. The whole shebang."

The wife spoke up to tell me something I had already suspicioned. "We just had a pressure water system put in. We're mighty proud of our new bathroom too."

When I returned from my ablutions, I complimented her on her lovely new bathroom. "That's nicer than anything in the Hotel Boise," I assured her, and she beamed.

Jack had returned from his flying trip to the henhouse, and I could smell bacon frying. "Gee, bacon too!" Jack sounded like he could hardly believe his eyes, ears, and nose.

I was motioned to the chair again. It was the biggest, most comfortable and lived-in chair in the front room. Obviously it belonged to the papa bear, but I sat down in it and exclaimed at how comfortable it was. That, of course, pleased the chairman. Jack got in his usual inept remark. "Yeah, it sure is, ain't it? You're lucky. Pa won't let me sit in it." That brought on an embarrassed silence while the host self-consciously seated himself in a less massive and much less comfortably upholstered chair.

After a moment's pause, the county chairman brought the meeting to order by getting right to the point. "Now, about me supporting you," he said in a businesslike way.

I said, "Yes sir," denoting that I was listening.

"Well, I supported George Donart in the 1940 primary," he announced.

I said, "Yes sir," denoting that I had no comment.

"And," he continued, "I guess I was the most surprised man in the state when you beat the stuffing out of him."

Before I could say, "Yes sir," again, Jack interjected, "Yeah, Pa was sure mad about that." Pa gave him a look that presaged bad news for Jack when I was gone.

Mrs. Acuff, who had come to the kitchen door to listen, tried to smooth things over. "Now, Jack, your father wasn't mad. He was just a little disappointed."

"I'll say he was," the irrepressible offspring vouched. "He darn near gave me a lickin' when I said I was glad the singin' cowboy won."

That was too much for the big shot of Kootenai County politics and his neck reddened as he pointed a gnarled forefinger and threatened, "Well, I'm going to give you a licking right now if you don't shut up and quit talking about things you don't know anything about."

Jack knew when he had pushed his luck far enough. He shut up and went over to the breakfast table, sitting down with a knife in one hand and a fork in the other, with the butt ends of the handles resting on the table, like he was waiting to carve a turkey.

Now that this was settled, the man of the house assured me that, while he had been for Donart in the 1940 primary, he had supported me in the general election. He also said I was probably the best speaker he had ever heard, but he didn't much like some of the things I had said, particularly that business about making just one big deal out of all the farms in Idaho.

I asked him if that wasn't what was happening now, and he agreed it probably was, "but it's a little hard to take all at one gulp," he lamely explained.

He changed the subject, or, to be more exact, brought us back to the subject we had been discussing before it got sidetracked. "Now, about supporting you," he reiterated.

"Yes sir," I reiterated in turn. (That's a good word, by the way, and I am just as good a reiterator as the next one.)

"I've sort of let it be known that I'm supporting Bothwell," he stated.

"Yes sir," I said, and began to feel that maybe I'd better say something besides "Yes sir" the next time it was my turn.

He waited a moment, his brow furrowed, as though he was making a tough decision, and then burst out, "But, by god, any man that'll come knocking on my door before daylight asking for my support, deserves all the support he can get, and you've got mine."

At that, Kathy ran to her father and threw her arms about him, smothered him with kisses and further showed her approval of his decision with an excited stream of words. "Oh daddy, you've made the right decision," she assured him. "I was so hoping you would. Mr. Taylor is such a nice-looking cowboy, and he sings and plays; and he's smart too. I heard him speak and he's a real cowboy, and he has such a beautiful horse." And with that clincher, she showered her father with hugs and kisses with such adolescent fervor that he made motions like he was trying to swim to the surface for a breath of air.

There was, however, no respite for this undemonstrative man. His daughter had no sooner backed away to admire her suddenly brainy parent than her mother took her place and while her demonstration wasn't quite as gushy as Kathy's, it was nevertheless plain that she was embarrassing this grownup farm boy by saying, "Jeff, I'm so glad. I told you Mr. Taylor was a good man when we met his wife and darling little boy in Idaho Falls." And, having delivered herself of that well reasoned judgment, the harassed chairman's wife proceeded to give her flabbergasted husband a big, sucking, country-style smacker—on his shiny bald head.

All these goings on were just too much for Jack. The sixteen-year-old "Son of Kong" just *had* to get into the act or bust. Forgetting his recent reprimand and the admonition to keep his mouth shut unless he was spoken to, Mr. Acuff's son and heir rose from the table and noisily clomped across the hardwood floor to where his father was sitting, embarrassed and red-faced from all that kissy-kissy business that he had just been forced to endure.

I'll have to say this for Jack. As he strode toward his discomfited father, the young muscleman looked, for all the world, like a sixteen-year-old boy trying to look like a man. With his shoulders squared and his chin thrust forward and with an expression as serious as a solemn-faced monkey, he grabbed his bewildered father's limp hand and intoned, "Congratulations, sir."

With a sickly half grin on his face, the poor bewildered parent started weakly shaking his son's hand; and then, all of a sudden, he seemed to come out of a trance, looked down to see what he was doing, and threw the hand away like it was covered with owl manure.

Finally, everything got quieted down and we ate breakfast. As we ate, the now recovered big-wheel politician explained that my moonlight appearance at his door was not the only reason he had decided to throw his valuable support in my direction. Not by any means! His wife, he said, had been after him since she first fell in love with the Taylor family at the Idaho Falls convention in 1940. In fact, she had, only a week ago, for the first time in their seventeen years as man and wife, told him that she was going to go against his advice and vote for me instead of Bothwell. At the mention of Bothwell's name he sat for a moment, staring pensively at his coffee, which he was absently stirring, and then he gave a little laugh, "Heh-heh-heh."

He stuffed his mouth with another hay-hand helping, and then decided to say something. His words were a little scrambled as they naturally would be, coming through two or three inches of scrambled eggs plus an ill-fitting set of dentures, but he managed. "I wonder," he mused, "what Bothwell will say when I tell him I've decided to support you because you snuck up on my blind side in the dark?" And with that he gave an explosive guffaw.

I was sitting opposite him, and now I had a couple of ounces of his eggs, plus my own. Mrs. Acuff was horrified. Mr. Acuff's lungs had been pretty well emptied by his gusty outburst and when he started to refill them, he sucked a goodly portion of the eggs still remaining in his mouth into his lungs and started having a big coughing fit.

Young Jack was sitting next to his father, and when it became apparent that her husband was in more-than-passing trouble, Mrs. Acuff shouted to their husky son, "Hit him on the back!" I suspect that this was just the opportunity Jack had long been waiting for, because he responded with alacrity and several times the force required in this ancient therapy. He hit his purple-faced parent so hard that, not only the rest of his mouthful of eggs, but his uppers as well, landed right in the middle of my already contaminated breakfast. Poor Mrs. Acuff gasped, "I'll get you more eggs," grabbed *my* plate, which was now topped off with her husband's "plate," and hurried to the kitchen with my unusual omelet.

Stangely enough, Mr. Acuff did not seem to appreciate what his "chip off the old block" had done for him. He was definitely getting better though. His face was turning a much lighter shade of purple, but then his eyes fell on his muscular offspring, and he started getting purple again. He pushed himself up from the table, clenched his fists at his sides, and, with all the stern authority he could command without his uppers, lisped, "Thack! Thont yew eber thu that again."

Jack was on his feet too. Prepared, I imagine, to run. "But, Pa, you was dyin'," Jack protested.

"Well, I'd rather thie a nathural death than be kilt by my own thun."

Fortunately, a showdown between father and son was averted by the opportune return of Mrs. Acuff with my eggs and her husband's teeth. The poor woman was so flustered she placed the teeth in front of me and gave my eggs to the chairman.

I guess I was a little flustered myself. I must have been, because I was all ready to fork Mr. Acuff's uppers when his good wife noticed her *faux pas* and shuffled the eggs and dentures.

In exasperation, she exclaimed, "Oh, foot!"

BABY OIL! While we finished breakfast, I told about how I had been so saddlesore the night before that the tears ran down my cheeks when I had dismounted.

Kathy clapped her hands delightedly and exclaimed, "Oh, we've got a remedy for that. The forest ranger told us about it last summer when we took a pack trip up the Selway. We all used it and it worked just fine."

With real fervor I said, "Well, if you know of a way to help me, it would certainly be appreciated. I've already started dreading getting off that horse tonight."

"Oh, it's simple, but you'd never guess what it was," the daughter burbled.

"What is it?" I asked.

"Baby oil," she squealed.

"Baby oil?" I repeated, somewhat taken aback and no little embarrassed.

Kathy wasn't embarrassed at all. "Yes," she said, "you know baby oil—the kind you rub on babies to keep them from chafing? I've got nearly a whole bottle left. You can have it. Isn't that exciting?" she asked no one in particular and everyone in general. "Imagine! A candidate for senator using my baby oil," and she giggled excitedly.

"Well, don't tell anybody," I pleaded. "The Republicans are poking enough fun at me just being a singing cowboy without letting them know that I'm a singing cowboy who's so tender he has to use baby oil." Everyone laughed, but it was no laughing matter. Just imagine what they would do with that one!

The meal was finished without further incident, and I prepared to leave. Kathy and Jack nearly came to blows over who was going to be allowed the honor and the privilege of bringing Ranger from the barn. The dispute ended when Kathy maneuvered into position by the door and, while Jack turned his head to appeal to his father, she yanked the door open and slammed it behind her.

Jack tried. He made an awkward sixteen-year-old leap, but just managed to get his proboscis in the way as the door was banged shut. He got a bloody nose and, as his mother led him to the kitchen for the cold water treatment, his father impolitely turned his back on me and walked over to look out the window on the other side of the room.

Now, one would think that with his son's lifeblood running out the end of his nose, a father's place would be at the side of his wounded heir, but there he was admiring the view. And not only that, his shoulders were jiggling up and down in that well known motion which denotes a suppressed chuckle. And if the shoulders move a little more noticeably, as Mr. Acuff's were, that denotes a stifled guffaw.

I stood there alone and ignored, twiddling my thumbs. Then Mr. Acuff got hold of himself, figuratively speaking, and turned to me with a straight face. But he had gotten too good a hold of himself and overdone it. He looked like he was going to a funeral.

As he took two or three steps toward me the struggle within was obviously still going on because his stomach and diaphragm muscles were contracting convulsively like the proverbial dog crapping peach seeds, and when he opened his mouth to speak, his stony facade crumpled completely.

Despite himself he snorted, slapped his thigh, and gave way to an unsuppressible fit of giggling. He made two or three false starts at speaking, only to relapse into another spasm of tittering. Finally he managed to control himself, wiped his eyes with his bandana, blew his nose, drew a big breath, and exhaled in an exaggerated sigh as though he had just put down a great weight.

He came close to me, still having difficulty speaking, and in a voice calculated not to reach the ears of his wife and son he whispered, "That girl Kathy—she's a humdinger, ain't she?" And with that he jabbed me in the ribs and gave one more snorting chuckle with his hand over his mouth. Obviously, his self-reliant tomboy daughter had given him profound vicarious satisfaction by doing to her brother what he had wanted to do all morning.

Now the time had come to say goodbye. Kathy was back from the barn, bright eyed and excited. Jack was back from the kitchen, glassy eyed and sullen, a wad of cotton visible in one nostril. My host got my white San Fran Stetson out of the guest closet next to the front door and handed it to me, after first blowing at a speck of dirt and then flicking it off with a thump of his finger.

They were all lined up to say goodbye. There was a dramatic moment of silence, which was shattered by Kathy loudly inhaling "Oh" and putting her fingers over her mouth. Her eyes were round and wide open like someone had just stuck a pin in her shapely little *derrière*.

"What's the matter?" her father asked on behalf of all of us.

"Oh, Mr. Taylor's baby oil," she squeaked, and ran down the hall. Everyone looked a little embarrassed, but before we were forced to contrive any small talk she came running back and proudly presented me with my very first gift of baby oil.

While I was trying to think of an appropriate speech for a gentleman to make when receiving, from a young lady, a bottle of baby oil to massage his private parts, the young lady herself grabbed me by the arm and started hustling me down the hall to the bathroom. "Now you just go in the bathroom and rub it— well you know—wherever you—well that is, wherever the saddle rubs you." I was relieved when she stopped at the bathroom door and shoved me in. I hadn't been quite sure.

Jack capped the climax of a climactic morning by bellowing, "Be sure to take your pants down."

There was a slight interval of silence, during which I imagine Acuff was grinding his teeth, and then I heard him say, "By God, I swear—"

He left it dangling, but his wife picked it up and scolded, "You certainly do, Jeffrey Acuff. You've been swearing all morning and you've got to quit it. You're setting a bad example for our son."

To which Jack added, "He sure as hell is," and while I didn't see it I had a mental picture of Jeffrey Acuff advancing upon *her* son with blood in his eye and mayhem in his heart, only to be confronted by his wife with her left arm round the boy and her right arm extended, palm outward à la 1890, to stop the assault.

Boy! This baby oil deal was embarrassing. I could just imagine them all standing out there, in dead silence now, each conjuring up their own undignified picture of a would-be senator, with his pants down, dousing himself with baby oil. It wouldn't have been much more embarrassing if they had all crowded into the bathroom with me, and I am sure that with them all crowded in that way they wouldn't have had nearly the graphic view they were seeing in their own mind's eye.

I let the water run full and loud and made a great show of washing my hands, having in mind the fact that I had yet to say goodbye and shake hands and I didn't want them to remember me as an oily politician.

When I emerged I tried to look as dignified as possible. I succeeded well enough that no one cracked a grin, not even Jack.

The family was once again lined up for the farewell ceremony. I took Mrs. Acuff's hand in both of mine and held it while I complimented her on her lovely, spotless home, her wonderful new water system and handsome bathroom, her fine family and the splendid breakfast.

Next in line, standing close to his mother, was Jack. It was easy to see that he was her pride and joy. Her firstborn, who returned her affection if for no reason than the fact that he needed the shelter of her loving arms when he had exasperated his male parent beyond human endurance.

I shook his hand and complimented him on his fine physique and promised that, should I be elected and if he were so inclined, I would be happy to arrange for him to take the exams for West Point. I felt certain, I said, that he had all the qualities necessary to become a leader of men.

Now to Kathy: I told her what a beautiful young lady she was and promised that if she should one day become a good secretary there would, if I got to Washington, be a position waiting for her in my office. "If all this comes true," I told her, "I will personally place your name in nomination to be queen of the Cherry

Blossom Festival." I was holding both her hands, one in each of mine, and when I had finished I leaned over and kissed her lightly on the cheek. She was blushing as red as a ripe Winesap.

Finally, I turned to the chairman. He was still looking open-mouthed at his son, Jack, trying to make some sense out of all the laudatory things I had said about him. Not until I held out my hand and said, "Well, so long, Mr. Acuff," did he snap out of it.

He came to with a start, clicked his dentures shut, and stammered, "Huh—uh—oh yes—yes—good-bye, Senator, and good luck." He wasn't county chairman for nothing. I wasn't the only one who worked at "winning friends and influencing people." He knew how to make a fellow feel good. "Senator!" What a spine-tingling preview.

I gave them all one last fond look, turned with a flourish, opened the door, stepped outside, and pulled the door shut behind me. *What the hell?* It was darker than a stack of black cats!

What the hell goes on here? I was sure it was daylight. Yes, I remembered looking past Acuff when he was looking out the window. I had noticed how pretty it was with the first rays of the sun slanting across the field and the forest beyond. Then what the hell was the matter? Maybe I had gone blind. I'd heard of people doing that, going blind instantaneously, for no reason at all. Surely this horrible fate could not overtake me. Not now. Not at this memorable instant when I had just been called "Senator."

But it was true. Here I stood in the glorious dawn of another day and all was dark. Stygian. Not a ray of light. I broke out with a cold sweat. Why didn't Acuff come to my aid? Why was everyone so silent? I was afraid to take another step for fear I would fall down the steps to the porch.

I thought of Dora, of Arod and my new son. *No! No!* This just could not be! Tremblingly, I held out my hand and recoiled when my fingers touched some furry creature. What the hell was this, anyhow? A bad dream?

That was it. A terrible nightmare. I was on the verge of calling out to Acuff to help me when a light began to dawn. Not the light of day, but the light of reason. That furry thing I had touched. That couldn't be a living creature standing shoulder high and confronting me here in the doorway of this house that belonged to the chairman of the Democratic Central Committee of Kootenai

County. I reached out my hand again. That furry thing was still there. It felt like, it couldn't be, but yes it was—a fur coat!

I was in the closet. My God, how embarrassing! Then I remembered that there were two doors—side by side. What an idiot! What to do? What was going on in the room I had just left? If I only had a saw—I could saw a hole in that wall and keep on going and never have to face those people again.

And then the ridiculousness of the whole thing struck me and I turned and opened the door. They were still lined up there. Exactly as I had left them years ago.

My grandiose departure into the clothes closet had left them in a state of shock. Immobilized. But then, when they saw me and the foolish grin on my face, they were yanked back to reality and the place rang with shouts of laughter. I joined in and we all laughed and laughed—until tears streamed down our cheeks. Finally we were all laughed out and then, when I told them of all the crazy thoughts that had raced through my befuddled mind during those few brief seconds when the door had closed behind me, we all laughed some more.

Finally, everyone was out in the yard and I was mounted on Ranger. He was tossing his head, snorting and impatiently stamping his hooves, anxious to start moving.

Kathy was rapturizing. "Oh Daddy, Mama, isn't he a beautiful horse?" I gallantly dismounted and asked the chairman if Kathy could ride Ranger around the yard.

"Sure. She can ride anything, even a bronco," he bragged pridefully.

The chairman's "pride and joy" didn't need a second invitation. She grabbed the reins and was in the saddle. "Keep a tight rein," I admonished her. Ranger outdid himself. He lifted his feet even higher and brought his dainty hooves down more precisely and with unbelievable vigor. Kathy nearly swooned for joy.

Jack was jumping up and down in front of his father, flapping his arms like the wings of a giant condor and shouting, "Can I ride him? Can I ride him?" Acuff was excited too. He was trying to see, but not getting a very good view with Jumping Jack leaping and gesticulating in front of him. "Yes, damn it, you can ride him," the chairman bellowed, grabbed the excited youth by the hand, and "popped the whip" with him so violently the loose-jointed offspring "off to buffaloed" twenty feet across the yard and banged into the woodshed.

After Jack had his ride Kathy squealed, "Now, daddy, you ride him."

The chairman protested sufficiently to appease his dignity as chairman of the Kootenai County Democratic Central Committee; then he had his ride.

As I rode away at long last, everybody was shouting at once. Above all, I heard the sweet music in the raucous bellow of the chairman. *"Good luck—Senator."*

"Senator!" No tough drill sergeant ever got the reflex action that this *"senator"* did. My back involuntarily straightened, and I rode ramrod stiff until Ranger had killed at least a bushel basket of snakes.

After that, the heat plus the pounding on the end of my spine caused me to gradually compromise my senatorial dignity, and I started slumping and moving around trying to find a soft spot in the saddle. Then all of a sudden it dawned on me. I was hurting because of the pounding my rear end had taken the day before, but it wasn't too bad, and I really wasn't chafed anymore. Kathy's baby oil was working like a charm. I sat up straight, and for the first time I began to enjoy the ride.

"THE WEST STILL LIVES" I was making slower progress than I had planned. It took time to stop at each farmhouse, although I was succeeding pretty well at avoiding political arguments with the plea that I had a tight schedule and had to keep moving.

I made less than twenty miles that second day out. I spent the night at Tensed in a room supplied rent free by the proprietor of a bar and restaurant. He also gave me my evening meal.

The room was only a cubbyhole tacked onto the rear of the place. The bar owner kept it as a service to his patrons who took a few too many and couldn't make it home. No sheets. Just blankets. It did not look or smell too clean, but freeloading drunks and senatorial candidates can't be too choosy. I picketed Ranger in the weed-grown lot behind the bar.

A farmer I met during the evening, while I was having a friendly (and free) drink, drove five miles to his place and got some oats for Ranger. I was meeting lots of nice people.

From Tensed I mailed another postcard to the AP and UP wire services in Spokane. It read: "Had Ranger shod here. No charge. Two days and two nights and haven't been able to spend a penny to feed or bed my horse or myself. The West still lives."

That line, "The West still lives," grabbed 'em and it appeared as the heading on my (nonpolitical?) little story in papers all up and down the state and in distant places.

RATS! The third night out from Coeur d'Alene I spent at a place where there was nothing but a combination bar and pool hall. The manager gave me permission to stay in the lot out behind his place. It was grown up with weeds two feet high, but there was some grass down among the weeds, so Ranger wouldn't fare too badly.

All I had to eat before turning in was a candy bar.

I stomped down the weeds in an area big enough so I could roll up in my blanket and slept well until two a.m., when I was awakened by a sharp pain in my ear lobe. Instinctively, I struck at the source of the pain. My hand struck a soft body and something furry scampered across my face. Boy, was that a rude awakening! I didn't move because I wanted to collect my wits before I let whoever or whatever had disturbed me know that I was awake.

Carefully, I felt around and found my flashlight and switched it on. The rustling all around me which I had heard, when whatever it was had brought me out of a sound sleep, stopped the instant I turned on the light. When the flash came on there were two eyes reflected in the beam. I moved the light slowly about. More eyes! I was surrounded by eyes and whatever the eyes belonged to! A form scurried across the beam of light. A rat! A big—fat—rat! The weeds were *alive* with rats. I felt my ear. Blood. I could tell by the feel, and I confirmed it by holding my fingers in front of the flashlight. That damned rat did a workmanlike job.

If I had decided to wear an earring right then I wouldn't have needed to have my ear pierced. I saddled Ranger and got the hell out of there.

NO RUMBLE SEAT My next overnight stop was the little town of Genesee. Again, I slept under the stars with the measured sound of Ranger munching grass to lull me to sleep.

The following morning I composed and mailed out my daily postcards, reporting on my progress, to the UP and AP. The gimmick I thought up for that day's message was printed in practically every paper and used on every radio station in the country. The clippings I have are invariably headed, NO RUMBLE SEAT.

What I wrote on my postcards was: "As I travel the highways and byways on my trusty steed, Ranger, in my quest for votes I am often asked why my wife and young son, Arod, are not accompanying me as they have in the past. My answer is simple. I would love to have them with me, but my conveyance has no rumble seat."

HAY HAND   After twenty-four grueling days, I at long last entered the Boise valley at the town of Weiser.

I could easily make the ride from Weiser to Boise in three days, but this was heavily populated country, and I wanted time to shake hands at the numerous farms and towns.

Right off the bat I lost nearly a whole afternoon. But, boy, it sure paid off! This clipping explains why. It is two columns wide by three inches deep and has a narrow line around it to make it stand out. That fact illustrates again the advantage of human interest stories, as opposed to quotes on the issues. Can you imagine these papers, none of which particularly loved me, putting some profound statement of mine in a box to attract attention? The heading is rather long but, as I have pointed out, there is nothing headline writers like better than an opportunity to display their cleverness at composing humorous captions.

This one reads: FRANKLY WE WOULD RATHER KISS 18—YEAR—BABIES.

Now that your prurient interest has been aroused let's see what goes on here.

A blistered hand today supported this story told by Glen Taylor, who is seeking the democratic senatorial nomination. It has to do with the hazards of campaigning in a farm state during a labor shortage year.

It seems that Taylor, who is campaigning on horseback,

called on a farmer in Payette county and found him putting up his hay. "Tell you what," the farmer suggested, "You take this pitchfork and just follow along and we'll talk about politics." Taylor seized the fork and started pitching. But every time he attempted to start a political conversation, the farmer demurred, "Right after the next load is on." They pitched through the afternoon. When the supper gong rang the farmer shook hands with the perspiring candidate and said, "Thanks for the lift. I just wanted to see if you've got what it takes. You have. Every senator should have a course in haying."

That's the article, but there is an addendum. The farmer got word to his four sons who farmed round about, and during the afternoon they all drove over and brought their wives to be introduced and see the distinguished hay hand in action. Counting the farmer's wife, that's a total of ten votes, not to mention the three other hay hands and their wives. Add to that the friends and relatives of all these citizens, and you have a sizeable bloc of voters. In addition, think of all the hundreds of farmers who read this story about a candidate who wasn't too proud, lazy, or soft, to pitch hay. I'll venture that this was the most profitable afternoon's work I ever did. But that isn't all.

I got a bounteous hay-hand supper—topped off with strawberries fresh off the vine and cream so thick you could have spread it like fresh churned butter.

Now wait a minute, that's not the end of it. I was put up for the night in a comfortable room with a down-filled tick on the bed. After supper we sat on the porch enjoying the cool evening breeze, smoking big fat fifty-cent cigars (bought especially for the occasion), and discussed everything under the sun—except the issues.

Now hold it. The real payoff is yet to come. The farmer's wife and the four sons' wives had been busy on the phone calling the neighbors, and we had scarcely finished our stogies when they started arriving in droves to shake my blistered hand and promise to vote for me. Not because they agreed with my stand on any issues, but because I had been a good sport and helped out their hard-pressed neighbor with the haying. That is grass-roots politics. Full steam ahead, and the issues be damned.

Next morning at daybreak the farmer stuck his head in the room and bawled loud enough to be heard at any or all of his sons' farms, "Time to start another day's hayin'!" Ordinarily, such a rude awakening would have brought me up standing, and that is in fact the message that my flash point flashed to my various receiving stations, but the response by my aching bones and muscles was something less than electric.

I finally made it to my feet to the accompaniment of anguished groans and the audible creakings of my abused joints.

At breakfast my wily host dangled in front of me the tempting promise that if I would help him out for one more day he'd have "twice as many voters over this evening," but I lied like a yellow dog and told him that, much as I'd love to, I had a press conference set up in Boise and I couldn't possibly miss it.

The sun was hardly up when Ranger and I hit the trail again, full of ham and eggs and chopped oats.

As soon as we were out of sight of the house I remembered, took to the bushes, and gave myself a baby-oil treatment. And I didn't bother trying to get all the oil off my hand either. If it was good for blisters on one part of the anatomy, it ought to be good for blisters on another.

Now that I was passing through larger towns reporters came to interview me. Papers which ordinarily would have snorted at the idea of printing my picture free were eagerly using pictures of me and my famous steed.

Generally, the pictures were quite large too—two columns by eight inches. It's difficult to squeeze a man and a horse into much less space than that. It is common knowledge that a picture of a person plus a horse, dog, cat, or most any living creature will be more readily acceptable to the press and create more reader interest than a plain old mug shot.

And so it went, and you can rest assured that an overwhelming majority of those I met when they stopped their cars or when I sought them out in the fields or at home could hardly wait to tell their less fortunate friends, or just anyone who would listen, that they had really seen that goddamned Taylor, and he was really riding that friggin' horse.

In the bars and general stores along my route the favorite subject was "that singin' cowboy" and his beautiful goddamn horse, which everybody had been hearing about on the radio and reading about in the newspapers.

I know this is true, because two or three times I left my white hat hanging on the saddlehorn, slipped on my light raincoat to cover the lettering on my shirt, and sneaked unobtrusively in the back door of these places to listen. It was amazing. Everybody in the place had seen me traveling every road at all times of the day and night, on every color and type of horse, going in all directions at once.

Heated arguments would erupt as to who had and had not seen me riding in which direction at what time.

TIME MAGAZINE   On August 10, the day before the primary election, *Time* magazine hit the stands with the most flagrantly untruthful, scurrilous, and damaging attack on me that I had suffered to date:

"Taylor boasts that he made better money campaigning for Senator in 1940 than he ever made in show business."

This statement makes me appear to be an outright idiot, which I would have to be to say such a fool thing, true or not, but particularly when it was not true.

That outright lie was quoted again and again, and for years I was attacked because of *Time* magazine's false and malicious charge.

Having appeared in *Time,* the fabrication was deadly and devastating.

I wired *Time* threatening to sue unless they printed a retraction. They printed my wire and said they stood by the article as printed. I saw a lawyer about suing *Time.* He said, "Forget it unless you have a million dollars." Despite *Time's* attack I was again nominated.

CLARK POLITICS   During the general election campaign there was a rumor going around that Clark, if elected governor, would resign and accept a federal judgeship while the lieutenant governor would become governor. When the votes were counted, it appeared that Clark was the winner.

The voters, however, threw a monkey wrench into the machinery. They elected a Republican lieutenant governor.

This meant that if Chase Clark resigned and took the judgeship he coveted, a Republican would become governor and all those political jobs would be filled by Republicans. Even the Clark machine couldn't get away with a deal like that, but wily old Chase wasn't to be denied.

Finally, after much conferring and scurrying about it was announced that "Bott" Bottolfson, the Republican candidate for governor, had won by 400 votes. The newly elected Republican governor appointed Democrat Chase Clark to the federal judgeship and everybody was happy except the Democratic voters who had voted for Chase, and particularly the Democratic rank-and-file party workers who were left out in the cold.

Unheard of? Not in Idaho it wasn't.

Late in the '42 campaign, the Idaho Businessmen's Committee mailed out the same package of Gillette's quotes they had used in 1940, and again I lost to Thomas.

Dora felt pretty low, but I cheered her up with a little simple arithmetic.

"In 1940," I pointed out to her, "we lost by 14,000 votes. This time we lost by only 4,000—next time we're in."

SANSKRIT   Before leaving '42, let's have a snifter to raise our spirits a notch or two.

Vardis Fisher was the most famous author that Idaho ever produced. One of his novels won a Pulitzer Prize, and that means you are pretty damned good.

At the time of the 1942 campaign Vardis was writing a political column which appeared in several Idaho papers. Shortly after the election, he wrote a piece reviewing the performance of various candidates. He had nothing good to say about anyone except me, and that pertained only to my ability as a writer and speaker.

> I listened to Glen Taylor every time I got a chance, not because he said anything, but because he said nothing superbly well.
>
> I imagine he must be one of the greatest speakers of our time. I'd place the President first. If I had hastily to make a second choice, I'd name Glen Taylor.
>
> I suppose that Glen wrote his own speeches. If he did, he can turn a phrase and round a sentence that make the

> speeches of all the other candidates sound like high school exercises, and his delivery is so flawless that I'd like to hear him even if he talked in Sanskrit.

Actually, I did not "write" my speeches. Sometimes in the early stages of a campaign I would make notes of what I wanted to talk about. I never referred to them. I just memorized them and started talking.

That is one of the most cherished compliments I ever received. It is no little honor to have a Pulitzer Prize winner say that one is second only to Roosevelt as a speaker. That is taking in a lot of territory. To have a critic of his acknowledged stature as a writer compliment me upon my speech writing ability makes me feel sinfully egotistical. Is this me he is writing about?

As soon as the election was over, I had to hurry back to San Francisco and my war plant job. War or no war, I would have hurried back because it was that or starve to death. My family was growing, and so was the pressure to keep my nose to the grindstone.

In politics, any and every defeat is generally considered to be another step toward oblivion. So far, I had proven that this old rule was not necessarily true. Inasmuch as I had made progress and come closer to winning each time I ran, I was determined to keep trying until I lost ground.

Working in the war plant, marking time until the 1944 election, was one of the most unhappy times of my life. To be happy I must be doing something meaningful, and have an ultimate objective in mind. All I was doing was collecting good wages for loafing. I was not cut out to be a loafer or a drudge.

I kept my sights on 1944. That was something to look forward to. The fact that I had a devoted wife and two fine sons dependent on me for their support gave me a feeling of worth, despite the make-work nature of my "cost-plus" job.

NUMBER 1 CHALLENGER The first bubbling of the 1944 political pot came in the form of a brief item in the *Idaho Daily Statesman* dated May 4, 1943. Commenting on possible entrants in the 1944 senatorial race, the article said that it appeared likely that Governor C. A. Bottolfsen might be the Republican candidate against D. Worth Clark, the Democratic incumbent, as though Senator Clark had the nomination all sewed up. "Democrats could hardly turn down D. Worth Clark, but Glen Taylor might try again" is the way the *Statesman* put it. Well, at least I was rated as the number one challenger, which was a place of honor never before accorded me by this very, very anti-Taylor publication.

On April 3, 1944, while I was still working in San Francisco, I formally announced my candidacy for the U.S. Senate. I was so strapped financially that I was forced to delay my return to Idaho as long as possible. This meant that I would have less time to campaign, which would gravitate against me and my personal contact style.

On April 5 there was a full-column rundown on Idaho politics datelined Boise, but appearing, of all places, in the *San Francisco Examiner*. Coming from Boise, you can rest assured that it reflected the prejudices of the *Statesman*. One paragraph says:

> Senator D. Worth Clark, up for renomination and election, will face stiff opposition in the primaries. His opponents for the Democratic nomination for Senator will be James H. Hawley, Boise attorney and son of a former governor of Idaho, and Glen H. (Cowboy) Taylor of Pocatello. The latter has a large following among the more radical elements of the state. Whatever the outcome of the Democratic primaries, the indications are that in November Idaho will send another Republican to the U. S. Senate.

Forgetting that gloomy prediction as *Statesman* hogwash, the entrance into the race of Hawley was great news. He came from the same clique as Clark and could only take votes away from him. Hawley's entrance also emphasized the fact that D. Worth's isolationism was so out of step and his contempt for the machine, unless he could run it, was so flagrant that the machine had decided to support Hawley. They must have felt that Hawley could win in a three-way race. Personally, I was convinced that no such blue-blooded, stiff-necked machine lawyer and politician like Hawley could seriously hurt me.

Another newspaper story dealing with my candidacy dealt Clark a gut blow by winding up with this sentence: "Clark, popular among his senatorial colleagues, has to live down an isolationist record in which he once said, "We have needlessly insulted Japan in the Pacific' and 'Bloody Joe Stalin, I am ashamed to say, is our new ally.' " This quote in the face of the fact that we were at war with Japan, and that Russia was our badly needed ally, was lethal. I intended to remind the voters of it again and again and again.

At this point, I suffered what I considered to be my most serious setback to date. I received a letter from former Governor C. Ben Ross, the old warhorse whose platform technique had inspired me to enter politics. In his letter he deplored my entrance into the race and informed me that he was supporting Hawley. The blow was more sentimental and psychological than real. Nevertheless, I felt as though my own father had turned against me.

HOMELESS   When we arrived in Pocatello, the people who were renting our four-room house refused to vacate. We were homeless as well as broke, with two small boys, two and eight. We had to stay at the home of a good friend and supporter, Wesley Mauzy.

To have to sponge off friends was a terrible ordeal for us as well as for our hosts.

After spending some two weeks imposing on these good people, we headed for Boise. On the way we stopped in Twin Falls to attend a big Democratic dinner to which all candidates for major offices were invited. The response I received in this very conservative, third largest town in Idaho was encouraging. Both Hawley and Clark were present, and each of us was given five minutes to address the assembled Democrats. There was no doubt about it, I received the best hand when I was called upon to speak, and the most enthusiastic applause when I finished.

Dora was seated next to D. Worth Clark, who kept playing with a twenty-dollar bill, running it through his fingers. Poor Dora. She told me later that she sat there enviously watching him and thinking how wonderful it would be to have a twenty-dollar bill to play with.

We went on to Boise, staying at the home of a dear old gentleman who was a staunch supporter. We were hopeful that we might get something to eat there, and we were not disappointed. Not only did he invite us to dinner, but he insisted that we make his home our headquarters while we were in Boise. Perhaps the invitation was simply meant as a friendly gesture, but being in such desperate straits we took him up on the offer.

We had done a tremendous amount of spadework before leaving San Francisco. We had a list of three thousand supporters, which Dora had faithfully recorded during previous campaigns, together with what other information she had been able to elicit, such as the wife's name, children, business, etc. We had sent them all Christmas cards from San Francisco. Then, some thirty days before we returned to Idaho, I had quit my job, gone to the dime store, and bought enough writing paper to write them each a personal letter in longhand. I had made it a point to include in each letter some personal item, such as asking by name how the wife and five children were, or how the alfalfa crop was coming along, or how the hardware business was doing, etc., etc. I had spent the last month at this task, writing at least ten hours a day.

The project was little more than half finished when we moved in, bag and baggage, on this devoted old friend in Boise, where I spent some three weeks writing the rest of the letters. We might have stayed longer, but on this certain day we had driven downtown, and when we returned we found that our personal effects had been crammed into our suitcases and placed in the middle of the room. I am sure that my friend never knew about this or he would have blown his stack, but we could hardly ignore such a delicate hint, as we announced that we must be moving on. I didn't blame the man's wife at all. The poor woman had been miraculously forebearing to put up with us as long as she had.

At long last our house was being vacated, so we headed for Pocatello. When we had first arrived from San Francisco we had inspected our house and knew that it was rundown and shabby. It would be cold and the larder would be bare, but this little four-room abode was our home, the only home we had ever known, and we were unutterably grateful at the prospect of not having to impose on friends and once again feeling the security of having a roof over our heads which we could call our own.

I had been shamelessly soliciting campaign funds since arriving in Idaho and had raised three or four hundred dollars, with twenty being a maximum contribution, so we were in no immediate danger of starving. Knowing of the thousands of dollars raised and spent in Idaho campaigns, I could only come to the conclusion that I was the world's worst fund raiser. I am, however, comforted by the conviction that no politician ever accomplished more with less money than I did.

TAYLOR TOPPER On May 15 we started the campaign. We were headed for north Idaho. We had spent a good part of what little money we had for handbills. Dora and I had worked long·hours handstamping the place and date on them, and wrapping and mailing them to the postmasters to be distributed to boxholders in the twenty communities where we would hold street meetings. The mailing took an even bigger chunk out of our puny funds.

Something happened and we never even made it to our first rally. All that time, effort, and money down the drain. What could have happened to cause such a dreadful waste?

Well, sir, it's a most unusual story.

By the time I was twenty-four I had become too bald to play romantic leads. I decided to buy a hairpiece, hoping that they had been improved since my acquaintance with that not-too-good job brother Ferris wore. I couldn't find anything I'd wear to a dog fight.

However, my interest in the subject had been aroused, and I had started thinking about how a really practical toupee should be made. Having other more immediate things to think about, I had sort of turned the problem over to my subconscious, like the headshrinkers say you can.

Fifteen years had gone by, and while I had a pretty good idea of how a hairpiece should be made, I had done nothing about it because I was no longer personally affected; that is, I hadn't been until I started running for office.

Then I noticed that as long as I was up on top of my car and had my hat on the gals seemed to be well pleased. They would ogle me, talk to one another behind their hands, nudge each other, and make it very plain that they weren't at all displeased with this singing cowboy.

But when the meeting was over and I climbed down off the

platform and politely removed my hat to shake hands with the ladies, thereby exposing my bald head—yuck! They would recoil like I had been scalped by Sitting Bull.

All this had been bugging me, but not enough to prompt any concrete action on my part. And so on this hot day as we headed north to campaign, we stopped for gas, and while the attendant "filled her up" I went in the station for a bottle of pop. Dora remained in the car. The two boys were in the back seat and Dora was sitting in front, where her lovely and amazingly youthful face was clearly visible to the attendant.

I came out with the pop, bareheaded and bald-headed, and asked the attendant, "How much?"

He turned to my beautiful, young-looking wife and then back to me, and in answer to my question he said, *"Your daughter paid for it!"*

Before she thought, Dora gave forth with a wide-mouthed "Hah—hah—hah!"

That did it! I turned the car around and started back toward Pocatello, and Dora asked, "Where are you going?"

"I'm going home and make myself a head of hair," I said, and I said it very positively. ("Positively" is a much better word than "stubbornly.")

"But—aah—why?" she asked.

"Because," I stated firmly, "I need hair." I started to let it go at that, and then I decided that I had acted like an ass long enough so I explained, "If I look like your father, it's no wonder I'm not getting enough votes to win these elections."

She digested that and then she realized how very, very deeply her husband, who was usually such a pleasant fellow, had been hurt. So she set about trying to repair my damaged ego.

"Oh, honey," she said cajolingly, "you don't need hair. You look *fine* without hair. I think your bald head makes you look distinguished and mature. I love you just the way you are."

"Well, maybe *you* do, but those female lady voters don't," I said with some heat. "You've seen how they look when I take off my hat."

She didn't have an answer to that. She had noticed, all right.

There was another reason why I wanted hair at this particular time besides the wisecrack that smart-alec service station boob had made. In all my previous campaigns I had been running against older men with no sex appeal to shower on the lady voters. I had always been the best-looking one in the pack, even with my bald head. This time things were different. D. Worth Clark was not only the same age as I was, he was also a damned good-looking son of a bitch.

Besides that, he had nice, dark wavy hair with just enough gray scattered through it to make him what Dora had just said, "mature and distinguished looking." I'd seen him operate with the ladies, and boy! He was a real wheeler-dealer. I'd heard more than one simpleton say, "Hell, the gals will elect D. Worth."

I needed hair, and I needed it bad.

I was at enough of a disadvantage running against D. Worth and the Clark machine without being handicapped by a bald head.

Always before, my campaigns had been a free-for-all, with everybody starting out more or less even. This time it was different. That goddamned D. Worth Clark was the senator. He was the incumbent, and everybody knew, or at least said, that being the sitting senator and the incumbent gave a man a big edge. Yes *sir*—I needed hair. If having hair could pick me up just 10 votes from those gushy females, they might be the very ones I'd need. This wasn't just another campaign I was in; it was also a beauty contest.

Dora asked me, "What about all the towns we've booked and billed?"

"I'll get out a press release saying I've got the flu," I said. She was horrified at the awful thought of all the time, effort, and money that would be wasted because of this bee I had in my bonnet.

Dora tried once more, though. She asked why we didn't drive to Salt Lake City, which was *only* two hundred miles from Pocatello, and pick up a ready-made toupee. That way we would only miss one day of all those towns we had worked so hard and spent so much money billing.

I knocked down that trial balloon with one shot. "They're not worth the powder it'd take to blow them up," I said firmly. We drove along a ways and then she got me started telling her how my toup—a—a—hairpiece would be different from others.

I think that by the time we got to Pocatello I had her pretty well convinced that maybe I had something.

We had to pass the dime store on our way home. We stopped and bought a couple of hair switches. In those days they cost only a dollar or so—genuine human hair, too. Dora matched it to mine right there before God and everybody.

When we arrived home I had Dora call the press and tell them I had the flu, and that all my advertised meetings were canceled until further notice. Then we went to work on my hairpiece.

The first thing I did was to ask Dora to get me a pair of her flesh-colored panties.

"Whu—a—whu—what?" she stammered.

"Get me a pair of your panties, goddamn it, and don't ask questions. Every minute we waste is that much time off from campaigning," I said impatiently.

She got the panties.

"Now, cut me a piece the size of my bald area," I directed her.

"But, Glen, they cost ninety-eight cents," she protested. I gave her a withering glance and almost tearfully she started whacking.

We then cut a piece of tan-colored felt to the same size, and I glued the two pieces together with rubber cement so it would remain flexible. Then I put my skeptical wife to threading needles with hair and sewing it through the "scalp," starting from the panty side and back through.

Then I took Dora's only bread pan, cut the bottom out of it, and shaped the piece of aluminum to the same size and pattern as the scalp. Using an old flat iron as an anvil, I started pounding the aluminum with a ball-peen hammer and gradually it assumed the shape and contour of my bald area.

This operation took half a day, what with all the fitting and pounding and pounding and fitting. When I had that job done, I joined Dora in the tedious and slow—very slow—process of threading needles with hairs and sewing them in and out of the "scalp."

It took us ten days to complete this phase of the operation.

Then I glued the "scalp" to the base, which I had drilled full of three-sixteenths-inch vent holes. Using the reaming blade of my pocketknife, I reamed holes through the scalp to match the ones in the base. I took an old leather belt and cut two pieces from it five-eighths inch by one inch and glued them to the underside of the base. One of these "pedestals," as I called them, I glued near the crown, and one about an inch from the front.

In forming the base, I had cupped it down at a gradual angle around the front to compensate for the thickness of the pedestals so that when the hairpiece was placed on the head there was an air space next to the wearer's scalp the thickness of the leather pedestals, but the front contacted the wearer's head, and the hair appeared to grow right out of the person's own scalp.

At this point my creation looked very good, except for the fact that the front hairline was a little abrupt and severe. It would need some camouflage to soften it, and make the hairline more casual.

I looked at Dora's hairline and there were countless short, new hairs of various lengths growing there among the long hairs. I also noticed that these shorter, new hairs tended to be more curly than the mature ones.

We tried curling some hair with Dora's curling iron, but as soon as we wet these experimental samples they straightened out. What to do? I was exasperated and sweaty, so I decided to take a bath.

While drying myself I looked down. The hair down there!—it was curly!—very curly!—and in spite of the fact that I had just bathed. Eureka!

I took the scissors and went to work. Very carefully, of course. This was a delicate operation. The success of my hairpiece, as well as my unimpaired manhood, were both at stake.

When I presented my handful of nice, curly hair for Dora's inspection, she was very happy. She asked me, "Where in the world did you ever find this?"

When I explained, she like to have died laughing. I asked her what was so funny, and she said, "Why Glen, I'll be afraid every time you are talking to someone they'll recognize what it is."

"Well, that is just too silly for words," I huffed. "Hair is hair, no matter what part of your anatomy it comes from."

So we glued the curly hair under the base across the front, and the effect was great! Perfect! I had nice, natural-looking, curly little new hairs growing all over the place.

I put a little quick-drying glue on each of the leather pedestals, put the hairpiece on my head, and when the glue had set for two or three minutes, Dora proceeded to wet the hair and comb it. She is quite handy at such things and put some fetching waves in it at least equal to anything of which D. Worth Clark could boast.

I had borrowed a pair of thinning shears from my barber, and Dora, while she was trembling with fear that she might at this last moment ruin the whole thing, proceeded to do a perfect job of trimming and thinning so that the hairpiece blended in with my own hair.

I stepped before a mirror and the years took wings. There I was, just like I used to be in those halcyon days of my youth.

No longer did I have the feeling of inferiority, that I looked like a freak. That old gung-ho pride in my appearance came surging through my veins. I wasn't old! That damned bald head had just made me look old beyond my years. I was a whole man again. I even looked taller. Of course, with hair on your head you *are* taller.

I threw my shoulders back until it hurt.

"Who is this lady killer D. Worth Clark, anyhow? Lemme at him!"

I returned to the campaign with renewed determination, new vigor, and a restored ego. No more did I see that startled, disappointed expression on the faces of lady voters when I removed my hat. I had new pictures taken for campaign literature.

Now if anyone was ever well known by reputation, sight, and sound, I was in Idaho in 1944. I had been in five campaigns. I had been nominated to run for the U.S. Senate twice. I had shaken hands with thousands of people. I had removed my hat and exposed my bald head to all the feminine voters, and I had had my picture in the papers dozens or perhaps hundreds of times, but do you know what happened when I suddenly blossomed forth with a full head of hair? Nothing. Absolutely nothing.

Quite often people would look a little puzzled and say something like, "Glen—this campaigning sure agrees with you. You look younger every time I see you." Or they might ask, "Glen—what's different about you?" When they did, I would just ignore the question and start talking about something else, and that would end it.

With Idaho politics being what they were, with all the petty criticism of my cowboy dress and my style of campaigning and with the *Statesman* even editorializing about me living in California when it was known to everyone that I was working in a war plant there because there were none in Idaho, then certainly if it had dawned on any Republican or any *Statesman* reporter that I was wearing a hairpiece they would have made a big deal out of it and ridiculed me to high heaven. It never happened.

So much for my brainchild. The important question is, "Would it do the job?" Would it really make a difference? After losing three elections, would the fact that I now had hair make me more acceptable to women voters?

Besides the high hopes I had for the efficacy of my new image, I had something else going for me. Something really big. If I could get past D. Worth, then FDR would again be heading the ticket in the general election.

I returned to the campaign trail steamed up and "rarin' to go."

GOODBYE, COWBOY   Now that I had a handsome head of hair and no longer needed to wear my Stetson I changed my entire approach. I bought a conservative business suit and a stylish hat. No more cowboy. I had done enough way-out things to become known. No need for more of that. Everybody knew Glen Taylor, either favorably or unfavorably. My job now was not to become better known, but to unscare those more conservative voters who had been so prejudiced by my unorthodox behavior that they had never attended one of my meetings.

Instead of spending all my time shaking hands on the streets or with employees in shops or stores, I now sought out the boss. He was the guy that had received the scare literature out of Boise. He was the one who had stayed in his office and shut the windows to keep out the awful blare of the loudspeakers on Main Street while his employees had deserted their posts to pack the sidewalks and be converted.

Sometimes I had to laugh, afterward, at the astonished expression on the faces of some of these lesser minions of capitalism when the soft-spoken, well dressed gentleman came walking into their office and introduced himself as Glen Taylor. That's all the introduction I gave or needed. I never added, "I'm running for the United States Senate." They knew.

Sometimes you could have "knocked their eyes off with a stick," they were so astonished at my conventional appearance and cultivated approach. I actually had more than one business-man say, in effect, after we had chatted a few minutes, "You know, I had gotten the wrong impression about you, Mr. Taylor. From what I had been told and read about you I thought you might have horns."

I spent a great deal of time knocking on doors, particularly in larger towns like Boise where my street meetings had been, to say the least, somewhat discouraged by the local police. I would get someone to chauffeur me about, stop at one house in a block, walk up to the door, and knock. I did not care whether or not the door was answered.

If it was, then I used the old street pitch, "I'm Glen Taylor, I'm running for the United States Senate and if you folks don't know anyone you'd rather vote for, I'd appreciate your votes." And for these home calls I added two words I had not used in my street contacts. I said, "Thank you," and got the hell out of there before I got caught in a web of useless conversation.

If there was no answer to my knock, then I had some four-by-four-and-a-half-inch memorandum sheets in six diffeent colors with a duplicated handwritten message, which was different on each color, saying something like, "Stopped to see you. Sorry you were out. Hope to see you later," and signed with just my given name, "Glen." When there was no answer to my knock I did not knock a second time. My time was precious. I simply left a memorandum sheet by opening the screen door and shutting it again so half the sheet was visible, and hurried to a house in the middle of the next block. The sheets were arranged so that I left a different message at each of six houses and then repeated the process. No two identical messages were closer together than six blocks apart, so it would be unlikely that any two note receivers would get together and discover they had a printed message. It was a good printing job, and each sheet looked like an original.

If by chance the receiver contacted the man in the next block or six blocks, they would see that the message was different and be convinced that they had indeed received a personal note from Glen Taylor. I was banking on the fact that most of those who got the note would spark as to who "Glen" was, and if they did not they wouldn't rest until they found out *who* he was. All of this would cause talk, and that's what I wanted.

At future meetings I had many of these new friends come up, wring my hand, and say, "I got your note," and then they would apologize all over the place because they weren't home when such a distinguished visitor came to pay them a call. None of the voters who had answered my knock ever approached me and mentioned my personal call. Obviously, the note technique was more effective. So when I knocked on a door, I began to hope devoutly that the householder was not at home.

DIPLOMAT   In commenting on Hawley's entrance into the senatorial race, the *Pocatello Tribune* ventured, A TRIANGLE MIGHT LAND TAYLOR ANOTHER NOMINATION. I was counting on it. Hawley was doing an effective job of cutting D. Worth down, too. He mailed out a damning piece of literature publicizing Clark's antipreparedness record. I would never have had the staff to comb Clark's record or the money to print and mail out the leaflets. It was most damaging because of the war orientation and patriotic fervor of the time.

To the best of my knowledge, Clark never made any effort to defend his voting record, either on the grounds that he was opposed to war or any other basis. Both Clark and Hawley chose to ignore me and concentrated on destroying each other, just as in my previous campaigns.

I managed to get enough small contributions, none over twenty dollars, to enable me to place some modest two-column-by-eight-inch ads shortly before the primary election. I did not mention either Hawley or Clark in these ads, although I had attacked Clark's record in my campaign speeches, which were reported in some papers but very sparingly in the *Statesman,* if at all. In contrast to previous campaigns, in which it had attacked me viciously, there seemed to be a less critical attitude on the part of the *Statesman.*

Because of the fact that Senator Borah, Idaho's most illustrious citizen, had helped scuttle the League of Nations after World War I, plus the fact that both Clark and Governor Bottolfsen, who was expected to be the Republican nominee, were known as isolationists, I bore down in my newspaper ads on the theme that I would work for an organization to maintain world peace.

I also changed my approach to reclamation projects. In the past when good farmland was scarce, reclamation had been somewhat of a fetish in the West, but circumstances had changed. In contacting farmers, I had found that they were not enthusiastic about bringing more land under cultivation when our farm problem consisted of surpluses, even in wartime. This made sense, so in the ads I said, "He is more interested in seeing that those presently engaged in farming are prosperous than he is in setting others up in competition with them."

In previous elections I had advocated a Columbia Valley Authority similar to the Tennessee Valley Authority, in order to have a coordinated development of our resources. However, the *Statesman* and the Idaho Power Company had scared farmers silly with insidious and false propaganda that their irrigation water rights would be used to make electricity. That, of course, was foolish because the more storage and power dams built, the more water would be available for irrigation, but farmers felt that while that Power Company propaganda might not be true, they just didn't want to take any chances.

Then, too, the word "Authority" was scary in and of itself. The farmers didn't want any "Authority" tinkering with their precious water rights. On the other hand, the Bonneville and Grand Coulee projects in neighboring Washington were a great success without any "Authority," so I used that approach. My ads said, "He will seek federal aid to develop projects in Idaho similar to Bonneville and Grand Coulee in order to bring new industries to the state. This will mean jobs for returning veterans. Workers with paychecks mean cash customers for our merchants and close at home markets for our farmers."

This politically diplomatic approach seemed to please everybody. At least I had pulled the teeth of their "anti-Authority" propaganda, and it ceased.

Incidentally, my ads included a picture of the candidate. A distinguished looking gentleman with a fine, wavy head of hair.

NOLO CONTENDERE Dora and our two sons were accompanying me on my campaign trips. Arod, who was eigh⸱

now, was a great campaigner, but P.J., who was only two and a half years old, became bored. He was a precocious and energetic child. During an evening meeting he had kept squirming and fidgeting, asking his mother when the meeting would end. He had not yet learned the art of whispering, so he had been a disrupting influence.

After the meeting I took him to task. He listened attentively to my lecture, which I wound up by saying, "You've got to be a good boy." Looking me squarely in the eye, he said calmly, "Well, if you'd make a good speech I'd be a good boy."

I burst into laughter, picked him up, and promised to try and do better.

CHICKEN? While my family had accompanied me throughout the campaign, we had sung no songs, used no loud-speakers, held no street meetings, ridden no horses, worn no cowboy regalia. Furthermore, I had not bombarded the press with my usual brief, pithy press releases, which had always been composed in a manner that required no editing. I am sure that the wire services, particularly, missed my daily epistles. I had planned this sneaky campaign hoping that my complete departure from past practices would be so mystifying that the press would be lured into speculation to keep my name before the voters.

It worked out as planned. The *Statesman,* and to a lesser degree the other Republican papers over the state, could not help but be aware of the strange quietude, and they couldn't resist the temptation to speculate. At least every other day they would wonder, somewhere in their columns, where I was and what in hell I was doing.

Maybe I had chickened out at the prospect of competing with Senator D. Worth Clark and fled back to the safety of California and the war plant. I was sick, perhaps. Dead? There was no end of speculation. The press coverage was almost as good as if I were dashing about on horseback.

I had a hunch I was in pretty good shape, and I didn't want to rock the boat.

IV

United
States
Senator

TOP DOG   On primary election night the first returns, as usual, came from Boise. As expected, Hawley made a good showing there. Clark was second, and I was not far behind.

A little later, as returns came in from other parts of the state where Hawley was not well known, he was passed by D. Worth, which eliminated him, because he had no further reservoirs of strength.

I passed Hawley, but still trailed D. Worth. I kept creeping up on him, though. At one point he led me by 1,000 votes.

By tens and twenties, I began to whittle away at Clark's lead. Now we were hearing from the "horseback" precincts. They were called "horseback" because they were beyond the ends of the telephone lines. As usual, I had bulled my way over ungodly roads back into these remote bastions of democracy while Clark had scorned such laborious grubbing.

Finally, and at long last, on June 24 the official count was announced. The black headline on the three-column spread in the *Pocatello Tribune* proclaimed: TAYLOR WINS BY 216.

With no sitting governor, I was the titular head of the Democratic Party in Idaho. My new head of hair had worked against curly-haired Clark; now we would see how I fared against the black-thatched governor.

TWO LIARS   An unimportant little incident got my name on page one. The caption reads, CANDIDATES SWAP INSINCERITIES. The ten-line quickie reads: "Glen Taylor, Democrat, and Gov. C. A. Bottolfsen, Republican, candidates for the U.S. Senate, met in Boise Thursday. 'What did you say to each other?' Taylor was asked. 'We exchanged the amenities and wished each other luck like a couple of liars' came the reply."

This little story appeared in papers all across the country.

As the campaign drew to a close, Bottolfsen, whom I had always felt was a rather decent sort of fellow, became desperate and resorted to outright falsehood when it was too late to refute such tactics effectively. He said, "Taylor told an audience in Ririe that the federal government should repudiate war bonds after the war to create a market for new bond issues to finance relief." That, I believe, is the most blatant attempt I ever heard of to frighten voters with an outright lie. Nearly every voter had money invested in war bonds. I was done for if they believed this lousy lie. We would shortly know whether his desperate scheme would be effective.

When asked by a reporter what I thought of the Republican campaign, I am quoted as saying, "At times I have been in doubt as to whether I was running for the senate or the penitentiary." The quote wasn't original. Abe Lincoln said it, but it was apropos.

SENATOR TAYLOR!   The first returns on election night were from my home county, and I jumped off to a 161-vote lead with the first radio report. I never did my best in the larger towns, and they always reported first, so it was no big surprise when Bottolfsen went ahead by 227 votes. But within an hour, on the basis of 110 precincts reporting, I forged ahead by 175 votes and Bott never caught up with me again. Eventually, I beat him by 4,723 votes and became the first actor ever elected to the United States Senate. Perhaps having hair does help.

There is something interesting and more than a little strange about those election results. There were 1,410 more votes counted in the senatorial race than in the race for governor. I wonder who they were counted for? And why?

All right, let's say there was more interest in the senatorial race than in the gubernatorial race. That's possible, but hardly likely. What about Roosevelt? What about the presidential race? Surely that would draw the maximum vote. It didn't.

There were 1,806 fewer votes cast for President than there were for U.S. senator. Is it likely or possible that 1,410 voters who went to the polls were so disinterested in the gubernatorial race that they just didn't bother to mark their ballot for governor, even though they were there with pencils in their hands? Stranger yet, 1,806 voters who had voted for U.S. senator were so disinterested in who should be President of the United States that they didn't bother to vote in that race. I mention this obvious crookedness because we will see more of it.

My reaction to my election was close to disbelief. After all the years, all the campaigns, all the struggles and heartaches and defeats, could this really be so? Dora remarked that in winning I was less excited than I had been on those election nights when I had lost. I was in shock. I had hoped to win, but knowing how crooked the machine was, I had prepared myself to lose, and this was just too much. I was afraid that this was a dream.

One would think that with the election over the Republican press might relent a little and give me credit for making a good fight, but it didn't happen. The *Recorder Herald* of Salmon, Idaho, had this to say:

> In Lemhi County Governor Bottolfsen, running against Glen Taylor for the U.S. Senate, polled the largest vote of any national, state or county candidate in which there was a contest. Lemhi County has reason to feel proud of that vote. It demonstrated good citizenship.

It may have been a demonstration of good citizenship, or it might have been a demonstration of bare-knuckle politics. There were twenty-eight more votes counted in the senatorial race in that little county than there were in the gubernatorial contest.

TORCHLIGHT PARADE   On the evening of the day the official result was announced, a woman friend of Dora's came over about six p.m. and told her that the citizens of Pocatello were planning a torchlight parade at eight p.m. celebrating my victory. It was supposed to be a big surprise, but Dora's friend was afraid that she might be in the very fix she *was* in, so she had felt it was her duty to warn her. Poor Dora had been down in the basement packing furiously and she did look terrible. Supper was forgotten while the neighbor lady helped her make herself and the house presentable.

The parade of a hundred cars or so arrived on schedule, torches blazing and P.A. system blaring. They drew up in front of our miserable little house and a voice started shouting over the loudspeaker system, "We want Taylor—We want Taylor."

And who do you think the enthusiastic celebrator was? None other than my old friend Nick Ifft, the columnist for the *Pocatello Tribune,* who once in a while said something halfway nice about me but generally used his column to run me down and question my fitness to be a dogcatcher, much less a United States senator.

Oh well. Somebody once said, "Politics makes strange bedfellows."

As soon as it was apparent that I had won, our family's privacy was ended. Reporters phoning and knocking on the door, well-wishers to congratulate me, politicians offering to organize and serve on policy committees. It was obvious what they were getting at: I just wasn't capable of handling the job so they would lead me by the hand.

I thanked them for their unselfish offers and told them we would get together later. In the midst of, around, and through, all this disruption we were trying to pack so we could get started for Washington.

We were on the verge of starving, but it didn't occur to anyone that such a thing as eating could possibly be a problem to a famous man who had just been elected to the United States Senate.

Finally, I borrowed fifteen hundred dollars from a long-time supporter who ran a country store and gas station.

PROPHET AROD At this point another phenomenon reared its lovely head. Several papers wrote factual articles (with pictures, yet) about my struggles and victory and family without saying anything at all derogatory about me. *This* is *the* day.

The *Coeur d'Alene Press,* for one, gave us a two-column story extending from top to bottom of the page with our family group picture. Another Arod story was included and reads:

> In regard to his candidacy Mr. Taylor has a story he likes
> to relate that indicates that his son Arod (age 9) may be
> something of a prophet.
> At the beginning of the fall school term the son came

home and said that he had been required to fill out a questionnaire, which among other things, asked "Father's Occupation?"

Mr. Taylor was curious to know whether the boy had termed him a singer, actor, radio entertainer or defense worker, any or all of which would have been correct, so he asked, "What did you say my occupation was?"

"Well," said Arod, "I didn't have room to write 'candidate for United States Senate' so I just put U.S. Senator."

WASHINGTON OR BUST   We left Pocatello in a blizzard, with a *Statesman* editorial calling me a demagogue ringing in my ears.

Our old Ford car, which had seen us through so many campaigns, was on its last legs.

Our trip was not too pleasant. It was cold. The backseat was leveled off from the top of the front seat to the top of the backseat with cardboard boxes containing clothing, pots and pans, and bedding. The boys would take turns riding in the front seat and lying down on top of the junk in the backseat.

The only suitcase we owned was in the car trunk with whatever other stuff we could jam in there, including two saxophones, a guitar, a clarinet, a ukulele, a trombone, a banjo, and miscellaneous other essential belongings.

Our second day en route to Washington we blew out a tire. We limped into Cheyenne, where I wired Compton I. White, the Democratic congressman from north Idaho's First District, asking if he could help us get some new (and rationed) rubber. Immediately, he called me on the phone at government expense and suggested that we go on to Denver, and he would make arrangements for tires to be awaiting us there.

We made it to Denver "on a wing and a prayer," as the wartime song put it. To be less euphemistic, we made it with boots in three tires, limping along at fifteen miles an hour. Five new tires (the very best) were waiting for us at the Denver ration board.

This was the first concrete evidence that there were certain advantages attached to being a United States senator.

AWOL   From Denver to Roanoke, Virginia, it was cold and the roads were snow covered and slippery, but the trip was uneventful except for frequent periods of cooling our heels while we got replacements for worn-out spark plugs, distributor points, carburetors, a new muffler, and a dozen or two other items necessary to keep moving. In Roanoke, Virginia, we again had it impressed upon us that senators weren't treated like just any-old-body.

Roanoke had streetcars and at intersections there were islands for boarding. I was concentrating on following the car ahead of me and did not notice the light change so I got a ticket. The motorcycle officer told us to follow him to the JP's, where I was brought into the presence of that worthy gentleman.

Preliminary to collecting tribute from another out-of-state driver, for which Roanoke was well known, the JP asked me a few questions. When he learned that I was the United States senator from Idaho on my way to take my seat in that august body, he turned two shades lighter and experienced some difficulty clearing his throat.

While I did not know it at the time, the Constitution of the United States is very clear on this point. A senator on his way to Washington is immune to arrest. You just can't do it. But they had done it.

There wasn't another word spoken. The judge simply looked at the arresting officer, gave a barely discernible jerk of his head, and they both went out through the back door. Impatiently, we waited for them to return. We wanted to pay our fine and be on our way.

When twenty minutes had passed I went over to the door where the law had exited and opened it cautiously. There was no one in this back room. The back door was open, so I went over and looked out into the backyard, which was surrounded by a board fence. There was no one in the backyard. There was no gate, so obviously the officer as well as the more elderly judge had "gone over the wall." It took a moment or two for the fact of this unseemly behavior to soak in. Detaining a senator was no joking matter. I went back to the room where my aborted trial had begun and ended, with only a sentence or two spoken and no sentence pronounced. Dora and I talked it over and decided that I must be more important than we had realized. I led my brood out to the car and we proceeded toward Washington, D.C.

THEM APPLES   Besides being infamous for the generous manner in which the city passed out traffic citations to out-of-state victims, Roanoke was famous as an apple-growing district. The Taylor family can vouch for the quality of Roanoke apples because we got a box of the delicious fruit absolutely free, and it wasn't given to us, either.

A few miles out of Roanoke the road was covered with apples. That's right. Someone had gone this way with a load of apples and a box had fallen off the load and burst open.

I screeched to a halt and we all jumped out and fell to with a will.

It did not occur to me that there was anything unseemly about a United States senator picking up apples on a busy highway, causing brakes to squeal and motorists to curse. Here was food, and our long years of fighting to survive during the Depression, as well as more recent privations, when obtaining food was our paramount problem, made it unthinkable that these apples, or any food, should go to waste.

So when we got to Washington we had a box of apples with no box. They were simply spread out in a fairly solid layer on top of everything else in the backseat.

When I worked in the war plant I had wasted thirty minutes getting to work and thirty minutes coming home each day, and I was determined that this wasteful expenditure of time should not happen in Washington.

We would use the Senate Office Building as the center of our house hunting and work outward.

We arrived in the Capitol in the early afternoon. Everyone got a big thrill as we passed the White House and the Washington Monument on our way to the Senate Office Building.

Our house-hunting efforts came to naught. We spent the afternoon looking for a "for rent" sign, driving up one street and down another with our backseat full of boxes and bedding, apples and kids.

It was getting late. We had to have shelter. The closest hotel to my prospective office was the Continental, just off the Capitol grounds. We were told that they had nothing available.

Dora was exasperated and said to me, "Surely there must be some provision for housing senators."

The clerk overheard her remark. "Are you a senator?" he asked with a sudden show of interest. When I answered in the affirmative, his whole attitude changed. "I'm sorry, Senator," he apologized. "I didn't know. Now let me see." He ran his finger down the register sheet. "Oh, yes, yes." In no time at all we were safe and warm.

Getting unpacked presented problems. We had only one suitcase to our name. Everything else was in paper bags or cardboard boxes. We had assumed that we would be moving into a house and hadn't planned on putting up at a hotel or we might have tidied things up a bit. It was embarrassing for a new senator to be carrying paper bags and boxes through the lobby of a fancy hotel.

I didn't do the carrying, although I couldn't escape being identified as the owner of the mountainous mess of crap. The shamefaced bellboys did the carrying, but even so the operation was delayed in getting under way. You see, the apples had jolted off the crib mattress we had on top of all the stuff in the backseat of the car, and when one of the fancily dressed bellhops opened the car door, our unboxed box of apples came tumbling out and we had to go through the same process of picking them up that had delayed our arrival.

The chore was even more laborious than it had been out on the highway. It takes time to pick up a box of apples, even with the help of two embarrassed bellboys, especially when most of the apples have rolled anywhere up to a hundred feet away on a sloping concrete parking lot, under parked cars and scattered all over a half-acre lot.

Now that they knew I was a senator, everyone was very courteous. Actually, the word should be "obsequious," overly courteous, fawning. This was our third lesson on the subject: "Senators are *not* ordinary people."

It cost us twenty-five dollars a day for two rooms. Twenty-five dollars! My God! As it turned out, this wasn't for just a one-night stay, either. This was December. We didn't find a house till May, and then we had to buy it.

BREAK-IN AT THE PENTAGON   The third day after our arrival in Washington, Congressman Compton I. White called and made an appointment to show us the town. Knowing his reputation as the world's worst driver, I would have declined the honor and the risk of the sightseeing tour, but before he told me what he had in mind he asked me if I had anything to do that afternoon. I was sure that this tour of our beloved capital city would be most exciting. I was not disappointed.

Comp averaged a new car about every three months, the previous new car having been hauled away to a junkyard. Knowing how insurance companies had a habit of canceling your policy after one or two wrecks at the most, I wondered how anyone with a record of wrecks like Comp's could get any insurance at any price. I asked Comp about that, but he assured me it was no problem. "They wouldn't dare cancel a congressman's insurance or raise his premium," he assured me. "If they get smart about it, just tell 'em you'll introduce a resolution calling for an investigation of their racket. That scares the hell out of them. No siree, they won't cancel you or raise your premium; they'll lower it. Every time they threaten me it winds up with me getting a lower rate. I've got a rate so low you wouldn't believe it."

We took off down Pennsylvania Avenue. Dora asked the congressman if he'd mind stopping at a store so she could buy a jar of cold cream. He gallantly mumbled "No trouble at all," and launched into the tour-guide routine which he used on all VIPs from Idaho.

As the car rolled down the traffic-heavy avenue, half of the time there was no hand on the wheel; Comp was too busy pointing out this, that, and the other landmark on both sides of the street at the same time.

We came to a green light. Comp stopped and started another phase of his spiel while the drivers piling up behind us began honking their horns. The only effect this had on Comp was to cause him to mumble, "Oh shut up, goddammit, I'm Compton I. White." The way he said it, with no particular emphasis and not really loud enough for anyone to hear, gave me the impression that he was a little "tetched" on the subject of his own importance.

We came to a red light and Comp drove calmly through while brakes screeched, horns bellowed, and irate drivers screamed imprecations. Comp simply repeated his mumbled "Oh shut up, goddammit, I'm Compton I. White."

"Now here's Woodward and Lothrop," Comp informed Dora. "You can get your cold cream here."

"Oh, that will be fine," she answered, but then as her eyes traveled on down the length of the block and beheld nothing but a solid phalanx of parked cars, she said disappointedly, "It looks like there's no place to park."

"Don't let that worry you none, young lady," Comp advised her and drove right up on the sidewalk, chasing from his accustomed place the liveried footman who stood on the sidewalk at the entrance to this snooty emporium.

This usurpation of his sacred precincts agitated the self-important doorman, and he protested vigorously, "You cannot park here, sir." Comp simply mumbled his magic words, "Go to hell, I'm Compton I. White, congressman from Idaho," gave Woodward and Lothrop's symbol of dignity an undignified push and we all trooped into Washington's foremost department store, leaving the "car door opener" with no place to ply his trade.

When we came out the footman was protesting loudly to a policeman, gesticulating and explaining how some crazy man had driven this car up on the sidewalk and walked off and left it. When we walked to the car and it became apparent that we were the brazen scofflaws, the policeman approached Comp as he was getting behind the wheel and said, "Could I see your driver's license, please?"

Such impertinence set Comp off and he shouted, "Aw, go to hell. Can't you read? Take a look at my license plate. I'm Compton I. White, congressman from Idaho." The poor officer recoiled like Comp had hit him in the face with a wet towel.

As Comp eased the car off the curb and we drove away, I looked back to see the officer look at the doorman, shrug, and spread his hands in the well known gesture which means, *What the hell can I do about it?*

This was our lucky day as well as Comp's. We had many near misses but no clash of metal.

Our tour manager headed off across the Potomac, explaining as he drove that he had to see a man at the Pentagon because a friend of his (Comp's) had a drafted son he couldn't get along without on the farm.

There is a brain-addling maze of cloverleafs as one approaches the Pentagon. Comp must have driven clear around the huge five-sided building at least three times, grunting and mumbling, turning this way and that, but never seeming to get any closer to our goal, no more than one hundred yards away.

Congressman Compton I. White's name more or less matched his skin. It was somewhat bleached from long days, weeks, months, and years at a desk either in his offices, a committee hearing room, or the congressional chamber.

Now, however, as we circled the habitat of the top military brass, a pink tide was working up from his collar. It hadn't risen far, no more than half an inch showing, when Comp gave the steering wheel a violent turn and headed off across the immaculately groomed lawns toward the elusive edifice which stood there in all its rambling grandeur, so near and yet so far away.

With this direct approach we were at the front entrance in no time. I looked back at the tire marks we had left on the well watered greensward. My heart was filled with fear at the very idea of doing what Comp was doing, but admiration for his numbskull courage.

There were parking lots all over the place, including one by the front. It was marked "reserved" and each stall was posted with a general's name. Comp selected the nearest empty one to the door and parked. There was no one about, so there was no argument. It probably had never occurred to the denizens of this architectural monstrosity that anyone would have the unmitigated gall to park in a space clearly marked "General Marshall."

We went in and Comp inquired of a girl at the information booth where he could find his man. "Do you have an appointment with the colonel?" she asked.

"No," mumbled Comp. "I'm Congressman Compton I. White of Idaho, and I've got some important business with the colonel."

That, as usual, did it. Identification badges were pinned on us and a uniformed guide took us in tow and threaded the mystic maze with astonishing facility.

There were several people waiting in Colonel Long's outer office. As we entered, the door to the colonel's inner office opened and a man came out. The departing person failed to shut the door, and we could see the colonel seated at his desk while his secretary handed him a cup of coffee. Obviously, the colonel was all set to take a coffee break.

The girl came toward us and literally shut the door in Comp's face. I could see he wasn't happy at being thwarted with his quarry in sight, but he controlled himself and went over to the receptionist. "I'm Compton I. White, congressman from Idaho," he mumbled. "I want to see Colonel Long."

"Do you have an appointment?" the girl asked.

"No, I don't," Comp said, his voice rising a little.

"Well, I'm sorry, sir, but you'll have to wait. These people all have appointments."

Comp was getting a little short on patience, and the red was beginning to show above his collar again. "Maybe you didn't hear me. I'm Compton I. White, congressman from Idaho, and I want to see the colonel—Now!" And old Comp banged the desk so hard that everything on it jumped a foot in the air.

The receptionist held her ground. "I'm sorry, sir, but—"

That's as far as she got. Old Comp wheeled, walked to the door of the colonel's inner office, and gave a hefty push on the door. When it didn't budge, he stepped back, raised his right foot, and slammed it against the door just below the knob, like cops do in the movies. Something gave, the door flew open, and Comp marched in, motioning for us to follow.

It was difficult to believe that Comp was always this rough, and I had a feeling he was perhaps overdoing it to impress upon us just how much weight he had in Washington.

When the door flew open and Comp stood framed there the colonel must have thought his time had come. Comp was mad. The colonel's jaw dropped and he turned white, from rage or fright or both.

"What the hell do you mean, breaking into my office unannounced?" he gritted through his teeth.

"I've got a little business with you, Colonel," Comp said.

"You have no business with me until you are properly announced," the colonel stormed.

"Calm down, Colonel, you don't want to talk like that to a congressman."

The man in uniform, who usually gave the orders, opened his mouth, but instead of anything coming out, the message soaked in.

"C-C-C-Congressman?" the flabbergasted colonel stuttered.

"Yessir," Comp said. "Congressman Compton I. White of Idaho."

The colonel's face, which had turned white, then red, was now turning white again. From being a mighty and imperious colonel, he instantaneously became a fawning sycophant as obsequious as the shoeshine boy in the Senate cloakroom.

"Uh, well, ah, I'm Colonel Long, Congressman. We're always happy to have you drop in on us. Here, sit down. Are these people your friends?" He wanted to be sure we had not just followed Comp in before offering Dora and me a seat.

"This gentleman," said Comp somewhat icily, "Is the Honorable Glen H. Taylor, newly elected senator from Idaho."

That did it. The poor colonel, who like all his confreres was under strict orders to never, never, under any circumstances, offend a congressman, much less a senator, was visibly shaken.

You never saw such politeness. Shaking hands, placing chairs, all the while outdoing Comp in the mumbling department.

Comp had hardly stated his business when the colonel assured him that he understood perfectly. The congressman was absolutely right. It was very important, most important indeed, that young men who were needed for farm work should remain on the farm. Someone had erred. The mistake would be rectified "immediately."

To further demonstrate his good intentions, he ordered his secretary, "Get me Colonel Ogilvy at Selective Service," and when the girl didn't jump, he barked in true colonel fashion, *"at once!"* Then she jumped.

While the girl was getting Colonel Ogilvy on the line, we were effusively ushered to the door and before the door closed behind us, we could hear Colonel Long telling Colonel Ogilvy what had to be done, "Congressman White, yes, *and* Senator Taylor—"

As the door closed Comp looked at me, smiled his toothless smile, and gave me a long, meaningful wink.

If Colonel Long's agitation seems a little overdrawn, let me explain why officers in any branch of the armed services are so desperately concerned that they should not incur the disfavor of any congressman or, and particularly, a senator. In the first place, the military are dependent on Congress for the appropriations which are their life's blood. Any officer who antagonized a senator or congressman would have to answer to the high brass, and his excuse had better be good or his career might just come to a screeching halt.

The second reason for these often overbearing and dictatorial officers to become uncustomarily humble in the presence of a United States senator is that their promotions and therefore their careers are dependent, not on how a group of senators might feel toward them, but on the whim and fancy of any one senator.

All promotions in the armed services above a certain rank must be okayed by the Senate. Periodically, a list of all contemplated promotions is sent to the Senate. If no senator objects, it is routinely approved, *but,* if one—just one—senator requests that any names on the list be passed over—then those promotions are held up. The military will contact the objecting senator, and if he is adamant, that officer's name is stricken from the list of those up for promotion, unless he can prevail upon the objecting senator to relent.

Senators are jealous of their powers and prerogatives, and should the military ever be so foolish as to ask for a vote on one of these "passed over" promotions, it is most likely that the Senate would hesitate and thoughtfully consider before voting to override the objection of a fellow-in-membership of the most exclusive club on earth. It is always in the back of each senator's mind that he may one day need the backing of his distinguished associates.

The display of senatorial power that I had witnessed awed me. I had always been resentful of any unduly harsh display of authority. While I had had a certain amount of authority as manager of my own show, I had always suggested rather than commanded. There are times, of course, when the authority of the head man of any undertaking, great or small, if his wishes are questioned or defied, must take off the kid gloves and assert his power in no uncertain terms. What I had seen on this afternoon caused me to resolve never to use this new power capriciously.

On the way back to our hotel, Comp said that he and Mrs. White were going to a party in the evening, that he had mentioned to the hostess that we were in town and had been asked to bring us along. Important people were giving the party and important guests would be there, Comp assured us.

We had not yet been to a Washington party, so we readily agreed.

Dora was all atwitter. She had bought a new "senator's wife's" dress, and this would be her first chance to wear it.

FIRST PARTY   Comp drove us to the party, but his wife was a pretty good backseat driver, so the trip was not as bad as the afternoon's. She made him stop for stoplights and signs and wouldn't let him stop on green lights to explain the passing scene.

The party was quite remarkable. The hostess was the daughter of one of our very top admirals. The house was hers. It was a row house, not large but expensively furnished. The host was the lady's boyfriend, and they made no bones of the fact that they were living together without benefit of clergy. This state of affairs was a little unusual at the time, to say the least, and certainly such scandalous goings on were several jumps ahead of the standards of acceptable behavior in Idaho.

Another guest was an editor of *Reader's Digest*, so you can imagine where *he* fit in the political spectrum.

Another gentleman who was, I'd say, around seventy turned out to be a former senator who had been defeated for reelection in the recent voting. He was a big man with a high, squeaky voice. I couldn't even imitate him because my vocal cords wouldn't stretch that tight.

I had cautioned Dora beforehand that we would have to be on our toes at all times because every senator except me was probably educated and knowledgeable and if I wasn't careful, my lack of education and culture would brand me as an unlettered ignoramus. So we were en garde as we found ourselves cozily seated in a corner with the former senator and his wife.

During the course of the conversation, which had gotten around to a book I had recently read, I mentioned that the following evening we planned, as was our custom, to take our sons to a western movie. That brought forth the following astonishing and reassuring statement from the ex-senator. "W-e-l-l," he falsettoed in his incongruous voice, "I never go to the movies. And I never read books. I never listen to the radio—and I never read the newspapers." And they got up and headed for a refill at the bar.

When this incredible statement had soaked in, I leaned over to Dora and whispered, "If he is an example of what I'll find in the Senate, I guess I won't have too much to worry about."

Now the admiral's daughter and her friend in residence came over. Since her distinguished father was still on active duty at the highest levels, his daughter could not be much over forty, but she looked older. She wasn't bad looking, mind you; in fact, she was quite striking, but she did look a little haggard.

Her friend was an unprepossessing character, but quite charming and suave. From the way he steered the conversation, it was evident that he was trying to find out whether I was here to save the world or to be more sensible and vote in a manner that could be capitalized upon. When I told him briefly of the principles I had espoused in my campaigns, he made no attempt to hide his disdain for anyone so foolish, unceremoniously getting up and moving to another group.

HOME ON THE RANGE   We were still homeless when the new Senate convened on January 3.

I had been familiarizing myself with the Capitol and the Senate Office Building. The day before Congress was to convene I had been shown my office, which was the same one vacated by my predecessor, D. Worth Clark. You cannot imagine how unreal it all seemed and the heart-thumping thrill when I saw *my* spacious and elegant offices with my name on the door, and sat in the massive, leather upholstered chair behind my equally massive desk. I had never even sat behind a desk, much less one that was my very own. I had difficulty breathing. I just could not bring myself to believe that all this was happening to *me. Is this really me?* I kept asking myself.

Now on this opening day of a new Congress, everything was hubbub. Photographers busy. Flashbulbs popping. Pictures of all the new senators in a group.

There were six of us. I was assigned a seat, in the back row where all new members must start. You move toward the front only as members are defeated or die.

Me? Here? Waiting to be sworn in as a United States senator? I, who had never belonged to any legislative or any other group? I, who so recently had been a day laborer? Could this be me among all these gentlemen whose hands felt so soft when I shook them with my callused one? I still expected to wake up and find that I had lost again and this was only a dream.

My heart skipped a beat when I thought of all the schooling represented here. There probably wasn't another man here with so little formal education.

A reporter for a newsreel buttonholed me and asked if I would sing something for their cameras. I said, "No, I'm afraid not, I didn't come here to sing. I am here on serious business." He coaxed and cajoled and finally I said, "See Colonel Halsey. If he thinks it would be okay I'll do it." He hurried away.

I was sitting in my new seat trying to get used to the idea of being a senator when Les Biffle, the secretary to the majority, came to my seat, leaned over, and whispered, "Colonel Halsey would like to see you, Senator."

When I followed Biffle into Halsey's office, the large room was jammed with what I soon learned was practically every reporter here to cover this important occasion and they were all here to urge the colonel to okay my appearance, on camera, to demonstrate the vocal technique that had made me world famous as the "Singing Cowboy" from Idaho. The badgered and beleaguered secretary was obviously torn between his desire to uphold senatorial dignity and his wish to keep in the good graces of the press corps. Biffle elbowed our way to the colonel, who explained the situation. I passed the buck back to him by saying that as a newcomer I would leave the decision up to him. If he thought it was not inappropriate I would be happy to oblige. After much vacillating amid shouted pleas from the press, which could recognize a good story a mile away, the beleaguered colonel harrumphed a time or two and capitulated. "I can see no real reason why Senator Taylor should not accommodate you boys if he is willing," he judged. "After all, he *did* sing his way to the United States Senate, and the millions of people who have read about his amazing feat would doubtless like to hear him sing. So if it's all right with you, Senator—" He left the sentence hanging.

A chorus of pleas rose from the never bashful newsmen, yelping like a pack of bloodhounds. "Come on, Senator!" "Give us a break!"

"Okay, okay," I shouted, and a cheer went up, or perhaps I mistook the baying of a pack of newshounds for cheers.

Now two or three ringleaders started arguing about where would be the best place to stage the event.

"On the Capitol steps with the dome in the background," it was decided.

It was ten a.m. We would have to make haste. The Senate would convene at twelve noon. While the young army of old-head reporters started milling toward the Capitol steps to get their equipment ready I went home—pardon me, to the hotel—to get my banjo and my family.

Dora had spent the morning getting herself and the boys ready for this, the greatest event of our lives, and she still had much to do, but she had to cut it short and we hastened across the Capitol grounds to the steps, where it looked like every cameraman in Washington was getting ready to film "The Great Train Robbery." About all that was missing was D. W. Griffith with a megaphone.

The steps and other vantage points were crowded with senators, secretaries, and tourists waiting to see this unprecedented event.

I have always contended that if a thing is worth doing, it is worth doing right. So, as long as we were singing, let's do it right. My instinct for publicity, aiming to intrigue the public, rouse their sympathy, and grab at their heartstrings, had been operating at top speed since it had been decided that this event would take place.

The papers were full of the housing shortage. Newly elected senators and congressmen were homeless, tramping the streets looking for a place to live. Most any old place rented at any outrageous price. Witness my own predicament. Cooped up in two small hotel rooms with two small children—at twenty-five dollars a day. That's seven hundred and fifty dollars a month!

In all my years in show business I had never paid more than two dollars and fifty cents for a room. Talk about inflation and highway robbery!

So, with the housing shortage on everyone's mind, I decided to capitalize on the situation. In the brief time since this thing had jelled I had been busy composing a song. Not really a new song, but some new topical words for a well known old favorite.

We would sing "Home on the Range," but with words that would make the event ten times more newsworthy. Pathos, comedy—we would make this a heartrending appeal for the homeless.

P.J. didn't sing but Dora, Arod, and I would harmonize. We were still frantically rehearsing our new words when one of the men manning the batteries of newsreel cameras shouted "ready," and raised his arms to silence the spectators. I strummed a few chords on the banjo as an introduction. Then we sang—for more people than we had sung for in all the times we had ever sung before, put together.

We had an audience of millions, and we knew it, but it didn't show. Whatever else we may have been, good or bad, one thing was certain. We weren't amateurs. We were old pros, and that went for Arod too. To the tune of "Home on the Range," we sang:

> *Oh give us a home,*
> *Near the Capitol dome,*
> *With a yard where little children can play,*
> *Just one room or two,*
> *Any old thing will do,*
> *Oh we can't find a pla—ce to stay.*

I looked about. Up there on the top steps I recognized some of the dignified senators I had met this morning. They were convulsed with laughter. The blasé newsmen who had thought we were going to sing "Home on the Range" were caught off guard and were laughing uproariously.

As the laugh started to subside, a round of applause bounced off the majestic steps and echoed across the grounds. Sightseers a block distant looked our way to see what was causing all the applause.

I was glad we were well received because Dora hadn't been too sure we were doing the right thing. She had felt I should be more dignified, and so had I, come to think of it. How in the hell had I gotten roped into this, anyhow?

Oh well, it was done. How would the coverage be? Good,

great, or amazing? It was amazing. The newsreels appeared all over the United States. Clips of our song were included in foreign newsreels, even when they didn't use the entire newsreel.

The picture and the pleading words of our version of "Home on the Range" appeared all over the world in every major language.

Some stiff-necked editors were shocked, but most applauded and said it was a relief to have a senator who wasn't too filled with his own importance to unbend a little.

Many predicted that our plea for a home would evoke a sympathetic response, and it did. We had numerous letters from people in supposedly housing-short Washington, D.C., offering to rent us rooms, let us live with them until we found something better, offering to move upstairs and let us have the downstairs. The response was unbelievable. If our plea had been for all the homeless instead of us alone we could have solved the housing crisis right there.

Unfortunately, all the offers were for makeshift quarters of a temporary nature. There just wasn't a house available in Washington, D.C.

The day after the episode on the Capitol steps, I was assured by a knowledgeable newsman that when this event attained its maximum saturation in a few days, more people would know the name of the new senator from Idaho than would know the name of any other senator living or dead. I'm not bragging, but that *was* what the man said.

As one would expect, the forever partisan Republican press of Idaho deplored my "disgraceful exhibition."

The *Statesman* editorialized, under the heading THE MELODY IS SOUR IN IDAHO, "While Glen Taylor, Idaho's New Senator gives proof of the misfortune of his election by crooning on the Capitol steps *The Statesman* hopes that those who are responsible for his being where he is have the courage necessary for the next six years."

The *Pocatello Tribune* ran an editorial in the same vein.

"It's too bad—too bad for Idaho and too bad for Mr. Taylor" (not Senator Taylor). "We blame the press for letting him get away with it" (the press set it up—not I).

Now that our astoundingly successful opening day publicity

coup had made me, for better or for worse, one of the best known senators, I set about trying to smooth the feathers of those who may have been offended and felt I was a frivolous knothead.

On January 8, I posed for a picture holding my old banjo and looking down at it with a sad expression. The caption read, FENCED IN NOW, and the text said, "Glen H. Taylor, former banjo-strumming cowboy crooner of Pocatello, Idaho, is shown above at Washington as he wistfully laid away his banjo in favor of more serious duties as Idaho's Senator in the new 79th Congress. Taylor strummed his way into the Senate after two previous campaigns were unsuccessful."

This picture and story were printed almost as widely as the Capitol steps episode. It was a natural follow-up to that scoop.

I do not know how it could have been improved upon. Anyone who had condemned me because of the original incident would now say, "Well thank God he intends to settle down and seriously attend to business." And everybody wishes a repentant sinner well.

THE OATH   Being sworn in as a United States senator is, I imagine, the most thrilling event that can possibly happen to most men so honored. It certainly was to me. After all my struggles and disappointments, and considering the odds against me, it was absolutely unreal.

I had hoped, when I first ran for office, that my father and mother could live to see me achieve this ambition, but they had passed on.

Mama was very proud of her sons and would have burst with pride if she could have witnessed this episode straight out of a fairy tale. As for Papa, I have already related how he had told me that he was convinced that if any of his sons ever scaled the heights, I would be the one. (If any of my siblings were alive, I would not mention this, but they have all joined Papa and Mama. I am the last survivor of thirteen children.) The grand occasion would have been complete if he could have lived to see his prediction come true. Nevertheless, it was one of the high points of my not uneventful life. Dora and our sons were in the section of the Senate gallery reserved for senators' families and the boys were waving to attract my attention.

It is customary for a state's sitting senator to accompany the newly elected senator to the well of the Senate chamber and present him to be sworn in. As the time neared for the swearing-in ceremony Les Biffle, the secretary to the majority, came to my desk and said Senator Thomas, the elderly banker and landowner who had defeated me twice and was now my senior colleague, did not feel up to the chore of escorting me down the aisle. Refusing to accompany a new senator to the well is a tactic used, although rarely, by senators who wish to show their contempt for the new arrival, even though they should work in harmony if the best interests of their state are to be served.

I am sure that John Thomas had a full measure of scorn for me, and subsequent events proved that the corporate political machine in Idaho was not above trying to embarrass me in this sleazy manner.

Senator Elbert Thomas of Utah assumed the chore, and I felt more at ease in the company of this good man than I would have had John Thomas deigned to assume the role.

While waiting to be sworn in I was introduced to Henry Wallace who, as vice president, was to administer the oath. I had time for a few words with him and I told him how greatly I admired him, and that having him administer the oath would make the event complete.

All the time I was walking down the aisle and taking the oath I kept figuratively pinching myself and asking, *Is this really me, is this Glen Taylor here, being sworn in as a member of this, "the most exclusive club on earth"?*

It was real, and from far away I heard myself saying, "I do," as I was being sworn in.

Later, I was still walking on cloud nine when Les Biffle came to my desk and whispered, "Mr. Wallace wants to know if you would care to preside over the Senate?"

I had never in my whole life presided over any sort of meeting. I had barely had time to thumb through *Robert's Rules of Order,* much less familiarize myself with the rules of the Senate. I didn't hesitate, though. I had come this far and now, by God, was no time to falter.

Again, I found myself center stage, exchanging a few words with Vice President Henry Wallace, and then I was alone, sitting in the seat where the great names of history had sat throughout the years. As I took the gavel and gazed out over that appalling sea of famous faces, again I had to mentally pinch myself.

It wasn't nearly the ordeal I had expected. The Senate parliamentarian was at my elbow whispering directions for every word I spoke and every move I made. "The chair recognizes the senator from Kentucky," he whispered and I repeated, "The chair recognizes the senator from Kentucky," and with that one brief sentence I had removed myself from the category of being just another senator. Most of these men could scarcely be heard in that vast chamber but I heard my own voice, trained by years in the theater, fill the great room from wall to wall and on up into the galleries, and at that moment I had established myself as the owner of a voice unusual, even in this assemblage of oratorical talent.

Later, I was somewhat deflated when I learned that presiding over the Senate was not necessarily considered an honor, but a chore to be avoided, if possible. Newer members were called upon to perform this routine task, and those with greater seniority seldom warmed the chair.

I do believe, however, that Mr. Wallace meant it as an honor in recognition of the compliment I had paid him. The ham in me made it a pleasure to act as presiding officer, and the many compliments on my fine voice from senators on both sides of the aisle did not, I must admit, lessen the pleasure I derived from performing this task.

MOVIE STARS   A change was taking place in the general attitude back in Idaho, relative to our stint on the steps of the nation's Capitol.

The newsreels starring the Taylor family were now appearing in theaters throughout the old home state. Reading about their new senator singing on the Capitol steps, together with acid Republican comments, was one thing. Having us appear on the screens of local theaters was something else again. We were movie stars, and what is more glamorous than a movie star?

Besides, we put on a good show. When seen on the movie screen, it wasn't like the Republican papers had made it seem at all. There was nothing garish or unseemly about the episode. It was soberly done with never a smile or a smirk. We weren't the cheap publicity seekers about whom the editors had scandalized. Don't you believe it!

We were simply a homeless American family. Everybody knew that every American family was entitled to have a roof over their heads. No American family should be homeless, much less a United States senator and his fine family. An American family being homeless was bad enough, but this was an Idaho family.

In fact, goddammit, this was the family of their United States senator, whom they had so recently elected. It was outrageous that old Glen should be forced to get up there on those god-damned cold concrete steps and sing to try and find some place where Dora and the kids could be out of the cold. And there was no doubt about it being cold. The cameras clearly showed every exhaled breath. It was as cold on those Capitol steps as it was on the steppes of Russia.

Newspaper editors who formerly wouldn't have walked across the street to see or hear me were forced by the terrific impact of the newsreels and our emergence as movie stars, to send reporters to view, and review, our film debut. They came away shamed because of the unkind things their papers had printed about me and gave us some rather decent reviews.

The heading on the piece in the *Idaho Daily Statesman* illustrates the changed attitude.

TAYLORS IN MOVIES, the heading proudly proclaims. IDAHO SENATOR SINGS FOR DWELLING, it says. The article is the one which accompanied our picture on the Capitol steps, but which the *Statesman* did not print, although they ran the picture of us committing the original sin.

In this story, following our emergence as movie stars, the *Statesman* included the follow-up piece relating how our singing had paid off with many offers of housing. This irrefutable evidence of the practical results of our singing gave our friends a solid base from which to attack my Republican critics.

Those of the TV generation may be a little puzzled as to why appearing in the newsreels was such a big deal.

Later, with the advent of TV, the networks were faced with the necessity of finding newsworthy stories for several thirty-minute telecasts a day. As a result of this wholesale need, relatively commonplace events and personalities get TV exposure.

On the other hand, newsreels came out just once a week, and they were only fifteen minutes long. Given one minute each, that would allow for the coverage of only fifteen events a week. Our singing, together with the explanatory comment, probably consumed three or four minutes. It is doubtful if D. Worth Clark, for example, ever appeared in a newsreel at all, so it is understandable that we created quite a furor when on our very first day in Washington we were probably given more newsreel footage than any other event that transpired in the whole world during that entire week.

On January 14, long enough after the Capitol steps incident for a sober evaluation, the *Denver Post* carried a twenty-eight column-inch story about me on its front page, telling of my life and my six-year struggle to reach the United States Senate. There was no hint of the contempt that the *Statesman* claimed practically all editors held for me.

HARRY TRUMAN   When we moved into our new offices we found that Senator Harry Truman, who was vice president–elect, occupied the next-door suite.

Each morning we would ride over to the Senate together on the underground railway, and we became rather good friends. He seemed to get a great kick out of some of my experiences outwitting and outmaneuvering political hot shots by singing songs and riding horses.

He was, to me, not an impressive man. The press accounts of how he had run a men's store in a small town and gone broke were much more believable than the fact that he was Vice President of the United States and very possibly would become President, considering the state of Roosevelt's health.

He had a warm personality that made me feel at home. I liked him, although I felt a certain resentment toward him for having replaced Henry Wallace, whom I considered to be the foremost advocate of the people and the most honest man in government.

The stories I had read about Truman's close association with the Pendergast machine and its unsavory ramifications and reputation didn't help matters either. Nevertheless, I looked forward to each morning's trip with him to the Senate chamber.

NEPOTISM   Nearly a month after we had arrived in Washington, we were still living in the hotel. It had become evident that my salary, which we had imagined would sustain us in luxury, would not even afford us a meager living.

I mentioned the matter to the always discreet and helpful Les Biffle, and he told me that mine was not an uncommon problem. To help overcome this deficit, numerous senators put their wives on their payroll. There was also the practice of accepting fees, euphemistically called "honorariums," for making speeches to, and serving as prestige window dressing for, conventions of such groups as bankers, and other well heeled organizations.

Because of the notoriety I had received and my soon earned reputation as a speaker, I was approached by a booking agency which procured such lucrative engagements for senators. I was assured that I could command as much as fifteen hundred dollars for each such moonlighting endeavor. I turned the offer down, which is solid proof of my integrity or simple-mindedness.

Reluctantly, I did put Dora on my office payroll for seventy-five hundred dollars a year, which was about half my own salary, and we figured that that would make ends meet.

My conscience did not bother me, because she had worked like a beaver for twelve hours a day from the moment we moved into my offices. Besides, this arrangement did not obligate me to bankers, labor unions, or any other groups who might expect me to reward their generosity.

Of all the senators' wives, only Dora and the wife of Senator Ball of Minnesota actually worked in their husband's offices, according to that super-snooper columnist Drew Pearson.

As soon as I decided to join in this practice, for which the dirty word is "nepotism," I issued a statement to the press declaring my intentions and the reason therefore. I knew that if I did not the matter would, sooner or later, become known and the Republican press of Idaho would have a field day.

DREW PEARSON AND DORA   Shortly after Dora went on the payroll, a bellicose gent came into the outer office and announced for all to hear that he was an investigator from Drew Pearson's office.

For the benefit of any youngish readers who may not recall

Drew Pearson, I would like to explain that he had a widely syndicated newspaper column largely devoted to exposing wrongdoers. It made no difference how important or influential the suspected transgressor might be, he was still fair game for Mr. Pearson's column. In fact the more important the suspect might be, the more apt he was to have Pearson probing into, and exposing, any shady activities in which he was involved.

If there is any doubt as to the potency of his staff of investigators and their ability to obtain deeply hidden facts, and even secret government documents, may I point out that the famed Jack Anderson was one of Pearson's leg men and the one selected by Pearson to be his successor. In that capacity Anderson acquired a degree of fame probably surpassing that of his mentor when he surreptitiously obtained, and made public, the "White House Papers."

So when someone said, "I work for Drew Pearson," you'd better be clean as the proverbial houndstooth or hunt your hole.

In this instance the dark and sinister looking bogeyman said he wanted to see Mrs. Taylor.

Ordinarily, such a request would be routinely handled by the receptionist. In this case the male secretary, recognizing that here was an occasion of more than passing importance, took over. He asked the scowling caller to wait a moment and opened the door to my office where Dora also had her desk.

All too often, when word reached the person being sought that a Pearson man wanted to see him, the hunted one would hastily vacate the premises via an escape exit. Pearson's boys knew this and didn't take chances on that happening.

So as soon as the secretary opened the door to my office, the legman unceremoniously elbowed him aside and charged through the door unannounced to confront his prey without affording her any opportunity to be alerted and flee.

I was out of the office, dutifully occupying my seat in the Senate chamber. Undoubtedly, Pearson's man had checked on me and selected this moment when Dora would not have her big, strong, perspicacious, and fearless senator husband at her side to protect her from his ravenous onslaught.

So there poor Dora sat, totally unprepared for her Gethsemane when Pearson's henchman, true to the bullish strongarm tactics used by his staff in their relentless pursuit of evil, confronted her.

"Are you Mrs. Taylor?" he asked accusingly.

Dora had jumped to her feet when the door flew open. Angrily she said, "I am the wife of Senator Taylor—and just who do you think *you* are forcing your way in here unannounced?"

"I," he grated menacingly, "am John Fox, I work for Drew Pearson, and I want to talk to you, lady." No doubt Mr. Fox had in the past seen such unceremonious entry, face-to-face confrontation, and the chilling announcement that he was the long arm of Drew Pearson, reduce strong men to blithering idiocy.

But Dora's conscience was clear and she is remarkably self-possessed in times of stress, not prone to panic. "Just what could an impolite ass like you have to say to the wife of a United States senator?" she asked icily.

"Nepotism, lady, nepotism," the impolite ass barked.

Dora was still unsure as to just what the crude intruder wanted and demanded haughtily, "Well—what about nepotism?"

"What about it?" he asked scornfully. "Nepotism is a crime, lady, that's what about it. You are on your husband's payroll and it's against the law for a relative, even the wife of a United States senator, to be on the payroll unless she really works. You know that, don't you?" he blustered.

Dora had gotten the picture. As I have told you, Dora is a quiet, gentle person but when occasion demands she can be tough as old shoe leather and cold as ice. This was that sort of occasion.

As she came round the desk to shake her finger under this wise guy's nose, she was white with self-righteous anger, and her eyes were spitting fire. "Listen, you," she grated, "I *work* in my husband's office. I work longer hours than anyone *in* this office except the senator. You understand? I was working when you broke in here and stopped me." Dora was ready to scratch somebody's eyes out, and Mr. Pearson's hired hand realized that fact.

This hard-to-fool investigator recognized the truth and calmed down immediately. "I'm sorry, Mrs. Taylor. Please accept my apology. I can see that you are really on the job and working. So many wives who are on the payroll do not. In fact, few do. I had to find out, and I have. I hope you will forgive me." And he stood there, hat in hand.

By now Dora was cooling off a little. "Well," she said, still a little huffy, "I can understand Mr. Pearson's interest in getting at the truth in such matters, but it does seem to me you could be a little more gentlemanly in how you go about it."

"I am truly sorry, Mrs. Taylor. I really am. Please forgive me."

"Why, of course, I'll forgive—this time—but next time please don't come rushing in here, scaring me half to death," she admonished the now meek tough guy who bowed and made his exit.

The next day Drew Pearson's column included this item. "While quite a few Senators' wives are on their husband's office payroll at the taxpayers' expense, few of them make more than an occasional token appearance at their alleged place of employment. The wives of Senator Glen Taylor, Idaho's singing cowboy, and Senator Joe Ball of Minnesota, are two hard working exceptions to the rule. These two charming ladies do work fulltime in their husbands' offices."

On that same day, by special messenger, we received an expensive square envelope with the name of the sender engraved in the upper left-hand corner. Dora brought it in to me and excitedly opened it. It contained an engraved invitation to a dinner at the Pearson home. *We were to be the guests of honor.*

PEARSON'S PARTY   That was our first venture into Washington high society. When it came to putting on the dog that dinner was a barn-burner. Drew, as he requested I call him, was a most gracious and charming host.

Pearson's home was what I'd call sumptuously shabby. Of course I had read about antiques and knew they were prized by those who could afford such highfalutin ideas. Everything in the place was old and well worn. The settee cushions looked so old and decrepit one might assume they were stuffed with passenger pigeon feathers.

I felt high-toned sitting in these glorified pieces of junk that looked like they had been borrowed from the Smithsonian Institution for a party celebrating the rein of King Charlemagne. I couldn't help speculating as to what important asses had once warmed these orginally valuable, and now priceless, relics.

We got along fine until it came dinner time. Then, as luck would have it, Drew announced that Mrs. Pearson was indisposed, and he asked Dora to sit at the head of the table and act as hostess in place of his ailing wife. Dora was petrified and my heart went out to her.

We had barely been seated when two Japanese servants, a man and a woman, were at Dora's elbow bowing and scraping. Dora retained her composure but I could see she was mystified as to what was expected of her.

Drew, who was on her left, leaned over and whispered something to her, and then said something to the obsequious servants, who bowed and retired from the scene. I wondered what Pearson had whispered to her and I'll bet you are wondering, too.

Well, sir, what he said to her was, "You've got your foot on the bell"—and when she felt around underfoot and still looked nonplused he explained, "It's under the carpet." Now how in the hell was Dora to know that the goddamned bell was under the carpet?

If all the silver on that table had been turned over to the mint we could still be using silver dollars. Neither Dora nor I had ever attended a formal dinner in our lives. The one Comp took us to was a buffet and we had helped ourselves to a glass of wine, the first we had ever tasted, but this was something else again. There were three wineglasses of various shapes and sizes lined up in front of us.

Here came the little Japanese girl with the first course. She made a beeline for Dora and stood there waiting for her to serve herself. Dora, bless her heart, had been reading Emily Post and practicing up a little without telling me anything about it. She took the two tablespoons, serving spoons, tongs or whatever, and did a passable job of getting the food on her plate.

We both got along okay until the Japanese houseboy brought the baked Alaska. Neither she nor I had ever heard of, much less seen, one of these culinary bonfires. There was an implement which came with it that looked like a trowel to me, but Dora picked it up and cut herself a piece of the now extinguished mystery. I had all I could do to keep from applauding her skill and derring-do but managed to restrain myself. Imagine my surprise when I tasted my barbecued whatever and discovered it was, of all things, ice cream. Who ever heard of cooked ice cream?

After that, things got worse. There was placed before each guest a plate. On the plate was a fancy doily. On the doily was what looked like a wide but shallow, overgrown wineglass. In the cut-glass container was water and floating in the water was a sweet pea. What the hell? Do you drink the water and eat the sweet pea or what?

I could see that Dora was stumped, too.

She got out of that tight place by leaning over and asking Drew some fool question like "When is the cherry blossom festival?" but all the while she was watching out of the corner of her eye to see what the others might be doing with this "enigma wrapped in a mystery," as Winston Churchill put it. At the same time she was hoping and praying that it was not incumbent upon the hostess to be the bellwether in this operation. Fortunately, it wasn't.

The other guests lifted the vessel of water, put the doily to one side, replaced the floating sweet pea and its container on the doily, and then sat waiting. It turned out that the plate was for salad. This was another surprise. In Idaho, and the West generally, the salad is served right after the soup, or first, if there is no soup, but in the East, including Washington, the salad is served last. The water with the posy in it was the fingerbowl. We had seen and used fingerbowls before. It was the sweet pea that threw us.

After dinner we all sat about and were served brandy in a snifter. There was a congressman at the party who really took that "snifter" bit to heart and sat there with his snifter clutched in both hands like he was afraid it was going to get away from him, and made a big deal out of sniffing his snifter. Pretty soon someone asked how I came to be called the "Singing Cowboy." That led me to mention our campaign techniques and that led to our days in show business barnstorming the wild and woolly West, etc., etc. I was urged on from one story to another for an hour.

I had enough sense not to want to monopolize the conversation, but they were insistent and no one seemed to be bored or to begrudge my being the center of attraction. In the end I simply had to say that I had already talked too much and shut up.

This came to be the format of practically every party we attended. At nearly every party henceforth there would be at least one person present who had heard my stories at some previous party and they would tell the assembled guests about how "fascinating" my tales were and although, as time went on, I grew increasingly embarrassed at hogging the show every place I went, my fame had spread ahead of me and I couldn't flatly refuse to accommodate a roomful of guests without appearing to be rude.

I have often wondered if I overdid it. I do not believe, really, that I was so stupid as to mistake a buttering up for a genuine interest.

Dora and I must have made quite an impression on Pearson despite our lack of finesse, because from that time on he gave me and the family so much space in his column it became obvious.

In Idaho a really serious rumor got around that Dora and Drew were cousins. At least that's the way I heard it. Knowing how vicious my home state enemies had been in trying to blackmail me and destroy our image as a closely knit and devoted family, it may have been that the rumor had Dora shacking up with Pearson and my friends had cleaned it up before passing it on.

Shortly after the Pearson party, Drew devoted several inches of his column's valuable space to a story I had told him about Arod. "Young Democratic Idaho Senator Glen Taylor has been having trouble with his nine-year old son Arod (Mrs. Taylor's name reversed)." (Note: The parentheses are Drew's, not mine. Isn't it terrible that I inflicted that name on my son and caused him to become a public figure at such a tender age?) "Senator Taylor came into his office the other day, saw a package addressed to 'Idaho's Junior Senator.' Opening it he discovered a toy for Arod from one of his friends back in Idaho with a card reading 'Dear Senator Arod, you are the only Senator I ever knew so I am sending you my fire truck that you liked so much. I liked it, too, but here it is.'

"That evening Taylor took the package home and asked his son 'Why does Tommy call you Senator?' With no hesitation and without apology Arod answered, 'Oh, I told all my friends in Pocatello that I was the junior senator.'"

LORD HALIFAX   Early in January of 1945, I received an invitation to attend a stag cocktail party given by a Major J. G. Lockkard, "to meet the British Ambassador Lord Halifax."

That "to meet" irked me a little. Why not say, "to afford the guest of honor, Lord Halifax, the British ambassador, the opportunity and the pleasure of meeting you"? However, the condescension implied was not sufficiently irksome to cause me to turn down the invitation. We went.

Lord Halifax was a tall, lean, and aristocratic gentleman. He was polished, suave, and at the same time friendly and likable. I stayed only about thirty minutes, as I had heard was customary at these "run 'em through" events, where more people are invited than the premises could possibly hold at one time. Later, I learned that affairs like this constituted a sort of screening process so the ambassador could look the guests over and decide which of those he met, rather informally, would be suitable and worthwhile courting as guests at the numerous formal dinners to be given at the embassy from time to time.

Evidently I made a rather favorable impression on "His Lordship," because no more than a week later we received an invitation to the very first embassy dinner of the season.

The one Washington social event which stands out from all the others was that dinner at the British embassy. It also happened to be the first opportunity Dora and I had had to dress formally. She bought herself a long elegant evening gown and was most lovely. I wore my new "tails."

At every Washington dinner there is always one honored guest who takes precedence over all the others in the Washington pecking order.

At this elegant, full-dress function, I was the prestige item of the evening. There were generals, admirals, and congressmen, but I was the only senator.

It was drizzling when we drew up in front of the embassy, but even though there was a marquee extending out over the sidewalk the footman who opened the car door held an umbrella to keep the rain off us for the brief two or three feet intervening.

Another liveried footman escorted us to the massive carved doors and opened them for us. We were delivered to a third liveried servant who asked for our engraved invitation and announced, "The Honorable Glen H. Taylor United States Senator from Idaho and Mrs. Taylor," and passed us on to the ambassador.

Lord Halifax's right arm was withered and his hand barely extended from his side far enough for us to shake hands.

He welcomed us suavely, recalled meeting me the previous week, and, like the good politician he was, mentioned that he had visited Idaho as a young man. He presented us to Lady Halifax, who was equally aristocratic and self-assured. A maid stood waiting. Lady Halifax said to Dora, "Mildred will help you freshen up," and proceeded to lead the way to the grand staircase.

When we had been announced the hum and buzz of cocktail conversation had stopped. Everyone wanted a good look at this famous "Singing Cowboy" who had been monopolizing the headlines. We were objects of interest far beyond the fact that I was a senator. All eyes were upon us.

At this critical moment I committed my first boo-boo. In my verdant ignorance of such things, I started to follow Dora and Mildred up the steps. It wasn't too noticeable. I had no more than put one foot on the first step than Mildred, who was obviously an old hand at handling stray cowpokes, gently suggested, sotto voce, "Perhaps, Senator, you would care to join the gentlemen."

The "gentlemen" were standing about, each with a drink. Apparently we were the last of the guests to arrive because Lord and Lady Halifax had abandoned their station in the foyer, she to follow Dora upstairs while his Lordship hastened toward me.

I learned later that the time on our invitation had been some half hour later than the others for the very purpose of having the other guests present when we, as the guests of honor, made our grand entrance.

Lord Halifax took me by the arm and suggested, "Senator, would you do me the honor, sir? I would like for our guests to have the privilege of meeting you." He steered me toward the nearest group and, with a marvelous display of memory, introduced me to every one of the dozen or so male guests, naming them all. Then he hastened away and up the long, imposing flight of stairs.

A few minutes later the string orchestra struck up a tune. All eyes turned toward the stairway. I looked up and there, at the head of the stairs, Dora stood, in all her self-assured loveliness, on the arm of the handsome, debonaire ambassador, with Lady Halifax on his other arm. Keeping time to the music but in a perfectly relaxed way, they came down the steps with all the other female guests behind them.

Evidently these ladies had been entertained up there somewhere while waiting for this "grand entrance." Later, Dora told me that this was the most thrilling moment of her life with the exception, she hastened to add, of that memorable occasion when she said, "I do." Dora did not share my "common man" complex, at least not 100 percent, and all this pomp and circumstance was right up her alley.

Lord Halifax seated her with courtly dignity on his right, and I was seated on the right of Lady Halifax. Both Dora and I had to watch our Ps and Qs to avoid any breaches of etiquette, but with the experience we had gained at the Drew Pearson party and by being just a little slow and observant we managed to get through the evening with a good score in deportment, I'd say.

The first opportunity I had to speak to her I whispered, "Can you believe this is us?" and she whispered back, "I just love it." I felt sure that she could have stepped into the shoes of Lady Halifax and carried on with all the grace and charm of that gracious and charming lady. In Washington society she was as much of an asset as she had been all through the years of strife and struggle. Senators and generals, admirals and congressmen, stood about her three deep to bask in her loveliness, charm, and, let's be frank about it, sex appeal. I was exceedingly proud of her.

After dinner "all us gentlemen" retired to a massive room filled with bookcases, heavy leather-upholstered furniture with obviously rare and precious statuary tastefully scattered about and priceless rugs under foot.

Cigars were passed about and when the distinguished guests were lit up, sure enough, someone asked me how I acquired the sobriquet of the "Singing Cowboy." That story held my sophisticated listeners spellbound, laughing, and at times applauding and slapping each other on the back. I held forth for a time, and when I finished talking there was spontaneous applause and polite cries of "More—more." I was properly reluctant and looked to Lord Halifax for guidance. He said, "By all means, Senator. Your stories about your incredible experiences are delightful and most entertaining."

So I gave them an account of my horseback jaunt and after I had unsuccessfully tried to stop a time or two, and nearly an hour had gone by, I became embarrassed. I politely begged off and started asking admirals and generals questions about their experiences in the Pacific and managed to stay out of the limelight, although when things slowed down there would be pleas for me to tell them more.

As we were leaving, Lord Halifax squeezed my arm and said, "Our guests have told me that, thanks to you, this was the most memorable and enjoyable affair they have ever attended."

As the word spread, we were deluged with invitations, and I was told that I was the most talked-about man in Washington.

COMPLIMENT FROM PRESIDENT PRO TEM While I had entered into the debates on the confirmation of Wallace and Aubrey Williams, my first real effort was when the Senate was considering a bill to draft labor for the war effort on the grounds that there was a shortage of labor and that some jobs which were essential to the war effort, but more or less undesirable for various reasons, were going begging. The idea was to be able to assign any man to any job whether he liked it or not.

After the debate had tapered off I made what was probably the most effective speech of my career in the Senate, if the effectiveness is judged by the number of votes it may have influenced. I simply told the story of my war plant experiences.

As I began speaking, there were probably twenty or thirty senators in their seats. Almost immediately others started coming in from the cloakrooms, which were at the rear of the chamber and separated from it by a ten-foot-wide passageway which extended around the entire rear and sides. Both the Republican and Democratic cloakrooms were being emptied with an urgency I had not previously witnessed. A few minutes later, when sufficient time had elapsed for those senators who were in their offices to have been alerted, they also started arriving and taking their seats.

Imagine! My first major effort, and here they came until there was scarcely a vacant seat. I do not believe I have ever known a greater personal satisfaction or a more thrilling experience. Or-

dinarily, those few senators in their seats would be reading newspapers or carrying on low-voiced conversations while some illustrious colleague delivered a well written argument, buttressed
with quotes, facts, and figures. No senator, much less a new
member making his first speech, could ask or recieve a greater
compliment.

I told of how people were hired, not because they were needed,
but in order to increase costs so management could collect a
greater amount in the way of the 10 percent profit on whatever
they could spend. I told how there was seldom enough work to
keep the workers busy. If there was work, then there was a
shortage of tools to work with, and if not a lack of tools, then
there would be no materials to work with. I told how, when
young navy officers who probably had no idea what they were
doing would come through the plant "inspecting," we were
alerted in advance and expected to look busy whether or not we
had anything to do.

I told the senators that the trouble was not a lack of workers,
but a lack of materials due to poor planning at the top. There
were too many men in fabrication and not enough working in
heavy industries producing steel, aluminum, and other materials
needed to keep production lines operating.

When I had finished, there was a hushed silence and then a
buzz of low-voiced conversations and a nodding of heads, obviously in agreement with what I had said. Senator Kenneth
McKellar, the president pro tem of the Senate, a dignified and
conservative old Southerner, was in the chair. Ordinarily, he
would have rapped his gavel the instant the speaker resumed his
seat and gotten on with the business at hand, but now he sat there
mediatating for perhaps thirty seconds before he roused himself,
rapped the gavel, and silenced the hum of earnest conversation.
As the next speaker took the floor, McKellar started writing on a
scratch pad. When he had finished, he crooked his finger at the
alert group of page boys and one of them hastened to his side.
The venerable president pro tem handed the boy the note with a
few words of instructions. The lad came directly to my seat and
handed me the pink slip of paper.

The handwriting was a large, irregular scrawl, not easily decipherable, as might be expected of a man in his middle seventies. It read, "Senator, you made a fine argument. I congratulate you." And it was signed "McKellar."

I instinctively looked up at the old gentleman. He nodded and smiled.

KUDO FROM VP   The day after I made by speech, Vice President Truman was presiding over the Senate. I noticed him busily writing while some senator droned on. When he finished he beckoned to a page boy. To my surprise, the boy came to my desk and handed me the communication. It read:

"Glen, I wasn't here yesterday when you spoke. Just read your speech of yesterday. I made dozens of inspections in all sorts of plants and I heard your story everywhere. I am—"

At this point the page is filled, and in the very cramped space left in the lower right-hand corner, written in script so small as to be scarcely legible, is the word "over." On the reverse side of the memo slip the note continues:

"—most happy that you told them about it. I would have done it if it were possible for this former member to do it. You did a good job."

The note was signed with the vice president's initials, "H.S.T."

When I had finished reading his generous compliment I looked up at the chair, and the vice president was waiting for me to do just that. Our eyes met, and he made the okay sign by forming a circle with his thumb and forefinger.

Naturally, I was pleased and proud to be extended this personal recognition by the Vice President of the United States.

VIETNAM QUOTE   "I am as much in favor of economy as anybody, but I think we would do well to build up our own nation by spending a little money here at home rather than trying to support phony governments in places like Indo-China."

If you had to guess who said that and when, what would you say? Much as it sounds like those liberal politicians who started denouncing our involvement in Vietnam only after Eugene McCarthy's success in the 1968 New Hampshire primaries and after subsequent polls revealed that the American people were fed up with the Vietnam war, you would be wrong if you attributed the above quote to any of them.

I had started writing a weekly news column which we mailed out to every paper in Idaho. The above quote is taken verbatim from that first week's news column, "Report to the People," as it appeared in the *Glenns Ferry Gazette*. The date was March 9, 1945.

MY BROTHER   On April 11, I was paid the most glowing, all-encompassing compliment to date. This item appeared in the *Chicago Sun*, and the heading is WHAT RADIO TECHNIQUES WILL DO. The article explains:

> Most nimble talker in the Senate appears to be Glen H. Taylor (Dem., Idaho), whose speaking voice has the smoothness that comes from a long background of radio crooning and whose explanations are equally smooth. An outstanding example:
>
> In explanation of his vote against the Manpower Conference report, "I do not feel that I am against the Administration. If my brother were doing something which I felt in my heart was wrong and I tried to dissuade him, I do not believe it could honestly be said that I was against him. I would be for him. I am for the Administration. I want to keep the record straight."

"INVITE" TO HARRY   About two weeks before the family took a fishing trip to the primitive area at the head of the Salmon River in Idaho, I sent a wire to Harry Truman, now President. When I received no answer I was a little miffed. To my surprise, when I returned to my office, I found that my message to the chief had received wide publicity, and not of my doing, because I had not told anyone (the press) about the matter.

The wire I had sent read: PRESIDENT HARRY S. TRUMAN, WHITE HOUSE, WASHINGTON, D.C.—MR. PRESIDENT— The telegram dispensed with formality at this point:

DEAR HARRY, WOULD YOU HONOR THE STATE OF IDAHO
AND YOUR FORMER NEIGHBOR S.O.B. BY SPENDING A DAY
OR TWO AS MY GUEST? STOP. NO SPEECHES, NO BAN-

QUETS. STOP. WE'LL GO FISHING. STOP. WE WILL FLY OR
DRIVE INTO THE PRIMITIVE AREA OF THE MIDDLE FORK
OF THE SALMON RIVER. STOP. YOU HAVE TO HIDE BEHIND
A TREE TO BAIT YOUR HOOK. STOP. MORE FISH THAN
THERE ARE DEMOCRATS IN ALABAMA. STOP. I WANT TO
GO FISHING AND I'M LOOKING FOR ANOTHER COMMON
PLUG TO ENJOY THE GOOD TIME. STOP. ANSWER HERE
TILL JUNE 12TH, THEN AT BOISE, IDAHO. STOP. YOU ARE
DOING A SWELL JOB. STOP. EVERYBODY IS PLEASED,
SENATOR GLEN TAYLOR OF IDAHO.

True to his reputation of having the common touch, he answered, albeit after we had already started our fishing trip. His
wire said:

WISH I COULD ACCEPT YOUR INVITATION. IT WON'T BE
POSSIBLE THIS TRIP BUT I WILL TAKE A RAIN CHECK. MY
BEST TO THE FAMILY. HARRY S. TRUMAN.

I heard that he mentioned the matter to newsmen, and when
they evinced further interest, gave them copies of the wires. He
had a warm feeling toward me to indulge in this byplay.

While I did not really expect it would be possible for him to
join me, I am sure he would have been a great fishing companion. He was that sort of person.

INFINITE ODDS   Here is an example of what can be accomplished in the way of keeping your name before the public if
you are on your toes, can recognize a good story, and write it up
so the press can quote it verbatim. This is printed exactly as it left
my office in the form of a press release. The introductory paragraph is all that was added, and I feel it is quite a tribute to my
ability as my own press agent. The mention appeared in the
Philadelphia Inquirer. It reads:

We are happy to print, as an example of senatorial enterprise in making the newspapers, the following "press release" from Senator Glen H. Taylor (D., Ida.):

"Way back in 1928 a musical comedy company came to
Great Falls, Mont. The *Great Falls Tribune* sent a 21-year-

old cub reporter to interview the leading man and get a story. The 21-year-old reporter and the 24-year-old actor and singer spent a pleasant half hour.

"Glen H. Taylor came to the U.S. Senate at the beginning of the present session. He is the thespian in the above story and made good use of his singing ability in his campaign for election.

"Shortly after Taylor was sworn in, a new senator was appointed from the state of Washington by the name of Hugh Mitchell. He was given the next seat to Taylor. You guessed it. Hugh was the reporter who interviewed Glen."

ODYSSEY   I was one of the sponsors of the Full Employment Act. Naturally, I made a speech in behalf of our bill. It elicited the most extravagant account to date of my ability as a speaker and, more important, attracted the attention of the blasé senators and presumably influenced their subsequent actions.

The author of the account you are about to read, Tris Coffin, was a writer and radio commentator of considerable fame. This was part of a script for one of his radio broadcasts.

A pale, handsome man rose from his seat in the last row of the Senate. A young reporter sitting next to me—a little self-consciously cynical—snickered something about "the singing cowboy." The senator was Glen Taylor, who was, as he admitted, a poor, ham actor.

Then, the senator began to speak. The rustlings and whisperings in the gallery were stilled One row of ten servicemen across from me leaned forward, put their arms on the rail, and watched the pale, angry face. A girl in a blue dress behind me gripped the seat in front of her until her knuckles were white. She sat, frozen stiffly. The sneer dropped off the face of the young reporter like snow sliding off a roof.

Even the senators—long accustomed to ignoring their colleagues—swung their chairs around to listen to this bold, audacious address.

His speech was an odyssey, the odyssey of a man who has come up a long way—an actor playing for potatoes and cabbages in desolate country towns, a sheet metal worker in a war plant. There were times when he didn't eat. Not because he forgot. Because he didn't have any money.

314 / Senator Glen H. Taylo

He began to think—dangerous, penetrating thoughts. Why was it that sometimes men went hungry in a land of seeming plenty? He read books, and often looked up from his page to see the sun coming up from behind the hills. He talked to all kinds of people—businessmen, Socialists, Communists. Then, he started running for Congress. He finally made it last year.

This was all a preface to his main theme—a demand for the passage of the full employment bill.

He said, "I know how the common people feel when they can't get jobs. I have seen the time when I would have signed up for $25 a week for the rest of my life. I wouldn't have done it, if I were the only one to consider, but I had a family, and they needed medical attention, and I couldn't afford it. In such circumstances, it isn't a matter of favoring private enterprise or something else. It's a matter of life and death."

Senator Taylor went on, "I would like to see the private enterprise system continue, although I admit I am not so closely wedded to it as are some others. But, frankly, if the stopper is kept in the kettle, and we refuse to allow any changes to take care of changing circumstances, the thing may blow up. . . . I know how the people feel. I know how easy it would be to persuade them to throw the whole thing overboard. They have seen what we can provide in war in the way of jobs and a high standard of living. If we break down again, we are bound to lose our private enterprise system."

When Glen Taylor sat down, the Senate was suddenly still. The gallery began slowly to relax, and almost automatically file out, ignoring the patient, sincere words of the next speaker, Alben Barkley. Some of the senators were bent in their chairs, as if they heard from a distance the angry rabble of unemployed demanding food.

That speech of Glen Taylor's was something of a landmark. A man had actually arisen in the United States Senate and questioned the free enterprise system.

PROFANE MOPPET   The constant efforts of the Republicans to block all social legislation must have really gotten to me Apparently I carried my aggravations home and berated the GOl and their tactics to Dora, and in front of my sons, because vividly remember the following incident. This reads, I know, like something Bob Hope's writers might turn out, but it is absolutely true and it really happened.

I had been walking up and down our living room letting off steam telling Dora bout the perfidious doings of the Republican minority. Three-year-old P.J. was playing on the floor with some little cars and apparently paying no heed to my tirade when all of a sudden, out of a clear blue sky he exploded, "Damn those Republicans!"

After a moment's stunned silence, Dora "seen her duty and she done it." "P.J.," she scolded, "don't you ever use that naughty word again."

Without stopping his play, P.J. innocently inquired, "What word is that—Republicans?"

SENIOR SENATOR On Tuesday, November 14, 1945, Idaho's Senior Senator John Thomas died. After having served for just seven and a half months I became the senior senator from Idaho.

Senator Thomas had no sooner been interred than speculation was rife as to whom conservative Governor Gossett would appoint to succeed him.

A commentary in the *Idaho Daily Statesman* relative to the dilemma Gossett faced said of the prospective new senator "he must be a conservative." In less euphemistic language, that meant, "he must be subservient to the machine."

The three most likely prospects, as named by the *Statesman*, were Judge James R. Bothwell of Twin Falls, George Donart of Weiser, and James Hawley of Boise.

When I read this list I had some difficulty suppressing a grin. All of these distinguished gentlemen shared the same claim to fame. Each of them had met defeat in the dust stirred up by a sound-equipped car or the galloping hooves of a horse named Ranger, both the property of a certain "Singing Cowboy."

There wasn't a man left in Idaho of sufficient stature to be worthy of this plum who had not tasted that bitter dust.

Not unexpectedly, Gossett resigned. The lieutenant governor, who automatically succeeded him, then appointed him United States senator.

THE OLSON STORY   It had come to pass that the position of "Register of the Land Office at Blackfoot, Idaho" was vacant, and it was up to me to make the appointment. I knew Frank Olson to be a good, honest, intelligent, and hard-working man as well as a deserving Democrat. Besides that, he had ten kids to support.

He had also—just incidentally, you understand—worked diligently in my behalf in all my campaigns. He would take his kids and they would descend on a community like a swarm of locusts and distribute my literature.

So, when this plum came up for grabs I thought of dear old loyal Frank, and I appointed him to the job. What a blessing, what manna from heaven, this unexpected reward would be to Frank, and what joy would reign in his ramshackle old home when he received the good news!

You can imagine my surprise when, in due time, I received word from the Bureau of Land Management that their investigation had turned up the sad and astonishing fact that Frank Olson had, in 1933, been convicted of and served ninety days in jail for the heinous crime of bootlegging. He was unacceptable, not only because he was a jailbird, but also because his educational attainments did not include a college education. Well now—this was ridiculous.

Here I had only five years of schooling and I could appoint Frank to this job, but he couldn't serve because he only had a high school education. I asked a couple of senators how you handled a case like this. One said, "Forget it. You'd never get any senator to vote to confirm a man with a record even if you could get the Interior Department to send his name up, which is about as unlikely as the cow jumping over the moon."

The other one said, "You are in luck. You have paid off any debt you may have had to this bootlegger, and now you can use the job to pay off another one—kill two birds with one stone."

Such cold-blooded cynicism didn't appeal to me. Whatever else may be said of me, I do not forsake my friends in their extremity.

I was sure Frank could read maps and do simple arithmetic. That would be all that was necessary. The office would go on functioning even if Frank was an idiot, which I knew he wasn't.

I called my old friend and apprised him of the sad fact that he had a black mark on his escutcheon.

Frank said he was surprised because the last time he had looked at his escutcheon there wasn't any black mark on it.

So after we had a good laugh at this joke I told him what was cooking, and he told his story.

He had, he told me, pleaded guilty to protect two nephews, and felt that everyone thought the better of him for having done it.

I told Frank that he'd better get busy and send me some letters from responsible people attesting to his character and qualifications. In no time at all I had eight really remarkable testimonials unequivocally endorsing the appointment and bearing witness to Frank's good character and high standing.

I took all the testimonials and went down to see the commissioner of the Bureau of Land Management.

After exchanging small talk, we got down to the subject of my visit. For openers, he said, "Senator Taylor, I'm awful sorry we couldn't okay your man, but we had an unsolicited communication from your state reporting the facts and we couldn't very well just ignore it."

So that's how it was. That goddamned, heartless gang of rich political dictators—the machine—trying to blast old Frank's only hope of ever knowing anything better than the lifelong struggle and deprivation which had been his undeserved lot.

"Do you have another name to submit, Senator?"

"No," I said, "I don't."

He looked a little puzzled and asked, "Then what are you here for?"

"I'm here," I said, "because I want to appoint Frank Olson to be Register of the Land Office at Blackfoot, Idaho."

"You mean," he asked incredulously, "that you're stickin' with him after—after—?" He left it hanging.

I produced my bundle of laudatory recommendations. "Read these, Commissioner," I said with just a trace of senatorial command.

When at length he had the taxing job done, he sat for a moment with his eyes closed, meditating. Just as I was about to decide that he was napping, he slammed his big old hand down on his desk with such vehemence that I jumped half out of my seat.

"Aw, what the hell," exclaimed the commissioner, "what if he did bootleg a little? Lots of people bootlegged in those days," he declared belligerently and then, like the old Democratic wheelhorse that he was, he shifted the blame for everything onto the universal scapegoat of all true Democrats by expounding, "Old Herbert Hoover's depression was still with us. Frank Olson had to support ten kids. He couldn't just let 'em starve. What if he did bootleg a little?" He glared at me menacingly, as if challenging me to dispute his logic. When I didn't, he said, "I'll tell you what, Senator. We'll send this nomination to the Senate, but with no recommendation that it should be or should not be confirmed. You can understand, Senator," he said pleadingly, "that we can't give this nomination our unqualified endorsement without running the grave risk of getting our tit caught in the wringer and laying the bureau open to a charge of dereliction of duty if anything ever went wrong. You can see, Senator, what a spot I'd be in if Olson ever committed some indiscretion while holding office or if a stink is stirred up about the matter by the Republicans in the Senate."

I assured the commissioner that I understood his position and his concern for the bureau. I congratulated him for his statesmanlike handling of a complicated problem, and we shook hands on it.

Well! I had Frank over that hurdle. Now all I had to do was get his nomination through the Interior and Insular Affairs Committee, of which I most fortunately happened to be a member, and after that Frank's nomination would have to run the gauntlet of the Senate, half of which was Republican.

But, the information about Frank's fall from grace was in the report of the bureau to the committee and there was no "Do Pass" recommendation.

While I had not tried to railroad Frank's nomination through the committee, neither had I called attention to the last paragraph, and I had kept my fingers crossed hoping that no one would read that far, but I did not reckon with the sharp eyes of the senator from Iowa, Mr. Hickenlooper.

While the committee was considering another matter, he spotted the tidbit in the bureau's report and interrupted to ask, "What about this report on Frank Olson from the Bureau of Land Management? I think Senator Taylor should make an explanation to the committee." I assured him that I would be happy to answer any questions the senator might have, and that if I was asked to do so I would make a statement on the floor of the Senate.

At this point the committee chairman reminded us that the Olson report was not the business before the committee at the moment and that we would get around to it in due time. Shortly thereafter, Senator Hickenlooper hurried from the room. I imagine, although I do not know, that he was hastening to tell his fellow Republicans that he had something with which they could embarrass me and was seeking advice as to how to proceed in order to get the most mileage out of my nomination of a bootlegger.

Olson's nomination came up a few moments later. The chairman asked if there were any questions or comment. Hickenlooper had not returned, so there were none. I heaved a sigh of relief, and the nomination was sent on its way to the Senate, where it would appear on the calendar without the report.

When Olson's nomination came up in the Senate, Senator Hickenlooper got the floor and asked me if I had any statement to make. I was caught flatfooted.

I had not been informed that Mr. Hickenlooper expected me to make a statement, so I said, "I do not understand what the senator from Iowa means." Hickenlooper did not explain but addressed the chair. "Mr. President, this nominee, Frank Olson, has been convicted and served a jail sentence for bootlegging. Since the senator from Idaho is not prepared at this time to make a statement I ask that the nomination go over."

That's all it takes in the Senate: one objection, and the nomination goes over until the next reading of the calendar.

About three weeks before the nomination was due to come up again, Charlie Gossett, the new senator from Idaho, arrived in Washington. When he was settled in his office, I went over to discuss with him the unusual circumstances of the Olson appointment.

I said, "Charlie, I have come to discuss the appointment of Frank Olson." With an airy wave of his hand, Gossett replied, "Glen, that appointment is strictly your business. You made the appointment before I got here so it is none of my concern."

That would have been the proper attitude ordinarily, but I wanted to explain about the bootlegger charge, so I said, "But Charlie, I—" He interrupted with an upraised hand to stop me and said, "No, Glen, that appointment is yours. If you want Frank Olson, that's it."

I had tried. If this was the way he felt, that was it, and I left.

A short time later, just long enough for him to have gotten the Bureau of Land Management report, look it over, and call the machine out in Idaho, he was in my office. "Glen," he said, "about that Olson appointment."

"What about it, Charlie?" I asked.

"Well you didn't tell me that he had served a jail sentence for bootlegging," he complained.

"I tried to, Charlie, but you wouldn't listen. Remember?" I reminded him.

"Well, Glen, I can't vote for a bootlegger," he informed me righteously. "I'll have to vote against his confirmation."

"That's your privilege, Charlie," I said, with no attempt to explain or to cajole him into going along on this matter, which could very well set the tone of our future relations.

"I'm sorry, Glen," he wagged his head.

"That's okay, Charlie," I said, although I didn't feel that way, and my displeasure probably showed despite my words.

He left.

The day arrived when the Senate would act upon the nomination of Frank Olson.

My jocular cloakroom reminders to my colleagues, that on this day I would try to get my bootlegger friend confirmed, had added to the interest. By now I was known as a clever and entertaining speaker who could be expected to say and do the unexpected. This added to the buildup.

As the time drew near, the Senate chamber began to fill up.

By the time Frank's name did come up, the number of senators in attendance was phenomenal. There was scarcely a vacant seat, and the atmosphere was like that of an audience before the curtain goes up on a stage production. There was an air of puzzled expectancy. What argument could the cowboy from Idaho possibly advance to try and get this august body to go against tradition and persuade its members to run the risk of criticism and adverse publicity by voting to confirm a confessed and convicted bootlegger?

Without debate and with a desultory smattering of "ayes," as was customary, the gavel fell as the last name preceding that of Frank Olson was confirmed. The buzz of conversation ceased. Senators returned to their seats. There was silence.

If Frank Olson was to be confirmed, my appeal would have to be to the emotions of these blasé senators who prided themselves on being poker faced and unemotional. If logic prevailed, the facts were irrefutable. Frank Olson *had* been convicted of a crime and *had* served a prison sentence. He did not deny it. I could not.

I thought, *This is ridiculous—all this just over Frank Olson.* But this tenseness! Somehow I had to relax things or I might fall flat on my face.

Our crochety old president pro tempore, Senator McKellar, intoned, "The question before the Senate is, Will the Senate advise, and consent to the nomination of Frank Olson to be Register of the Land Office at Blackfoot, Idaho?"

I stood up. "Mr. President," I addressed the chair.

Old Senator McKellar croaked, "The senator from Idaho," and the words of his recognition spoke volumes. The way his voice went up instead of down on the word "Idaho" seemed to ask, *Do you really want to go through with it, Senator? You can still back out, you know. But if you are determined to go ahead, she's all yours. I don't know what the hell you're going to say in defense of your bootlegger but she's all yours.*

With my first sentence, I cut the gordian knot of tension. I looked seriously about the crowded chamber and said, "Mr. President, a few moments ago I was thinking about suggesting the absence of a quorum." Then, before that had a chance to soak in and get the little laugh it might have rated, I quickly added, "But I guess that won't be necessary." That obviously ridiculous observation got a belly laugh that lasted much longer than one might expect. And why was that? Because I was using the measured-blink technique and looking as though I was trying to figure out what was so funny.

The ice was broken. They were in a jovial and receptive frame of mind.

"Mr. President," I started over, "I am loath to take up the time of the Senate and inconvenience senators in this manner at this late hour of the day, and I would like to reassure them that this is not the first in a series of speeches each day at adjournment time on the merits of Idaho potatoes."

This got another back-slapping belly laugh at the expense of Senator Wiley of Wisconsin, who had the obnoxious habit of starting a speech just before adjournment time, on the virtues of Wisconsin cheese.

I started again. "Mr. President, the nomination of Frank Olson has been passed over several times and I would like to have it acted upon," and I added in a rather sad and hopeless tone, "one way or the other."

I kept a straight face, as though I were so desirous of being rid of this vexing matter that I just might be relieved if I had to accept "the other." This got another laugh. If you intend to try and work on people's emotions, it's a good idea to get them laughing first. Laughter and tears are closely related; people sometimes "laugh till they cry."

After each of these interruptions, I started over and addressed the chair. This gives an impression of great respect and seems to indicate a certain uncertainty and humility. Nobody likes a cock-sure wise-ass. So I began again. I said, "The matter before the Senate is a most serious and important one." After three belly laughs they were in a mood for more, and this ridiculous assertion got another lesser laugh but when I stood there deadly sober, as if I could see absolutely nothing to laugh about, the laugh grew and, when I still failed to crack the faintest hint of a smile, the laugh grew some more.

Do you know what they were thinking? I can tell you. Even as they laughed they were thinking, *Is this guy serious? Does he really think that this bootlegger thing is important? Aw, come off it. Nobody could be that dumb. But he looks absolutely serious.* Then, when they looked at my face with its innocent-of-guile expression, they laughed all the harder.

When the laugh finally started to subside, it was by fits and starts, with residual snorts and guffaws coming from one individual who was trying to suppress his mirth, and then another. First over there to my left, and then over to the right somewhere.

At length I was able to proceed. "Mr. President," I began for the fourth or fifth time. "The confirmation of Frank Olson merits very serious thought and consideration on the part of every one of the distinguished, learned, and most honorable senators in this hallowed chamber."

This overblown statement, delivered in all sincerity, again set them wondering, *Just who is kidding whom?* I was laying groundwork for another belly laugh. "Mr. President, Frank Olson has been nominated to a position of great importance. A position of trust requiring unimpeachable honesty and integrity and ability of the highest order. Frank Olson has been nominated to the position of—" and I hesitated for a count of two before I added, "Register of the Land Office at Blackfoot, Idaho." There was an instant of silence while the ridiculousness of my pronouncement soaked in. The name "Blackfoot" gave my words an added humorous connotation.

Even the name "Idaho" conjured up visions of a backwoodsy state way out there in the folksy, wild, and woolly West.

The great guffaw that ensued shook the dear old place so violently that a piece of plaster gingerbread broke loose and fell to the floor of the passageway at the back of the chamber. A page boy retrieved the egg-sized fragment and later presented it to me as a souvenir of the occasion.

When I could again be heard, I doggedly started over again. Even my oft-repeated "Mr. President" got a ripple of laughter. I looked about, very slowly as though I was profoundly puzzled by all the merriment, blinking my eyes in a measured manner and leaving them shut for a count of one between blinks.

Lest you become outraged to think that a senator would use such a device in the United States Senate, let me assure you that this measured blinking is in no way hokey or obvious. Actually, it could probably be classified as a subliminal technique. I'll wager that not one senator recognized that he was being "hookwinked" and "taken into camp," so to speak.

All they knew was that I looked so innocently puzzled as to why on earth they were laughing that they were convulsed anew.

I had to start over and say "Mr. President" three times before I could proceed.

"Mr. President," I finally managed to say, with no reaction other than a few scarcely heard snorts suppressed and muffled by pocket handkerchiefs, "let me give a brief history of how and why the nomination of Frank Olson came to be at issue here.

"When I first recommended Frank Olson for the position of Register of the Land Office at Blackfoot, Idaho, the Civil Service investigators looked into his record and found that in 1933 he had served a jail sentence of ninety days following a conviction under the Volstead Act—in plain English, for bootlegging.

"Accordingly, I had the U.S. marshal make an investigation.

"He wrote to me as follows:

" 'Whatever the seriousness of Frank's ancient mishap may be, it should certainly be erased by the conduct of his life since that time, and is more than overcome by the high regard in which he is held by everyone to whom I talked.'

"Mr. President, may I at this point, relate the facts relative to the offense to which the U.S. marshal refers?

"It seems that way back there in the dark depths of the Depression, when people had so little to eat they drank quite a bit, their neighbors, quite a lot of them, brewed and peddled a good deal of 'moonshine likker.' When one of these dispensers of the only commodity that could make you forget Herbert Hoover got caught, everybody but confirmed bluenoses were sorry to hear about it. I'm not apologizing for Frank. I don't need to because he was one of the minority who never made, or spent a nickel for, bootleg whiskey.

"He'd take a drink if somebody offered him one, but he had all those kids to support and just plain couldn't afford to squander money for a bottle of his own.

"Well it seems Frank had two young nephews who had reached the embarrassing age where tradition dictates that they leave the nest and go out on their own. The boys needed shelter so Frank let them occupy an old deserted cabin over on the east forty.

"These young men, like so many others, were hungry but instead of going on relief and raking leaves they went in business.

"The 'revenooers' came along, found the still the boys had put together, and busted it all to pieces. The young men were in town for groceries at the time, a few sacks of grain and some sugar, etc., when the law came along, so the officers arrested Frank because the still was on his property.

"Frank, being the good-hearted soul he is, took the rap for the boys because he didn't want them starting life with a black mark on their record. And may I add, Mr. President, that the boys learned their lesson and appreciated what Frank did and they have lived upright and honorable lives to this day.

"Mr. President, I have here several letters from prominent citizens testifying to the good character of Frank Olson. Some are quite lengthy, so I will read only a sentence or two of each. The first is from the editor of the *Oakley Herald,* Mr. Charles Brown. He writes:

"'Mr. Olson is a talented writer and an authentic humorist with honesty and intelligence. I regard him as one of the truly interesting and useful men of our State.

"'The appointment is popular with the readers of my paper.'

"I now read a letter from the chief of police at Burley, Idaho, which is the county seat of the county in which Mr. Olson lives. Chief W. W. Williams writes:

"'My hearty approval of the nomination by you of Mr. Frank Olson.'

"Mr. President; I would like at this point to call the attention of the Senate to what, I believe, is a very important and pertinent fact. The W. W. Williams who wrote this sincere testimonial is the same man who had no choice other than to arrest Frank Olson on that bootlegging charge so many years ago, when he refused to implicate his nephews.

"I now read a letter from the Olson family doctor, who writes:

"'Mr. Olson can do his district, his county, his State more good as land commissioner at Blackfoot, Idaho, than any other man you may hand pick from Idaho or our neighboring states. Dr. G. E. Craner.'

"I now read a letter from a prominent attorney in Burley, the county seat:

"'I believe that Mr. Olson's character and intelligence is such that he will perform the duties of the Office of Register with credit to himself and the Democratic Party,' and the letter is signed Kales E. Lowe, Attorney.

"I now read a letter from a prominent contractor in that section of the state, Mr. Dan J. Cavanagh, of Twin Falls, Idaho, who writes:

" 'This letter is an unqualified endorsement of Mr. Olson. He has a wide knowledge of reclamation, irrigation, and range problems.

" 'He is a sober, industrious man of unquestioned integrity and honesty.'

"Mr. President, the letter which I now read is from Honorable Henry W. Tucker, probate judge of Cassia County:

" 'Mr. Frank Olson is a fine, outstanding citizen of his community and this county.'

"Mr. President, I feel it is significant to note here that the judge who wrote that fine character reference is the same judge who had the unpleasant duty of sentencing Frank Olson to a minimum term of ninety days when he refused to defend and exonerate himself by telling the truth and marring the lives of his nephews, and left the judge no other recourse.

"Mr. President, having read those letters, I wish to say that Frank Olson has raised a large family of ten or eleven children on a dry-land farm. Recently, when I attended the funeral of Senator Thomas in Idaho, I saw Mr. Olson, and his hands were deeply cracked from the hard work he had been doing on his farm. I sympathize with him. I myself am one of thirteen children, and I know that while my father was a fine and capable man he never was able to get ahead very far financially because of the large family he had to support. After we were grown and left home, he did very well financially, and I am sure that, but for the fact that he had such a hard time financially during the earlier years, he might have been here in the Senate long before I came here. I feel the same way about Frank Olson. I am sure he is an honest and capable man. I am convinced that he never committed the offense for which he was sent to jail, but rather that he took the blame for someone else.

"I wish to say that it was a misunderstanding which resulted in having this matter come up in the first place. The senator from Iowa [Mr. Hickenlooper] understood that I was to make this talk on the floor of the Senate. I offered to make it in the committee, but I did not understand that I was expected to do so. The senator from Iowa understood that it had been agreed that I would make the talk and explain the circumstances. So when the nomination came up in the Senate, the senator from Iowa rose to his feet and asked me if I had any statement to make. I really did not understand what he meant at that point, and I so stated. He then made the statement that Mr. Olson had been convicted and served a jail sentence. So now I am making my statement.

"In conclusion, Mr. President, I wish to say that Frank Olson is a wounded veteran of the First World War. He has had two sons in the service in this war, and a daughter who is taking nursing training. I have absolute confidence in his integrity and ability.

"This appointment was made long before the junior senator from Idaho became a member of the Senate. He has taken the position that, inasmuch as an issue has been made, he wishes to have the opportunity of voting against the nomination. However, I wish it to be known beyond any doubt that the nomination is not of his sponsorship, but that it is of mine, and I take full responsibility for it.

"Before I relinquish the floor, Mr. President, I would ask the indulgence of my fellow senators that I may tell a little story which I believe bears out the good things said about Frank Olson in the letters I have read.

"For many years Frank Olson has supplemented his meager income and helped sustain his large family by tending a government beacon on a mountain near his homestead. We are all familiar with these beacons. There are many hundreds of them all over the country. Each one is part of a network by which airplanes are guided on their way during the hours of darkness. Their importance to aviation is obvious and the necessity of keeping them flashing their guiding and warning signals is a matter of life and death.

"The job which Frank Olson undertook to perform was to keep that beacon on top of the mountain shining, twenty-four hours a day, three hundred and sixty-five days a year. Once a week Frank had to climb the mountain, on foot, carrying the two five-gallon cans of fuel which were necessary to keep his beacon shining. Two full five-gallon cans of gasoline are a very heavy load, Mr. President, and Frank Olson is not a muscular man. In fact, his spare frame reminds one of Abraham Lincoln, but I do imagine he is strong in the thong leather tradition of the West. But, rain or shine, blistering summer sun or howling winter blizzard, in sickness or in health, Frank Olson never failed to struggle up the mountain. I imagine, Mr. President, that there were thousands of dedicated men who shared with Frank Olson the responsibility of keeping a light shining in the night.

"There are lots of good responsible people in America, Mr. President, but do you know what? Frank Olson's beacon was the only one in all that vast network that, not for one day, or one hour, or one minute, for years on end never—ever—went out.

"He has a letter of commendation testifying to his trustworthiness and his simple, dogged devotion to duty." I hesitated a moment and then, with all the heartfelt sincerity I truly felt and with a rising inflection on Frank Olson's surname, denoting a hope rather than a request, I said, "I hope—" and there was a catch in my voice that I could not have helped if I had tried, "—the Senate will confirm Frank Olson."

As I sat down, there was a profound silence, broken only by a random senator here and there and some in the gallery quietly blowing their noses.

The patriarchal president pro tem roused himself, dabbed at his eyes with his breast pocket handkerchief, and ended the spell by informing the Senate, "The question is, 'Will the Senate advise and consent to the nomination of Frank Olson to be Register of the Land Office at Blackfoot, Idaho?'"

Charlie Gossett got to his feet and half mumbled, "Mr. President, I would like to be recorded as voting 'no' on the confirmation."

That scarcely audible statement carried a world of meaning to the assembled senators. It told them that here was a newly arrived senator seeking to embarrass his senior colleague. It was even more notable because both were of the same party. If there is anything a senator despises it is to have a colleague who seeks to tear him down and destroy him. Charlie had gotten off to a very bad start. At that instant, I made up my mind to place high on my calendar the little matter of getting rid of my esteemed colleague.

What happened then was completely unprecedented. I had never seen or heard anything even remotely approaching it in the nearly a year I had served, nor did I in all the time I was a senator.

After Senator Gossett made his halfhearted request and sat down the president pro tem intoned, "It shall be so recorded," and then, referring back to the question before the Senate he said, "All those in favor say 'Aye.'"

Ordinarily, this invitation results in a smattering of weary "ayes." If the matter being voted upon is controversial, there may be a more general response. On this occasion, when all those in favor of the confirmation of Frank Olson were given an opportunity to register their feelings, there was a full-throated roar of "Aye."

The senators shocked even themselves by their unseemly enthusiasm and in the self-conscious silence that ensued the chair looked right at Senator Gossett and invited him to implement his expressed desire—"Opposed?"—and poor old, sorethumb Charlie could barely manage to get out a squeaky, solitary "No" and slump down in his seat as low as his beefy hulk would permit.

If he was blessed with the slightest degree of ESP, he must have faintly heard some of the unsenatorialish epithets his colleagues were silently thinking and to which they would later give voice in the cloakroom.

I was pleased to have so many of my colleagues congratulate me for turning what had seemed like a hopeless defeat into a roaring vote of vindication for Frank Olson.

I was happy to put up with a great deal of good-humored ribbing from my colleagues, individually, and in groups, the general consensus of which was "Now look, Taylor, we voted for your bootlegger, now it seems the least you could do to show your appreciation would be to pass out a few samples of his product." All this friendly funnin' came from Republicans and Democrats alike, as had that blessed chorus of enthusiastic "ayes," God bless 'em.

During the ensuing years I had nothing but good reports about my bootlegger Register of the Land Office at Blackfoot, Idaho.

SO SOLLY, CHOLLY　The first event of consequence to happen in the new year of 1946 occurred while I was in Idaho on January 8. The *Statesman* reports the matter thusly:

"Glen Taylor said today that he would support Geo. Donart of Weiser in his bid to defeat incumbent C.C. Gossett for the 1946 senatorial nomination."

And so the fight is on. War has been declared. Donart was not the ideal candidate but he was the best available.

Not as reactionary as Gossett. More independent of the machine. But "so god-awful slow," both in his movements and his speech, not to mention the snide and snotty remarks he had made about me in the past. But you can't beat somebody with nobody.

I persuaded Donart to run by promising to campaign for him.

I campaigned against Gossett with my sound car. In winding up each talk I made, I told the story of how Gossett was the only senator to vote against good old Frank Olson. Gossett was popular among the sporty element and that story, casting him in the role of a hypocritical, self-righteous bluenose, cooked his goose.

The clout I exhibited in bringing him down received national attention. Grudgingly, the *Statesman* admitted:

"Sen. Glen Taylor, who made the campaign a personal issue, must be recognized as the top dog in the Democratic party in Idaho."

TRUMAN SIRES McCARTHYISM   I am confident that if I had strung along with Truman here in the early months of 1946, instead of denouncing his "get tough" foreign policies, I could quite possibly have been his vice-presidential candidate in 1948. But it was not to be. I chose to follow my convictions.

Henry Wallace was a voice "crying in the wilderness" against our policy of vilifying the Russians and pushing us closer to a war of extinction. A third-party movement dedicated to peaceful coexistence was starting to take form.

President Truman set the tone of things to come, including the terrible excesses and injustices of the Joe McCarthy era, by issuing a statement on April 1, suggesting that Henry Wallace should "go to the country he loves so well and help them against his own country."

I was always revolted and enraged at this demagogic, small-town, Ku Klux Klan type of patriotism. Wise-ass remarks like that are well nigh impossible to answer. To do so, you must explain at some length that such utterances are not in accord with our traditions of freedom of opinion and speech, and to accuse anyone of being a traitor simply because he does not agree with your point of view is viciously un-American.

The more you condemn an appealing cliché like that, the more you publicize it. And the more you explain, the more it looks like you have done something that needs explaining.

Frankly, I think that this sort of demagogic attack would be used by only two types of people: those with no real understanding of how precious and necessary the right of dissent and free speech is to the preservation of democracy, or those mountebanks who have no regard for fairness, decency, or the welfare of the people of our nation or the world.

I would place Mr. Truman, with his small-town Chamber of Commerce background and mentality, in the first category. I doubt if it ever occurred to him that his attack on Wallace was a blow below the belt.

It was just an effective, easily remembered, and quotable cliché that gave those who repeated it a feeling of cleverness and a satisfying glow of patriotism.

What Truman said was what his old pals in the Independence Chamber of Commerce would probably have said. That's what his old American Legion buddies would have said. That's what his old cronies in the Pendergast machine would have said. That was the kind of talk he was hearing, day in and day out, from the top brass who had his ear.

During the more than three months that he and I had made the morning ride to the Senate chamber together, chatting informally, I came to know him quite well, and therefore it seems to me that the opinions I formed of him might be of interest to some. As I have said, I liked him personally, so none of my thoughts or conclusions are in any way tinged with personal dislike or envy of his astonishing political success.

Truman's unwarranted, unmoral, unfair, un-American, kick-in-the-groin attack on Wallace set the stage and style for a "new politics." Coming from the President of the United States, it established the moral tone, or lack of it, that encouraged Joe McCarthy, Richard Nixon, et al., to launch one of the most vicious assaults in the history of our country upon the constitutional rights of the people, wherein dissent became disloyalty.

I was in San Francisco making a speech attacking the "cold war" idea when Truman made his infamous reference to Henry Wallace. The only senator to speak up, condemn Truman's outrageous remark, and defend Henry Wallace as a great and loyal

American was Senator William Langer of North Dakota. At a time when other senators were being intimidated, tucking their tails, and running from appearing at any kind of liberal meetings for fear of being smeared as a "Red," old Bill Langer went his merry way talking to any group that would pay a fee. That may sound crass, but it was better than being beholden to special interest groups. His courage in addressing leftish groups amounted to foolhardiness in the eyes of other senators.

If further proof is needed that Harry Truman's attack on Henry Wallace was the actual starting point for one of the most hateful, bigoted, and shameful periods in American history, here are two gems from Idaho papers that follow his lead almost verbatim.

The *American Legionnaire,* published in Boise, had this to say in its May issue:

> Since Henry Wallace obviously has no love or loyalty to the U.S., exile him permanently—or put him out to graze with his braying stooges Claude Pepper and Glen Taylor.
>
> They are revealed once and for all as radicals who would deliver America over to the Communists.

The *Caldwell* (Idaho) *News-Tribune* of May 5 added its bit by editorializing:

> All Henry Wallace now needs to complete his barnstorming tour of Europe is Glen Taylor, Idaho's warbling senator, and his banjo. It's a pity that both of them cannot be exported to Russia and be compelled to live with Stalin and his red regime, whom they seem to admire so much.

All this, of course, is simply putting words in our mouths. Neither Wallace nor I had praised either Russia or communism. We *had* condemned the "cold war" and our "get tough" foreign policy.

I believe that the establishment (big business–military) had decided that the only way to head off a postwar depression was via an armament economy. In order to get the people to go along with the huge expenditures for armaments, there had to be a bogeyman to scare the bejesus out of them. For countless years Russia had been cast in this role. Then Hitler appeared, and overnight the Russians became "our gallant allies." Now Hitler was gone. They had to have a new bogeyman and Russia was the only possible selection. Again almost overnight the old "Godless Communists" theme was revived and "The Heroes of Stalingrad" had once again become "The Villains of the Kremlin."

This was no time for statesmen to warn of the contrived and synthetic nature of the sudden about-face. This was a time for politicians who hoped to be reelected to tuck their tails and run. Climb on the bandwagon and cheer on the inflamed mob.

No matter if annihilation threatened. No matter if civil rights went down the drain. This was a time for smart men to "rise above principle," if there ever was one. This was a time for yesterday's liberals to start baying like southern coonhounds.

Almost from the moment returns started coming in on the 1946 general election, it was apparent that the Democrats were taking a bad beating.

After Donart's primary victory, the *Statesman* wrote two or three editorials bemoaning the fact that a fine man like him would accept aid from a character like Glen Taylor. Mr. Donart was "big enough and strong enough to get along by himself" was the line they used. Donart fell for the play on his vanity and informed me that he wouldn't need my help in the general election.

He was soundly defeated.

Frankly, I am not at all certain I could have pulled him through. The red scare had been used to the hilt everywhere during the general election campaign, and with devastating effect.

The Republican red-baiting campaign, not only in Idaho but all across the nation, was a success beyond their fondest hopes and firmly established a technique they would expand upon and use successfully in campaigns across the nation for years to come.

Little did Harry Truman realize the potency of the weapon he was presenting to the Republicans when he made his shocking remark that Henry Wallace should "go to the country he loves so well." It would wreak havoc on Democratic stalwarts who would bite the dust in this and succeeding elections.

The Democratic Party would be pilloried for years as a result of the ruthless use the Republicans would make of the Pandora's Box that Mr. Truman had recklessly opened.

BILBO   The opening day of the first session of the Eightieth Congress was filled with excitement.

Along with other newly elected and reelected senators who would present themselves to be sworn in on this day was a certain Theodore G. Bilbo. Because he had flouted the Constitution and his oath to uphold it by urging the white citizens of Mississippi to use force to prevent blacks from voting I was determined that he should not be seated.

I learned that the Republicans planned to have Senator Homer Ferguson introduce a resolution barring Bilbo from taking his seat. I went to see Alben Barkley, the Majority Leader, relative to the catastrophe that was about to befall us. What were the Democrats going to do? Nothing—absolutely nothing.

Barkley agreed that something should be done, but no Democratic senator wanted to attack a fellow Democrat. I informed him that I had no such scruples and no false sense of loyalty to individual senators. I felt that the welfare of all the people was more important than it was to protect a senator who had clearly forfeited any right to serve in the Senate and whose head, in any event, would probably roll as a result of the action contemplated by the Republicans.

I received Barkley's promise to aid me in any way he could. We got together with Leslie Biffle, the secretary to the majority. This was necessary because at the start of a new Senate, the secretary to the majority occupies the chair until all the new members have been sworn in. I told him what I planned to do, and he agreed to recognize me when Bilbo was presented.

Here are some quotes from a most complimentary story about my effort to stop Bilbo. It occupies the full space devoted to the syndicated column of Marquis Childs.

DRAMA IN THE SENATE: A STAR IS BORN IN
MOVIE SENATE SCENE
If Hollywood had written the script, the drama on the first day the Senate met could not have been sharper. It was a situation for a movie producer. The triumphant Republicans were handshaking and back-slapping.
The atmosphere on the Democratic side of the aisle was subdued, because the Republicans were going to try and deny Senator Theodore G. Bilbo a seat and thereby score a

great propaganda victory, particularly with the Negro voters of the country.

Then, from the back row on the Democratic side, the young hero sprang up. It was perfect typecasting. Glen Taylor, Senator from Idaho, could be played by James Stewart or Gary Cooper. As it was, Taylor did very well by the part.

In the first place he had to be clever and quick to beat the opposition to the draw. On the other side of the aisle, Michigan's Senator Homer Ferguson was waiting for the moment.

But Taylor was in there first. He put in his resolution and therefore it had precedence. What is more, he was prepared with a speech and a good speech. On top of that, he could read his speech in a voice that had some dramatic quality. It could be heard even above the disorderly buzz of the Senate. Perhaps more politicians should try the radio before they come to the Senate.

As though any further drama were needed, at the peroration of Taylor's speech, Bilbo came over and sat down a few feet from the speaker. He sat there glowering up with an arrogance rarely equaled in Senate history.

(Bilbo was not seated.)

VISIT WITH THE PRESIDENT   On February 12 I was called to the White House by President Truman. This was the second visit in less than a month. I use the word "visit" advisedly, because that is what we did. We did not discuss any specific legislation. We just visited.

I was somewhat puzzled, but the significance was not lost on me. Was it that he just liked to talk and enjoyed my humorous little stories of my campaigning days? I had a hunch that he might be considering me as his vice-presidential candidate to offset the popularity of Henry Wallace with the liberal wing of the party, and wanted to get to know me better.

FREEDOM OF THE PRESS   Recalling the treatment accorded me over the years by the *Idaho Daily Statesman,* perhaps it might be in order to include here a direct comparison of how they invariably handled me as opposed to machine-blessed politicians—in this instance, newly elected Senator Dworshak.

The legislature had just beaten back an attempt to scuttle Idaho's primary law and return to the convention method of selecting candidates. This was quite a personal victory for me, inasmuch as the move had been aimed at me solely.

The *Statesman,* in commenting editorially, said: "There will be time to correct the primary law before Senator Taylor runs again. We must put a halt to candidates of the Taylor type and stop the election of such incompetent public officials."

Now, let's see what they say about dear Henry's Lincoln Day speech. "U.S. Senator Henry Dworshak deftly depicted on a broad canvas a moving picture of the party's urgent need for 'unity' and 'courageous leadership.'" (Wow! Ain't that wunnerful?)

TOO STUPID FOR WORDS   On April 15 I made a five-hour speech in opposition to the President's proposal to bypass the United Nations and bolster the Greek monarchy with two hundred and fifty million dollars plus a comparable amount to Turkey.

On this occasion my objective was to delay a vote because the Gallup Poll showed that a majority of the American people opposed our bypassing the UN and that their opposition was increasing. I was hopeful that a delay would give this growing sentiment time to soak in and cause the Senate to accept a substitute proposal by Senator Pepper and myself to channel any and all aid through the UN. It had come to the point where matters of great importance were decided by the single-minded criterion of whether the communists were for or against it. This headline puts it in unmistakable terms: SPEED ON MIDEAST BILL LIKELY AS REBUKE TO WALLACE.

That's quite a basis on which to decide how you are going to vote, isn't it? But that's the way it was. If the communists were *for* it—vote *against* it. Wallace was saying we should try to get along with Russia, so he must be a communist, so if he was against the bill, then vote *for* it. Prove your loyalty and anticommunism at all costs. Even if you had to let them (the communists) determine how you should vote. Henry Wallace wasn't a communist, but he *was* a New Dealer and "communist" had now become synonymous with "New Dealer" as well as "liberal."

The communists *wanted* us to aid dictatorships and make all the people who were fighting for self-determination angry at us. So they enhanced their image as the friend of oppressed peoples by standing *against* us helping military dictatorships. The fact that the communists were publicly opposed to us aiding penny-ante dictators all over the world forced senators to vote *for* such measures lest they be branded as fellow travelers, dupes, or commie sympathizers. As a result, the communists had their cake and ate it, too.

It's all too stupid for words, but *that* is the way it was. How the Russians must have gloated over our mindless idiocy.

"STATE OF WAR" DEPARTMENT In my fight to abort the borning of what came to be known as the "Truman Doctrine," I had contended that we no longer had a State Department and a War Department, but a "State of War" Department. Lest you fear that I was overly concerned and exaggerate, may I quote from my final speech before the vote was to be taken. I said:

"The *Army and Navy Bulletin* of January 18 contained this boast: 'Today the army has virtual control of foreign affairs, commencing on the home front with General Marshall (Secretary of State) and his Assistant Secretary of State (for occupied areas), Major General John H. Hildring, who directs the military commanders controlling our foreign policy in occupied Europe and Asia. The chain of control in diplomatic hot spots, both in the execution of basic policy and in the formulation of ad hoc arrangements, lies almost totally in the hands of the military authorities.' "

That's plain enough, isn't it?

LOYALTY TESTS President Truman had ordered into effect a program for testing the loyalty of all government employees. In the *Chicago Times* of August 18, 1947, I am reported to have made the following statement on the floor of the Senate in discussing the matter:

"Some prominent and valuable citizens have been taking a pushing around because they are related by blood or marriage to other persons who are suspected of being communists. I understand that in the State Department, in their loyalty investigation, they asked these two questions among others: Were you in favor of the Taft-Hartley bill? And were you in favor of tax reduction? That is a good one. I should like to know what that has to do with anyone's loyalty."

This was just the beginning. Soon I would join the company of those "prominent and valuable citizens" just mentioned.

VP OFFER   On December 12, 1947, or therabouts, I was waited on by a delegation representing Henry Wallace and asked if I would accept the vice-presidential nomination to run with him as head of the new peace party.

I said I would take the matter under advisement.

Immediately, I asked for and was granted an appointment with President Truman. I wanted to find out if there was any possibility of a change in our foreign policy to a more conciliatory attitude toward Russia. If there was, I would not feel obligated to run with Wallace.

As soon as we had sat down together, Truman started denouncing Wallace. "What's this I hear about you thinking of running with that nut?" he asked me. At length, I had an opportunity to ask the President if there was any possibility of us getting along with the Russians. Truman's reply was, "All the Russians understand is force," and he repeated the popular cliché at least three times during our conversation. I got the impression that he had heard the phrase and liked it, and his repetitious use of it reminded me of a parrot.

Any hope that Truman was even considering an effort to resolve our differences with Russia at the conference table was shattered by this visit.

V

Running
With
Wallace

TOUGH DECISION   Dora pleaded with me for weeks not to join Wallace. She had such high hopes that our sons would be afforded an opportunity to attend college and, as she pointed out, this would almost certainly be the end of my political career. There was little or no prospect that I could carve out a new career for myself at my age. When I finally made my decision and told her I had decided to run with Wallace, she wept.

I hoped that I would never again be placed in a position where I would, as a matter of conscience, be forced to inflict such pain and anguish upon her. It was a terrible ordeal for both of us.

She was fortunate in having the release of pent-up emotions afforded by tears. I did not. Her last plea was, "Think of your sons. How are they going to get an education?" My answer was, "If they are atom bombed, it doesn't make much difference whether or not they are educated."

During the week preceding my announcement that I would run with Wallace, Dora lost ten pounds.

"BIRMINGHAM JAIL"   On the thirtieth day of April 1948, we traveled by train to Birmingham, Alabama, to address the Alabama organizing convention of the new party. Dora, Arod, and P.J., as well as Foy Blackburn, my secretary, accompanied me, as they almost invariably did. As we emerged from the station, newsboys were shouting, "Senator Taylor to be arrested." Dora was terrified.

Foy bought a paper. The story headline on page one of the *Birmingham Post* did indeed say, SENATOR TAYLOR MAY BE ARRESTED. The story read:

Sen. Glen Taylor, of Idaho, vice presidential running mate on the Henry Wallace ticket, is scheduled to speak tonight before the Southern Negro Youth Congress.

If he speaks before a nonsegregated gathering of white and Negroes, in violation of the Birmingham Code, the police will arrest him and any other guilty offenders.

He (Connor) declares that he has the support of the Klan in his efforts. "I have instructed these Negro ministers about our segregation laws and informed them we intended to enforce them to the letter," said Eugene "Bull" Connor. "I have been elected three times by the people of this city as police commissioner to enforce our laws. I don't intend for this youth congress or any other similar organization to violate our segregation laws."

(A story in the *New York Times* quoted Connor as saying, "There's not enough room in town for Bull and the commies.")

A reporter for the Birmingham paper said that when I was asked for my reaction to Bull Connor's threats to arrest me, I "gazed distantly down the street and calmly said 'Safety Commissioner Connor can go to hell. I do what I think is right, let the chips fall where they may.'"

Shortly before the appointed time for me to appear at the evening meeting, the two organizers who had been at the church overseeing last-minute details came rushing into the hotel lobby, where I was waiting for them to pick me up. They brought word that Bull's gestapo had broken the brave resolve of the minister in whose church our meeting was to be held. No segregation—no meeting.

As they explained it, the situation was this. The building was approximately twenty-five feet wide, with the wooden benches extending to the walls, with only a center aisle. After the minister had capitulated, the police had placed an old door on its side across the aisle near the middle of the church and nailed it there. This effectively separated the front half from the rear half. Whites, of course, would sit in front of the barrier and Negroes behind it.

I had the picture, except for one very important detail that they failed to explain. The omission would prove to be of considerable consequence.

What to do? The crowd was there waiting. Finally, we decided that it was more important that the organizing convention should proceed so we would be on the ballot than it was to insist on no segregation. We also agreed that I should go out to the meeting place and at least let these really brave people see and hear me, no matter how briefly. I would not make a speech, but would tell them that the policy of Wallace and Taylor refusing to speak to segregated meetings was preventing me from making my scheduled address.

There would be no violence, no insistence on holding a non-segregated meeting, no showdown with Connor as we had planned, which would surely have resulted in my arrest and no telling what other complications. Violence was out. We couldn't ignore the wishes of the minister. Everything would be nice and peaceful.

Foy and I took a taxi. We pulled up before the church, paused at the corner, and asked what all the police were doing there. I had addressed my question to the two dozen or so curious by-standers who had congregated, hoping to see this "carpetbagger nigger lover" get his comeuppance from good old Bull. These "poor white trash," as their more affluent betters called them, just stood there with no more expression than so many Hereford steers looking through a fence.

There were at least a dozen or two harness bulls standing around. Guns, clubs, the whole bit. Three or four reporters were standing there waiting, doubtless hoping for some fireworks after an hour-long vigil. I started toward the front door. Two party workers, perceiving my intention, caught me by the arm and drew me back a step.

They told me what they had failed to tell me before. Negroes were to enter through the front door and sit in the back, and whites were to walk down the gloomy side street and go in a "back" door, which was really a side door near the back of the building, and sit in the front. That's when our carefully laid plans hit the fan. If it had been so decided, I would have come here and raised hell, insisted on having the door across the aisle removed, and personally kicked it down if the police refused to do it. That would have created a big ruckus and gotten a lot of publicity, and I would probably have wound up in the hospital with a busted head. That wasn't the plan, though. Everything was to be nice and peaceful.

But when they told me that I would have to sneak down that side street to a back door, fifty feet away, when there was a perfectly good door right there in front of me, it was too much. I saw red. This had ceased to be a matter of nobly fighting for the rights of others. It had become a personal matter. I was the one who was being discriminated against. I was a United Sates senator, and by God, I wasn't going to slink down a dark alley to get to a back door for Bull Connor or any other bigoted son of a bitch. I'd go in any goddamned door I pleased, and I pleased to go in that door *right there*. That's when I said, "I'm going in the front door." The two organizers tried politely to hold me back, but I shook them off and headed for the door.

There was a little porch, probably four by six feet and two feet high, in front of the door. A big, uniformed policeman stood guard there. He was really a huge man. Six feet two at least, I'd say, and he probably weighted two-twenty or -thirty, if he weighed a pound.

As I came up the three or four steps, my intentions were plain. As I approached the entrance, the officer stuck his massive arm across the door in front of me.

According to the press, the great hulk confronting me told them that he said to me, "I'm sorry, sir, but this door is for Negroes. Please use the white entrance around the corner." What he actually said, in a snotty tone of voice full of sinister purpose, was, "I'm sorry, buddy, but this door is for niggers. The door for white folks is around there." He pointed with a big, fat finger.

I said, "I'm not particular about those things," and stepped forward. When my chest made contact with his arm, he swept me back to the edge of the porch with no more effort than if he were shooing a pestiferous fly from his Sunday dinner table. I stepped forward again, hoping to get by before he got his arm back across the door.

I might as well have "choosed" King Kong. This time he really pushed me. So hard I teetered on the edge of the porch. I would have regained my balance, but someone grabbed me from behind and yanked me to the ground. I managed to light on my feet, right beside another unlovely big cop.

Something very strange happened then.

For years I labored under the impression that the spooky manifestation was peculiar to me alone, but I have since learned that what happened to me does on occasion, and at similar times of impending danger, happen to others.

Everything went into slow motion. Just like someone pressing a button on a movie projector.

I saw the man next to me, slowly, v-e-r-y s-l-o-w-l-y, clasp his hands together, and then, in the same slow motion, move his arms and clasped hands sideways away from me, stop, and then start back toward me. Still, ever so slowly, when that elbow hit me in the ribs, it knocked me the three or four feet against the building, and I bounced another two feet off the wall. At that point my slow motion apparatus ceased to function.

When I bounced back toward the bruiser who had given me the elbow, he grabbed my arm and other minion of the law grabbed my other arm, and they started hustling me across the tiny lawn toward a waiting white patrol car.

Now something happened that was ludicrously funny, although at the time it seemed damned serious to me (it is difficult to see anything funny in a situation when you are being manhandled by infuriated segregationists, acting in the name of the law).

There was a single strand of wire around the churchyard about a foot from the ground, tacked to stakes driven in the earth, probably to keep people from cutting the corner across the lawn, which was no larger than a prize ring. In the excitement, all those Ku Klux, Keystone, Kops seemed to have forgotten about that wire. The light was dim, and the wire was difficult to see.

When I started toward the front door instead of down the side street, the officers who had been lounging about on the sidewalk became alert. Obviously, the prepared script was not being followed. At the point where I was unceremoniously jerked from the porch, and it became apparent that the action had started, the officers on the sidewalk made a concerted rush for the scene of activity, and every last one of them fell over the wire.

There they were, all dozen or more of them, floundering about like huge porkers drunk on sour mash, cursing and grunting as they struggled to rise, only to fall over each other and perpetuate the burlesque scene. I imagine that complete mystification was the unanimous reaction. There they were, all floundering about, trying to regain their feet, wondering what in the hell was going on.

My two captors must have seen this, but apparently they failed to understand what had caused the mass prostration, so they preceeded headlong with their bum's rush to get me to the patrol car, and the three of us also fell over the wire. No one had as yet scientifically analyzed the situation, so no one knew why a baker's dozen of Birmingham's finest were down and flopping around like mudcats out of water.

When I went down, with my arms held, there was no way for me to break the fall except to hunch my shoulders forward. Fortunately, I fell with my face past the edge of the concrete sidewalk and on the strip of grass between the sidewalk and the street. Despite that lucky break, I was badly shaken up and half stunned. Later, I remembered thinking in a dazed sort of way, *This is it—they are going to beat me to death.*

At this point there is a discrepancy between what I recalled and what Foy had seen. In a speech to the United States Senate, I said that I deliberately refrained from violence, but Foy said that this statement wasn't exactly correct. He said that after the fall I got up slugging in all directions. I like that version best. I'd hate to think that at a time when I was convinced I was being beaten, possibly to death, I would submit meekly.

Foy said that I was apparently dazed from the shock of my face hitting the ground and that, while I was swinging with a will, I was doing so blindly. Luckily for me, I hit no one before the officers again grabbed my arms, hustled me to the patrol car, and shoved me into the backseat. Ever faithful Foy tried to climb in after me, but a couple of hefty cops yanked him back and violently pushed all one hundred and twenty pounds of him across the sidewalk back onto the lawn.

There was a delay of several minutes while the police tried to find out what had happened. They finally figured it out. The wire! That goddamned wire had tripped them all.

There was a burly officer in the front seat and a small one in the backseat beside me. I don't imagine he weighed more than one hundred and seventy-five pounds. That was little compared to most of the platoon.

In an effort to recoup some of my senatorial dignity and present a facade of insouciance, I fished in the breast pocket of my coat and brought out a badly battered cigar and lit it. I had taken no more than a puff or two when my companion in the backseat ordered menacingly, "Throw that goddamned thing out. They make me sick." In view of the treatment accorded me to this point, I decided it would be folly, not to mention downright suicidal, for me to stand up for my constitutional right to smoke a cigar, so I threw it out the window.

Finally, the patrol car dug out. As we passed under the occasional street lamps, I was afforded fleeting glimpses of the pinched face belonging to the unprepossessing specimen sitting beside me. I recall thinking that his eyes were glittering with malice and hatred, reminding me of the chilling glitter I had often seen as a boy in the eyes of cornered rattlesnakes, and he was ready to strike. He had his back in the corner, and his hand on his gun. I had no doubt that one false move on my part, and he would be overjoyed to let me have it.

We were traveling so fast that at each intersection, where there were dips in the street, I was being bounced against the car roof. In order to keep from having my neck broken, I had to clasp my hands atop my head. I had scarcely completed that self-defense measure when it occurred to me that we had slowed down. Way down. The streets were dimly lit and deserted. There was no mistaking it—we were cruising in a factory district, dirty brick buildings, streets full of potholes. A perfect setting for mayhem or murder, with not a witness in sight.

The officer sitting in the front seat kept up a steady barrage of provoking personal questions, any one of which would have caused me, under normal circumstances, to tell him to go to hell. It was quite evident to me, though, that he was trying to provoke me into some word or action that would give them an excuse to murder me.

Preposterous? I don't think so. Why were we aimlessly cruising these deserted streets after the breakneck speed a few minutes ago? And why did we drive out in the country and back again? And why did we finally reach the jail ten minutes after Foy had gotten there in the taxi?

The reason I use the term "murder" is this. In view of the

prodding, provoking questions asked me, I can conclude only that the police had violence in mind. That being the case, they would have been fools to beat me up and leave me alive to exhibit my bruises to the nation. An even more compelling argument against a nonfatal attack on me would be the fact that I would be alive to testify against them. Dead men tell no tales. They could easily have said that I attacked them. What Alabama jury of the time would have convicted these fine, upstanding officers for defending themselves against a radical, integrationist commie? By swallowing my pride and playing it cool, I cheated Bull Connor out of a chance to be a genuine folk hero to more redneck red haters, north and south, than you could ever imagine.

We finally arrived at the famous Birmingham Jail of song and story. As I was escorted through the door, a big, fat policeman was standing with his back to me talking through a window to the desk sergeant. He did not know I was right behind him, and he was saying, "Yeah, he's right outside here. Don't be afraid of him. Treat him rough. Give him the works."

I was ordered to empty my pockets. I forgot my breast pocket handkerchief. One of my "booking agents" jerked the handkerchief from my pocket, and with it came my last dog-eared cigar.

After they had cleaned me out, I was shoved into the large holding cell commonly referred to as the "bull pen."

So there I was. A United States senator, the Honorable Glen H. Taylor, locked up in a stinking cell with all that night's crop of drunks, dopes, pimps, pickpockets, and a variety of other petty offenders who had been brought in during the evening. One thing was for sure: I was the only one in that Birmingham jail who was there for defending *anybody's* civil rights.

The fifteen or twenty gentlemen of leisure who were there when I was shoved in and heard the lock click behind me, were an unprepossessing, dirty-looking lot. They were down at the heels and down at the far end of the fifteen-by-forty-foot tank, clustered about a card game.

The area where I had been searched and booked was no more than ten feet from the cell where I was confined, and I could see what went on there. I had an opportunity to observe the difference in the way white and black prisoners were treated.

Whites were simply told what to do with no abusive language

or manhandling. One Negro was brought in while I was watching. He was a gangling youth of about twenty, frail and skinny. In addressing him, the police repeatedly used the word "nigger." Instead of asking him to turn around and allowing him to do so voluntarily, as they did with the "white folks," the officers would say, "Turn around here, nigger," and without giving him time to comply, they grabbed him and violently turned him around. The term "nigger" was used at every opportunity and no excuse to manhandle him was overlooked.

The booking area was the only place that was unsegregated, but when you were being booked, there were two windows, side by side. One for "white folks" and one for "niggers." As soon as he was booked, the "nigger" was led away to a segregated "bull pen," and of course there were no "niggers" in the cell where I was. Couldn't have our fine, white criminals sharing a common cell with "niggers."

After a bit, a seedy-looking, unwashed character detached himself from the crowd at the other end of the cell and shuffled down to stand looking at me where I was sitting on the wooden bench that extended clear around the room. After sizing me up, he said, "My name's John, John Martin," and he stood waiting. Obviously I was expected to answer in kind, so I said, "My name's Glen, Glen Taylor."

"They got me for pukin' on the sidewalk," he volunteered. "Vagrancy." His stained, shabby clothing confirmed his statement, as did the gagging odor emanating from the caked evidence of his "crime" embedded in the whiskers of his unshaven chin. Since I had not volunteered the information, he asked, "What's your racket?"

"I am a United States senator," I said. "And I was arrested for trying to enter a meeting through a colored entrance."

A look of shocked disbelief greeted my statement. Then he backed cautiously away. He edged sideways to the far end of our mutual habitation, crossing one foot over the other as he retreated, never taking his eyes off of me. Obviously, he thought I was the craziest kook in the place. Once among his companions of the evening, he felt safe enough to turn his back on me and join the group round the card table. There followed a whispered dialogue.

At first it was evident that the motley crowd of lawbreakers were loath to believe the well dressed stranger was really crazy enough to imagine that he was a United States senator. I gathered this impression from the furtive looks of disbelief cast in my direction. Then one of the disreputable characters sparked and grabbed up the newspaper he had been reading, which he had discarded to join the powwow. For a few minutes my presence in the flesh was forgotten as their attention was focused on the newspaper story and my picture. Occasionally one of my cellmates would glance in my direction, no doubt comparing my face with the picture.

After a few minutes, it was plain that they all agreed. They did indeed have a real, live senator in their midst. A real, live, *integrationist* senator, bent on destroying the ego-satisfying arrangement which kept them from occupying the lowest rung on the social ladder by relegating "niggers" to a position a good rung or two below the lowliest white criminal.

The grouping round the card table dissolved as the standees moved unobtrusively away. Those seated stood up, one at a time, and unhurriedly a general movement started in my direction. One at a time and with elaborate nonchalance they drifted toward me. They stopped to study holes in the decrepit plaster on the walls. With great interest they explored rough spots in the floor with the toes of their shoes. Even cracks in the ceiling were eyed speculatively, as if the characters slowly but inexorably closing in on me were a crew of painters hired to renovate the smelly place, estimating how much spackle and time it would take to get the joint smoothed out for the paintbrush. With the inescapable certainty of death and taxes, the unsavory sampling of Birmingham's lower echelons moved toward me.

I began to get apprehensive. Being an honest crook was one thing. Being a "nigger lover" was something else. I had read about men being beaten up in jail. Beaten to death, in fact. I stood up, trying to appear as nonchalant as possible in the face of the slowly approaching enigma.

What did they have in mind?

I prepared to defend myself, because I expected them to rush me.

The closest one, a hatchet-faced, mean-looking customer, was no more than three feet from me. He stuck out his hand, and I moved back a foot or so toward the corner before I perceived that he was offering to shake hands. Still unconvinced, I put one foot well forward and prepared to jerk my hand free if this was a trick to yank me off balance. We shook hands, and with that, they all crowded about smiling and friendly, anxious to shake the hand of their distinguished fellow lawbreaker. We had a pleasant visit for perhaps thirty minutes. They showed no animosity over the race issue.

By now we were at the card table. They had courteously given me one of the four stools, and their ringleaders were seated on the other three. They had started tearing pieces off the margin of the newspaper, and I had just started signing autographs when the cell door opened. The big cop who had told the desk sergeant to "give him the works" stood there crooking his finger at me.

I got up, only to find myself surrounded by a phalanx of extended hands. Being a true politician, I hurriedly shook hands all round with my newly found friends while assuring them that I would appreciate their votes. And if any of them ever managed to get his poll tax paid, I wouldn't be at all surprised if I didn't pick up a few votes in the Birmingham Jail.

As I was winding up this unusual electioneering stint, my liberator became irked. "What the hell's going on here, anyhow?" he impatiently demanded. I wasn't at all happy to leave the company of my newfound friends to go with this bruiser who had advised all and sundry to be "tough" with me. If he had it in mind to act upon his own advice, he had the weight and the muscles to hurt you—real bad.

My fears proved groundless. I was told that bail had been posted, and I was released. Frankly, I had hoped that the decision would be not to post bail and let me stay in jail in order to capitalize on the crummy happening and get the maximum of publicity possible at the expense of Bull Connor, but Foy had called Beanie Baldwin, the chairman of the new party organization, and the orders were to bail me out. "It's more sensible and the better part of valor," Beanie had said, "for the senator to remain a live and ambulatory candidate than to become a crippled up and/or dead hero."

I had scheduled a radio talk for ten-thirty. It was after midnight. The radio station, feeling that they had a big scoop that would attract the largest listening audience in the station's history, had agreed to hold time open for me whenever I got out of jail. Meanwhile, the station had been furiously plugging my appearance, promising the listeners that I would tell them firsthand exactly what had been going on.

When we arrived at the radio station, an unfriendly group of fifty or so had gathered and we had to push our way through the hissing, booing, and spitting mob to the door of the building. Fortunately, the station was several floors up, and the elevator operator was instructed not to bring unknown persons up or the station would probably have been vandalized. I say that because when we reached the studio, the frightened manager said they were being swamped with obscene phone calls threatening dire consequences for allowing "that nigger lovin' son of a bitch" on the air. They had finally quit answering the phone, but it was ringing without letup, and it continued to ring all during the broadcast. As we left the station, the phone was ringing more frantically than ever.

I told the radio audience what I have told you about the evening's happenings, not forgetting the comedy sequences. I imagine Bull Connor and his boys could have bitten nails in two when I described how they had stupidly failed to case the joint and notice the wire and how they had all fallen over it.

When we left the building, the mob had grown to much larger proportions. Mostly young ruffians looking for diversion. We were pushed and shoved, booed, hissed, and spat upon as we struggled through the threatening crowd, but we finally made it to the car. After we had gotten in and locked the doors, the mob pounded on the car and rocked it back and forth until we were afraid they would tip it over. The driver had the engine going, and we pushed our way through the milling hoodlums and headed for the hotel.

Here another crowd had gathered, but they were better dressed and older, and while they were just as hate-filled as those at the radio station, there was no outward sign except for the sullen stares.

When we reached the room, four stalwart party workers had thoughtfully been stationed outside our door by the two organizers. Our guards were on the ball, and if you think I had courage to face what I had endured for these past long hours, just think of those brave souls. I was leaving, but they had to stay on in this hate-filled seat of segregation and violence. Eventually they would leave, too, of course, but think of the local Negroes who had rallied to our cause. They lived here. They had to stay here, at the mercy of the unspeakable Bull Connor, his brutal officers, and his Ku Klux gangs of cross-burners, castrators, and tar-and-feather experts. These downtrodden and oppressed people were the really brave ones, and their only hope was that the federal government would exercise its power and save them before it was too late.

But the help would have to come quickly. If Bull Connor got away with treating a United States senator like this without feeling the heavy hand of the federal government, there would be no stopping him.

Just wait, I thought. *Just wait until I get back to Washington and tell my colleagues of the abuse I have suffered and the lack of respect shown for the office of United States senator.*

Ordinarily, Dora and the boys would have accompanied me to the meeting where this travesty of justice had started, but because of the threat of violence I had left them in the hotel where they would be safe and sound and get some badly needed sleep.

They had indeed gone to bed at eight o'clock, not knowing that I was still down in the lobby trying to figure out what was best to do after I had been informed that, after all, Bull Connor had prevailed and the meeting would be segregated. They had slept peacefully until I was arrested and jailed and the glorious news was flashed over the radio that a United States senator had met his match in good old Bull Connor. (That name is not something I thought up to add color to this story. The press and everyone else called him "Bull" Connor, probably because he was, in true southern politican style, a great "bullshitter.")

The despised northern carpetbagger who had come to their fair state to stir up trouble among the happy and contented "darkies" had been manhandled and unceremoniously thrown into jail for defying the God-given segregation laws of the great state of Alabama, plus a few thought up by the city dads of Birmingham. "Hooray for Bull!"

Shortly after I was arrested at the church, Dora was awakened by the insistent ringing of the phone. Half awake, she took the phone from its cradle and sleepily said, "Hello."

A woman screamed in her ear, "Your husband got just what he deserved!" The voice was shrill and choked with hate. "That will teach you nigger-lovers to come down here and stir up trouble."

Poor, frightened Dora started to ask, "What's happened to my husband?" but the woman hung up, leaving her in an agony of suspense, not knowing whether I was alive or dead. As she paced the floor trying to decide what to do, the phone rang again. It was another venomous woman screaming approximately the same words, only this one did stay on the phone long enough for Dora to ask, "What has happened to my husband?"

"He's in jail. That's what happened and that's where he belongs, the nigger-loving son of a bitch!" If that dear lady had only known how she had relieved Dora's mind by letting her know that I was alive, she would have bitten her tongue off.

Dora had scarcely hung up the phone when there was a knock on the door. Frightened half to death, she wasn't about to open it—for *anyone*. She inquired through the locked door, "Who's there?"

A man's voice answered, "I have just heard about your husband being arrested. I am an attorney, and I want to help him."

Dora answered, "Well, write your name on a card and slip it under the door. I'll give it to him, but I'm not going to open the door." And she didn't. The man tried to reassure her, but she was taking no chances.

Later, it turned out that he was a Negro attorney, and he did in fact help represent me in court. Knowing that he would not be allowed in the hotel as a guest, he had taken the grave risk of sneaking in a back door and furtively walking up several flights of stairs to our room.

There were several more phone calls, one from a woman pleading with Dora to find me and leave town before something "terrible" happened. She told Dora that her husband had become involved in a similar incident in behalf of Negroes. He had been unmercifully beaten. His skull had been fractured. He had been kicked, which had aggravated an old hernia condition that had to be operated on while he was still unconscious. She said her husband was practically an invalid now, and she pleaded with Dora to please, *please* take me away before something like that happened to me.

By the time the broadcast was over and I had returned to the hotel, it was after one a.m. No one had phoned Dora to tell her about the events of the evening because no one had thought about the matter. If we had, we probably would not have called because we did not know of the venomous phone calls, had no idea that she had been harassed, and would have felt there was no reason to disturb her sleep.

She had suffered a great deal more than I had.

The next afternoon, as we passed the newsstand in the lobby on our way to the airport, I picked up an *Atlanta Journal* and a *Birmingham Post*. Both papers carried exhaustive accounts of the night's happenings.

The *Atlanta Journal* quoted me as saying about the Birmingham police, "They treated me very rough. Anything but gentlemanly. God help the ordinary man."

On the flight to Washington, I read the *Birmingham Post* from cover to cover. I learned something. Every ad for a service establishment, such as barbershops and beauty parlors, had a line at the bottom reading "Discriminating Service" or "For Discriminating People." There was no end to their cleverness in composing euphemistic variations without using the term "segregated."

The next day on the Senate floor I described my unbelievable adventures in Birmingham. I expected that when I had finished every senator, at least those from above the Mason-Dixon line, would express indignation and outrage at the physical mistreatment I had endured and the indignities which had been heaped upon a colleague and fellow member of "the most exclusive club on earth." I reckoned without due regard for the effectiveness of the red smear and communist witch hunt and the fear it had instilled in the chicken breasts of my colleagues.

Not one senator opened his mouth. Not even senators Lister Hill and/or John Sparkman of Alabama rose to apologize for the shameful treatment accorded me in their state or to repudiate the brazen words and brutal actions of Bull Connor. Even that great liberal and constitutional authority Wayne Morse of Oregon saw nothing sufficiently threatening to the Constitution to merit his learned comment.

Nowadays, when I tell college groups what Wallace and I endured, they find it difficult to believe. There have been profound changes for the better since 1948, and it is a source of real satisfaction to know that Wallace and I were responsible for getting the ball rolling.

GALLUP 51 PERCENT   In mid-July a Gallup Poll showed that 50 percent of those polled felt that the Progressive Party was communist dominated. What else could be expected when the media were solidly united in a vicious campaign calculated to frighten the people into believing that it was? The wonder is that only 51 percent believed the charge, or said they did. With newspapers printing lists of all those who signed our petitions and many losing their jobs and any hope of future employment, how many frightened people do you imagine said "Yes" to that stark question rather than run the risk of being branded subversive and losing their jobs?

ARREST OF COMMUNIST LEADERS   In New York, on July 20, the top leaders of the Communist Party were arrested. Timed to coincide with our "new party" convention, it was an obvious ploy to embarrass us. Headlines and stories covering the two events were intermingled until one could get the impression that Wallace and I were the ones arrested. The news coverage of one event often mentioned the other, to add to the confusion.

The whole Machiavellian scheme was a political move calculated to force us to come to the defense of the communist leaders and their right to exist as a party.

Although Wallace and I knew that by denouncing the move as unconstitutional we were doing great harm to our own cause, there was no other course open to us unless we were to give the lie to our belief in civil rights and political freedom.

We denounced the action as unconstitutional, and the establishment politicians and media belabored us unmercifully.

The asininely vicious depths to which the press descended in their frantic efforts to paint the Progressive Party red was illustrated by an article in the *Daily Statesman* about our convention:

"The Rules Committee even met in the Pink Room at the Bellevue Stratford Hotel. And the badges passed around to the press were—bright red."

Oh, for Christ's sake! Can you imagine such crap? We didn't paint the damned room pink, and the badges had to be *some* color.

Syndicated columnist Marquis Childs revealed the temper of the times:

> If war with the Soviet Union should come, the FBI would move at once to confine thousands suspected of allegiance to world communism rather than to the United States. And it is no secret that some of those who would be confined are here at this convention.

The *New York Times* for Saturday, July 24, 1948, carried a factual, unprejudiced, and dispassionate account that gives one the "feel" of the convention's first day:

> The Progressive Party convention opened here tonight. Where old-party delegates had been blasé, indifferent, the new party delegates were eager, attentive, orderly and more spontaneous.

Our platform called for an end to racial discrimination and supported antilynching and antisegregation legislation. Voting rights for eighteen-year-olds was also promised. We advocated a national health insurance program, a one-hundred-dollar-a-month old age pension, an increase in the minimum wage to one dollar an hour, and repeal of the recently enacted peacetime draft. Boy, were we a radical outfit!

Think of the untold billions of dollars and the untold lives wasted on the Vietnam war. Think of the ruinous inflation it set off, which certainly would not have happened if Wallace and I had been elected. I did my best. I tried.

I also insisted that nationalization of the railroads be included in the platform. As you can see, I was to the left of all these "commies" whom the press was yapping about. A howl went up from the railroad lobby, but not too many years later, when passenger service became unprofitable, that white elephant was unloaded onto the government and is now maintained at terrific cost to the taxpayers.

NOMINATED   On the afternoon of July 24, Wallace and I were nominated as the party's presidential and vice-presidential candidates. The *Philadelphia Bulletin* said of the event:

> Taylor was the first of the two candidates to enter the hall. He carried his youngest son, Greg, their two other sons followed him and his wife Dora onto the rostrum.
>
> The crowd shrieked itself hoarse for five minutes. Shouts, screams, cheers, and in some cases sobs came from the throats of the crowd. When the crowd had shouted until it could scream no more, it began to whistle. Not a person in the hall was seated.
>
> Then, as these delegates have done whenever their emotions were aroused, they broke into song.

Thirty thousand people crowded into Shibe Park, the baseball stadium, to hear Wallace and me make our acceptance speeches that evening. For the first time in history, those who came to a party's national convention to see and hear and lend their support to a political party paid to get in. Most seats were two dollars and fifty cents; others sold for as little as sixty-five cents in order to avoid undue hardship.

In answer to charges made during his presidential campaign in 1972, Senator George McGovern "admitted" that he had been a supporter of the Progressive Party but dropped out because he became convinced that "they [Progressives] were a bunch of fanatics."

That seems to be a case of the pot calling the kettle black. Did you see George's convention in Miami? Of course we were fanatics. At least I was. You have to be, by commonly accepted standards, a fanatic or some kind of nut when you place your future, your job, and your prospects of educating three sons on the line in a predestined losing battle in the cause of peace. I wasn't the only one, either. Many, many people, college professors and many others in all walks of life, lost their jobs and had their lives ruined or irreparably damaged because they dared run for office on, or even support, the Progressive Party ticket.

During the Progressive Party campaign I was accused of being a Russia-lover and a communist dupe because I said that I was convinced that the Russians did not want war and that they were in no shape to wage war. They were having to exert every effort to try and repair the terrible damage inflicted on them by Hitler's legions. I also pointed out that the Russian economy was not dependent on armaments to sustain it.

It is ironic that, in the midst of all the calumny being heaped upon me, one of America's most conservative business publications, *U.S. News and World Report,* should bear me out completely.

In its issue of August 20, 1948, we read:

> War preparations by Russia are defensive, not offensive, in nature. Russian industry is being shifted eastward, back of the Urals. Russian communication lines to the west are not being highly developed. Russia, by her shifting of industry eastward, by her neglect of lines of communication westward, is weakening, not strengthening, her offensive positions. Russian military preoccupation is with defense, not offense.

Did anyone apologize to me for the attacks against me for saying precisely what *U.S. News* now told their big business readers? Did the press reprint this reassuring news? Did Truman say that all his "get tough" talk had been based on misinformation given him by his military buddies that we were in mortal danger from the Russians?

No. Nothing like this happened. The cold war has gone on for thirty more years. An armament economy using Russia and the threat of imminent attack as the straw man drained the American economy until the dollar started losing its value, and once the slide started there was no stopping it.

Why in the world would *U.S. News and World Report* print such stuff and let the cat out of the bag? Because, dear friends, businessmen don't pay good money for hogwash. They want the facts.

But don't worry. Relatively few ordinary people read the *U.S. News and World Report* and the press would go right on giving Joe Blow and John Doe the old cold war line.

The polls had shown Wallace with 11.5 percent of the vote in February, but as the cold war and the red smear mounted in ferocity our vote diminished accordingly: 7.5 percent in April, 6 percent in June, 5 percent in August, and 4 percent in October, and on election day we received just 2.37 percent of the vote.

As time for my reelection campaign drew near, the machine was desperate for a candidate to run against me. In his column of May 15, 1949, John Corlett said in the *Statesman:* "Former Sen. D. Worth Clark is being touted as Taylor's principal opponent. That could be, but in Washington, D.C., where Clark is an attorney, he indicated it would be pretty difficult to give up a lucrative law practice."

On May 25 Clark announced. Apparently the machine had made him an offer that would be more lucrative than his law practice.

VI

Post-Wallace

Days

NO DOUGH   During the 1948 Progressive Party campaign I had a great many people assure me vehemently that should Wallace and I lose they would not forget how I had "so courageously" put my future on the line, and that they could be depended upon to help me financially in my effort to be reelected to the Senate.

It was June 1950. Time to get the campaign rolling. I mailed out twenty letters to the most affluent prospects selected from the lists of heavy contributors to the Progressive Party. But the red smear had mounted to such a fever pitch that few dared stand against it. I received five contributions totaling three hundred seventy-five dollars. The other fifteen did not answer.

I was dumbfounded. Another chunk of my faith in mankind was chopped away.

SNOT?   On April 19, 1950, the annual dinner of the Democratic State Committee of New York was held at the Waldorf-Astoria Hotel in New York City. Dora and I were invited.

The trip to New York was via a chartered railway coach plus a club car with cocktail lounge and dining room. On the way I had some cramming on senatorial business to do, so Dora got out a deck of cards and moved across the aisle to a pair of seats which were vacant and turned face to face. She had the steward bring a table and started playing solitaire.

Senator Hubert Humphrey was roaming about talking to all and sundry, as was his habit. He stopped at Dora's table, and shortly they were playing cards together. To be more specific, they were playing "eights."

The reason I recall this is because they were absolutely uninhibited, laughing and talking excitedly. Dora is ordinarily rather reserved, but Hubert's contagious ebullience had gotten to her, and she was almost as loud as the senator. All this might have slipped my mind except for the fact that at one point, when Dora had obviously scored heavily, Hubert banged the table so hard everything jumped in the air and shouted, "Oh, you little snot!"

SPIES, STOOGES, AND DUPES   On April 28, D. Worth Clark kicked off his campaign for the Democratic nomination for U.S. senator with a statement that gave us a pretty good idea of how Clark's campaign would be conducted. He said:

"Make no mistake about it, we may be moving into something more than a 'cold war' with Russia. Some shooting has already started.

"For many years, we have been harboring all sorts of Russian spies, agents, stooges, and just plain dupes. These dupes may be any place—in communist-front organizations—in atomic energy plants, yes, even in the halls of Congress. We must eliminate our Henry Wallaces from high places." (Say, now! That was a pretty clever one D. Worth pulled off there, wasn't it? Using Henry as my stand-in to get his idea across without using my name.)

KOREA   The campaign was proceeding nicely. Our crowds were big and friendly. Things looked good. Very good. Then the earth opened up and the roof fell in. The Korean War started.

Immediately, of course, the cry of "red" and "communist," which had become shopworn, was renewed with an orgy of name-calling, accusations, and denunciations to make all that had gone before seem feeble.

DESTROY HIM!   In an early primary in Florida, Senator Pepper was defeated by a fantastically expensive red smear campaign, with full-page and even page-and-a-half ads purporting to prove that Pepper was sympathetic to "reds" and "niggers."

Down in that country, at that time, politicians just did not shake hands with blacks. Senator Pepper broke with tradition, and for the first time a major candidate *did* shake hands with Negroes, and every day the papers would run at least one picture of Pepper shaking hands with blacks.

The Idaho bipartisan corporate political machine and the

Statesman secured the plates of the Pepper smear, and for the last thirty-six days of the campaign they ran a full page of the defamatory propaganda each day. All about Pepper, mind you. The only connection between me and the smear material would be comments by the *Statesman* saying that all this applied even more to Glen Taylor than it did to Senator Pepper. In addition to the smear material which had been used against Pepper, the *Statesman* culled the columns of the *Daily Worker* and reprinted everything laudatory that paper had ever said about me, including pictures of me with Wallace and Paul Robeson, the famous black singer, shaking hands with Panyushkin, the Russian ambassador.

Lest you might find it difficult to believe that the *Statesman* was as vitriolic and unprincipled as I have pictured it to be, I would like to quote from a book written about my political career, beliefs, and actions. The book is *Prophet Without Honor,* written by F. Ross Peterson and published by the University Press of Kentucky. Dr. Peterson did a fantastic amount of research, and in pursuance of the truth and the facts he had occasion, in 1967, to interview John Corlett, the political writer for the *Statesman.* In referring to the campaign waged against me by the *Statesman* in that year of 1950, Mr. Corlett said to Dr. Peterson, "That was the only time I ever set out, under the direction of my publisher and editor, to completely destroy a person."

In addition to the material calculated to destroy me which was being printed by the *Statesman,* I was being red-baited by my opponent D. Worth Clark as well as by the Republican candidate, Herman Welker, who hoped to run against me in the general election.

The election reports were almost a replay of the 1944 primaries, in which I had nosed out Clark by a bare 220 votes. First he was ahead, and then I would jump into the lead.

Too often to be coincidental, populous precincts which usually reported early remained unreported. Clark and I were neck and neck. Then the tardy precincts began to report. They were invariably for Clark, and he began to pull away.

The Clark machine was in gear. The final vote was: Clark, 26,897; Taylor, 25,949.

STRANGE HAPPENINGS Some strange things happened in that election. There were two senatorial races. There were five contestants in the race for the four-year term. Only three candidates, including myself, in the six-year race.

If there was to be any discrepancy between the totals in the two races, common sense would seem to suggest that five candidates, each presumably with a personal following, would poll more votes than three candidates for the same office. That was not the case. The exact opposite was true.

There were 63,304 votes cast in the five-man race for the four-year term. There were 67,445 votes cast (or counted) in my three-man race. That would be 4,141 *more* votes cast or counted in my three-man race than in the five-man contest.

Where did those 4,141 votes come from?

Could these extra votes represent Republicans crossing over and voting in the six-year race to try and get me in the primary? If this were the case, then there would have been fewer votes cast in the six-year race in the Republican primary. As a matter of fact, this did happen. There were 616 fewer votes cast in the six-year race on the Republican side than in the four-year race. Assume they were Republicans crossing over: 4,141 minus 616 still leaves 3,525 more votes cast or counted in my race than in the four-year race.

Examination of the vote by precincts in the Boise area showed that I got a vote fairly consistent with past elections, but in certain precincts I would fall flat on my face and Clark would almost make a clean sweep.

In Minidoka County, the supply of ballots had been exhausted by six p.m. The polls were scheduled to close at eight p.m. Several hundred voters were turned away. Mostly working people, and my supporters.

Idaho had no recount law, so there was no recourse there. I flew to Washington and finally prevailed upon the Senate Elections Subcommittee to investigate the Idaho election. It was agreed that six precincts of my selection would be counted, and if that should show a discrepancy sufficient to change the result if projected to the total vote, there would be a recount.

The committee counsel arrived the evening before the recount. He was in such condition he could hardly walk. The next morning at ten everything was in readiness. The accountants were there, the ballot boxes were there. Everything was there except the committee counsel.

My attorney and a bailiff went to the hotel to see what was detaining the counsel. He had taken the early plane and flown away without notifying anyone that he intended to do so. No counsel—no recount.

Investigation revealed that a well known attorney who passed out corporation money to machine-backed candidates had shown up in the hotel the evening before with a fat briefcase.

The machine had scored again.

If I had been able to get the recount and found that my suspicions were groundless, I would have forgotten politics and set about building a new life. As it was, I just couldn't accept the idea of quitting on such a sour note. I felt obligated to those steadfast friends who had been cheated just as I had. I made up my mind I would run again.

I realized that the only way I could win would be to get so many votes the machine could not steal enough to beat me.

In the general election Herman Welker gave D. Worth Clark the worst beating in the history of Idaho politics: 124,237 to 77,180.

The only Democrat elected was our old friend Ira Masters, who won his race for secretary of state. Ira had always been a vocal supporter of mine, so now my supporters could say, "See, Glen's old friend and supporter was the only Democrat to win. It's as plain as the nose on your face that if Glen had been the senatorial nominee, he would have won along with Masters."

And what did I do? I gave 'em hell, boy. The *Lewiston Tribune* carried the statement I issued the day after the election. The heading on the editorial said TAYLOR'S CAMPAIGN BEGINS (and truer words "was never spoke"). I jumped into the void left by yesterday's catastrophe with both guns blazin' and issued a "fire and brimstone" pronouncement to the press. The *Lewiston Tribune* says I said it, and I happily plead guilty to saying it, as follows:

"The catastrophe which befell the Democratic Party in the Idaho election Tuesday was the result of a callous determination on the part of a small group of willful men to rule or ruin the Democratic Party in Idaho," Taylor declared. "This close-knit, bipartisan group of tinhorn economic royalists have controlled Idaho politics for so long that they cannot bear the thought of even one man holding an important office who is not beholden to them.

I for one am not going to take the underhanded tactics and unscrupulous political methods of these schemers lying down. I am going to fight to the finish against the self-seekers who play politics for the benefit of their moneyed masters and whose blackhearted disregard for the hopes, aspirations and the needs of the people has brought the Democratic Party to its lowest ebb."

And the Tribune added this footnote:

Seldom does a new senatorial campaign open so quickly after the collapse of another, but Senator Taylor is noted for doing things that seldom have been done, and the fact remains that it *was* Clark and *not* Taylor who was defeated by the Republicans.

It may prove to be the luckiest event of Taylor's political career that he was *not* involved in the debacle of the Democrats Tuesday.

CORPORATION PRESIDENT While my golden opportunity to denounce the machine and put the blame on them for the disastrous defeat had given my spirits a temporary lift, my most pressing problem remained. How in the hell was I going to feed my wife and kids?

I could have had money to throw at the birds if I had signed up with that outfit in Washington that booked big shots for speaking engagements, but *no*, I had been too honest for that. All I had was my speaking ability, a strange and unfathomable power to sway audiences. But who wants to hire a defeated senator as a speaker or in any other capacity?

But don't worry. Help came in the form of two angels, and, believe it or not, they were male angels. One angel was chewing tobacco and the other one was smoking a stogie.

I was sitting in our twelve-by-fourteen front room trying to see the light at the end of my tunnel of unemployment when there came a knock on my bell-less front door. There was a bell, but it was kaput, and new bells cost money.

Since my defeat, callers had been few and far between. Who

could this be? Well, what do you know? The Coryell boys, Verl and Cody. They were contractors, in a modest way, and I had performed a little senatorial magic by getting their problems with the FHA straightened out.

As soon as I had lost the election, they figured that I might be open for a business offer. They wanted me to be president of a construction company they were starting.

To start with, my pay would be nothing sensational, say five hundred dollars a month. Now while five hundred dollars a month probably wouldn't seem like much to most men who had drawn a senator's pay, it was five hundred dollars more than nothing. It was a deal.

Cody told me frankly that the main reason they were presenting this proposition to me was that the brothers couldn't get along together, and they wanted me to be the court of last resort and adjudicate their quarrels. The Coryell brothers were Irish through and through, with the fiery, hasty tempers and other foibles of that lovable race of quick-witted brawlers.

Another reason why they were offering me this life-saving job was that the rich gent who was going to bankroll the undertaking thought it would be helpful to have a former senator associated with the new venture to lend prestige.

GOOD GUY HARRY   Shortly after I was defeated in the 1950 primary, Harry Truman sent word that he would like to see me. I couldn't imagine why. After all, I *had* run with Wallace, and it was no secret that the President bitterly despised him.

To my surprise, Truman was very cordial. After we had exchanged mutual assurances of how glad we were to see each other, the President said, "Well, Glen, I'm sorry about what happened to you, but I did my best. I warned you to stay away from that nut. Bu-u-ut, that's water under the bridge. What are you going to do now? Have you got a job?"

I explained about the contruction company and told him frankly that it was a blind venture, and that for some time at least it would be pretty lean pickings and tough sledding. At the end of my not-too-rosy recital, Truman said, "Well, Glen, aside from that Wallace thing, you've been a pretty good Democrat. You've got maybe the very best record of party regularity of anybody. I could always count on you except for your votes on foreign policy, and they didn't matter because those votes were nearly unanimous anyhow. You've been a lot better Democrat than some of those goddamn Dixiecrats. I guess you did what you thought was right when you left the reservation for old screwball Henry, and I think you are a hell of a lot more deserving than a lot of others. It sounds to me like you need a job, so you name it and it's yours. Anything at all within reason in the fifteen-thousand-dollar range."

Such generous treatment was the last thing on earth I expected from this rough, tough, Pendergast-trained politician. God, but I was tempted, but I had already decided that of all the things on this earth that I didn't want, it was to wind up as a political hanger-on. A bureaucrat to be browbeaten and chewed out by senators and congressmen, not to mention superiors in the chain of command. I felt like hugging old Harry and crying on his shoulder, but instead I told him how grateful I was for his offer and how generous it was of him, but that I couldn't think of imposing on him because we both knew what a storm of criticism and red baiting would be set off if he appointed me to some job—any job.

"Oh, to hell with that!" he exclaimed. "I've been red-baited by experts."

We both laughed at that, but I told him that my mind was made up. I did not want a political job. I might run for the Senate again, but would not settle for anything less. My pride just wouldn't permit it.

He looked at me a little unbelievingly, I thought, and then he shrugged and said, "Okay, Glen, it's you for it. If you change your mind, the offer stands. Just let me know."

JOHN GUNTHER　John Gunther was probably the country's best known "roving reporter" during the forties and fifties. He wrote *Inside U.S.A.* and a whole series of "Inside" books. He interviewed me in my Senate office, and one of the nice things he wrote about me was, "He has already proved himself one of the most useful Senators the country has." This was in the 1947 edition. Later, in 1951, there was another printing of this best-seller and the compliments Mr. Gunther had paid me were deleted.

The reason? I had criticized our involvement in Indo-China which some years later evolved into the Vietnam war. Consequently, I made the lists of suspects whose loyalty was in question. If U.S. senators were not exempt from the McCarthy witch hunt, who was? The fact that a writer of Gunther's stature could be forced to edit out any plus references to a man gives us a pretty good idea of how all pervasive and all powerful McCarthy had become in 1951.

Reprinting portions of the same page from both editions will best prove my point. I have italicized the complimentary portions that appeared in the 1947 edition but were deleted from the 1951 edition.

1947 EDITION

"No."

"A teller or a clerk?"

"No."

"What, then?" finally asked the puzzled Wagner.

"I was a depositor," Taylor replied.

He got the appointment.

Glen Taylor, no matter what people in Boise or Pocatello, Idaho, may tell you, is not a clown, not a hillbilly, not a buffoon. On the contrary he is an extremely serious man. He has a nice dry wit, abundant common sense, fertility of mind, and a modest enough sense of showmanship. Above all his character shows pertinacity of almost incredible dimensions. Bilbo sneered at him once that he might make a senator in "about five years," but he has already proved himself one of the most useful senators the country has.

Taylor's career is picaresque to say the least. He was born in Portland, Oregon, in 1904, and brought up in the hamlet of Kooksia, Idaho, one of the eight children of a retired Texas ranger who was also a minister. He quit school when he was twelve, and has never had any formal education since. The contrast to *his friend* Wayne Morse, an intellectual by profession, is immense. . . .

1951 EDITION

"No."

"A teller or a clerk?"

"No."

"What, then?" finally asked the puzzled Wagner.

"I was a depositor," Taylor replied.

He got the appointment.

Taylor's career is picaresque to say the least. He was born in Portland, Oregon, in 1904, and brought up in the hamlet of Kooskia, Idaho, one of the eight children of a retired Texas ranger who was also a minister. He quit school when he was twelve, and has never had any formal education since. The contrast to Wayne Morse, an intellectual by profession, is considerable. . . .

SECURITY RISK   In the Fall of '51, the Coryell Construction Company was nearly a year old. We were nearing the end of the project we were working on and it would be quite profitable. A substantial share of the profit and a pay raise would be forthcoming. In order to live until that happy day, we sold our Washington house and moved to San Jose, California.

One day Gregory, my youngest son, sailed a little balsa wood plane and it lit on top of the garage. I retrieved it and then jumped off the garage. In doing so I suffered a severe back injury. I was bedridden for several weeks. I finally wound up wearing a heavy canvas belt extending from my rump to my rib cage.

By occasionally dipping into the seventy-five hundred dollars we had netted on the sale of our Washington house to supplement my five-hundred-dollar-a-month salary we managed to live very, very meagerly.

The Coryell boys decided to go to Guam to look at a job there that was up for bid. Military clearance was required before a passport was granted. The Coryells had no trouble, but *my request was turned down*. I was considered to be a "security risk." That, of course, made me a handicap to my benefactors.

There was only one thing I could do. I submitted my resignation. There was no object in trying to find another job. People were not about to hire a "security risk" for a responsible job.

The rich partner who had financed the Coryell Construction Company took a dim view of being associated with a company whose president had been branded a security risk, and he withdrew. The company folded.

Recently I sent for my FBI file, as the law now provides.

With relation to my being blackballed, losing my job, and the corporation going out of business, my FBI report has this to say:

"O.N.I. [Office of Naval Intelligence] Seattle has confidentially advised that the Navy really has no good reason for denying clearance for Taylor."

Understand that the foregoing communication was just an interoffice report, and I was never apprised of the good news. That's the way secret police work. Their job is not to see that justice is done. What if I *did* blow my brains out because I could not find a job? What if the goddamned corporation did blow up?

SHOW BIZ   We were desperate.

I did something that I would not have even considered if there had been an alternative, but the need to support one's family sometimes leaves no room for pampering pride. I decided that we would take a last, brief fling at show business during the school vacation period. Many people would still remember The Glendora Players and little Arod, the three-year-old who sang cowboy songs and yodeled, and they would be curious to see Arod as a young man. One other factor should attract the curious. The morbidly curious. All these Glendora fans were aware that Glen Taylor had gone almost directly from being an important part of their social life to the United States Senate. Perhaps they would be curious to see the man who had risen to the heights and was now back where he had started.

Crass? Shameful? What about your pride, Glen? Sure I thought about these things, but there was one other consideration. I had been well on my way toward carving out another niche for myself but my own government, a government in which I had served in a capacity only a notch or two lower than the presidency, had snatched it away from me. Admittedly for no reason, it had branded me a security risk and made it impossible for me to obtain other employment so I could provide my family with a decent standard of living and educate my sons.

If the fact of past glory would attract a few people to pay to see me, like a monkey in a zoo—what the hell?

There was another matter that was of greater concern to me, and that caused a twinge of conscience. I planned that the show would be strictly a family affair. No salaries. I was confident that it would be a good show, but what if it wasn't? Never, in all our years of trouping, had we failed to give the customers their money's worth, and more. The apprehension that a family show might not measure up bothered me more than the fact that I would, to whatever degree, be exploiting the office I had so recently held.

There were other worries, too. TV had come to the little community of Power, Montana. There were antennas reaching skyward everywhere—one for nearly every residence. Could we draw a crowd against such handy and formidable opposition? If we did have a crowd, could our five-people family show please this TV-satiated generation?

Much to my relief, the show went over with a bang.

As it turned out, our attendance was about what it used to be, and with higher prices due to inflation the gross was a few dollars more: $56.91. Our share was $42.65.

As always in the past, we sold candy after the third act. I made the same old pitch. I would have liked to have been spared that mortification, but we were in no position to skip the candy sale and the three or four, perhaps even five or ten, extra dollars it would bring in.

I had inwardly cringed at the prospect: a former United States senator doing such a penny-ante, undignified thing—but it wasn't too bad.

After the show, we played for the dance. As I sat there playing my old banjo and watched the dancers swirl by, it all seemed unreal. A dream. Would I wake up and find that this *was* just a dream and that I was still in the Senate, or would I wake up and find that being in the Senate was the dream and that we had never left show business at all? They couldn't both be real. The disparity was too great.

One thing was certain: Tonight I was getting a grim satisfaction by demonstrating, in a small way, that I could go on despite the stab in the back I had suffered from my own government in being branded a security risk. Other men who had been so stigmatized and found themselves unemployable, with no alternative means of earning a living, had, in many instances, committed suicide. I was certainly more fortunate than they.

In the forty-three days of trouping, we netted one thousand one hundred dollars, and by "netted" I mean that's how much more cash in hand we had than when we started. Not bad. We sure as hell hadn't saved that much on a senator's salary.

It was obvious that with the affluence prevailing we could have done better in show biz than we had done in the days before TV, but with three boys of school age that was out.

When we returned home we found a letter awaiting us from Cody Coryell, one of my associates in the late lamented Coryell Construction Company. He was in Redding, California, and wanted us to come down; he and I would build a house on a speculative basis.

It was something to do, and I had always wanted to build a house anyway. We went to Redding.

1954 CAMPAIGN It was terrifically hot in September. I had done little or no hard labor during my senatorial tenure, and certainly not since my back injury. Every muscle and bone in my body ached from the ten-hour days we put in, but after two or three weeks I became inured to it except for the discomfort of the heavy belt I had to wear. Besides causing me to sweat excessively in the hundred-degree-plus heat, the fact that I could not bend or twist at the waist was a handicap and an aggravation.

On weekends we put on shows and dances in surrounding communities.

When the time for the 1954 campaign finally came, we returned to Idaho and I announced.

As in the past I had three opponents, which worked to my advantage. I again won the nomination.

The general election campaign was going well when, on August 21, *Time* magazine again hit me below the belt with a false charge very similar to the one leveled at me in 1942 when they quoted me as saying, "I make more money campaigning than I ever did in show business."

This new alleged "quote" had me saying: "I want to be reelected to the Senate because I can't find another job."

That outrageous untruth was worse than the first one. More idiotic and damaging. It was quoted and requoted. Editorials were written about it, and with devastating effect.

Remembering the lawyer's advice at the time of the 1942 attack, when he said, "Don't start a suit against *Time* unless you have a million dollars," I swallowed my rage and didn't even bother to complain.

To add to my problems, Herman Welker, the lawyer who had

so murderously defeated D. Worth Clark in the 1950 general election, was now Joe McCarthy's right-hand man in the red-hunting business. In fact, he was chairman of a subcommittee all his own.

Welker came to Idaho bringing with him the infamous FBI informer, Matt Cvetic, and together they staged a red-baiting attack on me, charging that I was a communist dupe.

A TV series based on Cvetic's exploits as an FBI informer had made him famous. He worked northern Idaho where many mine workers have names like Cvetic. He reeled off names of persons he alleged were communists who had infiltrated the Progressive Party. He did not accuse me of any deliberate wrongdoing, but left the impression that I was a stupid dupe and not to be trusted with a high office.

In the meetings he held in the southern part of the state, Welker would hold up imposing looking books that he intimated were secret files and say: "If you could see the material on Glen Taylor in these files it would make your hair curl."

Two weeks before the election, the *Statesman* admitted that I was almost certain to be elected. Then, with massive aid from the press, Welker's red-baiting campaign took hold. On October 31, John Corlett, the political writer for the *Statesman*, said: "Five weeks ago there wasn't a Republican in the state who sincerely believed that Dworshak would be victorious. Today there is not a Republican in the state who does not believe Taylor will go down to a great defeat."

TOO LATE   On the evening of November 1, election eve, we held our final rally in Pocatello and dragged ourselves home, completely worn out. There was mail in the box, and one piece was a large envelope, the return address of which bore the name of the Pittsburgh attorney whom I had asked for information on Cvetic. He had defended numerous people who had been falsely accused by Cvetic of being communists.

When I opened the envelope and began to read I was astounded. The first item was a photostat of a complaint filed by Cvetic's sister-in-law, who charged that Cvetic had attacked her and broken her arm. Cvetic had been tried, found guilty, and fined three hundred and forty dollars. In court Cvetic had said, "Since when is it a crime to beat up your own sister-in-law?"

Another enclosure revealed that Cvetic was sued for divorce, and the court ordered the records impounded as "unfit for publication." Cvetic had twice been hauled into court for failure to support his two children. In a rural, straight-laced state like Idaho, how would the voters react to that sort of behavior?

But wait! Here is what we are interested in. Up-to-date proof that Cvetic is a liar without conscience, scruples, or pity. The heading on an item from the *Pittsburgh Press* of June 18, 1954, reads: CITY CLEARS CLERK OF RED CHARGES. NO EVIDENCE FOUND TO SUPPORT CVETIC. The article says:

> Barney Schmidt, a clerk in the Pittsburgh City Water Department, stood cleared today of charges that he is a communist. The accusation was made last Oct. 7 by Matt Cvetic, erstwhile FBI informant.
>
> At the time Mr. Schmidt said that Cvetic was "a contemptible liar."

And there was more—much more. Time and again Cvetic had been proven to be a liar, and people he had accused of being communists had been cleared. There were photostats of hospital records showing that Cvetic was an alcoholic. A psycho who had been restrained in a straitjacket.

After all the furor created by Cvetic's charges, imagine what the public's reaction would be to this damning and incontrovertible evidence proving that Cvetic was, as I had charged, "a contemptible liar." I was momentarily elated, and then the cold, bitter truth dawned on me.

Here I had in my hand information that would, with absolute certainty, turn the smear used against me into a gigantic boomerang, that would utterly destroy my enemies and assure my victory and vindication, but it was too late. Now wait a minute. It was too late for this election, perhaps, but Herman Welker would be up for reelection in two years. I was certain beyond doubt that with the material in the brown envelope I could murder him in cold blood. Tomorrow, while he strutted, preened, and crowed over the success of his lousy conspiracy with his sleazy, paid-to-lie stoolpigeons, he would not know it, but his doom was signed and sealed, so help me.

KAPUT   And so another "free" election, Idaho style, became history. I suffered a staggering defeat: Dworshak, 142,269–Taylor, 84,138.

The newspapers screamed, "A great victory for the decent, patriotic citizens of Idaho. Thank God for Welker! Thank God for that great patriot, Cvetic!"

This would surely be the end of Glen Taylor.

We lasted out the winter playing for a dance or two each week. We actually went hungry at times.

On the day that school was out, about June 1, I was talking to the business agent of the Carpenters' Union. He knew how hard pressed I was and how badly I needed a job, and when I mentioned that I had a carpenter's card he exclaimed, "Well, why the hell didn't you say so before? We have more jobs than we have carpenters. I can put you to work tomorrow." Gratefully, I accepted the offer.

Explaining how much work was available, he mentioned that there was even a shortage of apprentices, and when I told him that Arod was looking for a job he was delighted. Both Arod and I went to work the next morning. I was thankful that we were working on top of a flat-roofed building where the curious could not stop and gawk at the spectacle of their former senator doing the heaviest kind of manual labor. That is certainly what it was. The timbers Arod and I had to handle were two by fourteen inches by fourteen feet. I was of course wearing my heavy felt and canvas belt with the inch-wide steel stays up both sides of my spine to support my back, but by being careful to squat rather than bend over when I was lifting I was able to keep up my end.

The heavy work was much worse on Arod than it was on me. He was slightly built and weighed no more than one hundred and twenty pounds. The weather was very hot, hovering around one hundred degrees and going as high as one hundred and two, and probably considerably higher on that flat roof. More than once the heavy lifting and the heat caused Arod to vomit. I urged him to quit, but he refused and toughed it out all through his summer vacation.

That my frail son had to drive himself to help support the family was a constant reminder of the folly of my idealistic approach to life that had reduced us to this sad state.

On a wild and stormy night, Foy and I set forth on a do-or-die effort to raise money for my campaign to unseat Welker. We were driving our old car, which we had purchased in Washington six long years before. The dilapidated rattletrap's odometer registered one hundred and seven thousand miles. The tires were threadbare. A raging blizzard was whistling through the leafless trees along the deserted street. We drove away in darkness because I had worked that day at my carpentering job. We needed those few extra bucks.

Our first stop was San Francisco. We traveled from there to L.A., to New York and back, and all points in between contacting people I had met through the years. We traveled all through the long cold winter and returned with a piddling campaign fund of fifteen thousand dollars.

GET WELKER! The Clark political dynasty had run out of blood-line relatives to carry on their activities so in this 1956 election they had to place their bets on Frank Church, a young attorney just thirty years old. He became the dynasty's last hope by virtue of the fact that he was married to Chase Clark's daughter.

In its issue of May 25 the *Idaho Daily Statesman* printed an item that gave me a pretty good idea how much support I might get from Mr. Church and the machine, should I be the nominee. The article says:

> Frank Church, Boise, candidate for the Democratic senatorial nomination, Thursday issued a statement in reply to a proposal by Taylor in which he (Taylor) urged that all six senatorial candidates and all party leaders pledge themselves to support the party nominee in the coming primary election, whoever he may be.
>
> Church's statement says, "My reply to Mr. Taylor's proposal is this: I am a good Democrat. I will support any good Democrat who wins the coming primary election, in whose principles and integrity I can place an honest confidence"

I incorporated the material on Cvetic into a four-page tabloid. I had figured on it having a weighty impact, but nothing like the devastating blast that it was.

During the last week or two of the campaign, I learned that the machine had hired a plague of older party hangers-on who were busily crisscrossing the state spreading the propaganda line: "Yeah, Glen *was* a good senator all right. Probably the best senator we ever had—but we've just got to beat that dirty son of a bitch Welker. What he did to Glen with that goddamned bastard Cvetic is the most unprincipled thing that ever happened in Idaho. That man has just got to be beat. But, from all I hear, folks just don't feel Glen can beat him, so most people I've talked to say they're gonna vote for Church because Burtenshaw and Mac-Cormack don't seem to be getting anyplace and they figure Church is the only one can do the job."

The machine, with its thousand ears listening about the state, had discovered that my little paper, *The Democrat,* had so enraged the voters against Welker that "getting Welker" had become the all-important thing. Their desire to elect me had become secondary, and if necessary my election could wait. There would be other elections, and I could run again. The all-important thing now was to get Welker no matter what.

Recognizing this anomalous situation, the machine was using it, and with murderous effect. With each passing day I heard this story more and more often. Even some of my staunchest supporters were beginning to parrot the line and would still seem doubtful despite my efforts to buck them up and convince them that it was now or never for me.

I had done too good a job on Welker. My exposé of his perfidy in *The Democrat* was proving to be an overkill and the machine was capitalizing on this weird fact.

The first returns reported election night were from the Boise area, which was the citidel of the machine and the home of Mr. Church. He jumped into a lead of 1,000 votes.

My guts tied up in a knot. There was so damn much at stake. Everything. This was my last chance, my final fling. If I could win the nomination I was confident I could beat Welker.

For the first time in my political career I had spent beyond what I had received in contributions. I was deeply in debt, a thousand dollars or so. If I lost, how in the hell would I ever pull out?

A few minutes later the returns came in from my home town of Pocatello and Bannock County, and I pulled up even. Fifteen minutes later I was ahead by a few hundred votes.

It was obvious that the race was between Church and me. The others were falling farther behind with every report. I would inch ahead and then some big precinct that should have reported long ago would report, and Church would catch up.

All through the night it was a dingdong battle. Church was ahead by 100 or 200 votes most of the way but, true to form, I began to inch up on him as the far-out precincts came in. At one point it was a dead heat, with the score all tied at 27,000 votes each. With just a few remote precincts to report, I pulled into a 100-vote lead just as the radio station went off the air at two a.m.

That should be it. I always picked up a few votes in the remote, late reporting, and sparsely populated precincts. However, on this night there were still several larger precincts unreported, for some mysterious reason.

Dora, the boys, and Foy were jubilant. Then they noticed me sitting there showing no signs of being elated at my apparent victory. Dora asked, "What's the matter?"

"One hundred votes isn't enough," I told them. "The machine will have no trouble digging up that many votes."

I was sorry to put damper on their celebration, but I was certain that what I said was true. Past experience had proven that in close elections the machine always had at least a thousand or perhaps two or three thousand votes stashed away in precincts where they owned the election machinery lock, stock, and barrel. Don't forget the 4,000 extra votes that showed up in the 1950 primary that no one could account for. I was so certain that I would be counted out that I sat down and composed a statement, phoning it in to the AP and UPI.

> The election is so close that no matter who may be declared the winner, there should be a recount. Should I be the lucky one, as it now appears will be the case, I will be happy to join with Mr. Church in a request for a recount.
>
> Since a joint request from both candidates seems to be the only way in which a recount may be obtained, I am hopeful Mr. Church will agree to this proposal now before the final result is known and announced.

My seemingly overgenerous suggestion wasn't that at all.

With the prevailing situation, I was morally certain that I would be the one who would need the recount. My suggestion was an effort to put Mr. Church on the spot should he refuse to help me when I did request a recount.

I had no real hope that the maneuver would help. Not really. The machine just didn't operate that way.

When asked by the press what he thought of my proposal, Mr. Church said, "I will await the final outcome. Meanwhile, I am going to California for a vacation, and if, when I return, I am the nominee, I am sure I will have a united party behind me and we will go on to a glorious victory in November."

My hopes sank to rock-bottom.

"That isn't only a refusal of my proposition," I told Dora and Foy. "That is a victory statement. He knows what's going to happen. As for that California vacation bit, it's too ridiculous for words.

"What normal human being," I asked them, "when he is 100 votes behind, is going to head for California for a vacation? Any normal person would stay glued to the radio until the final vote was announced.

"What has happened," I said, "is that the machine boys have told Church, 'Now look, son, everything's going to be okay, but things may get a little messy, so you'd better get away, get clear out of the state, so none of it gets on you.'"

Sure enough, that's what happened. Church and his wife departed for California, and just as they crossed into Nevada the radio announced that enough "mistakes" had been found to put Church in the lead. He reported later that when they heard the news on their car radio he and his wife got out and did a dance in the snow to celebrate. Then they went on to California and were gone for several days.

Many errors were found when county canvassing boards checked the results. Some were in my favor; more and bigger mistakes were reported in Church's favor. The newspapers kept a running account of the ridiculous foulup.

30 FOR GLEN   On August 29, three days after the state canvassing board had officially declared Church the winner by 200 votes, the *Statesman* carried a report:

Discovery of a typographical error chipped 30 votes from Frank Church's 200-vote margin, but Atty. Gen. Graydon Smith said the State Board of Canvassers has no power to make a correction now and that Church's margin will remain officially at 200.

In the 1950 primary I had received 758 votes in Elmore County. In the 1954 primary, 719, yet in this year of 1956, when I had received more votes than ever statewide, I had received only 500 votes in Elmore County. The machine had put on a hell of a good campaign for Church, or something was wrong.

Precinct number 3 in Mountain Home heightened my suspicions. In the county as a whole, excluding number 3, I had polled 34 percent of the Democratic vote. However, in Mountain Home, number 3, I had received only 19 percent of the Democratic vote.

In view of this startling difference and the fact that it was the largest precinct in the county and therefore the most fertile field for "mistakes," I was convinced something was amiss.

In a last desperate effort to come up with something to force a recount, I decided to make a personal canvass of number 3 and see if I could get the voters there to tell me how they voted. People are notoriously touchy about having anyone invade their privacy by trying to ascertain this. I would have to be a champion diplomat to get them to answer that question without offending.

THE CANVASS   Foy and I rented a room in an old wooden firetrap of a hotel and went to work. We got the list of registered voters for precinct number 3 and checked it against the files of the water department and the Idaho Power Company.

Eight families had moved locally and had new addresses, and five had moved away in the thirty days since the election. We got the forwarding addresses of the latter at the post office and wrote them letters explaining at length just what we wanted and why, and enclosed a dollar bill to pay the notary fee. Foy and I were existing on hamburgers, and sending those five one-dollar bills really hurt. We impressed upon all those we wrote the urgency of the matter, and two of the five sent the affidavit saying they had voted for me. The other three failed to answer and kept the dollar bills. I allotted those to Church.

We then got a large street map and numbered each lot. After that we made a list of all the names and addresses, and gave each one a number so we could arrange our housecalls consecutively and know whom we were calling on.

When I started my house-to-house canvass I was already worn out from the prolonged ordeal I had been through. It was a man-killing job. The temperature was well over one hundred degrees. I walked from house to house, and Foy followed along in the car to haul me over the empty spaces, but there weren't many of them.

I urged each person I contacted please, *please* not to say they had voted for me unless they actually had. "It might make me feel good," I told them, "but it would render useless all the time and effort I am expending trying to arrive at the truth." I did not suggest that there had been any deliberate fraud. My whole approach was based on the fact that there had been so many mistakes found throughout the state, and it appeared that there might have been a major mistake made in this precinct. I had a sheet showing the election results in Elmore County, and I pointed out the strange discrepancies which I have mentioned.

I impressed upon each person that I was not interested in how they had voted except as a statistic. I told them that if the information I was gathering checked with the announced vote that would end the matter. If it didn't, I would ask that the precinct be recounted. I forewarned them that if my canvass showed a significant discrepancy I would be back to ask those who had voted for me to sign an affidavit to that effect.

People in general are not disposed to take lightly the signing of an affidavit. People who have voted for a winner are not disposed to be reluctant about saying so. Thus, I am quite certain the count on Church was factual.

For all these reasons I believe my poll was very, very close to being accurate. Another reason I felt that I generally got truthful answers is the fact that the totals for the other two candidates, McCormack and Burtenshaw, checked out almost exactly right.

POLICE   Everyone was aware of the great number of errors which had been discovered in all sections of the state because the ridiculous foulup had been headline material for weeks. Generally, the people I was polling agreed that if so many errors had been discovered just in checking the tally sheets, there might be as many or more errors found in the boxes themselves.

I had called on a dozen or so homes when a police car drove up alongside us, and the officer told me that the chief of police wanted to see me. At the station I was confronted by the mayor, an unprepossessing individual who was later arrested and fined for shooting an elk out of season. His Honor told me he had received "complaints" that I was "bothering" people and ordered me to stop my canvass.

"We have a Green River ordinance to stop such door-to-door activity," he pontificated.

We argued back and forth, and finally I called the county attorney, who said that I couldn't be restrained as long as I conducted myself in a gentlemanly manner.

I issued a press release about the threat to stop me via the Green River ordinance. It got generous headlines in the press and some editorial comment on the asininity of classing my poll as an activity covered by a Green River ordinance.

FIGURES   After five days of "legging it" door to door from nine a.m. until nine p.m., I had checked 443 of the 488 voters in the precinct. In the official count Church had been credited with 249 votes, and I had gotten only 71. I allocated the 43 voters I had failed to contact according to the figures I had on the 91 percent I had contacted. According to my poll, I should have received 107 votes instead of 71—a gain of 36. Church should have received 215 instead of 249—a loss of 34. Actually, only 168 people said they had voted for Church. This total for Church includes 26 given him because these persons refused to say for whom they had voted and one who was "uncertain," plus the three who had failed to answer the letter I wrote them.

I believe it is significant that I gained almost exactly what Church lost while the vote for McCormack and Burtenshaw came out almost right on the nose. The fact that Church lost votes is, I believe, significant because, as I have stated, people who vote for a winner seldom shrink from admitting it and are generally inclined to brag about what "good pickers" they are.

The gain of 70 votes for me relative to Church would be, in

just one precinct, nearly half of Church's winning margin state-wide.

At this point, September 15, the Democratic state convention was held in Pocatello. I temporarily left my canvassing to attend the convention because I wanted to make one more appeal to Church.

While not one of the twenty or thirty delegates who had supported me tried to argue that the election was honest, they were all urging me to be a "good sport" and support Church. Welker's poor showing in the primary had made a Democratic victory practically certain, and they wanted to be in on the kill. This acceptance of political thievery as a fact of life sickened me.

These friends had assumed the role of peacemakers and intermediaries. They came to me and said they had been authorized to offer me nine thousand dollars for ten speeches in behalf of Church. The offer, of course, was an attempt to bribe me. I was broke, in debt, and had no idea what I would do to earn a living, much less how to pay off my debts.

It was an attractive offer, but I turned it down. I told them that I couldn't be bought but that I would be glad to make the ten speeches, or any number, for nothing on condition that Mr. Church would go with me to see Senator Gore and get him to conduct a recount of just six precincts. Unless those six precincts showed a trend which, if projected, would change the result of the election, I would wholeheartedly support Church. (Senator Gore was chairman of the Senate Elections Subcommittee, and it just so happened that he was in Pocatello to make the keynote speech at the convention.)

At this point Frank Church appeared in the lobby. The "peacemakers" who had been sent to bribe me immediately grabbed him and literally propelled him by force of numbers over to where I stood. They asked me to repeat my statement to Mr. Church, which I did. All those round about started urging Church to accept my proposition. They pointed out that six precincts could be quickly counted, and that the campaign would not be seriously delayed. Everybody would be happy and the party would be united.

I am quite certain that Church did not like the idea at all, but the fervent pleas for him to accept the proposition and the presence of reporters had him at a disadvantage. He finally held up his hands to silence the clamor and said, "All right, I'll do it," rolled back his lips, gave his horse grin, and we shook hands.

Someone asked, "Who will set up the meeting with Gore?" and Church quickly said, "I'll have Glasby do it." If I hadn't been a trusting fool, I would have balked at such an arrangement.

Glasby was the county chairman of Elmore County. Mountain Home, where I was conducting my house-to-house canvass, was the county seat of Elmore County. Glasby was also Church's choice for state chairman. That post generally goes to a supporter who has done an outstanding job of rounding up votes and/or money for the nominee. Considering the lopsided vote counted for Church in precinct number 3, I'd say that Glasby filled the bill.

A half hour or so later I was told that Senator Gore was ready to see me. I looked around for Church, but he was not about, so I went upstairs, assuming that Church would be waiting for me there. He was not, so I waited in the hall for him to show up.

You can imagine my shock when the door to Senator Gore's suite opened and Frank Church backed out the door shaking hands with Gore. When he turned and saw me he flushed but didn't say anything. He simply ducked his head and hurried by me to the elevator.

Senator Gore was unctuously cordial. He said, "Why hello, Glen, come on in." I went in. Church, freed of the pressure which had caused him to agree to the proposition I had made in the lobby, had, I am sure, told Gore that he definitely was opposed to a recount. Gore parroted Church's contentions and said, "Glen, a recount of even six precincts would cause too much of a delay." I told him that was a lot of crap and stalked out.

I was heartsick. A resolution of the impasse had seemed so near, and now there was nothing. I was so worn out, and so tired of the unequal and hopeless struggle, that I would have been infinitely relieved even if the recount of six precincts had proceeded and I had been proven wrong.

I sought the reporter who had been present when Church agreed to my proposition and told him what had happened, and that as a consequence I was redoubling my efforts to secure a recount. I also told him about my poll in Mountain Home and that I had already found enough discrepancies to wipe out more than half of Church's lead.

The convention was on Saturday. Sunday morning I drove back to Mountain Home to continue my polling of precinct number 3.

THE BOX   The time had come to get signed affidavits.

A very good friend and supporter of mine was county assessor, so I went to the courthouse to ask him if he knew a notary I could get to help in my project. I parked behind the courthouse and entered via the back door.

The first floor of the building consisted of a room, or hallway, about thirty feet wide, extending from front to back, with offices on either side. About fifteen or twenty feet from the front door there was a stairway some ten feet wide leading to the second floor.

As I came in the back door I was, of course, viewing the stairs from underneath. This area under the stairs was enclosed by a wooden framework of two-by-fours covered with chicken wire; it was being used as a storage area. What was stored there in the flimsy enclosure made my heart jump and skip a beat.

Right there before me, protected only by chicken wire, which was no protection at all, were stacked the ballot boxes used in the recent primary.

The Mountain Home courthouse is not the busiest place on the earth. I spent several minutes examining the setup. Finally I saw it. The precinct number 3 ballot box!

How simple it could be to secrete myself in the courthouse at closing time, then late at night pull a few staples which held the wire in place. It seemed almost as if Providence had provided this golden opportunity, chicken wire and all. There it was. The proof I needed.

I was certain then, and I am certain now, that if I had gotten possession of that box I could have forced a recount, been declared the winner, and been reelected to the Senate.

I was never so frustrated in my life, but I tore myself away from the enticing prospect and called on my friend in the assessor's office. He was doubtful if any local notary would want to be associated with my project. We decided that my only recourse was to get a notary from Boise. We reasoned that, even if I could find a notary in Mountain Home willing to tackle the onerous job, those contacted might be reluctant to reveal to a local neighbor how they had voted.

I found an aged notary in Boise who was more than happy at the chance to pick up a few bucks.

When I returned to Mountain Home, Foy told me that he had been contacted by a political fixer and finagler who told him that the machine boys were ready to up the ante if I would come out for Church: twenty-five thousand dollars instead of the nine thousand dollars I had been offered in Pocatello. This new offer only confirmed my belief that Church knew all too well what the result would be if only one precinct of several I had in mind was recounted. At this point you may ask, "Why, now that they had their boys nominated on both tickets, didn't the machine let nature take its course?"

The machine was all out for Church because Welker was considered a bad risk. He was subject to fits of melancholia and violent outbursts of temper. He had become paranoid, was carrying a gun, and imagined that the communists were hiding behind every tree and were out to get him. The machine took a long-range view, and they were loath to try to elect a man who might not be around to succeed himself.

In Church, the machine had an ideal long-range investment.

I started out to get signed affidavits. The first man I called on signed the affidavit swearing he had voted for me.

While Foy and I were jubilating over the fact that I had encountered no hesitancy, a police car pulled up and the officer said, "The chief wants to see you at the station."

I was again confronted by the mayor, who again said that there had been "complaints" that I was "being obnoxious" and using "foot-in-the-door" tactics. I vehemently denied this, but he repeated his demand that I "ring it off." Obviously, the machine was desperate, or they would not have persisted in the face of the mounting criticism in the press.

For the first time the press was giving me rather sympathetic treatment because of the Hitler-like tactics being used to try and stop my canvassing of precinct number 3.

I was so exhausted physically and mentally that I couldn't

think straight, so I decided to go into Boise and rest a day or two at a friend's house before deciding what to do next.

After two days of rest, I decided that my only hope was in getting those affidavits at any cost.

FEAR!   I called the mayor and tried to reason with him, but he was adamant. If I came back I would be arrested. Finally I told him that I was returning to Mountain Home, so he might as well get ready to throw me in jail. He said, "That's your choice," and hung up.

When I got to Mountain Home I drove directly to the police station. The mayor wasn't in, so I told his office girl to tell him I was back, and that I intended to proceed with my project of getting affidavits.

The first people I called on were an old Basque couple. They were distraught. They wanted to help me, but the priest had come to see them and told them they must not sign anything for me or they "might get into a lot of trouble." The old man was so worked up he was trembling, and the wife actually broke down and sobbed. "We want to help you," she wailed. "We know you are a good man. You got our son out of the navy so he could take care of our farm and our sheep, but the priest, he say no." And, in anguish, she beat her forehead with her gnarled old fists.

We proceeded to the next house on our list. This man was in a grim mood. He told me that "someone," whom he would not identify, had called on him and told him he had "better not sign." He had talked to several other people, he said, and all of them had been warned. He defiantly signed, nevertheless, but his wife refused to do so and urged him not to.

At the next stop the man of the house came to the door. When he saw me, and without waiting for me to speak, he said, "I'm sorry as hell, Senator, but I've changed my mind," and shut the door in my face.

As I turned away, angry and frustrated because my high hopes were collapsing in ruins, I saw a police car coming down the street. The officer was in such a hurry his car was scattering gravel helter-skelter. He came to a sliding halt, churning up more gravel, some of which rattled against the side of my borrowed car. "What the hell is the matter with you, banging up the side of my car with the goddamned gravel?" I shouted.

"Now listen, mister, don't get smart with *me*. I've got orders to bring you down to the station," he informed me belligerently, and there was menace in his voice and bearing.

At the station, I was greeted this time by the chief with a respectful, "Hello, Senator," and he offered his hand, which I took, since I had no quarrel with him. He was being paid to do as he was told. "I'm sorry about this business, Senator," he said, "but I'm sure you understand my position. I only carry out orders."

I assured him that I harbored no ill will toward him personally.

"I've been ordered to tell you that unless you stop this business I am to put you under arrest."

I asked to see the mayor. He had "gone to Boise," and left the chief to do the dirty work.

The morning's experience had convinced me that I was licked. This conspiracy was more ruthless than I had imagined.

All I wanted was some halfway reasonable excuse to support Church without feeling that I was condoning corruption and betraying those who had voted for me. Winning the nomination was hopeless.

I just wanted to find a way out other than abject surrender, so I could go home and get some rest.

If Church had only unbent—just a little. But he did the opposite. He threw gasoline on the fire by announcing that he would open his campaign with a big kickoff rally in Mountain Home.

One reason he had chosen Mountain Home was to show appreciation to his new state chairman Glasby for the "splendid" vote he had turned in for Church in Mountain Home. That vote was the more amazing because Mountain Home was an old stronghold of mine. The other reason, of course, was to show his contempt for my puny effort to poll precinct number 3.

The emergence of write-in movements in various parts of the state convinced me that there were consequential numbers of voters who were as outraged as I was. If they were determined to keep fighting against corruption, I could hardly do less.

OUT-COUNTED The *Eastern Idaho Farmer* is a very conservative Republican weekly published in Idaho Falls. In its issue of September 18, there appeared a surprising editorial:

> Glen Taylor has been charged with violation of the "Green River" ordinance. That's the standard ordinance by which municipalities put a stop to unauthorized door-to-door sales efforts by out-of-town and fly-by-night slicker salesmen.
>
> Glen Taylor isn't selling anything. All he's trying to do is to establish a fact: Whether the official reported vote in one Mountain Home precinct is accurate. And darned if we aren't about ready to believe that he's entitled to a recount in Idaho if, for no other reason, than to be certain that he isn't, after all, the winner of the Democratic primary election in which Frank Church out-counted him.

That cynical statement puts the election in the category of a "counting contest" between crooked politicians in which Church just out-counted me. I am afraid that a majority fatalistically accepted that view.

Nevertheless, other editors were tentatively suggesting that perhaps I had a point, maybe somebody *should* find a way to count six precincts.

In the *Caldwell* (Idaho) *News-Tribune* for October 5, there is an editorial that includes this timely suggestion:

> Church should have stopped the Mountain Home "Hitler-like" affair in its tracks. He should have said "Glen, my friend, I don't like what went on in Mountain Home. The recount is yours." Police threats against Taylor's attempts to canvass that town were deplorable.
>
> Indeed, the Taylor-Church comedy of mathematical errors might be termed one of the most misdirected political operations in Idaho's history.

This was the first time any considerable percentage of the press had ever exhibited any sympathy for me or anything I said or did. But this mild spate of protest was as water off a duck's back to Frank Church.

John Corlett, in his "Politically Speaking" column for September 18, wrote:

> All Democratic leaders are convinced that the recount hassle will have an effect on Church's chances as long as it

is kept before the public. Many Democrats believe the easiest way to bring an end to the hassle is actually to recount a precinct or two and decide one way or the other whether Taylor has grounds for a general recount.

(We can rest assured that those who feel that some kind of recount is "the easiest way out" were not machine boys.)

Corlett goes on to say: "Some Democrats believe that the next legislature should set up legal machinery for a recount."

While I had long thought that a recount law was the most urgently needed political reform necessary to assure some measure of honesty in Idaho elections, it had heretofore seemed a hopeless proposition.

It had not occurred to me that my battle for a recount might be the one thing that could so spotlight the issue as to create sufficient demand to cause the legislature to enact a recount law. Corlett's column convinced me that the best possible thing I could do was to raise all the hell I could, regardless of what friend or foe might think of my tactics.

If by doing so I could bring about the enactment of a recount law, it might be my most important contribution to the state and its people and a fitting finale to my political career.

That I would be despised as a poor loser by many was beside the point. I had claimed to be a true friend of the people. This was my chance to prove it.

Quote:

> At a kick-off rally in Mountain Home to officially signal the start of his campaign against Herman Welker for the United States Senate, youthful Boise attorney Frank Church really got off to a flying start. The Democratic senatorial nominee played his trump card as he was joined on the platform by his chief primary opponent, former Senator Glen Taylor who told the audience that "several days of checking has convinced me that the recount is unnecessary and I hereby pledge my wholehearted support to Mr. Church."

Foy had typed that press release.

What I had planned was this: I would go to Church and tell him that if he would take a lie detector test, in private, and satisfactorily answer one question, I would support him. The question would be: "Do you think you got the nomination honestly?"

This was not an attempt to "smoke him out." I really hoped that he could and would accept this proposition. The press release I had prepared was a "visual sales aid" to help sell him on the idea.

The more I thought of it, the less I thought of it. Unless he could answer that question with a clear conscience he would have no part of the deal, and if he had a clear conscience he would long ago have consented to counting six precincts. I gave up the idea.

In politics one has to expect to be lied about, and I have been the victim of some prime examples, but an article in the *Emmett Messenger* beat them all. It was worse than anything the *Statesman* ever turned out.

> Soon after the nominating election, when the Democratic Central Committee was offering to pay all costs of a court inquiry into Glen Taylor's demand for a ballot recount and when many Democrats were in a mood to appease Taylor in a frantic effort to avoid messing up the fall election, Taylor wrote a letter to Senator Welker pledging his support to Welker in this fall's contest.
>
> The original of that letter, according to reliable rumor, some way disappeared from Welker's office and is now in "friendly" safekeeping.
>
> Now why should Taylor, if he is an honorable man—and some people still insist that he is—why should Taylor make such a compact with the one man in the United States he has cause to hate and despise above all others? And what could Welker offer Taylor that would be so enticing as to induce Taylor to forfeit his last shred of integrity in a fraudulent pretense that he is fighting both Welker and Church in a noble, self-righteous write-in campaign?
>
> If Taylor ever had a political future in Idaho, he is cashing it in now. After November 6 he will be done, utterly and completely washed up. Whether the Taylor-Welker compact succeeds in this election or not, Idaho may draw a deep, pure, refreshing breath in the certain knowledge that at long last it is done with one certain Glen H. Taylor.

(The offer to pay for a court inquiry, mentioned in the first sentence of the article, was made only *after* I had been stopped in my effort to get affidavits from the voters of precinct number 3. John Glasby, who made the offer, forgot to mention that there was no provision in Idaho law for a court inquiry into an election.)

The brazenness of the big-lie technique used by the newspaper stunned me.

In thinking the matter over, I recalled that some seven or eight years ago, during my last year or two in the Senate, a brother of the editor of the *Messenger* had written and asked me for a job. I had nothing available at the time.

Inquiry now revealed that this same son and his wife had worked at Church headquarters during the primary and were still working there. I also heard that a promise of a "job" or "jobs" had been involved as a reward for their efforts. I could only conclude that the fabrication and printing of the totally untrue "letter" must likewise have been part of the price exacted for the promised jobs. I could think of no other explanation for such an infamous act.

I contacted a lawyer and filed suit against the *Emmett Messenger*. When the trial occurred a year or so later, the only witnesses for the defense were the couple who had worked for Church in the election and were then employed in his Washington office.

They told a vague story of how "someone" had brought the "letter" to Church headquarters. No one had bothered to get the name of the party.

The editor's brother had shown him the letter and he had printed it. The letter had "disappeared."

The court ruled in favor of the defendants because I had not shown that there was any "malice" on the part of that dear sweet editor. So much for justice.

After filing my lawsuit, I went to the radio station and bought fifteen minutes' time for October 22 at eight-thirty p.m. for the purpose of announcing my write-in candidacy.

After that I went over to the Hotel Boise to see what was happening in that hub of political activity. The place was deserted, so I would pick up no political scuttlebutt. However, I did pick up a copy of the *Pocatello Journal*, which someone more affluent than I had bought and discarded.

I made myself comfortable in one of the black leather easy chairs in the lobby.

The paper carried a story based on a press release that I had gotten out the day before:

> Former Democratic Sen. Glen H. Taylor has spiked rumors that he is getting funds from the camp of incumbent Republican Sen. Herman Welker to finance his write-in campaign.
>
> "Of course my opponents would say that," Taylor said in commenting on persistent reports that his proposed write-in campaign is being financed by Republicans who see it as an opportunity to siphon off votes from Democratic senatorial nominee Frank Church.
>
> "If Frank Church will take a lie detector test and state that he voted for me for senator (in 1954) I'll take one that I'm not getting money from Welker," Taylor added.

END OF THE TRAIL   By now it was late in the afternoon. Time to swallow my pride once again and take my place at the dinner table of the elderly and dedicated booster who had fed and sheltered me for the past several days. I was hungry, but I continued to sit there, in my borrowed car, in front of the Hotel Boise.

I was thinking. Thinking about "the rewards of virtue." I was now faced with the very real likelihood that my family might go hungry, even before election day. If our overextended credit had been cut off, perhaps they were hungry at this very moment.

The three or four grocers, among whom we had so generously distributed our "on-the-cuff" business in order to keep each account within reason, were beginning to show an embarrassing reluctance to "put it on the bill" even before I left Pocatello, and so had the several gas stations among which we had divided our business.

If I managed to last until after the election, then what? It wasn't like it used to be, when three days after an election we could have The Glendora Ranch Gang back in action bringing in grocery money, at least.

As I sat there huddled in my borrowed old Cadillac, like a

fetus in the womb, I had to face the bitter fact that I had come to the end of the trail. I had no profession, no training to qualify me for any except the most menial of jobs, and of course there was that loyalty risk charge against me.

I was fifty-two years old.

It was most unlikely that I could find work, even as a "nail driver" carpenter, with so many younger men vying for those none-too-plentiful jobs.

Barring a miracle, I would have to abandon the idea of sending my sons to college, and condemn Dora to a life of household drudgery, which she despised. I was faced with the task of starting anew at the foot of the ladder.

I had spent eighteen of the best years of my life sincerely trying to help my fellow men, fighting an uphill battle against the machine. Now I had to finally admit that my struggle had been hopeless from the beginning. I was licked. Once and for all.

A really honest man is licked before he starts in politics. You just can't get the money necessary to carry on a successful campaign if you are strictly honest. Not only will the vested interests *not* contribute their money without a quid pro quo, but they will spend it on whatever scale is necessary to defeat you. They want someone they can deal with.

I might have overcome that handicap with my acknowledged ability as a campaigner, but what I could not cope with was the vote stealing and smear tactics. Without a recount law, the machine could steal elections without fear or hindrance.

In the minds of many people, the very word "politics" is synonymous with graft, corruption, and dishonesty. I had been honest, painfully honest. Now, at long last, I realized that I had been "laughably honest."

I still felt obligated to see this write-in thing through to the finish for two reasons. The people who felt that their votes had been stolen should at least be able to cast a protest vote, and I was the only one who could make that possible. Second, I wanted to raise just as much hell as I could to try and drive home the necessity for a recount law. If enough support for the idea could be created, the legislature would act.

So this write-in campaign wasn't a vainglorious grandstand play. I could render the State of Idaho, its people, and any future

Glen Taylors who might come along no greater service than to be instrumental in bringing about recount legislation. Even the *Statesman* just a few days before had admitted that my activities were spotlighting the need, but yesterday John Corlett had said in his column that the wise guys were predicting I would get no more than 5,000 votes. Some were convinced I'd get no more than 3,000.

I'd have to do better than that, considerably better, if the protest was to have any significance. But I couldn't do better, perhaps not that well, unless I had money.

THE PLOT THICKENS Without at least ten thousand dollars, there would be no way to get to the voters a coherent story of the sordid events which had transpired since the primary. My write-in candidacy would fall flat on its face and end up as a pitiful joke.

I might as well face it. The only way I could get any money was to accept Church's offer of twenty-five thousand or nine thousand or whatever, if indeed he was still interested in buying me off at all. He might not be, because it was becoming obvious that my exposé of Welker's perfidy had destroyed him so completely that Church could win in a walk.

Nevertheless I would have to make the try, crawl on my belly like a whipped dog, and publicly lick the boots of Mr. Church. I would have to fabricate some flimsy, untrue excuse for supporting him. To qualify for whatever sum of money I might get to sustain my family while I sought some means of livelihood, I would have to mislead those who trusted me by publicly stating that I thought Mr. Church was an honorable man, worthy of their support. It would also mean that I would have to abandon my campaign to force the enactment of a recount law.

As I sat in my car in front of the Hotel Boise and thought of having to make laudatory speeches about Frank Church, my spirits fell to such a low ebb that I began to feel drowsy, or perhaps it would be more accurate to say that I began to "lose consciousness."

Then, all of a sudden, I was waking up, with a start. I was puzzled for a few seconds until I looked around and recognized where I was.

How long had I been asleep? I looked at my watch. Fifteen or twenty minutes.

Something told me to probe those minutes.

I did, and there were all the answers. All the answers to all my problems falling in place like the letters in a linotype machine.

I had not been thinking straight. The place where I could get money was from Herman Welker, and I wouldn't have any reason to feel guilty, either.

Welker was the darling of the most reactionary elements in the nation, as well as in the state. Those eastern and Texas reactionary McCarthyites! That's where the real dough was, and Welker would have plenty. More than Church? Yes, more than Church.

As the editor of the *Boise Journal* had pointed out, Welker's campaign was going badly. His only hope—if indeed he had any hope—was my write-in campaign.

I could shake Welker down and parry any charges against me with the ploy I had used in today's press statement, wherein I challenged Mr. Church to join me in a lie detector test to see who was being truthful and who was not. The technique was foolproof. All I had to do was pass the buck to Church. By now I was certain that he would not and could not accept my lie detector challenge.

On the other hand, I could truthfully say that my decision to run as a write-in candidate had in no way been influenced by Welker or the Republicans, since I had already made this decision and reserved radio time for my announcement.

I could effectively answer any charges by countering with the challenge to a lie detector test. "You, Mr. Church, answer the question, 'Do you believe you got the nomination honestly?' and I will answer the question, 'Was your decision, Glen Taylor, to run as a write-in candidate influenced in any way by Welker and/or Republican money?' " The more they made the charge, the more opportunity it would afford me to throw the lie detector challenge in Church's teeth and convince the voters that he was guilty and *could not* accept my challenge.

To be sure, I would have to lead Welker to believe that my "write-in" decision depended upon my raising a certain sum, but I had no qualms about misleading him. None at all. Welker had blackened my name and cheated me out of being reelected to the

Senate in 1954. He owed me plenty, and anything I might get out of him I would consider as a payment on account for the damage he had done me.

I contemplated the idea with considerable glee, and with a clear conscience.

ACTION!   The first thing I had to do to get the ball rolling was to find someone to act as intermediary. One could nearly always find some big-shot Republican hanging round the lobby or the coffeeshop at the Hotel Boise, so I climbed out of my car and sauntered into the place.

There was no one in the lobby. I tried the coffeeshop. It was obvious that my plan was blessed because sitting there at the counter was the one Republican of all the Republicans in the state whom I would have chosen to meet at this precise moment. The hour was five-thirty p.m. and the place was practically deserted.

The guy sitting there enjoying a cup of coffee and a cigarette was known as an all-out Welker man, which meant that he was a McCarthy man, which meant that he despised Democratic institutions and people who prated about such trash and stuff. It also meant that he hated me with a passion.

Nevertheless, I slid into the upholstered stool next to his and ordered a cup of coffee. He was reading a paper spread out on the counter and didn't see me, so I said "Hello."

We'll call him "Bill." That wasn't his name, but there would be no object in revealing it here.

When he turned and saw who was "helloing" him, his mouth involuntarily flew open as though he had bitten his tongue. Before he answered my hello, he glanced furtively around the coffeeshop to see who was witnessing this hard-to-explain circumstance.

Having satisfied himself that for the moment at least we seemed to be alone, he mumbled, "Hello, Taylor, how's your write-in coming along?"

That was just wonderful. I couldn't have asked for better "openers" if I had written the script myself. His question also pretty well revealed what was uppermost not only in *his* mind, but in the hidebound minds of his reactionary *and* despairing cohorts as well. Friend "Bill" hadn't just happened to ask that question. It had popped out because my write-in was Welker's last hope, and he and his Neanderthal gang knew it.

"Aagh, not so good," I answered disgustedly. "I am pretty certain I could put up a good race and teach that gang a lesson if I had some money, but I just can't find any."

"No?" he asked, and started wiping his mouth with his napkin preparatory to leaving.

"Yeah," I said. "I had planned to announce my candidacy on the twenty-second, but no money. That ad I put in the paper just isn't paying off like I had hoped. I'm going over to the radio station now to cancel my air time and get my money back. I'm fed up with this whole goddamned mess. I'm going to head for Pocatello tonight."

Bill had gotten up as I started talking, but as I outlined the situation he eased back into his seat and when I finished he studied me a moment as though trying to decide whether I was just talking or saying something. I had evidently made it plain enough without being too obvious because he asked, "Is money all that's keeping you from running?"

I evaded a direct answer by saying, "Well, you can't run a campaign without money."

"You can say that again," Bill mumbled fervently.

I continued my none-too-subtle approach by saying, "I'm sure that if I had some money I could put on a campaign that would surprise a hell of a lot of people. See you around." I got up and made as if to terminate the conversation.

Bill stopped me with a hand on my arm. "Wait a minute," he said, "I want to talk to you some more about this business. My car's out back in the parking lot, I'm a yellow Cad," he added, with amazing if unintentional candor. "Wait for me out there, will you? I want to make a phone call," he growled. He had meant his words to be sotto voce, but lowering his naturally deep voice resulted in a chesty rumble that echoed all over the coffeeshop.

I almost laughed out loud because it occurred to me that I have that same problem, and that for the past several minutes we had been rumbling at each other like two angry Hereford bulls on either side of an irrigation ditch.

I strolled out to the parking lot and climbed in the Cad. It was a brand new beauty. I envied the son of a bitch.

Bill came out in less than five minutes, climbed under the wheel, and without a word headed for parts unknown. I slumped down in the seat with my elbow on the armrest.

Bill drove up on the bench east of town and turned off on a side road. We went over a rise, and there we were in the city dump. Great piles of trash and garbage, with roads running every which way. Bill seemed to know where he was going. He must have been here before. To empty a can of trash? Or perhaps to keep a secret rendezvous such as this.

It was getting dark fast, and the car lights made the skeletons of old cars in the dump look spooky. Bill stopped and turned off the lights.

No names were mentioned, but I was told that Bill and his friends would put up the money if I'd go ahead and run.

"Well, I'd sure like to run, all right," I said. "But it will have to be on my terms."

"What do you mean by that?" Bill asked somewhat truculently.

I told him I had already been offered a very substantial amount by the supporters of Frank Church but had turned it down because I couldn't endorse and campaign for Church. "After the lousy way he has double-crossed me and stolen the election I wouldn't do that for any amount of money," I said, adding, "If you know anyone who is willing to contribute to my campaign with no strings attached I would accept such a contribution."

Our friend Bill seemed more than a little puzzled and remonstrated, "But if we're financing your campaign, we'd certainly expect you to go easy on Welker." When I started to interrupt he added hurriedly, "Of course you'd have to make it look good, but we certainly wouldn't expect you to be any rougher than necessary."

"No, I won't make any such promise," I said. "Any contribution I accept will in no way affect what I say or do. I already have the copy for my announcement prepared and, believe me, I'm as tough on Welker as I am on Church. I will campaign exactly as though there had been no contribution at all."

We sat there silently in the darkness while Bill tried to figure what kind of a nut would insist on such a fool arrangement.

Finally he said, "Well—I'll have to talk this over." He didn't say with whom.

"Okay" I agreed, assuming that the deal was stagnated until he could confer with his superior.

I was surprised when, instead of starting the car, he asked, "How much is this going to cost?"

I had given some thought to this matter, so I wasn't caught unprepared by the sudden, direct question. "Fifty thousand," I said.

There was dead silence for several seconds, during which I wished it wasn't so dark so that I could see his expression. Finally, with no particular emphasis or emotion, he said, "Fifty thousand—that's a lot of dough."

"Yes it is," I agreed, "but you know that both Welker and Church will spend several times that amount."

"W-e-l-l—I don't know. We were thinking more like twenty-five." Evidently Bill and his cohorts had discussed this possibility.

"Well, if twenty-five is their limit, we might as well forget it," I said with finality. "I couldn't put on any kind of campaign for twenty-five thousand dollars."

"Now, wait a minute," Bill said, holding up his hand. "Let's not be in too big a hurry. Would you take thirty?"

We settled on thirty-five thousand. It was agreed that we would meet here at eight p.m. on the twenty-first, at which time the "contribution" would be given me in bills of twenty dollars or less. Bill explained that the transfer could not be effected sooner because someone would have to make a trip to either Seattle or Salt Lake City to get that amount of cash without creating suspicion.

We had no sooner come to an understanding when a car came careening into the dump followed by a second car. Both cars started racing around the dump, darting in and out among the piles of junk like crazy. We were blocking a road, and all of a sudden one of these idiots came barreling around a pile of garbage and almost crashed into us from the rear. Brakes screamed and skidding tires threw up a great cloud of dust and garbage. The road leading out of this dismal place was blocked.

Friend Bill looked back and exclaimed, "What the hell?"

The second car, which had taken a circuitous route, came out of nowhere and nearly ran into us head on. More squealing brakes and more dust and garbage. We were hemmed in.

Bill grabbed me by the lapels and snarled, "What the hell is this? Have you framed me, you son of a bitch?"

I was in a tight spot. Bill was a big bruiser, four or five inches taller than I and fifty pounds heavier.

I don't know what might have happened, but in the momentary quiet that followed his outburst, the laughing and shouting of teenagers came from both cars. Then the kids backed up and took off, roaring out of the dump screeching and yelling like wild Indians.

As the noise died away in the distance, Bill relaxed and let go of my lapels. He took a deep breath and mumbled, "Son of a bitch that scared me. I thought it was some kind of a frameup." He settled himself and took hold of the wheel.

I was congratulating myself on getting out of the situation with a whole hide when he turned on my as savagely as before. "This *ain't* no frameup, is it?" he demanded.

I was glad that I could honestly say, "No, this is not a frame-up. I give you my word on that."

"W-e-l-l," he growled. "It had better not be." I believed him.

As for me, I had no fear that I was being framed. What good would it do Welker to frame me? What he wanted was to get reelected, and framing me would not help him.

This was the best financed of all my campaigns. I couldn't possibly have spent even half of Welker's "contribution" without causing undue speculation among not only my enemies, but also my supporters, as to where the money was coming from.

I did spend fifteen thousand without being obvious. Most of that went for newspaper ads graphically explaining how my supporters should "write in" my name, and for some TV time.

While I had spent a little more than fifteen thousand in one or two previous campaigns, never had I spent so much in such a short time.

No one raised the question of where the money was coming from. The half-page ad I had, in desperation, placed earlier in the *Statesman* appealing for contributions pretty well removed this sting, and my challenge to Church that I would take a lie detector test and swear that my decision to run had not been influenced by Republican money if he would say he thought he got the nomination honestly had silenced the opposition and/or the press.

After paying our overdue grocery, gas, and advertising bills, plus the money we had borrowed, we had about seventy-five hundred dollars left to sustain us until I could find a job or come up with some bright idea for a business venture.

"13,415"   After a last-minute trip around the state, John Corlett stuck to his guns and again wrote me off by saying, "Taylor's support is of such small proportions that I do not estimate more than 3000 write-in votes for the former senator."

Actually I received 13,415 votes (counted, that is). I was satisfied. I had received nearly four times the vote Corlett had predicted.

Church defeated Welker, 149,096 to 102,781. Welker's poor showing demonstrated that anyone, including me, or a "yaller dog," could have beaten him, and it made the primary steal an even more bitter pill to swallow.

RECOUNT LAW   The ball game wasn't over.

Two or three weeks after the election I had rested sufficiently to do a little thinking. I called some key people and asked them to sound out sentiment to see if my "give 'em hell" strategy had, as I had hoped, created any great demand for a recount law. It had. A solid majority felt strongly that something should be done to prevent a recurrence of the unsavory mess that had developed after the primary.

I got busy and personally wrote a recount law. Contrary to most legislation, it was short, clear, and to the point. No lawyer would have been caught dead writing such a bill bereft of "whereases" and "wherefores." It simply said that any candidate, for any reason, or no reason at all, could demand a recount of one precinct or any number of precincts upon posting a bond of one hundred dollars per precinct. If a statewide office was involved, and a recount of ten precincts showed a discrepancy that would, if projected, change the result of the election, the deposit would be refunded and a complete recount would be undertaken at the state's expense. For a county office, if a recount of two precincts showed such a discrepancy, the county vote would be recounted at county expense.

It was much more difficult for the machine to rig an election for the state legislature because of the relatively small number of votes cast, so I had a good many friends in the legislature that would meet shortly after the first of the year. One of these friends in the House agreed to introduce my bill. He suggested one change. Understandably, I had included a provision that any ballots presently being held in custody would be subject to the provisions of the bill. My friend pointed out that such a provision would be like waving a red flag at a bull—the bull being the machine and Mr. Church, who was now the senator-elect, with all the clout associated with this office.

If no mention was made of the matter there was a long chance that it might slip through unnoticed. If there was no mention of those ballots they would automatically be subject to a recount.

The machine wasn't overly exercised. I was the only person who had successfully challenged their racket for decades, and they had no apprehension that another Glen Taylor would come along in the foreseeable future. They were equally certain that my write-in campaign had finished me politically.

I had high hopes that passage of the bill might yet enable me to get a recount. If this had happened I was, and still am, morally certain that it would have resulted in my being declared the winner in the primary and the victor in a rescheduled contest with Welker.

Sentiment was so strongly in favor of the measure that even those legislators tied to the machine wanted to vote for it so they could face the voters when they came up for reelection and say they had voted for clean politics. But in order to be able to have their cake and eat it too—that is, to be able to say they voted for clean politics without helping the victim who had created the demand—they insisted on one simple little amendment. Just one sentence specifying that any ballots cast in the last election were not included, or subject to, the relief afforded in the new law. They knew, damn them, that the election had been rigged, and the sharp-eyed machine attorneys were not about to be caught off base.

The machine held the balance of power. With their boys who

wanted to pose as "Mr. Clean" voting for it, the measure would become law, and in the future candidates would be afforded some measure of protection. Without the amendment, it would be defeated.

With a heavy heart, I agreed to the subversion of justice and kissed my last hope goodbye.

My recount bill passed with no sweat, but I would never be able to benefit from it. It was comforting to know, though, that I had been responsible for this desperately needed reform.

ETHICS   You may be asking, "What about the ethics of 'collecting damages' from Welker?"

No sweat. There were no laws relating to campaign contributions or expenditures in a general election. The sky was the limit. No reports to file.

As for the ethics of my running as an independent and not supporting Frank Church—don't make me laugh. My conscience was clear.

Welker's contribution had enabled me to put on a modestly financed campaign that resulted in the enactment of a recount law.

TAYLOR TOPPER REVISITED   Thanks to Welker's generosity, we were not facing immediate starvation. Nevertheless, the first order of business following the election was the question of how, in the long run, I was going to support my family.

I wasted no time nursing my wounds. The *Pocatello Journal,* in reporting a postelection interview with me, quoted me as saying, "I am planning on launching a business venture but I am not prepared to divulge the details at this time."

The business venture I had in mind was the last thing in the world anyone would have imagined.

Remember my offhand invention of a better hairpiece that helped me get elected to the Senate? All right, I would go into the hairpiece business. Surely a practical, detection-proof, easy-to-put-on, easy-to-take-off, easy-to-keep-clean hairpiece would sell.

It wasn't quite that simple, of course. Pounding out the base from a piece of aluminum, with its time-consuming hammering and fitting, pounding a little more here and a little more there, was hardly feasible. I had to find a better, faster way.

Threading needles with hairs and sewing them one at a time into a piece of cloth was fantastically slow and would result in out-of-the-question production costs that would have priced us out of the market.

I set about experimenting from daylight till dark, trying to find ways and means of making my hairpiece commercially feasible. It was a frustrating task.

I would make one hairpiece after another and then throw them away. Dozens and dozens of them. Such tedious work goes against my every instinct, but I managed to keep myself in hand and persist. I had to. It was my only hope. My nerves were on edge. If I had been the type, I might have enjoyed a nervous breakdown. I took a walk. And here is another of those strange coincidences. It's even a coincidence that I happened to walk in a certain direction.

I passed a house where a man was fiberglassing his boat. I stopped and watched the process. It worked! The base problem was solved!

Now, all I had to do was figure out how to root hair in another, more flexible layer of plastic. This feat made the solving of the base problem seem like child's play. Day after day passed, week after week. Our money was dwindling away despite the fact that we were sticking to our diet of beans, macaroni, and hamburger, plus a green salad. I knew the solution was there, and I was convinced it would be relatively simple when I stumbled upon it.

After all those months of futility I came wide awake in the wee, small hours, and I had it. Straight from my subconscious. A simple, fast, inexpensive way to root hair in plastic. Sorry I can't tell you about that—it's a trade secret.

It was April. November to April. It had been a long, agonizing experience.

CUSTOMER NUMBER 1   I dropped in to the Singer Sewing Machine store to buy some ribbon or something for Dora. I knew the man who ran the place. He was fifty, and he was bald.

He asked me what I was doing nowadays, and I told him about my wonderful new hairpiece and gave him a demonstration with the one I was wearing, which was the first one I had made using my new techniques.

He asked, literally begged, me to make him one. Boy, what a cinch this was going to be! I'd be rich before you could say "Jack Robinson."

Other hairpieces were selling for fifty bucks. I charged him one hundred.

It took Dora and me less than a day to make his "Taylor Topper," as I had decided to call my product. It would take longer when we had "hired help." We considered it a labor of love to make a hairpiece for an anxiously awaiting male. For obvious reasons having to do with human nature, employees would feel otherwise.

The Singer man's was the first Taylor Topper we sold. I saw him a day or two after we had trimmed in his new Topper, and he was ecstatic. "Oh, thank you, Senator Taylor," he said with tears of gratitude in his eyes. "You have no idea how I suffered, working here day after day, bending over this customer with my sweaty bald head just a foot or two from my lady customers. I died a thousand deaths, I was so mortified. But now, I prance right up here and stick my head out and say to myself, 'Look it over, goddammit, I've got a better head of hair than nine-tenths of the men in Pocatello.' "

Boy, this was great! Not only was I going to get rich, but people were going to love me. Put a Topper on a guy and, no matter what his religion, politics, or nationality, *you had a friend*.

BABY FACE On October 14, 1957, *Newsweek* magazine carried the first mention of Frank Church I had seen in a nationally circulated publication since immediately after his election. The heading on the item was THE NEW RATINGS:

> After an admittedly unscientific poll of Washington women, International News Service reporter Ruth Montgomery submitted a list of what she described as the capital's "most kissable" dignitaries. Among them:
>
> *Frank Church, 33, Idaho's Democratic Senator, "to accommodate the maternal type who prefers 'em fresh-scrubbed and baby-faced." [Author's comment: "No comment."]

Seeing Frankie's baby-faced likeness made me realize I suffered the disability of having a genuine antipathy for him.

It is not good to live with such an emotion. So, in another effort to rid myself of the aversion I felt, I wrote yet another letter to Church. I had tried supplication, so now I thought I would see if gratitude and loyalty to an old friend and benefactor would move him to take an hour or so to perform a simple chore and thereby salvage the political hopes and aspirations of said friend and benefactor.

I knew in my heart that it was hopeless. Nevertheless, on January 18, 1958, I sent Church the following letter:

> Dear Frank:
>
> Once again I am writing to you to ask you to agree to take a polygraph test and answer the question "Do you believe that you got the 1956 senatorial nomination honestly?"
>
> If you agree to this and successfully answer the question, I give you my word I will not enter the governor's race in 1958 and I will not be a candidate for the Senate in 1962.
>
> If you so wished the matter need never be made public. I would come to Washington personally to help arrange the test.
>
> Upon the satisfactory completion of the undertaking I would issue a statement that for good and sufficient reasons had become convinced that I had been mistaken in questioning the outcome of the 1956 primary and that I would not be a candidate for governor.
>
> If I have not heard from you in two weeks' time (January 27th), I will assume that you do not feel that any of the considerations I have stated are of sufficient importance to warrant your cooperation and I shall proceed accordingly.

Church ignored the letter.

In doing so, he cut the ground out from under his good friend and erstwhile state chairman, John Glasby, who had managed his successful campaign and had recently announced his intention to run for governor. I started making statements that I would run against Glasby if he were a candidate. He was backed by the machine and of course by Frank Church.

Up to that point he had been considered the front-runner, but the fear that Glasby could not win over my opposition caused party leaders to desert him and he abandoned the race.

This display of ingratitude on the part of Mr. Church toward the man who had as county chairman of Elmore County not only delivered such a handsome vote for Mr. Church in Mountain Home precinct number 3, but had gone on to manage his victorious general election campaign, strengthened my conviction that he had guilty knowledge and *could not* come to Glasby's aid. Perhaps the Washington press corps has him tagged. I recently read that during the 1976 campaign, when Church was scrambling for the second spot on the ticket with Carter, the best joke going the rounds in the nation's capital was that an appropriate description of such a combo would be "the peanut butter and jelly ticket."

I have long wondered why the State of Idaho, which in the past enjoyed a reputation for breeding big, strong he-men, including rock-hard miners, tough-muscled farmers, tall lean ranchers, and thong leather cowboys, would elect and reelect a person who is the very antithesis of that concept.

Of course I haven't kept up with Idaho politics, and it may be that the machine has things so well under control that no one would think of challenging them.

I've got to hand it to Church, though. He sure as hell has the formula for perpetuating the Clark machine in power and himself in office despite being labeled "Baby Face" and "Jelly.'

I am not surprised. In a mimeographed letter I mailed out during my '56 write-in campaign I predicted that, if Church was elected, the Clark machine, which had dominated Idaho politics for thirty years, would be in control for another thirty years. As of this writing, Church is serving his twenty-third year as senator.

To any charge that I am a bitter and vindictive man, my answer is "Yes, I am bitter." Not because Frank Church attained the senatorship, but because of the unprincipled tactics he used in the process. I have a passionate belief in the sanctity of the democratic process and in the absolute necessity of maintaining that process unsullied if our country is to endure. As I write, the confidence of the people in our elected representatives and in our form of government is at a low ebb because of a lack of political morality.

By his deeds and actions, Frank Church has contributed to the erosion of the public's faith and confidence in politics and politicians.

NOUVEAU RICHE   It was difficult for Dora and me to get used to the idea of spending money. There was always the memory of those lean years we spent trouping during the Depression, and the even more destitute times we shared campaigning on a shoestring. Even when I was in the Senate we had to scrimp. Dora wore a cheap cloth coat while other senators' wives wore mink and sable. She did not complain but I am ashamed when I think of the humiliation she must have suffered.

In extenuation, I can only say that I have tried to make it up to her since our ship finally came in.

Our astonishing success and affluence enabled us to put our sons through college with no sweat, and to live the good life. It made me very happy to be able to buy Dora a four-carat diamond to replace the one-carat job we hocked and lost so many years ago.

Since childhood, Dora's most cherished dream was to go to Hawaii. Since 1962 we have gone to the islands four times a year.

Two of our three sons, Greg and Arod, live close by, and P.J. is only fifty miles away.

Arod and P.J. are dentists, and Greg manages Taylor Topper, Inc.

P.J.'s wife Sally, on her own, is in the llama business. That's right, she raises and sells llamas. Doing real well, too. On the average, she sells them for thirty-five hundred dollars a head. Who buys them? All sorts of people. They are the latest status item in the pet business.

Arod has four beautiful children. Two boys, two girls.

Dora is still beautiful and looks half her age. Her lovely ivory complexion is the envy of women of all ages.

When people ask me how I'm feeling my stock answer is, "If you're feeling as well as I am, you're doing all right." Honestly, I don't feel any older than I did when I was twenty-five.

People often ask me how I feel, after all these years, about King C. Gillette's blueprint for plenty, *The People's Corpora-*

tion. All I can say is that a cooperative society such as Gillette envisaged is a beautiful pipe dream. It won't work because people just aren't built that way. There has to be an incentive to excel, like striving for a better job at better pay or being able to start a business of your own to make people really dig in and give it their best efforts.

Winston Churchill once said, "Democracy is the worst form of Government ever devised except for all the rest." I agree with Winston, and I would like to get in my two bits' worth by adding, "Capitalism is the worst economic system ever invented except for all the rest."

SPARRING PARTNER   You will recall my old Republican sparring partner Nicholas Ifft, who wrote a daily chitchat column for the rabidly Republican Pocatello paper, the *Idaho State Journal*. He had more pseudonyms than a San Quentin con. His name was Nicholas Ifft, everybody called him "Nick," and he signed his column "Ing."

Come campaign time and old Nick would swear on a stack of bibles that, while I might be a likable fellow, the U.S. Senate was just no place for an actor and banjo player. After the heat and hurrah of the campaign was over he would tell me he felt badly saying those things about me, but being a good Republican he just had to say something or lose face with his friends.

I understood, and to compensate he would, between campaigns, say some real nice things about me. You know, like "He's a handsome devil," and things like that. How can you dislike a guy who butters you up that way?

You may recall that Nick forgot his Republicanism to the farfetched extent of manning the microphone in the sound car my supporters hired to lead that torchlight parade when I was finally elected to the Senate back there in 1944.

Just to show that I forgive Nick for his compulsory badmouthing of me, we'll quote one of his columns.

It seems that as late as 1970 Nick was still around, and he must have mentioned my name in his column. I do not have that clipping, so I don't know just what he said, but it moved a lady to write to him.

Here is her letter and "Ing's" answer, which appeared in his column, "Buzz of the Burg":

DEAR ING:
Your remarks about Glen Taylor brought back many memories to me. In the 30's and early 40's when I was a child and teenage girl in central Montana a Glen-Dora show was a great treat. They were fast, funny, and novel. If the laughs were good, sometimes Mr. Taylor would outdo himself and become mildly risque. The dance music was good and we always saw all our friends. His shows and radio program had a large and loyal following.
Now that I think of it, his political career was pretty humorous too. I am sure that whatever Glen Taylor has tried he has had fun and left a few laughs behind.
Sincerely,
Christine Bassett

Here's Ing's answer to Christine:

Dear Christine Bassett:
It is our belief that Glen Taylor is the cleverest and most effective man on the campaign trail Idaho has produced in several decades. Also it is our opinion he could have stayed in the U. S. Senate at least up to the present time if he had not followed Henry Wallace into the wilderness. The Old Guard in the GOP feared him and certainly tried every ruse to get rid of him. Conservative Democrats belabored him in public but behind the curtain in the voting booth usually put their "X" behind his name. We always admired him, and he was always kind to us despite the swipes we took at him.
Ing

The *Idaho Daily Statesman* said:

The man is an idiot and a mountebank.

On October 17, 1978, the *San Francisco Chronicle* said,

Glen Taylor may well have been the most honest man in American politics this century.

INDEX

Aberdeen, Idaho, 164, 165
Acting and singing, at Bluebell, 30–33;
    on Capitol steps, 289–93, 295–97;
    "Home on the Range," 289–93,
    295–97; introduction to, 19–22. *See
    also* Glendora Players; Glendora Ranch
    Gang; "Tab" shows
Acuff, Jeffrey, family, 237–49
Afton, Wyoming, 116
American Falls, Idaho, 161
American Legionnaire, 332
Angel, financial, 217–18
Anticommunism, 336–37. *See also*
    McCarthyism; Red-baiting
Apples, 279–80
Arco, Idaho, 119
Arizona Rose (play), 20
Arlington, Oregon, 127
Army and Navy Bulletin, 337
Athena, Idaho, 127
Atlanta Journal, 355

Baby oil, 243–46, 249, 253
Back, injury to, 372
Baldness, of P. J. Taylor, 16–19. *See also*
    Taylor Topper
Baldwin, Beanie, 351
Ball, Joe, Senator, 301
Bannock County, Idaho, 380
Bannock County (Idaho) Central
    Committee, 208
Barkley, Alben, Senator, 314, 334
Baseball game, 125
Bassett, Christine, 414
Beacons, 327–28
Bellevue Stratford Hotel, 357
Biffle, Les, Senator, 289, 294, 298, 334
Big Horn Basin, Wyoming, 114, 152
Bilbo, Theodore G., Senator, 334–35,
    371
"Bill," bribe payer, 400–4
Birmingham, Alabama, 341–56
Birmingham (Alabama) *Post,* 341–42,
    355
Blackjack, 73–76
Blackburn, Foy, 341, 343, 346, 351,
    378–79, 381, 382, 383–96
Blackfoot, Idaho, 174, 316–29
Blacks, 364. *See also* Segregation
"Blink technique," 174–77, 321–23
Blisters, 251–53. *See also* Saddlesoreness
Bluebell, the, 22–35, 43, 47–
    48, 69–71, 73–77, 80–84, 85
Bob (pony), 13, 17–19
Boise, Idaho, 207, 257, 258, 259, 266,
    366, 371, 380, 390

Boise Hotel, 199–200, 395–96, 398, 400
Boise (Idaho) *Capitol News,* 214
Boise (Idaho) *Journal,* 399
Boise (Idaho) *Statesman,* 186
Bonneville Dam, 269
Bootlegging. *See* Olson, Frank
Borah, William E., Senator, 150,
    175–77, 183, 268
Bosses, political. *See* Clark, Chase;
    Older, Bob. *See also* machine, political
Bothwell, James R., Judge, 194, 240,
    242, 315
Bottolfsen, C. A., 218, 255, 256,
    268–69, 273–74, 275
Bray (manager of Rainbow Players), 129,
    132–33, 138
Brown, Charles, 325
Burley, Idaho, 325
"Buzz of the Burg" (column), 414

Caldwell, Idaho, 202
Caldwell (Idaho) *News-Tribune,* 332, 392
Calf, incident with, 50–52
Campaign cards, 233–34
Campaign shirt, 232–33
Canvass of votes, 383–96
Capitol, 279, 288, 295
Carpentering, 378
Carpenters' Union, 378
Carter, D. L., 204
Carter, James, President, 411
Cascade, Idaho, 129
Cassia County, Idaho, 326
Cavanagh, Dan J., 325
Chicago Times, 337–38
Childs, Marquis, 334–35, 357
Church, Frank, Senator, 379–96,
    398–407, 409–12
Churchill, Winston, 303, 413
Clark, Barzilla, 206
Clark, Chase, 195–96, 206, 207, 216,
    218, 224, 254–55
Clark, D. Worth, Senator, 206, 257, 258,
    262, 268, 270, 288, 297, 360, 364,
    367, 376
Clark machine, see machine, political
Clearwater River, 11, 15–19, 124–25,
    175
Closet, entered by mistake, 247–48
Clubs, service, 167
Cocklebur campaign buttons, 164–67
Coeur d'Alene, Idaho, 205, 227, 229,
    234; Fourth of July parade in, 229–33
Coeur d'Alene (Idaho) *Press,* 186, 276
Coffin, Tris, 313–14
Cold war, 359, 360

Columbia Valley Authority, proposed, 269
Communist Party, 356
Congressional campaign (1938), 151–81
Connell, Idaho, 127–28
Connor, Eugene ("Bull"), 342–44, 348, 351, 352, 353, 355
Conscription, 215, 357
Continental Hotel (Washington, D.C.), 279–80
Cookies, 189–90, 208
Cooperatives, 204
Corlett, John, 205, 360, 365, 376, 392–93, 398, 405
Corrupt Practices Act, 209–10
Coryell, Cody, 369, 372, 375
Coryell, Verl, 369, 372
Coryell Construction Company, 372–73, 375
Cost-plus, 256, 308–10
Coulter, Robert, 195–96, 208–9, 210–11, 217
Cowboy boots, 203. See also cowboy hat; Mix, Tom, clothing
Cowboy hat, 186, 204, 245. See also cowboy boots; Mix, Tom, clothing
Cowboy image abandoned, 266–67
Craner, G. E., Dr., 325
Cvetic, Matt, 376–77, 378–79

Daily Worker, 365
Davenport Hotel, Spokane, Washington, 94
Defense, national, 215
Democrat, The, 380
Democratic Central Committee of Kootenai County (Idaho), 247–48. See also Acuff, Jeffrey, family
Democratic National Convention (1920), 219
Democratic State Committee of New York, 363
Dentures, 242–43
Denver, Colorado, 277
Denver Post, 297
Depression, Great, 118, 123, 126–28, 171, 279, 318, 324, 412
Diary, Dora's, 126–28
Donart, George, 184, 185, 186, 191–92, 194–95, 196–97, 204, 237, 239, 315, 329, 333
Dove Creek, Colorado, 141–42
Draft. See Conscription
Driggs, Idaho, 147, 151
Dworshak, Henry, Senator, 335–36, 376
Dynasty, Clark, See Machine, political

Eastern Idaho Farmer, 391–92
Election irregularities, 224–25, 365–68, 381–96
Elections Subcommittee, Senate, 366–67, 386
Elmore County, Idaho, 383, 384, 387, 411
Emmett (Idaho) Messenger, 394, 395
Employees, excess. See Cost-plus

Farmers Union, 204
Federal Bureau of Investigation, 372–73, 376
Federal Communications Commission, 173
Ferguson, Homer, Senator, 334
Fight, in Bluebell, 73–75
Fight, after baseball game, 125
Fingerbowls, 303
Fisher, E. T., 199
Fisher, Vardis, 255–56
Fishing, 140–41
Fletcher, Henry, 173
"Floating Act," 43
Forest fire, 11–19
Fourth of July parade, 229–33
Fraud, election. See Election irregularities
Freedom, Wyoming, 116–19
Free enterprise, 313–14
Full Employment Act, 313–14
Funds, plea for, 207, 363

Gasoline rationing, 228–29
Genesee, Idaho, 250–51
Geraldine's (house of prostitution, Silverton, Idaho), 88, 97–101
Gillette, King C., 120–22, 155, 195, 222–23, 255, 412–13
Glasby, John, 387–91, 395, 410–11
Glendora Players, 110–38, 159, 373–75, 414
Glendora Ranch Gang, 138–44, 152–53, 155–64, 396
Glenns Ferry (Idaho) Gazette, 310–11
Gore, Senator, 386, 387
Gossett, Charles, Governor (and Senator), 315, 319–20, 328, 329–30
Grand Coulee Dam, 269
Grange, 204
Grangeville, Idaho, 200, 203, 207, 215
Great Falls, Montana, 107, 128, 312–13
Great Falls (Montana) Tribune, 312–13
Green River ordinance, 385, 392
Griffith, D. W., 290
Guam, 372
Gunnison, Colorado, 77
Gunther, John, 370–72

Hairpiece. *See* Taylor Topper
Hale, Calvin, 178–81
Halifax, Lady, 306–7
Halifax, Lord, 304–8
Halsey, Colonel, 289
Hand, injury to, 235–36
Hat. *See* Cowboy hat
Hawley, James H., 257, 268, 315
Haying, 251–53
Health insurance, 357
Heppner, Idaho, 127
Hickenlooper, Senator, 318–19, 326–27
Hildring, John H., General, 337
Hill, Lister, Senator, 355
Hirohito, Emperor, 226
Hitler, Adolph, 220, 332–33, 359; early opposition to, 225–26
"Home on the Range," 289–93, 295–97
Hood, Leo, 179–81
Hoover, Herbert, 318, 324
Hoovervilles, 126
Horseback campaign, 227–54, 315
Humphrey, Hubert, Senator, 363–64

Idaho Businessmen's Committee, 221–23, 224, 255
Idaho Daily Statesman, 184, 193–94, 199, 201, 205, 215, 220, 256–57, 266, 268, 269, 270, 292, 296, 297, 329–30, 333, 335–36, 356, 360, 364–65, 376, 379, 382–83, 394, 398, 404, 414
Idaho Falls, Idaho, 196, 205, 206, 207, 229, 241, 391
Idaho Falls (Idaho) *Post*-Register, 205–6
Idaho Pioneer, 200
Idaho Power Company, 198, 269, 383
Idaho State Journal, 413–14
Ifft, Nicholas, 276, 413–14
Incarceration. *See* Birmingham, Alabama
Income, limit on, 227
Independence, Missouri, 331
Indians. *See* Nez Percé Indians
Indo-China, position on, 310–11, 357
Ing. *See* Ifft, Nicholas
Inside U.S.A., two versions, 370–72
Integration. *See* Segregation
Interior, Department of, 316
Interior and Insular Affairs Committee (Senate), 318
Ione, Idaho, 127
Idaho County, Idaho, 200
Irregularities. *See* Election irregularities

Jail. *See* Birmingham, Alabama
Joseph, Chief, 125
Justice of the peace (Roanoke, Virginia), 278

Kahlotus, Idaho, 128
Kamiah, Idaho, 124–26
Kellogg, Idaho, 19
Kentucky Sue, 139
Kooskia, Idaho, 20, 158, 175–76, 188, 371, 372
Kootenai County, Idaho, 229, 231, 232, 239, 247–48. *See also* Acuff, Jeffrey, family
Korea, 364
Ku Klux Klan, 330, 342, 353

Lander (Wyoming) *Post*, 114–16
Land Management, Bureau of, 316, 317–19, 320
Langer, William, Senator, 332
La Sal, Utah, 122–23
Laughter, uncontrollable, 42–43, 52–53, 244–45
League of Nations, 268
Lemhi County, Idaho, 275
Lewiston, Idaho, 20, 187, 220
Lewiston (Idaho) *Tribune*, 187, 367–68
Liberty Theater (Great Falls, Montana), 97, 110
Lincoln, Abraham, 274, 327
"Lion of Idaho." *See* Borah, William E., Senator
Lockkard, J. G., Major, 304
Long, Colonel, 283–85
Long, Mr. (theater manager), 127–28
Lovell, Wyoming, 114
Lowe, Kales E., 325
Loyalty tests, 337–38

McCammon (Idaho) *News*, 186–87
McCarthy, Eugene, Senator, 310
McCarthy, Joseph, Senator, 330, 371, 376. *See also* McCarthyism; Redbaiting
McCarthyism, 330–33. *See also* Redbaiting
McComber, Bob (Mona's husband), 38–40, 93, 100–103
McComber, Mona, 25–61, 62–84, 86–88, 91–92, 98–104
McDonough Stock Company, 20, 85, 103
Machine, political, 197–99, 224–26, 254–55, 262, 294, 315, 360, 364–68, 379, 381–96, 406–7, 410, 411. *See also* Pendergast machine
McGovern, George, Senator, 358
McKellar, Kenneth, Senator, 309–10, 321
Manpower Conference report, 311
Margarita (employee at the Bluebell), 33, 47–48, 61–62
Marriage, to Dora, 109
Marriage, first, 107, 210–13

Marshall, George, General, 283, 337
Masters, Ira, 163–64, 179–81, 367
Miami, Florida, 358
Michael in Society (play), 115
Miller, Bert, 179–81, 211
Minidoka County, Idaho, 366
Mississippi, 334
Mitchell, Hugh, 312–13
Mix, Tom, clothing, 159, 160. *See also* Cowboy boots, Cowboy hat
Mona. *See* McComber, Mona
Monkeys, 174–75
Morse, Wayne, Senator, 355–56, 371, 372
Mountain Home, Idaho, 383, 387, 388, 393, 411
Mussolini, Benito, 220

Nampa, Idaho, 209, 213, 216
Nampa (Idaho) *Free Press,* 196, 213–15
Negroes. *See* Blacks; Segregation
New Deal, 201
New Hampshire primary, 310
Newsreels, 295–97
Newsweek, 409
New York City, 363
New York Times, 342, 357
Nez Perce, Idaho, 201
Nez Perce (Idaho) *Herald,* 201
Nez Percé Indians, 124–26
Nixon, Richard, 331
Norcus, Rafe, 39–40, 60

Oakley (Idaho) *Herald,* 325
Oath of office, 293–94
Ogilvy, Colonel, 285
Older, Bob, 229–33
Olson, Frank, 316–29, 330; speech on behalf of, 320–28
"One-two," the. *See* "Blink technique"

Parade, Fourth of July, 229–33
Parade, torchlight, 275–76
Park, sleeping in, 125
Parliamentarian, Senate, 295
Parole Board, Idaho, 89, 91, 92, 95
Parties, cocktail, 286–88; Drew Pearson's, 301–4; for Lord Halifax, 304–8; Taylors' first in Washington, 286–88
Peaches, 189–90, 208
Pearl Harbor, 226
Pearson, Drew, 298–304
Pendergast machine, 297, 331
Pendleton, Oregon, 227
Pentagon, 280, 282–86
Penthouse suite, 199–200

People's Corporation, The, 120–22, 222–23, 412–13
Pepper, Claude, Senator, 336, 364–65
Petain, Marshal, 201
Peterson, F. Ross, 365
Philadelphia Bulletin, 358
Philadelphia Inquirer, 312
Pierce City, Idaho, 22, 89–90. *See also* Bluebell, the
Pittsburgh, Pennsylvania, 376–77
Pittsburgh Press, 377
Plantages Theater (Seattle, Washington), 93
Plate (false teeth), 242–43
Pneumonia, Arod's, 153–55
Pocatello, Idaho, 110, 152, 190, 212, 218, 226, 227, 228, 229, 262, 371, 376, 380, 386, 389, 409
Pocatello (Idaho) *Journal,* 396, 407
Pocatello (Idaho) *Tribune,* 159, 202, 208, 221, 268, 273, 276, 292–93
Pope, James, 206
Port Isabel, Texas, 141, 142
Portland, Oregon, 159, 371, 372
Potatoes, Idaho, 322
Potomac River, 282
Poverty, Dora's fear of, 152
Poverty amid plenty, 313–14
Power, Montana, 374
Private enterprise. *See* Free enterprise
"Production for Use," 121, 155, 204
Progressive Party, 356, 357–60. *See also* Wallace, Henry, Vice President
Prophet Without Honor, 365
Props, stage, 111

Radio broadcasts, 129, 152, 351–52
Rainbow Players, 129–30, 132–33
Rainbow Theater (Great Falls, Montana), 109
Ranger (horse). *See* Horseback campaign
Rats, 250
Ray, Doc, 179–81
Reader's Digest editor, 287
Reclamation, 215, 269
Recount. *See* Canvass of votes; Election irregularities
Red-baiting, 356–58, 360, 364. *See also* Cvetic, Matt; McCarthyism
Redding, California, 375
Register of Land Office (Blackfoot, Idaho), 316–29
Resources in Idaho, 197
Roanoke, Virginia, 277, 278, 279
Robert's Rules of Order, 294
Rodeo performing, alleged, 218
Roosevelt, Franklin D., President, 201, 206, 218–20, 224, 274; letter to, 225–26

Ross, C. Ben, Governor, 147–51, 206, 258
Rubber rationing, 228–29, 277
Rupert, Idaho, 187–88
Russia. *See* Soviet Union

Saddlebag cards. *See* Campaign cards
Saddlesoreness, 243–46. *See also* Baby oil; Blisters
St. Anthony Chronicle, 205
Salmon (Idaho) *Recorder Herald*, 275
Salmon River, 311
Salt Lake City, Utah, 174, 403
San Benito, Texas, 141
San Francisco, California, 219, 259, 331, 379; working in, 226, 256, 257
San Francisco Chronicle, 414
San Francisco Examiner, 257
San Jose, California, 372
Santa Claus, 221
Schmidt, Barney, 377
Seattle, Washington, 93, 403
Security clearance, 372–73
Segregation, 334, 341–56
Senate campaign (1940), 183–224
Senate campaign (1942), 226–56
Senate campaign (1944), 257–70
Senate campaign (1950), 364–68
Senate campaign (1954), 375–77, 399–405
Senate Office Building, 279, 288
Shoshone County, Idaho, 224
Silverton, Idaho, 96
Sinatra, Frank, 173
Singing. *See* Acting and singing
"Singing Cowboy," 207, 218, 239, 243, 253, 289, 307, 313–14, 315. *See also* Glendora Players; Glendora Ranch Gang
Soda Springs, Idaho, 187
Southern Negro Youth Congress, 342
Soviet Union, 332–33, 336–37, 338, 357, 359, 364
Sparkman, John, Senator, 355
Speed traps, 123–24
Spokane, Washington, 227, 228, 250
Stalin, Joseph, 258, 332
Stalingrad, Heroes of, 333
Star Valley, Wyoming, 116–19
Stern, Joe, 20–22
Stetson. *See* cowboy hat
Stites, Idaho, 19
Sufferage for eighteen–year–olds, 357
Sutcliffe, Epha Taylor, 119
Sutcliffe, "Sut," 119–20
Syringa, Idaho, 13–14

"Tab" shows, 107
Taft-Hartley Bill, 338
"Talkies," 114, 116
Taylor, Arod. *See* Taylor, Glen Arod
Taylor, Dora (wife), 109–44, 151–55, 160–64, 170, 178–81, 187, 188–91, 202, 207, 212–13, 216, 221, 226, 227, 234, 255, 258–65, 269–70, 275, 279–88, 290–91, 293, 296, 298–308, 314–15, 341, 353–55, 363, 381, 382, 397, 408, 412; first meeting, 109; marriage, 109; working in Senate office, 298–301
Taylor, E.K. (brother), 19, 85
Taylor, Eleanor (sister), 119
Taylor, Ferris (brother), 19, 107, 113, 260
Taylor, Gladys (sister-in-law), 127, 129, 134–37, 178–81
Taylor, Glen Arod, 138–40, 141–42, 152–55, 161–62, 164, 170, 187, 188–91, 202, 216, 221, 227, 234, 269–70, 276–77, 291, 293, 296, 304, 314–15, 341, 353, 373, 378, 381, 397, 412; birth, 130; naming, 131; pneumonia, 153–55
Taylor, Gregory (son), 358, 372, 381, 397, 412
Taylor, Jack (brother), 109
Taylor, Lena (sister), 12, 15
Taylor, "Mama" (mother), 11–19, 293
Taylor, Nell (Ferris's wife), 19
Taylor, P.J. (son), 269–70, 291, 293, 296, 314–15, 341, 353, 381, 397; birth, 226, 412
Taylor, Paul (brother), 12, 109, 127, 129, 134–35, 137–38, 152–53, 178–81
Taylor, Pleasant John ("P. J.") (father), 11–19, 76–77, 80–82, 84, 140–41, 176–77, 219, 293
Taylor, Slade (brother), 107, 112
Taylor Quartet, 24–25
Taylor Topper, 407–9; curling hair, 264; first wearing of, 265–66; invention of, 263–65; need for, 260–61
Taxes, 197
Tennessee Valley Authority, 269
Texas, 140–41
Theaters, movie, working in, 19, 85
Thomas, Elbert, Senator, 294
Thomas John, Senator, 184, 195, 202, 218, 225, 226, 294; death of, 315
Time magazine, 254, 375
Tires, 141, 277. *See also* Rubber rationing
Toupee. *See* Taylor Topper
Toynbee, Arnold, 172–73

Traffic ticket, 278
Truman, Harry, Vice President (and
    President), 297, 310, 330–33, 335,
    338, 359, 369–70; invitation for
    fishing, 311–12
Trumped-up charges, 123–24
Tucker, Henry W., Judge, 326
Twin Falls, Idaho, 325
Twin Falls (Idaho) *News*, 218
Twin Falls (Idaho) *Times*, 217

United Nations, 336
U.S. News and World Report, 359

Vietnam, position on, 310–11, 357
Volstead Act, 324
Vote stealing. *See* Election irregularities

Waldorf-Astoria Hotel, 363
Wallace, Henry, Vice President, 294,
    295, 297, 330–33, 335, 336, 338, 363,

369, 414; presidential campaign, 341–
    360, 363
Wallace, Idaho, 19
Walla Walla, Washington, 127
War plants, working in, 226, 256
Washington Monument, 279
Weiser, Idaho, 185, 251–53, 329;
    newspaper, 204
Welker, Herman, 365, 367, 375–76, 377,
    379, 380, 386, 389, 394, 399, 405,
    407
White, Compton I., Congressman, 277,
    280–87, 302
White House, 279
Wig. *See* Taylor Topper
Williams, Aubrey, 308
Williams, W. W., Chief, 325
Williamson, Big Jim, 76–77, 82
Willkie, Wendell, 214–15
Willow Creek, Idaho, 200
Woodward and Lothrop (emporium), 282
Worley, Idaho, 236
Write-in campaign for Senate, 399–405